Succeeding as a Frontline Manager in Today's Organizations

A volume in
Contemporary Human Resources Management:
Issues, Challenges and Opportunities
Ronald R. Sims, *Series Editor*

Succeeding as a Frontline Manager in Today's Organizations

Ronald R. Sims

College of William and Mary

INFORMATION AGE PUBLISHING, INC.
Charlotte, NC • www.infoagepub.com

Library of Congress Cataloging-in-Publication Data

A CIP record for this book is available from the Library of Congress
http://www.loc.gov

ISBN: 978-1-64802-363-7 (Paperback)
      978-1-64802-364-4 (Hardcover)
      978-1-64802-365-1 (E-Book)

Printed in the United States of America

Contents

List of Tables

List of Figures

Acknowledgments

I am indebted to George F. Johnson at Information Age Publishing, Inc. who continues to provide the collective outlet for my ideas. A most deserved thank you and acknowledgement goes out to all those who continue to serve in front line management.

A very, very special thanks goes to my colleague, Herrington Bryce who continues to serve as my colleague, mentor, and valued friend. The administrative support of the Raymond A. Mason School of Business at William and Mary is also acknowledged.

Thanks and appreciation goes to my family who have supported me throughout my work over the years. I am truly thankful for all of you.

1

The Effective Front Line Manager

What They Do

Alfre Simone and Andy Dawkins are employees in one of the Jackson Industries' largest facilities. Jackson Industries is a manufacturer of computer chips. Both have been with the company approximately five years. This morning, while attending a training program, their manager, Jack Jurveic, gave Alfre and Andy a big shock. He asked both of them if they would like to become front-line managers (FLMs). Kevin explained that two of the FLMs in different parts of the company were being promoted and that he needed two new FLMs. Kevin also stated that he felt Alfre and Andy would make good FLMs because they both (a) were highly recommended by their current FLMs, (b) knew the job, and (c) knew people in the two departments that were losing the FLMs. Kevin asked both of them to think it over and let him know their decisions the next day. Later, Alfre saw Andy at lunch and they began discussing the possibilities of the new jobs. Both of them agreed that they had never given much thought to being an FLM. They wondered just what the job of FLM would entail.

If you are like Alfre and Andy, you want to learn what being an FLM means. According to businessdictionary.com, frontline management is

Succeeding as a Frontline Manager in Today's Organizations, pages 1–27

defined as "the first or second managers (line managers, office managers, supervisors) directly responsible for production of goods and services, and supervision of clerical staff and shop floor employees." Others may describe frontline managers as those who are responsible for the critical, day-to-day operations of an organization. This group of people is often an organization's largest population of leaders.

Managing on the front-line is a challenging and sometimes taxing activity. FLMs are responsible for the work of others as well as their own work. They must solve problems, make decisions, and take action. They experience pressures from top- and middle-level managers, their employees, and an ever changing world of work and society. FLMs never seem to have enough time to get their work done.

On the other hand, managing in the trenches is also a very exciting and rewarding experience. FLMs can experience a real sense of accomplishment when their work team is cooperating and performing effectively. Knowing that you have helped your employees develop their knowledge, skills, abilities (KSAs), and other characteristics can be satisfying. Helping to create an environment that employees find rewarding also provides satisfaction.

Managing is an increasingly important activity in today's society, as the role of the FLM continues to grow and be appreciated in organizations. How can you become an effective FLM? Experience is one answer. You can be placed in an FLM position and learn from your successes and failures. However, experience is not the only answer. A systematic study of management can also help your performance. By studying concepts that FLMs have found helpful, you can prepare yourself to meet the challenges of an FLM's job. While study alone cannot make you an effective FLM, it can help you profit from your experience. Learning from the trials and successes of other FLMs can make you an effective FLM more rapidly.

You are about to begin a systematic study of management on the front-line. This book will introduce you to the challenging and rapidly changing world of FLM. This chapter first discusses the role of the FLM, the FLM process the basic skills required of an FLM, and provides an overview of major challenges facing today's organizations and the FLMs in those organizations.

What Is a FLM?

When you talk to people in today's organizations you get a variety of descriptions of the FLM's job. You find that FLMs perform many different activities and face different problems. The FLM job can differ greatly from one organization, or even one department, to the next.

These differences are to be expected. FLMs work in a variety of organizations like retail banking, retail and manufacturing organizations, healthcare, travel and logistics, fast food restaurants, schools, government agencies, and not-for-profit organizations. Their jobs may vary widely, depending on the goals and structure of the organization, and their level within the organization. Certainly the personalities of FLMs and their employees and the kind of jobs to be done all influence the role of the FLM. The problems faced by FLMs, and the activities they perform, therefore, vary greatly.

While FLM jobs do differ there are some common elements that define a job as an FLM position. First, all FLMs have people working for them. FLMs are responsible for directing the work of others and accomplishing goals. They accomplish these goals by managing or supervising their employees to meet the performance goals set by higher-level managers. FLMs work in the trenches: on the plant floor, in the secretarial pool, or in the customer service office.

In its broadest sense, FLMs are central to creating an organization's culture. Because they are the leaders most employees interact with the most, they have a tremendous impact on whether the workforce as a whole buys into an organization's values or culture (e.g., "the way we do things around here"). FLMs are central to, for example, creating an innovation or entrepreneurial culture. Because they are the leaders most employees interact with the most, they have a tremendous impact on whether the workforce as a whole is inventive, agile, and entrepreneurial. And since they span the boundary between customer experience and corporate strategy, they are uniquely positioned to spot new product possibilities as well as better ways of operating. As a result, great ideas often come from FLMs.

With the impact FLMs have on an organization's culture, first and foremost, FLMs are managers, and all managers are involved in meeting performance goals. However, this book will be devoted primarily to the FLM who serves as the important link between operating employees and middle management. The remainder of this section examines the environment inside the organization in which FLMs must function. It identifies the settings where FLMs work, the day-to-day activities that utilize much of their time, and some generalized skills necessary to cope with the internal environment. We begin by briefly describing various levels of management, then focus on FLM skills.

The Various Levels of Management

Most organizations function on at least three distinct but overlapping levels, each requiring a different managerial focus and emphasis. They include the *operations level*, the *technical level*, and the *strategic level*. Managers at each of these three levels must plan, organize, lead, and control.

Operations Level

Every organization, whether it produces a physical product or a service, has an operations function. In any organization the operations level focuses on effectively performing the function necessary to produce or do whatever the organization produces or does. A physical product, for instance, requires a flow of materials and management of the operations. Banks must see that checks are processed and financial transactions are recorded accurately and quickly. The operations function is at the core of every organization. The FLM's task at the operations level is to manage in a manner that results in the best allocation of resources that will produce the desired output.

Technical Level

As an organization increases in size, someone must coordinate the activities at the operations level as well as decide which products or services to offer. These problems are the focus of the technical level. A dissatisfied customer complains to the unit FLM. A retail FLM mediates disagreements between customers and salespeople. Production or maintenance schedules and amounts to be produced or equipment to be prepared must be planned for an automobile manufacturer or a residential facility.

At this level, the managerial task is really twofold: (a) managing the operations function and (b) serving as a liaison between those who produce the product or service and those who use the output. In other words, for the operations level to do its work, FLMs at the technical level must make sure they have the correct materials and see that output is sold or used.

Strategic Level

Every organization operates in a broad social environment. As a part of that environment, an organization also has a responsibility to other entities' environment. The strategic level must make sure the technical level operates within the bounds of society. Since the ultimate source of authority in any organization comes from society, the organization must provide goods and services in a socially acceptable manner. Thus, the strategic level determines the long-range objectives and direction for the organization—in other words, how the organization interacts with its environment. The organization also may seek to influence its environment through lobbying efforts, advertising efforts, or educational programs aimed at members of society.

Front-Line and Other Managers

Understanding the various levels of management can be helpful in determining the primary focus of FLMs' activities at different levels in an organization. For example, terms widely used in organizations include top management, middle management, and first-level management (led by FLMs).

Top management reflects a group of people responsible for establishing the organization's overall objectives and developing the policies to achieve those objectives. Titles typical of top management positions include chairman of the board, chief executive officer, president, senior vice president, and cabinet secretary.

Middle management includes all employees below the top-management level who manage other managers. These individuals are responsible for establishing and meeting specific goals in their particular departments or units. Their goals, however, are not established in isolation. Instead, the objectives set by top management provide specific direction to middle managers regarding what they are expected to achieve. Ideally, if each middle manager met his or her goals, the entire organization would meet its objectives. Examples of job titles held by middle managers include division manager, district manager, vice president of finance, unit manager, commissioner, or division director.

FLMs, like top and middle managers, are also part of the organization's management team. Because FLMs oversee the work of operating employees they are often referred to as first-level or front-line managers. The kinds of job titles likely to identify someone as an FLM include shift FLM, operations delivery manager, HR associate manager, security manager, welding foreman, front of house manager, and receiving and warehousing FLM to name a few.

Basic FLM Skills

Certain general skills are needed for effective managerial performance, regardless of the level of the manager in the hierarchy of the organization. However, the mix of skills differs depending on the level of the FLM and other managers in the organization. These basic skills—human (interpersonal), technical, and conceptual—are needed by all FLMs and managers. The application of each of the three types of skills depends not only on the level of management, but also the type of organization.

FLMs must accomplish much of their work through other people. For this, it is essential that the FLM possess and demonstrate *interpersonal skill*. A reflection of an FLM's leadership abilities, interpersonal skill is the ability to work with, communicate to, and understand others.

The importance of interpersonal skill is most obvious in those managerial jobs that involve extensive interactions with other employees. FLMs are particularly in need of interpersonal skills because they spend so much of their time interacting with other employees. FLMs must provide ongoing feedback to employees regarding interpersonal and performance problems. They have the responsibilities to motivate employees to change or improve performance. FLMs must also oversee the other activities involved in supervising individual and team performance.

Communication skills are an important component of interpersonal skills. They form the basis for sending and receiving messages on the job. Different types of communication skills are important for FLMs. Speaking and writing skills are of obvious importance. Listening is also an important skill. The ability to recognize differences among people aids effective communication because the communicator can adapt the message to be more receptive to the receiver. Chapter 11 offers more discussion on communication.

Technical skill enables an FLM to apply specific knowledge, techniques, and resources to perform work. Technical skills have the greatest relevance for FLMs. This is true for two reasons. First, many FLMs perform technical work as well as managerial work. In contrast to other levels of management, the distinction between the individual contributor and first-line FLM is often blurred. Second, FLMs spend more time training and developing their employees than do other managers. This requires FLMs to have a greater technical knowledge of their employees' jobs than that needed by middle- and top-level managers.

For today's FLM, technical skills include the ability to prepare a budget, lay out a work schedule, program and work with more technically sophisticated tools. Well-developed technical skills can facilitate an individual's rise into management. For example, many an FLM launched his or her career by being a competent member of their operations or work unit. In spite of the importance of technical skills, the successful FLM must recognize that being technically competent alone will not help them achieve their own, their team's, or their organization's success. The ultimate challenge for the FLM is always to get things done through others. This challenge requires that the FLM have strengths in interpersonal and conceptual skills along with technical skills.

Conceptual skill is the ability to see the relationships of parts of the organization to the whole and to one another. For an FLM, conceptual skills include recognizing how the department's work helps the organization achieve its goals and how the work of the various employees affects the performance of the department as a whole. FLMs with conceptual skills understand all activities and interests of the organization and how they interrelate.

All three skills are essential for effective performance. As noted earlier, the relative importance of the three skills to a specific FLM or manager depends on their level in the organization. Interpersonal skill is critical at the lower level of management. For instance, because they deal with the day-to-day interpersonal problems in a particular unit or team, FLMs need more interpersonal skills than higher level managers in the organization.

The importance of conceptual skills increases as managers move up in the organization. This is due to the type of problems they encounter and the decisions they make at higher levels. The higher a manager is in the hierarchy, the more involved they become in longer-term decisions that can influence many parts of the organization or the entire organization.

Generally speaking, the higher a manager rises in an organization, the more the problems he or she faces tend to be complex, ambiguous, and ill-defined. These problems require custom-made solutions or nonprogrammed decision-making. In contrast, FLMs generally have more straightforward, familiar, and easily defined problems which lend themselves to more routine or programmed decision-making. Ill-structured problems and custom-made solutions make greater conceptual demands on managers than do structured problems and programmed decision-making. See Chapter 5 for more discussion on decisions and the different levels of decision-making.

Breaking down skills into these three categories or levels is helpful. However, it is also somewhat artificial. FLMs must use a combination of skills to deal with different situations. In fact, all three types of skills will come into play in most situations. While placing these skills into categories can be helpful in understanding behavior in organizations and learning how to become a more effective FLM, it is also important to consider other skills like the following:

- *Versatility.* FLMs need to be able to keep up with the ever-developing technological and business changes that occur in every organization. The ability to learn quickly from experiences and then turn around and use that knowledge to recognize, analyze, and address new problems gives FLMs the learning agility to deal with a variety of problems.

- ▪ *Ability to set attainable goals.* FLMs need to know what is important not only to their department, but the overall organization, and why. They become better able to develop strategies that can focus their own team on what actually matters. Part of setting goals is the ability to set milestones for their teams to monitor progress.
- ▪ *Motivating and inspiring others.* FLMs' ability to inspire their teams is a crucial skill. Providing meaningful feedback to their teams on both areas to improve and what they are doing right will give them direction and can create clear understandings of their roles. This may include motivating employees to exceed expectations or put in extra effort.
- ▪ *Ability to adapt and learn.* Adaptability is a crucial quality in FLMs. In today's dynamic environment, adaptability is an essential skill for FLMs to have to keep pace with shifting technological and work environment changes. To be able to adapt and learn FLMs will need three specific skills: creative thinking, a forward-facing mentality, and open-mindedness.
- ▪ *Business knowledge.* Knowing and being trained in the principles of their organization allows FLMs to understand their organization's priorities and strategy, and how best to help contribute to achieving them. This way, FLMs not only have the ability to connect their work and the work of their teams to the vision of the organization, hence they can more effectively demonstrate to their direct reports how their work contributes to the organization's overall success.
- ▪ *Strategic goal setting.* Once FLMs know what's important to their organization and why, they become better equipped to develop strategies that focus the efforts of their team on what matters. Whether the goal is to increase sales, better quality of service, or a lower average handle time, once defined performance standards have been set, FLMs can let their teams know what is expected of them, and how they will be evaluated.
- ▪ *Task execution to achieve milestones.* When goals are established, FLM leadership can set milestones for their teams, then monitor progress and give them direction on how to achieve those milestones. Conversely, FLMs need to be able to observe when progress is stalling or goals are in danger of not being met, so they can course-correct in a timely manner.

FLMs are an essential part of building both the employee and customer experience. Whether it is navigating a diverse workforce, solving a variety of problems, or addressing customer and employee needs, FLMs must develop the above skills in order to be able to handle their responsibilities. Additionally, the FLM uses resources and carries out four FLM functions to achieve an objective. These functions are planning, organizing, leading, and controlling. Each function is a method of managing the various resources used by the FLM.

Resources Used by FLMs

FLMs use resources to accomplish their purposes, just as a carpenter uses resources to build a porch. An FLM's resources can be divided into four types: human, financial, physical, and information.

Human resources are the people needed to get the job done. An FLM's goals influence which employees they choose. For example, Fernando Garcia, an FLM at a major chain restaurant has the goal of delivering quality food to her customers. Among the human resources she chooses are order clerks, cooks, delivery drivers, and other part-time employees. The types of human resources the director of the environmental protection agency chooses will be much more numerous because the goals of that huge federal agency are much more varied than the goal of Fernando's company.

The money that the FLM and the organization use to reach organizational goals is a *financial resource.* The financial resources of a business organization are profits and investments from stockholders. The financial resources of community agencies come from tax revenues, charitable contributions, and government grants. The financial resources of a particular department come from the budget developed by the FLM and approved by middle- and top-level management. See Chapter 4 for more discussion on budgets.

Physical resources are an organization's tangible goods and real estate, including materials, office space, production facilities, office equipment, and vehicles. Organizations use a variety of vendors to supply the physical resources needed to achieve organizational goals.

The data that the FLM and the organization use to get the job done are *information resources.* For example, to supply members of a safety unit with data from inspections and monitoring activities, many organizations rely on computers to store and process data on company history, and so forth.

To accomplish goals, the FLM performs four FLM functions related to the management of these various types of resources. These functions are planning, organizing, leading, and controlling.

Planning

The planning function involves defining and setting goals, figuring out ways for achieving these goals, and developing a comprehensive hierarchy of plans to integrate and coordinate activities to reach the goals (Chapter 4 provides a more in-depth discussion of the concept of planning). Setting goals keeps the work to be done in its proper perspective and helps organizational members keep their attention on what is most important. Planning is considered the central function of management, and it pervades everything an FLM does. In planning, an FLM looks to the future, saying, "Here is what we want to achieve, and here is how we are going to do it." Decision-making is usually a component of planning, because choices have to be made in the process of finalizing plans.

For example, once Alfre Simone took over the FLM's job at Jackson Industries, she and her manager Kevin Jurveic set a goal of improving computer chip manufacturing cost savings by $900,000 over a 12-month period. As the end of the eighth month approached, her unit was $157,000 short of reaching their goal. Adding to this shortfall was the realization that in spite of the unit's best efforts, mandatory certification training for several of her team members was behind schedule. Alfre and the rest of her team realized that they had an important decision to make. If they postponed the certification training for at least another month, they would have an excellent chance of achieving the computer maintenance cost savings objective for the year. Alfre made the decision to postpone certification training, leaving her team in position to spend the time they needed to achieve their cost savings. Team members were able to make up the training at a later date. In this case, Alfre and her team made the right decision. As you will see, in our discussion in Chapter 5, decision-making is also involved in the other functions of management.

Organizing

Organizing is the process of making sure the necessary human and physical resources are available to carry out a plan and achieve organizational goals (Chapter 4 provides a more detailed discussion of the organizing function). Organizing also involves determining what tasks are to be done, assigning activities, and dividing work into specific jobs and tasks. For example, Alfre Simone began addressing the charge of the computer chip manufacturing cost savings and certification training for her team by better organizing her team's computer chip manufacturing projects and scheduling the necessary training.

Another major aspect of organizing is grouping activities into departments or some other logical subdivision, and specifying who reports to whom, and when decisions are to be made. The activities of an organization are often divided into departments, such as production and marketing, or territories, such as northern and southern. FLMs like Alfre often have the major responsibility for dividing work into manageable components and coordinating results to achieve objectives.

Leading

Leading is influencing others to achieve organizational objectives (Chapter 8 discusses the concept of leadership). Leading involves dozens of interpersonal processes: motivating, communicating, coaching, and showing employees how they can reach their goals. When FLMs motivate employees, direct the activities of others, select the most effective communication channel, or resolve conflicts among members, they're engaging in leading. Leadership is such an important part of management that managing is sometimes defined as accomplishing results through people.

As suggested above, leading or influencing people, requires many different actions by the FLM. A typical act of leadership for an FLM like Alfre is to praise a team member who has done an exceptional job. In this way, Alfre tries to motivate the employee to continue performing at such a high level (see Chapter 9 for more discussion on motivation). Alfre's discipline of a team member who has violated safety rules is also an example of leadership behavior.

Controlling

The final function FLMs perform is controlling (see Chapter 4 for a more in depth discussion of the controlling function). Controlling is ensuring that performance conforms to plans. That is, after the goals are set, the plans formulated, the organizing arrangements determined, and the people hired, trained, and motivated, something may still go amiss. To make sure that things are going as they should, Alfre and other FLMs must monitor their organization's and unit's performance. Alfre must compare actual performance to the previously set goals. If there is a significant difference between actual and desired performance, Alfre must take corrective action.

A secondary aspect of controlling is determining whether the original plan needs revision, given the realities of the day. The controlling function sometimes causes an FLM to return to the planning function temporarily to fine-tune the original plan.

The large-scale use of computerized information has contributed to the complexity of the controlling process. Compared to the noncomputerized past, there is now much more information available to measure deviations from performance. The process of monitoring, comparing, and correcting is what comprises the controlling function.

Planning, organizing, leading, and controlling are important FLM functions. FLMs like Alfre Simone who are concerned with being successful must develop an understanding of these four functions.

Working Through Others

All FLMs' jobs have several common characteristics and chief among them is working with and through operating employees to accomplish established work-unit goals. This function separates employees from FLMs. Consider Seiya Chen. As an individual contributor (or direct report), one of her responsibilities was to maintain the boiler and other equipment in proper operating condition. When Sieya became an FLM, however, her function was supposed to change. Sieya is still responsible for some operational activities that her team performs. In many instances, however, she is not expected to actually do the operational work herself. She is expected to train other employees, provide them with direction, coordinate efforts, and give them the necessary resources and assistance so that *they* can maintain the equipment. In short, as an FLM, Sieya is supposed to achieve the maintenance goals through the efforts of other members of the team.

Project Management

Many attempts have been made over the years to paint a realistic picture of what managers, in our case FLMs, do. Like the various skills presented earlier, this emphasis on skills is very much in tune with today's results-oriented organizations. While there is no unanimous agreement among those responsible for teaching and training FLMs, certain skills have surfaced as being more important than others. The FLM's role and skills in project management is one such example.

Most of us accept the notion of projects in our personal lives as the opportunities and problems encountered in our daily living. Projects are elements of change. Projects are conceptualized, designed, engineered, and produced (or constructed); something is created that did not previously exist. A strategy is executed to facilitate the support of an organization. Projects, therefore support the ongoing activities of a going concern.

Project management provides for the creation and delivery of something while meeting costs and schedule objectives. The use of FLMs and the project teams they lead play a key role in preparing the organization to respond to the changing world of work. For example, FLMs are expected to use projects to capture opportunity in new technology and transfer existing technology in changing economic, environmental, political, and social conditions, which leads to enhanced organizational performance and survival. To fulfill their project management role FLMs must recognize that projects, like organizations, always are in motion as each proceeds along its life cycle. Projects go through a life cycle (planning, implementation, and close out) to completion, hopefully on time, within budget, and with the attainment of the performance objectives.

Successful project completion requires that the FLM use conceptual, technical, and interpersonal skills as he or she must determine if the project is really worth doing. This is the point at which the project is tied to the organization's strategic goals and objectives. A good analysis conducted at this point will provide more information and details on how to properly define and manage the project later. Some of the things that the FLM must do during this phase include:

1. Determine the technical and financial feasibility of the project.
2. Examine alternative ways of accomplishing the project objectives to include alternative projects.
3. Provide initial answers to the following questions: What will the project cost? When will the project be implemented? What will the project do? How will the project be integrated and coordinated with existing work and systems?
4. Identify the human and nonhuman resources that are required to support the project.
5. Select the initial project designs that will satisfy the project objectives.
6. Determine the initial project interfaces
7. Establish a project team organization.
8. Verify the "strategic fit" of the project.

The FLM must also more clearly define the project. A clearly defined project states, in more detail, what it is we want to accomplish, when we want to accomplish it, how we shall accomplish it, and what accomplishing it will cost. The purpose of this phase is for the FLM to establish project costs, schedules, performance objectives, and resource requirements. This phase dictates that the FLM stop and take time to see whether this is what is really wanted before resources are committed to put the project into operation.

The FLM's role in project management will be most evident in the forthcoming discussions on planning, organizing, leading, and controlling. In the presentation of each of these topics it will become increasingly clear that the FLM must deal effectively with people if they are to achieve successful results in general and in project management in particular.

To this point this chapter has defined FLM, important FLM skills, functions, and project management. The remainder of this chapter will examine some of the major challenges and developments that are likely to affect FLMs like Alfre Simone and the FLM process.

The FLM's Changing Environment

Throughout the foreseeable future, FLMs will have to understand and deal with many complex environmental factors and trends. These factors and trends influence the FLM. To be effective in today's changing world of work, FLMs must be adaptable and maintain their perspective in the face of a rapidly changing environment. For instance, global competition, the knowledge and information explosion, and diversity represent not only some of the latest buzzwords, but also a harsh reality currently facing FLMs.

During the past 20 years issues like workforce diversity and globalization have been increasingly important in the lives of FLMs and their organizations. There have been many solutions offered on how to deal with these complex challenges. Yet the simplest but most profound solutions may be found in the words of Sam Walton, founder of Wal-Mart and richest person in the world when he died. When asked for the answer to successful organizations and management, Sam quickly replied, "People are the key."

A look at some of the challenges that will continue to confront FLMs and their organizations include:

- *Focus on individual leaders and their personal performance.* The pace of change demands that FLMs work more closely with one another to be able to come up with integrated solutions in a more rapidly moving environment.
- *Business financials and shareholder returns are the primary outcomes.* Changing demographics and employee expectations, in particular among millennials (and Generation Zers), are challenging FLMs and their organizations to focus on profits and purpose instead of just profits.

- *Executing financial and investment stewardship.* The pace of change demands that FLMs and their organizations be able to sense, lead, and extend their capabilities to meet and exceed financial goals.
- *Delivering consistent and stable results.* The constant influx of new technologies means that FLMs and their organizations need to be able to operate and lead in an environment of continuous innovation where what is coming next is often uncertain.
- *Executing marketing and customer service.* Changing customer expectations are prompting organizations and their FLMs to create a distinctly human experience that creates a personal connection to the customer beyond the product or the brand.
- *Maintaining operational efficiency and performance.* The rapid pace of change across industries is forcing FLMs and their organizations to innovate and improve in a constant cycle that never turns off.
- *Managing structured career and talent programs.* Changing demographics and employee expectations are challenging organizations and FLMs to appeal to a diverse range of workers through lifelong learning, movement among and between jobs, and bringing meaning to work.
- *Supervising technology programs that enable common processes.* The influx of new technologies demands that FLMs be tech-savvy regardless of their current position.
- *Managing risk and quality.* Changing customer expectations are forcing a higher focus on risk and quality, as any single issue can quickly erode the value of an organization's brand.

In addition to the challenges or issues listed above, FLMs will also be impacted by other challenges, trends, and issues. Some of these are discussed below.

Globalization

FLMs and other employees throughout an organization must perform at higher and higher levels because the world has been changing more rapidly than ever before. The world is presently operating as one village, whereby people are able to communicate efficiently and conveniently with one another. This has been facilitated by the growth of computer and internet technology. The growth of air transport has also been of significant influence to the enhancement of transport. With these developments, communication, and transport have been heightened thus enhancing global relations in terms of business and other activities.

The rise of *global organizations*, organizations that operate and compete in more than one country, has and will continue to put severe pressure on many organizations to improve their performance and to identify better ways to use their resources and impact the FLM. Substantial investment continues to be made in U.S. firms by the British, Germans, Swiss, Canadians, Japanese, and others. Identifying the various cultural/value systems and work ethic differences is beyond the scope of this book. However, the FLM must recognize that management practices differ culturally and structurally in these organizations compared to the U.S. owned and operated companies. Today's FLMs will need to learn to operate in a one-world market made up of differing cultures and leadership styles, especially at the FLM level.

More than ever before, talented people will be needed to represent firms on a global basis. Clearly, there is increasing evidence that globalization will impact FLMs and their organizations. Today's FLMs who make no attempt to learn and adapt to changes in the global environment will find themselves reacting rather than innovating, and their organizations will often become uncompetitive and fall.

Harnessing the Power of New Technologies and Avoiding Security Threats

The digital transformation continues to have a profound effect on FLMs and their organizations. In some cases, it facilitates the functioning of an organization, but in others, it may render working models obsolete. FLMs and their organizations must make sure that the data, tools, and resources that come with technological advances don't result in security threats that negatively impact an organization's ability to effectively provide products and services. Security threats, which in some cases might be overlooked despite the fact that cybercriminals increasingly target organizations to get access to sensitive data and information.

Many organizations have been completely revamped because of technological advances, computers, artificial intelligence, robotics, automation, changing markets, and other competitive influences that demand both internal and external adaptations. The great expansion of information technology will continue to profoundly change the workplace.

The advances in technology reduce the number of people needed in various jobs and, thus, in turn, the number of FLMs needed to manage those people. In other words, technology has affected management greatly, either by automating work formerly done by employees directed by FLMs or by giving employees direct access to information and people without having to go through an FLM. This change has freed FLMs to devote more time to other tasks, such as better planning, more coordination of work among teams, management of suppliers or vendors, and assisting their work groups or teams to improve processes.

Increases in information availability and technological change will increasingly require FLMs to have increased technical skills. Furthermore, these changes require more skilled and trained employees. This then increases the importance of the FLM's role in training and overcoming resistance to change as discussed in Chapter 7. Therefore, FLMs must keep up to date on the latest developments so that they can effectively train their people. Higher level skills and training require new approaches to motivation and leadership. Thus, FLMs like Alfre Simone need more skills in the interpersonal area.

Workplace Demographics and Diversity in the Workforce

The composition of the workforce continues to change; specifically it continues to become more diverse, with more women, minority and group members, and older workers in the workforce. Some employers call "the aging workforce" a big problem. The problem is that there aren't enough younger workers to replace the projected number of baby boom-era older workers (born roughly between 1946–1964) who are retiring. Many employers have been bringing retirees back (or just trying to keep them from leaving.

Workforce diversity refers to the wider variety of today's employees, who vary with respect to gender, age, culture, and ethnic background, and who may have physical and/or mental disabilities or challenges. Whereas, globalization focuses on differences between people from different countries, workforce diversity addresses differences among people within a given country. An important FLM challenge will be valuing the uniqueness of each employee, while forming cohesive work groups and teams with people of different backgrounds and values. FLMs also must be prepared to deal with racial discrimination or sexual harassment, should either problem arise (see Chapter 3 for a discussion of both these concepts).

Workforce diversity has important implications for FLM practice. FLMs and their organizations will need to shift their philosophy from treating everyone alike to recognizing differences and responding to those differences in ways that will ensure employee retention and greater productivity while, at the same time, not discriminating. This shift includes, for instance, providing diversity training and revamping benefit programs to make them more "family-friendly." Some organizations are not only changing the range of benefit choices they offer, but also changing the basic structure of their benefits as they recognize that the "one-size fits all approach" to employee benefits does not work. Diversity, if positively managed, can increase creativity and innovation in organizations as well as improve decision-making by providing different perspectives on problems. When diversity is not managed properly, there is potential for higher turnover, more-difficult communication, and more interpersonal conflicts.

Some employers find millennial employees (those born roughly between 1981 and 2000) a challenge to deal with, and this isn't just a U.S. phenomenon. Some say that millennials want meaningful work and frequent feedback. And while many employees spend about an hour per workday on their social media, millennials spend more. On the other hand, millennials grew up with smartphones and social media and are experts at collaboration online. "Generation Z" (born 2000–2020), having seen their millennial predecessors struggle to find jobs, are in many instances "not willing to settle" and "extremely self-motivated."

Trends in How People Work

At the same time, work continues to shift from manufacturing to service in North America and Western Europe. Currently, over two-thirds of the U.S. workforce is employed in producing and delivering services, not products. By 2024, service-providing industries are expected to account for 129 million out of 160 million (81%) of wage and salary jobs overall. So, in the next few years, almost all the new jobs added in the United States will be in services, not in goods-producing industries.

Human Capital

One big consequence of globalization and technological trends or advances is that organizations are more dependent on their employees' knowledge, education, training, skills, and expertise—on their "human capital." Professional jobs always required education and knowledge. Today, even production assemblers as well as bank tellers, retail clerks, and package deliverers need a level of technological sophistication they wouldn't have needed a few years ago. The point is that in the knowledge-based economy, "the acquisition and development of superior human capital appears essential to firms; profitability and success."[1]

The challenge for FLMs is that they have to manage such employees differently. For example, empowering them to make decisions presumes the organization has selected and trained them to make more decisions themselves. Related to this challenge is the broader trend towards employee engagement.

Employee Engagement

One of the biggest challenges today is the increased focus on employee engagement. Employee engagement is the extent to which employees feel passionate about their jobs, are committed to the organization, and put discretionary effort into their work. Research shows engaged employees are more productive, creative, and less likely to leave. Therefore it's not surprising, more and more organizations are seeking to improve employee engagement. In fact, a key challenge for FLMs is how they keep engaging their direct reports throughout the employee life cycle.

Unfortunately, about one-third of U.S. employees are not engaged in their work for a variety of reasons. Many don't feel a strong connection with their company or the mission—if there even is one.

With just over one-third of the U.S. workforce engaged, that leaves a staggering two-thirds who are not. That cascade effect is powerful. Expensive too, as some estimates suggest that disengagement runs companies about a third of the disengaged worker's salary in lost productivity. Actively disengaged employees cost the U.S. economy $483 billion to $605 billion each year in lost productivity.

FLMs shouldn't need a study to tell them how many problems disengagement creates for an organization or the benefits of engaged employees who show up to work each day as their best self by passionately adding value, and proactively seeking to achieve their company's mission. Creating this sense of belonging with each employee requires more than free lunches or interesting work perks, it's a commitment from FLMs and other organizational leaders to focus on the specific and individual needs of every employee.

The Quality Impact

Today's organizations continue to operate quite differently than in decades past. For them the watchword is not "getting by," but, "making things better," which has been referred to as the *quality revolution* (or *impact*). The best organizations are ones that strive to deliver better quality goods and services to customers at lower prices than ever before. Those that do so flourish, and those that do not tend to fade away.

There is increasing evidence that the delivery of quality products and services to customers has a direct impact on the success of organizations.

The key, of course, is to realize that the people in the organization, not advertising slogans or statistical quality control, deliver quality goods and services. The challenge for FLMs and organizations across the world is to have their employees deliver quality products and—especially—services to each other (internal customers) and to customers and clients. In the future, organizations will continue their efforts to improve quality and service through various organizational practices.

Outsourcing

Organizations are continuing to restructure in efforts to do more with less by completely eliminating those parts that focus on non-core sectors of the business (i.e., tasks that are peripheral to the organization), and hiring outside firms to perform these functions instead—a practice known as *outsourcing*. Contracting with outsiders to do work previously done within the corporation, is not a new phenomenon, but becomes easier with technological advances as organizations continue to look for ways to cut costs. Thus, the increase in farming out many varieties of work previously done by regular employees, resulting in layoffs and internal reorganization. By outsourcing secondary activities, an organization can focus on what it does best, its key capability—what is known as its *core competency*. For example, by outsourcing its payroll processing, a company may grow smaller and focus its resources on what it does best. Outsourcing, of course, creates layoffs and the associated problems, including union-management frictions which all undoubtedly pose challenges for FLMs.

Telecommuting

Question: What current organizational activity continues to simultaneously help alleviate child-care problems, reduces traffic jams, and cuts air pollution and fuel consumption, while also saving millions of dollars on office space? The answer is *telecommuting* or teleworking—the practice of using communications technology to enable work to be performed by employees from remote locations, such as the home or a nearby telecenter. Imagine the following example: An after-hour request from one of Johnson Industries' customers is made for some assistance on a computer problem. Everyone has gone home for the day. A call is made to the on-call computer technician who has a computer/modem at home for diagnosing and addressing the customers' problem. The request is completed, the customer is happy, and no one had to make a trip back to the Johnson Industries office.

Telecommuting results in increased separation from the principal office, while, at the same time, it increases connection to the home.

Telecommuting is perhaps one of the most profound examples of how technology will continue to impact work, jobs, and FLMs.

Contingent or Alternative Workforce

Increasingly, organizations are employing more part-time employees. That is, instead of eliminating entire organizational functions and buying them back through outside service providers, organizations are eliminating individual jobs and hiring people to perform them on an as-needed basis. Such individuals comprise what has been referred to as a *contingent workforce*. This workforce is comprised of people hired temporarily, part-time, or as contract employees who work as needed for finite periods of time.

The temporary or contingent workforce has grown rapidly, paralleling the restructuring and layoff phenomena. The contingent workforce is of considerable size and includes specialists of all kinds, including nurses, accountants, lawyers, engineers, and computer and software experts. A growing number of middle managers and top executives are also part of this temporary workforce.

The "leasing" of employees by staffing service companies has become a rapidly growing industry because of the demand for temporary workers. Additionally, for many years people viewed contract, freelance, and gig employment as "alternative work," options considered supplementary to full-time jobs. Today, this segment of the workforce has gone mainstream, and it needs to be managed strategically. Given growing skills shortages and the low birth rate in many countries, leveraging and managing "alternative" workforces will become essential to business growth in the years ahead.

How will the FLM motivate employees who consider themselves, at best, transient—that is, just working at the present organization until something better comes along? Numerous studies have indicated that lower productivity and increased accidents occur when employees are not fully committed to their jobs. Motivating employees who are not fully committed will be another FLM challenge.

Changes in Job Design

Changes in *job design* (the process of determining and organizing the specific tasks and responsibilities to be carried out by each member of the organization and/or teams) has and continues to drastically change the nature or work itself in many instances.

The widespread and growing use of self-managed teams is an example of changes in job design. Organizations have moved toward the use of such teams to increase the flexibility of their workforces. They are redesigning work and jobs to allow employees with unique skills and backgrounds to tackle projects or problems together and to perform a wide variety of tasks, including dividing up the work, monitoring quality, ordering parts, interviewing applicants, and so on. The use of self-managed teams also frequently involves many organizational changes, including changes in technology, workflow, selection, training, and compensation.

As organizations continue to redesign jobs they will also reshape the relationship between FLMs and the people they are supposedly responsible for managing. You will find more and more FLMs being called coaches, advisors, sponsors, or facilitators. And there will be a continued blurring between the roles of FLMs and their employees. More and more decision-making will be pushed down to the operating level, where workers will be given the freedom to make choices about schedules, procedures, and solving work-related problems. Organizations will also continue to put employees in charge of what they do. And in doing so, FLMs will have to learn how to give up control to employees who must learn how to take responsibility for their work and make appropriate decisions. Empowerment (putting employees in charge of what they do) will change leadership styles, power relationships, the way work is designed, and the way organizations are structured.

The Job Skills Gap

The U.S. service sector continues to experience much faster growth than the manufacturing sector. Service, technical, and managerial positions that require college degrees will make up half of all manufacturing and service jobs in the coming years. Unfortunately, most available workers will be too unskilled to fill those jobs (i.e., *job skills gap*). Even now many companies complain that the supply of skilled labor is dwindling and that they must provide their employees with basic training to make up for the shortcomings of public education systems.

Although in the last decade the overall education level of Americans has increased in terms of schooling and even fundamental literacy, so also have the demands of the workplace. As a group, high school graduates are simply not keeping pace with the kinds of skills required in the new business world. The report card on college-educated workers is not particularly flattering either.

To deal with these problems, some businesses have developed agreements in which their companies join with public schools to form a compact that reserves jobs for high school graduates who meet academic and attendance requirements. A second strategy is in-house training for current or prospective employees through formal training and on-the-job training programs. Companies currently spend in excess of an estimated $83 billion in 2019 on a wide variety of training programs. This is in addition to the more than $19 billion spent on training programs by the federal government in the same year. Nonetheless, the job skills gap or shortage is likely to remain a challenge for FLMs and their organizations in the United States while also providing an opportunity for FLMs to better understand the skill needs of their organizations and contribute to organizational strategy and success through optimizing planning and understanding how to position their workforce for the future of work.

Changing Attitudes Toward Work

American workers are changing their attitudes toward work. Employees continue to demand better coordination between lifestyle needs, including family and leisure, and employment needs. Leisure pursuits have become more highly valued than work goals. Even previously loyal employees have become cynical of the corporate world. This cynicism has spawned a new interest in organized labor and collective bargaining, even among professionals.

Working habits are also changing rapidly, as technology transforms working arrangements and people's understanding of what matters at work shifts. American workers are more interested in jobs with meaningful work, which allow for self-fulfillment and work satisfaction. They want jobs that provide greater challenges and enable them to use more skills and knowledge. These changes in employee attitudes and values require that FLMs and their organizations use different organizational strategies than those used in the past.

Lifestyles and expectations about life circumstances are also changing. Where people are willing to live and work is becoming a serious issue for a significant number of workers. People are prone to have decided preferences about where they want to live, whether in the city, the suburbs, or a rural setting, and in what region and climate. In addition, more and more people express concern about the appropriate balance of work and family and leisure and other aspects of their lives. They may not want the job interfering with taking a child to a Little League game or to a Girl Scout meeting or going to church. Thus they may be less willing to accept overtime assignments or to work long hours or weekends. However, fear of layoffs undoubtedly produces considerable acquiescence to management's wishes, but with resulting job dissatisfaction for many people.

These trends present both a significant challenge and a real opportunity for FLMs and their organizations. For example, one challenge for FLMs is that the diverse workforce contains those who have traditionally been discriminated against. Thus, diversity takes on ethical implications of how FLMs and the rest of management can eliminate all forms of discrimination (age, sex, race, ethnic origin, religion, disability) and provide equal opportunity in all aspects of employment. Also stemming from the heightened sensitivity that results from the realization of a diverse workforce is a focus on problems such as sexual harassment, the glass ceiling effect, and work family issues. FLMs and organizations that formulate strategies that capitalize on employee diversity are more likely to survive and prosper.

Meeting Today's Challenges

It has often been said that the only thing that remains constant is change— and it's true! (See Chapter 7 for more discussion on change.) Today's FLM must increasingly be prepared for changing events that will have a significant effect on their lives. Some of the more recent changes and challenges have been highlighted throughout this chapter. The last section of this chapter takes a closer look at how some of these changes are affecting FLMs in organizations.

Globalization affects FLMs in many ways. An increasingly globalized world introduces new challenges for FLMs. These range from how FLMs view people from different countries to how they develop an understanding of these immigrating employees' cultures. A specific challenge for FLMs is recognizing differences that might exist and find ways to make their interactions with all employees more effective.

FLMs may be heavily involved in implementing the changes. They must be prepared to deal with the organizational issues these changes bring about. For example, when an organization downsizes an important challenge for FLMs is motivating a workforce that feels less secure in their jobs and less committed to their employers. FLMs must also ensure that their skills and those of their employees are kept up to date and that they are marketable. Employees whose skills become obsolete are more likely to be candidates for downsizing. Those employees who keep their jobs will more than likely be doing the work of two or three people. This situation can create frustration, anxiety, and less motivation. For the FLM; this, too, can dramatically affect work unit productivity.

An emphasis on quality focuses on the customer, seeks continual improvements, strives to improve the quality of work, seeks accurate measurement, and involves employees. Each FLM must clearly define what quality means to the jobs in his or her unit. This needs to be communicated to every staff member. Each individual must then exert the needed effort to move toward "perfection." FLMs and their employees must recognize that failing to do so could lead to unsatisfied customers taking their purchasing power to competitors. Should that happen, jobs in the unit might be in jeopardy.

Effective quality initiatives can generate a positive outcome for FLMs and employees. Everyone involved may now have input into how work is best done. A focus on quality provides opportunities for FLMs to build the participation of the people closest to the work. As such, quality can eliminate bottlenecks that have hampered work efforts in the past. Quality can help create more satisfying jobs—for both the FLM and his or her employees.

Few jobs today are unaffected by advances in technology. How specifically is it changing the FLM's job? One need only to look at how the typical office is set up to answer this question. Today's organizations have become integrated communications centers. By linking computers, smartphones, fax machines, copiers, printers, tablets, and the like, FLMs can get more complete information more quickly than ever before. With that information, FLMs can better formulate plans, make faster decisions, more clearly define the jobs that workers need to perform, and monitor work activities on an "as-they-happen" basis. In essence, technology today has enhanced FLMs' ability to more effectively and efficiently perform their jobs.

Technology is also changing where an FLM's work is performed since they have immediate access to information that helps them in making decisions. Technological advances assist FLMs who have employees in remote locations, reducing the need for face-to-face interaction with these individuals. On the other hand, effectively communicating with individuals in remote locations (for example, teleworkers), as well as ensuring that performance objectives are being met, has become a major challenge for FLMs.

The implications of changing demographics and workforce diversity for FLMs are widespread. However, the most significant implication for FLMs is the requirements of sensitivity to the differences in each individual and generation. That means they must shift their philosophy from treating everyone alike to recognizing, valuing, and responding to these differences in ways that will ensure employee retention and greater productivity.

Today's successful FLMs will be those who have learned to effectively respond to and manage change. FLMs will work in an environment in which change is taking place at an unprecedented rate. New competitors spring up overnight and old ones disappear through mergers, acquisitions, or failure to keep up with the changing marketplace and customer demands. Downsized organizations mean fewer workers to complete the necessary work. Constant innovations in computer and telecommunications technologies are making communications instantaneous. These factors, combined with the globalization of product and financial markets, have created an environment of never ending change. As a result, many traditional management practices—created for a world that was far more stable and predictable—no longer apply.

New governmental and societal issues will continue to complicate the FLM's job in the future. Numerous environmental concerns will remain as serious long-term problems for FLMs and their organizations. Energy availability and costs will continue to be of great concern internationally and domestically. These types of issues and societal pressures have to become part of the FLM's and organizations planning and operations.

Federal (and state and local and international) legislation affects the FLMs. In addition, state and local governments have laws and regulations that impact business. The effect of such legislation can be quite costly, and FLMs and their organizations may be required to change their methods of operations in order to comply.

All indications are that these pressures will remain intense. In some instances, today's FLMs have to be more of a lawyer, cop, teacher, accountant, political scientist, and psychologist than a manager. While this may be overstating the point, this reflects a realistic aspect of every FLM's contemporary role. FLMs must be more flexible in their styles, smarter in how they work, quicker in making decisions, more efficient in handling scarce resources, better at satisfying the customer, and more confident in enacting massive and revolutionary changes. As management writer Tom Peters captured in one of his best-selling books, "Today's FLMs must be able to thrive on change and uncertainty."

In bringing this introductory chapter to a close it is important to recognize that the workplace of today and tomorrow is indeed undergoing immense and permanent changes. Organizations are being challenged to change or be "reengineered" or "transformed" for greater speed, efficiency, and flexibility. Teams are pushing aside the individual as the primary building block of organizations. Command-and-control management has given way to participative management and empowerment. Authoritative leaders are being replaced by charismatic and transformational leaders. Employees increasingly are being viewed as internal customers. All this creates a mandate for a new kind of FLM today.

FLMs will need a broader set of skills to achieve and maintain both their own, the department's, and organization's success today. The areas in which they will need to develop expertise include strategic planning; budgeting; quality management, benchmarking and best practices; and telecommunications and technology; and interpersonal relationships. Aside from honing these skills, FLMs can better prepare themselves for today's challenges by gaining a better understanding of the needs of their internal customers, recognizing the need for effective information systems for employees, building relationships with the best service providers, and aligning the FLM's unit and organization strategies and their processes.

Like other levels of management, today's FLM must be a true strategic partner and coach in the organization. Each FLM must effectively respond to the ever changing world of work and the role FLMs are expected to successfully play in that world. As the pace of change quickens, FLMs must become a tougher and more durable, albeit more flexible, interface between their organization and the bumpy road of a changing environment. And they must do this while maintaining the highest level of integrity.

Note

1. Crook, R., Combs, J. G., Todd, S., & Woehr, D. J. (2011). Does human capital matter? A meta-analysis of the relationship between human capital and firm performance? *Journal of Applied Psychology, 96*(3), 443–456, p. 444.

2

On Becoming a Front-Line Manager

"You're Not in Kansas Anymore"

Being a new FLM is never an easy thing to do, but it is important for new FLMs to make as smooth a transition as possible. Why? If they get it wrong these might be some of the consequences:

- A reduction in the FLMs self-confidence/self-esteem as they struggle with the responsibilities of the role.
- FLM finds transition so tough they subsequently step down from the position.
- Day to day supervision and management of employees is disrupted or neglected resulting in increased absence costs, reduced productivity, and so on.
- Increase in grievances and grumbles by employees who are struggling to adjust to a new FLM. An unsettled environment often creates conflict.
- Reduced employee morale due to badly managed transitions/changes. This can in turn lead to reduced quality and customer care.

Succeeding as a Frontline Manager in Today's Organizations, pages 29–56
Copyright © 2021 by Information Age Publishing

■ Other potential FLMs might in the future reject offers of pro-motion to FLM role having seen what can go wrong. This will negatively impact an organization's succession planning and also might increase recruitment costs.

Not surprisingly, these possible consequences are a fact of life and may re-sult when any individual moves into a new FLM role. We will revisit these challenges later.

New FLMs often experience doubts as they start their first manage-ment jobs, due to the many challenges they face and the need to change their relationships oftentimes with their former co-workers. But if a person makes advance preparation and is willing to continually learn, the job can be fulfilling.

Today FLMs and their organizations must compete in changing domes-tic and global environments using diverse workforces. As a result, the prac-tice of management is continually changing. Many of today's organizations are giving the employees who do the work more authority for planning and controlling what they do by empowering them. In addition, these organiza-tions continue to establish teams and place a high premium on teamwork. Of course, any group of people working on a job could be considered a team; after all, the individuals do work together in one way or another.

As organizations have done more to empower individuals and teams FLMs have taken on more responsibility as "facilitators" or "team leaders." However, FLMs still have important tasks to perform, but they don't spend much time telling people what to do or watching to make sure they do it. So what do they do instead? The following comments reveal the new focus of FLMs:

Some of the teams I coordinate really don't need me much. They're run-ning their own operation. They let me know when they need something or have a problem they can't solve. I've been working on a task force to imple-ment a new computer system. I'm getting pulled into decision-making and planning tasks I never had time for before.

I do a lot more coaching and training now. We are developing a multi-skilled team where people learn to do every job in the work unit. That means a lot of cross-training. Also, we are adding some new responsibilities into each employee's job. I play a big role in conducting training and working with others to plan, implement and evaluate the training.

In the quest for increased performance and customer satisfaction, today's organizations are giving more of the everyday responsibility for scheduling work and solving problems to employees working in teams. This chapter begins by discussing the transition from individual contributor to FLM. Next, the focus is on the pros and cons of being an FLM. The chapter then discusses how to make a smooth transition to the role of FLM. Next, the chapter offers some factors important to being a successful FLM. The chapter then offers a discussion of a contemporary perspective of the FLM before concluding with a look at how organizations can best help new FLMs address various challenges and make a smoother transition to their new role.

From Individual Contributor to Front-Line Manager

Moving from an individual contributor (e.g., a person without management responsibilities who contributes to an organization) to an FLM is an undeniably large shift. At a minimum, it means a person needs to accept that they've chosen a path that alters their relationship with those around them and with themselves. They have to throw away the playbook that got them where they are today, and swap it for one that gives them the ability to challenge assumptions. That alone is a large enough change for someone who is used to staying head down in her or his own work. However, stepping into an FLM role also involves distinct evolvement in responsibilities.

When tasked with managing others, the work that person had grown so used to doing (and likely even was most passionate about) fades away, for example, often in favor of attending meetings, overseeing budgets and timelines, and ensuring the success of others directly reporting to them.

Most new FLMs are promoted from the ranks of front-line employees they are asked to manage as an FLM. Senior management usually selects employees with a good grasp of the technical skills needed to perform well in the department for FLM jobs. The individual also might have more seniority than many of the other employees in the department. Good work records (and work habits) and leadership skills are also reasons for selecting an employee to be an FLM.

In reality, none of these criteria for promotion guarantees an individual knows how to manage. When computer specialist Julie Jardone was promoted to departmental manager, she was unprepared for some aspects of managing a group of computer specialists. Instead of receiving any type of training in management, Julie says, "I was just kind of dropped off the end of the plank." She was especially challenged by determining how to lead her former colleagues. Recalling an early effort at handling a computer specialist's poor performance, Julie says, "She messed up, and I yelled at her. She started crying. I didn't expect that reaction, and my boss just looked at me and shook his head." Fortunately, over time Julie learned how to better manage people, and she has since moved up to a middle level management position at the same company.

For those like Jenny who become FLMs, the shift from individual contributor to FLM is sometimes difficult, as it is a shift from doing work yourself to getting work done through others. The new FLM must suddenly be more adept at using his or her people skills and devote more time to planning ahead and keeping an eye on the department's activities. These and other changes are bound to lead to some anxiety. It is natural to wonder whether you are qualified or how you will handle the problems that surely will arise. The remainder of this section looks at what it takes to become an FLM and the challenges FLMs face in this new leadership role. The following comments from a recently promoted FLM capture the dilemma many new FLMs face when they're promoted from the ranks.

> It wasn't easy to make the move from being one of the unit specialists in the department to being the FLM. On Wednesday I had been one of them. Then, Thursday of the next week, I became their boss. Suddenly, people I had joked around and socialized with for years were distancing themselves from me. I could see that they were apprehensive. They weren't sure how, or if, I could be trusted. I didn't think our relationship was going to be much different. Hey, we were friends. We went out together Fridays after work. But I'm management now. I still think I'm like them, part of the group. But they don't see me that way. Even when I join them for drinks, it's not like it used to be. They have their guard up now. It's been a hard adjustment for me. I've become a part of management and sometimes I'm even the target of blame or anger when they resent company policies.

Many new FLMs report feeling a sense of isolation, added responsibility, and a lack of control. They are no longer one of the gang and they are not sure what is expected of them. They are responsible for the results of other people's work and not just their own.

Moving from one middle-management job to another or from a middle-management position to one in top management rarely creates the anxiety that comes when you move from being an individual contributor to an FLM. Because middle managers already have some experience with the challenges of being in a management position, they know what to expect.

The experience of many new FLMs helps us to understand what it's like to become an FLM. Even though most of these new FLMs had worked in their respective organizations for a number of years, they have simplistic expectations of their FLM roles. Each had originally been a star employee. But the requirements of an individual contributor are very different from the demands on an FLM—and few of these new FLMs understood that. Ironically, their previous successes as individual contributors may actually have made their transition to management harder. Because of their strong technical expertise and previous success, they had depended on their FLMs less than the average worker. When they became FLMs and suddenly had to deal with low-performing and unmotivated employees, they were unprepared.

New FLMs encounter a number of surprises. The major changes they face as they transform themselves from individual contributors to FLMs are listed below. The FLM

- becomes responsible for the output of other people, usually for the first time;
- acts as a leader rather than a "boss";
- stays informed on technical issues, but realizes that this is no longer the primary focus of the job, nor the primary determinant of success or failure;
- acquires many new and unfamiliar administrative duties, which may relate to personnel, procedural, and budgetary issues;
- deals with employees and their problems, but no longer as a co-worker; and
- faces many new situations in which the action to be taken is unclear and requires a judgment call rather than reference to a rule book.

Moving from individual contributor to FLM thus requires a change in behavior and orientation and the development of a managerial point of view. With experience most new FLMs succeed in making this shift. They learn to get their sense of achievement through the accomplishments of their co-workers. They learn that while their employees may not always perform a specific task exactly as they might, jobs still get done and get done well. New FLMs learn that their new activities are quite different from, and even more important than, their old activities.

Doesn't Everyone Want to Be an FLM?

Working as an FLM can be challenging and exciting. As with anything worthwhile, however, certain trade-offs are necessary. Some of those who decide to enter management later reverse the decision and return to their previous jobs. They may say something like:

- ■ "There is just too much hassle involved."
- ■ "I hated all the meetings. And I found the more you did for people who worked for you, the more they expected. I felt like I was coming in every day and people were expecting me to meet their needs. I was a counselor, motivator, psychologist, and financial master."
- ■ "With technology changing rapidly, you can never slack off these days if you're on the technical side."
- ■ "It's a rare person who can supervise, keep up on the technical side, *and* handle an FLM job, too."
- ■ "You're a backstop, caught in the middle between upper management and the workforce."
- ■ "I felt like I was being pulled in 15 different directions by my bosses and employees and I had a hard time with all the complaining."

Although the issues discussed in this section are often matters of perception rather than reality, they present serious trade-offs for many FLMs. First, FLM positions are not easy. Even if an individual has been a superstar as an employee, this is no guarantee that the individual will succeed as an FLM. The fact that a person is capable of doing excellent work is a big plus, but there are many factors to consider.

Second, employees usually come to work, do their jobs, and then go home. The FLM, by contrast, often is on the job before regular working hours begin and is still there after the employees have gone. So, it should be no surprise that FLMs work long hours. The job of an FLM can literally be a 24-hour, 7-day-a-week job. That's not to be interpreted as being on the job every hour of every day. But when an individual accepts the responsibility of managing others, they really never can "get away" from the job. Things happen, and they'll be expected to deal with them—no matter when they happen, or where the FLM is. The number of hours tends to increase as an individual climbs the organization ladder.

Third, some FLMs think their pay is low in relation to that of their employees. In some instances, the difference in pay is insignificant. In fact, some beginning FLMs may make less than their most senior employees. In many organizations, a raise in an FLM's base pay when they become an FLM does not translate into higher annual earnings. How so? Consider that, as an FLM, you are no longer eligible for overtime pay. Instead, in most organizations, FLMs get compensatory (comp) time (i.e., time off). As a front-line employee, your organization is legally required to pay you a premium rate (typically time and one-half) for overtime work. Most likely that will not be true when you move into an FLM position.

Fourth, in addition to their own concerns, FLMs are affected by the problems of others. Employees may bring to the job a variety of off-the-job problems. Perhaps one employee is going through a divorce and simply wants to talk. Another might ask for advice on financial problems. Employees can choose to worry only about their own problems, but FLMs cannot. They have some responsibility for the people working for them, who have different personalities, aspirations, and problems. For some FLMs, this can be too great a burden.

Fifth, FLMs are responsible not only for their own actions but for the actions of others as well. Whereas employees need only be concerned about meeting their individual objectives, FLMs must make sure that all members of the team are working together to achieve team or departmental goals. Daily, weekly, monthly, and even annual performance standards must be met. Some FLMs find it hard to maintain a positive attitude under such pressures.

Sixth, FLMs are sometimes not given enough control to get the job done. Often they are only permitted to recommend certain actions. For instance, an FLM thinks an employee is unable to do the work properly and should be fired. The FLM may have to request upper management approval before taking this action and may in all likelihood be prepared to have the request tabled. Which means they will have to find a way to work with the employee and still get the job done.

Seventh, an FLM's work is fragmented; activities are often brief. Given an FLM's high activity level, they have little time to devote to any single activity. Interruptions, crises, and problems are the rule as the FLM is constantly juggling the needs of the organization (completion of tasks) and the needs of employees. The need to recognize these concepts and establish priorities is essential.

Eighth, an FLM, particularly one promoted within, is no longer one of the front-line groups. In many organizations the "us-versus-them" mentality develops. The newly promoted FLM is not now one of "them." Therefore, the FLM needs to develop a professional rather than a personal relationship with employees.

Ninth, some FLMs do not enjoy making the tough decisions that go with the job. Disciplining an employee, especially a former co-worker, is uncomfortable, to say the least. Firing an employee can be very traumatic. The same can be said of demoting or laying off employees or giving an employee a negative or less than sterling performance appraisal.

Finally, the movement toward more employee participation, along with the growth of the human resources department, is perceived as an erosion of the FLM's authority. At the same time, it has been suggested that the majority of the FLM positions in U.S. corporations are redundant. These notions are threatening to many FLMs.

The possible trade-offs described above will deter some people from becoming FLMs. For others, however, they simply increase the challenge and excitement associated with the work.

Despite all the aspects of the job an FLM cannot control, the FLM is not excused from doing his or her best. The FLM will have to make sure that they don't become discouraged or cynical. With time, FLMs learn to recognize their limits, their opportunities, and which difficult situations they cannot change. Today's FLMs must believe that they can do the job and make a contribution to their organization's success.

Given the discussion in the previous paragraphs, it is important to think about why you want to be an FLM. Managing others can be rewarding as evidenced by the discussion in the next section. It is important to understand exactly what your motivation is for becoming an FLM—and what tradeoffs you're willing to make to become the best FLM you can be.

Being an FLM Can be Satisfying

Being an FLM can be an immensely satisfying experience for you and those who work for you. By managing the efforts of others, you have more opportunities to make your ideas come to life. You can be a leader, a mentor, and a coach. You can be a person of vision and action, respected and rewarded for your contribution to your organization's success and the quality of work life.

There are a number of reasons why it is worthwhile for individual contributors to give up their comfortable, familiar jobs to become FLMs. One obvious reason is that FLMs get more rewards. Greater rewards come with greater contributions to the success of the organization. Some rewards are financial, some are perquisites (e.g., parking space) and some are psychological. Additionally, the accomplishment of various tasks is rewarding, particularly when others thought it was not possible.

Second, becoming an FLM opens the door to future promotions and opportunities to grow personally and professionally. Change can be uncertain and, at times, even uncomfortable, but employees are attracted to the ranks of management because they believe they are ready to learn something new, practice new skills, and solve bigger problems. Instead of just doing mechanical and technical tasks, FLMs perform the much more complex job of managing people. Each day they face new situations. For many FLMs, there is personal satisfaction in handling these situations successfully that is simply not available at the front-line employee level.

Third, many people enjoy the respect and influence normally accorded the FLM. In some instances, individuals are also thrilled by the prospect of being the boss. It is natural to want to have influence over others. The opportunity to make decisions and be held accountable for those decisions is satisfying. Increased involvement in decision making is a positive benefit to many FLMs.

Fourth, FLMs can make more of a difference as a supervisor than as an employee on the front-line. People above and below them in the organization listen to their ideas. Generally, the higher a person moves in the organization, the more that individual can affect the success of the organization. An FLM can find great satisfaction in helping employees reach their full potential.

Fifth, FLMs have greater flexibility than their employees. FLM experience provides experiences and learning that no textbook can provide. They are usually paid a salary rather than wages based on hours worked and are often allowed some flexibility in their working hours. That is because their job is to make sure that the tasks actually get done, as opposed to doing the tasks themselves.

Sixth, FLMs may enjoy the excitement of being involved in a wide range of technical activities. More than other managers FLMs are knowledgeable about the job performed at the operating level. The FLM is able to share in the experiences of several employees, which adds variety and interest to the job. For example, during any given hour an FLM might interact with a manager, a specialist in the work unit, or an employee from another department each doing very different and sometimes specialized tasks. An FLM gains satisfaction from the opportunity to use a wide variety of skills and gains valuable experiences. FLMs are rarely bored.

Finally, the FLM has a special opportunity to help people. Employees have personal problems that can sometimes be solved by referring them to counseling. If these problems involve conflicts with the organization, no one is in a better position than the FLM to go to bat for the employees or to help them understand the organization's needs. The FLM is also able to train employees and help them prepare for advancement or taking on additional responsibilities. An FLM can find great personal satisfaction in helping others reach their full potential. By constantly looking for the good in other people an FLM will uncover some personal strengths. They can then build on these strengths.

The Rewards or Benefits of Being a FLM

Many employees want not only to make money but also to make a difference. The reality is that most employees care about more than money. They want work that is challenging and engaging, that enables them to exercise some discretion and control over what they do, and that provides them with opportunities to learn and grow. Becoming an FLM offers many rewards apart from money and status, as follows:

- ▪ You have a newfound sense of job satisfaction. At the end of the day, job satisfaction is what will drive you to keep coming back to work. The sense of accomplishment you will get from managing a group or team or department will fill you with personal and professional pride at the end of the day. In your capacity as an FLM, you will be helping a group of people work together towards a common goal, earning their admiration and respect in the process.
- ▪ You get more responsibility. You will be trusted to make important decisions and be in charge of such things as employee schedules, budgeting, and interviewing, hiring and promoting people.
- ▪ You get more accountability with the responsibility. You will have a higher level of accountability as an FLM. While entry level employees may be able to hide poor performance behind teammates or even blame FLMs—as an FLM you won't have it so easy. The "buck stops with you," and you will be held accountable for not only your own performance, but the performance for all of your direct reports, as well.
- ▪ You will make more money. Making more money for you may be the best thing about becoming an FLM. After all, since you will be working harder, there is no reason your pay should not get a sizable bump.
- ▪ You and your direct reports can experience a sense of accomplishment. Every successful goal accomplished provides you not only with personal satisfaction but also with the satisfaction of all those employees you managed who helped accomplish it. You are truly able to experience what it feels like to get things done through people.
- ▪ You can stretch your abilities and magnify your range. Every promotion up the hierarchy of an organization stretches your abili-

ties, challenges your talents and skills, and magnifies the range of your accomplishments. Besides, you will be fulfilling a career goal that has you progressing from an entry-level position to a role of increasing responsibility.

- You build a catalog of successful products or services. Every product or service you provide becomes a monument to your accomplishments.
- You know what it is like to be valued in your organization. Your influence on the organization is multiplied far beyond the results that can be achieved by just one person acting alone.
- You will be able to manage yourself and your career. You can build your management skills in areas such as self-management, listening, handling change, and coping with organizational politics.
- You can become a mentor and help others. You can share your experience with others, provide guidance to someone new to the workplace, and help them advance their careers.

Cons of a FLM Job

- You just may not have what it takes to be a good FLM. Being a good FLM presumably requires skills that you do not currently have. Learning new skills is usually a good thing, but, if work in general has been a challenge for you in your entry-level job, an FLM job might just be too much for you.
- You may experience potential alienation from former coworkers. Being alienated from former coworkers may be a concern for you when you transition to FLM. You may fear the people you once worked with will view you differently because you are now in a position of authority.
- You will need to make tough decisions. Part of being an FLM is making some very difficult decisions. You may find yourself having to do dreaded tasks, such as disciplining, laying off, or firing employees. Although some FLMs enjoy exercising their power in this way, you may hate having to let people go or criticize them. As an FLM you will have to make a lot of unpopular decisions for the good of the organization.
- You will be under a lot more pressure. Not only will you have your manager breathing down your neck about cutting costs, you will have your employees demanding everything from more money to more vacation time. You will be the one held responsible every time something goes wrong.

- You will definitely do more work. Nights. Weekends. Holidays. Gone are the days when you could call in sick—even when you are—you are an FLM now and have way too much work to do to call in sick!
- You may experience a poor work-life balance. Because you will be doing more work, your heavier workload will most likely impact your having a health work-life balance. You may experience lower morale and job satisfaction may decrease. You will be working excessive hours, continually have to change shift patterns, or bring work home with you.

The reality is that being an FLM or manager is not for everyone. So, make sure you approach becoming an FLM with your eyes wide open!

Making a Smooth Transition to Front-Line Management

The new FLM can begin enjoying the benefits of being an FLM and making a better transition to the job by getting started right. Their immediate challenge is to establish their credibility by demonstrating that they are the best person for the job. Why is personal credibility so important? Because the weight of the FLM title is not so great that the individual can simply command people to get things done. The new FLM needs to work with everyone above, below, and beside them on the organizational ladder. If the new FLM is perceived as a person with little credibility, they will not be taken seriously, which means they will not be able to achieve their goals.

Personal credibility is easy to lose and hard to get back. It is determined by others and built on those values the individual learned as a child:

- Say what you mean, and mean what you say.
- Follow through and follow up.
- Don't let your teammates down.
- Be yourself.
- Deciding to play it safe by doing nothing, keeping a low profile, and generally avoiding conflict is almost always the wrong approach.
- You are more than a placeholder.
- Be smart, not just safe.
- You are not doing your job if you do not take a few risks.
- In the long run, your best security rests on your reputation for getting results.

As soon as an individual moves into the FLM job they shouldn't worry too much about establishing their management "style," which is a convenient way of describing how you interact with people. The new FLM's unique style will evolve as they get comfortable with the new role. They should concentrate instead on the substance of their job. What they choose to accomplish will affect their credibility. Selecting the right work to do, and finishing it on time and within budget, will show people that they are indeed competent to handle the new job. This is where the new FLM has to do some careful thinking and planning. They cannot afford to fail at their first management tasks, so they should choose them wisely.

An FLM may learn that one or more employees (possibly those he or she is now managing) had been candidates for the FLM's job and therefore may be jealous. One constructive approach that an FLM might take in addressing this problem is to acknowledge the other person's feelings, ask for the employee's support, and discuss his or her long-term goals. Julie Jardone did this with one of the other computer specialists who had been considered for the same job for which Julie was chosen. The computer specialist said that his goal was to "move into management." Julie said, "I told him, without making false promises, that I would do what I could to help him." Until this employee moved into a management job 9 months later, he was one of the top performers among Jenny's employees. An important aspect of this approach is that the FLM is helping employees to meet or exceed their own goals. For example, as an FLM, Julie can help a potentially jealous employee improve his or her performance. Julie shouldn't be surprised that employees regard her as a much better manager when she helps them make more money and achieve their career goals.

New FLMs must remember that their main responsibility is to see that all the work of their department gets done and gets done properly. The FLM must plan and organize the resources to accomplish the objectives of their department, and they must understand that they will be held accountable for the team's or department's results. The new FLM must be prepared to help everyone else complete their assignments successfully. This means that they will have to

- understand how their department contributes to the organization's goals;
- set and communicate the priorities that guide the work-units day-to-day activities;
- develop and implement effective work plans that get the required work completed right the first time, on time and within budget; and

▪ provide the necessary direction and feedback and coaching to employees about their job performance.

Once on the job, the new FLM must be concerned with big picture questions rather than focusing on one isolated bit of work. For example, what work do we have to accomplish? What work is in progress? What do we have to do to get ready for and complete the work? Who is doing what, and what will prevent them from finishing on time? What resources must we commit to solving the quality and service problems that employees and customers identified? Are we able to stay within budget? If not, why not? The new FLM must learn to make wise choices about where they direct employee efforts.

The new FLM needs to continue the learning process. It is very important that the new FLM learn as much as they can about the employees in the department or the work unit. Who are the quiet but productive employees, for example, and who are the unofficial leaders? To get to know employees, an FLM can talk to his or her own manager and read performance appraisals, but the most reliable sources of information are the employees themselves. Particularly in the early days on the job, an FLM should take the time to discuss goals with employees and observe their work habits.

Enthusiastic new FLMs are commonly trapped in the "I can do anything for everyone" mind set, so they say *yes* to too many people too soon. Their first few days as an FLM are filled with meetings, introductions, and other hazardous distractions. They have to say *no* to requests! If they don't, after a few days they will be over committed. The only way out of this dilemma is to work 24-hour days to catch up, explain to everyone why you are going to disappoint them, or pretend that nothing is wrong until your team members start complaining. Chronically over-committed FLMs cannot be successful. Most of the management tasks they are doing are new, so it will logically take longer to get them done in the beginning. They must schedule themselves accordingly.

Instead of rushing into risky commitments indiscriminately, FLMs like Julie should pick a few near-term challenges which she knows she can quickly accomplish. If these challenges have a high profile and Jenny receives rave reviews, so much the better. But Julie shouldn't jeopardize her relationship with her work team for any reason. These people are pivotal to Julie's success. Julie's first priority is to take care of them. She must establish her credibility with her work team with a few early successes, however modest.

When people like Jenny first become a new FLM it is more important to decide what should happen in the short-term (tomorrow and in the coming weeks) than to plan months ahead. Julie should think carefully about what she needs to accomplish, and then make lists of her short-term goals.

One of the more difficult tasks confronting new FLMs is the need to communicate with more people, more often. It is the FLMs job to know what is going on and to keep employees informed about what is going on so that everyone can work together smoothly. New FLMs must recognize that they will need to build and manage their information channels. While they are still new to the job, they should take the opportunity to ask employees the following questions:

- What are the goals of the department?
- How is the department evaluated?
- Who are the department's customers, both inside and outside the organization, and what do they say about us?
- How is the department doing?
- What prevents us from better serving our customers—both internal and external—in the ways they want us to?
- Do we have a common vision that we share for the department?
- Do we agree on what the department's priorities are?
- What are the department's short-, medium-, and long-term plans?

Some employees will be reluctant to share what they know because they are not willing to accept the responsibility that goes along with being an empowered employee. Other employees will give too much information because they want to impress the new FLM with their accomplishments or campaign for their favorite work assignments or projects. In either case, the FLM must be prepared to develop the information and communication flows necessary for working with their employees.

A further complication for the new FLM is that they will be blitzed with various communications in the form of memos, correspondence, and trade journals landing on their desk. What's really important? What information needs to be passed on to others? What other information aren't you receiving and needing to go out and get? Is everyone getting the information they need to do their jobs? Is everyone learning what they need to know? Are you getting an accurate understanding of what's going on in and between departments? It is important for the FLM not to get too many surprises. Few surprises are pleasant. If there are too many surprises then there may be unclear or incomplete communication which means that the FLM will need to make sure that they get more of the right information.

Finally, the new FLM is one of the partners important to the organization's success. The FLM is a resource for everyone else in the organization and vice versa. The partnership with the FLM's new boss and other upper-level managers. The FLM is in partnership with other FLMs, front-line employees, and even various vendors. In reality, the job of the new FLM is to work collaboratively with their partners so they can all work together for the success of the organization.

What Makes a Successful FLM?

Like most FLMs there are many things that will determine whether or not an individual will be successful. The following are particularly important characteristics critical to success as an FLM:

1. *Having a passion for the job.* Many individuals who have no passion to be FLMs are promoted into FLM merely because of their technical skills. Regardless of one's technical skill, the passion to be an FLM is necessary for success as an FLM. That passion encourages a person to develop all of the skills necessary to carry out the FLM responsibilities. Some people are happier using the technical skills of their profession or area of expertise. People who prefer this type of work to the functions of managing may be more content if they turn down an opportunity to become an FLM. In contrast, people who enjoy the challenge of making the plans and inspiring others to achieve the goals are more likely to be effective FLMs.

2. *Accepting the change in role.* Individuals who have been promoted to an FLM must recognize that their role has changed and that they are no longer one of the gang. They must remember that being an FLM may require them to make unpopular decisions. FLMs are the connecting link between the other levels of management and the front-line employees and, as such, they must develop expertise in representing both groups.

3. *Being a good role model.* FLMs must always remember that employees look to them to be a good role model by setting a good example. Front-line employees expect (and deserve) fair and equitable treatment from their FLM. Unfortunately, too many FLMs play favorites and treat employees inconsistently. FLMs who play favorites or whose behavior is inconsistent will lose the support and respect of their employees, and thus not be able to lead effectively. When FLMs make assignments and decisions based on who they like best, they will not necessarily make the assignments and decisions best suited to the organization. Effective FLMs are individuals who are consistent in their actions and practice what they preach. Lead by example. The FLM can set a good example by being on time and

refraining from doing personal work on the job—the same behavior requested from employees.

4. *Having a positive attitude.* Another part of being a role model is that employees tend to reflect the attitudes of the people in charge. When the FLM's attitude toward work and the organization is positive, employees are more likely to be satisfied with and interested in their work. Managers and co-workers prefer working with and for someone who has a positive attitude.

5. *Delegating.* Most FLMs were promoted from front-line jobs and have been accustomed to doing the work themselves. As a result, an often difficult, and yet essential, skill that these FLMs must develop is the willingness to delegate work to others (i.e., to give their employees authority and responsibility to carry out activities). FLMs tend to have excellent technical skills needed to perform job tasks, yet delegating those job tasks to others may be a challenge. They may resist giving an assignment to an employee who cannot do the job as well as they would. Nevertheless, FLMs cannot do the work of the whole department. Therefore, they must assign work to employees. Equally important, an FLM must give employees credit for their accomplishments. This, in turn, makes the FLM look good; the employee's successes show that the FLM is able to select and motivate as well as delegate effectively. (Chapter 3 discusses delegation in greater detail).

6. *Using authority wisely.* A number of FLMs let their newly acquired authority go to their heads. It is sometimes difficult to remember that the use of authority alone does not get the support and cooperation required in working with today's front-line employees. Learning when *not* to use authority is often as important as learning when to use it.

7. *Communicating effectively.* Employees and other managers depend on the FLM to keep them informed of what is happening in the organization. Employees who receive clear guidance about what is expected of them will not only perform better but also will be more satisfied with their jobs. Good communication also includes making contact with employees each day and listening to what they have to say. (Chapter 11 takes an in-depth look at the communications skills that FLMs need to develop).

8. *Leading a diverse workforce.* FLMs will need to establish relationships and friendships with individuals outside their own culture, beyond work relationships. Even if they are not fluent in other languages, they will need to understand enough of another language or two to feel comfortable around people who do not speak English. Additionally, it is important that today's FLM be open-minded. They

must be willing to break from the past, willing to do things that have never been done before, and willing to look at people and their viewpoints from a new perspective.

There are several other important things FLMs need to know if they are going to be successful in today's organizations. There are a number of personal issues they must address. First, FLMs must recognize that they are part of management as an FLM. This means that they must support the organization and the wishes of management. Although FLMs might disagree with those wishes, as FLMs, they must be loyal to the organization. As a part of the management team, they must take actions that are best for the organization. This may include making decisions that are unpopular with employees. In such situations, FLMs must recognize that taking on an FLM job means they cannot always be "one of the gang."

Next, the FLM must develop a means of gaining respect from the employees they manage, as well as from their peers and boss. If the FLM is going to be effective as an FLM, they must develop their trust and build credibility with them. One means of doing this is to continually keep their knowledge, skills, and competencies up-to-date. The FLM must continue their education, not only because it helps them, but also because it sets an example for their employees. It communicates that learning matters.

Finally, today's FLM must be sensitive to the needs of his or her employees. FLMs must learn to tolerate and even celebrate employee differences. Success, in part, begins with the understanding of what being flexible means.

FLM: A Contemporary Perspective

The primary responsibility of today's FLMs is to effectively manage their organization's most important resource—its people. It is the people upon which any organization ultimately depends. Effective management of people starts with selecting the right people to fill job openings and then teaching those individuals to do the job. It continues with ongoing training and development, motivation, and leadership, preparing employees for promotion.

Thus, FLMs will have to constantly strive to become true masters at managing others with a growing professional perspective. They must be attentive to the importance of trends influencing human behavior and observe how these trends impact the management of people in an ever changing and complex environment.

In all of this there is an imperative to take the professional perspective, which recognizes the need for constant self-improvement and self-renewal.

No amount of formal or informal education can ever be enough to fulfill an FLM's personal program of self-improvement. Today's FLMs must recognize that they, too, can become obsolete unless they constantly take measures to update their own knowledge and skills through a program of continuous self-development.

FLMs who acquire the knowledge and master the ideas and skills presented in this book will make considerable progress in terms of personal development, but just acquiring the knowledge and mastering the ideas and skills is not enough. Today's contemporary FLM must constantly seek new ways to apply their knowledge and skills in the challenging, complex, and dynamic situations they will encounter.

It is important to remember that too often the new FLM is forced to sink or swim, using a trial-by-fire philosophy. The newly hired FLM should consider the following pitfalls to avoid, training suggestions, and basic success strategies.

Pitfalls to Avoid

- Trying to be "popular" instead of effective.
- Failing to ask for advice.
- Overlooking the role of supportive problem solver.
- Failing to keep employees informed.
- Micro-managing by overemphasizing policies, rules, and procedures.
- Acting like "the boss" rather than a coach.

Training Suggestions

- Network with other FLMs.
- Identify a potential mentor.
- Participate in FLM development workshops and seminars.
- Register for FLM courses at local colleges and universities.
- Subscribe to periodicals and FLM training journals and magazines.

Basic Success Strategies

- Admit mistakes rather than attempting to cover them up.
- Show consideration.
- Provide details to all members of the team.
- Exhibit confidence and belief in your team members.
- Provide ongoing feedback, praise, and recognition.

Transitioning to the FLM Role: What Organizations Can/Should Do?

The beginning of this chapter took a brief look at some of the challenges faced by FLMs moving into their first FLM role and possible consequences if they do not make a smooth transition. New FLMs should expect their organizations to help them make as smooth a transition as possible when it comes to such challenges. This final section offers a closer look at each one of these challenges and offers some suggested ideas for solutions an organization's leaders or FLMs can use to help new FLMs achieve their full potential.

New FLM Challenge 1

I'm not sure I can do it. Just because an employee is great at meeting and greeting visitors does not mean they will be great as the FLM of the reception team. It's a different skill set entirely. This is seldom discussed though when an employee is offered an FLM job. Perhaps the employer just assumes the employee fully understands how different the role will be.

New FLMs are unproven. Not just to you, the employer, but to themselves as well. This creates the first challenge: I'm not sure I can do it. When supporting new FLMs, the first thing organizational leaders have to do is acknowledge that many will have huge self-doubt about whether they will be successful in this new role. With this in mind, organizational leaders should take time to regularly boost their confidence, provide moral support, reassure them of their support, and provide daily coaching as they begin to develop their skills.

Organizational leaders should also talk to them about their fears. Let them know it is normal and even senior leaders in the C-suite, in their first few months in a new role will often speak to their business coaches about, "What if people find out I'm not up to it?"

New FLM Challenge 2

I don't know how to do it. Responding to instructions is a different skill set to assessing requirements and then giving instructions! Not everyone knows where the fine line is between assertiveness and aggression and in our desire to assert our authority in a new role many of us can step over the line at times. Not everyone understands how they come across to others. Not everyone is self-aware. In reality, most of us are not great listeners and haven't taken the time to learn and/or develop this critical skill.

Training in soft skills training during the first 12 months of being an FLM on questioning and listening skills, communicating confidently, motivating and engaging direct reports and others, delegating confidently, self-reflection and presentation, and leading a team. FLMs immediate managers can provide them with daily coaching to ensure everything that is being learned in the formal training sessions is being put into practice day in day out. Additionally, FLMs can be appointed a mentor to learn from and share challenges with or otherwise setting up a buddying scheme.

New FLM Challenge 3

I'm not sure what to do. In most instances, a new employee is given an induction, shown where everything is and told what is required. However, in too many situations, when an employee is promoted to a new role, people seldom have formal inductions meaning that often they are left not being sure or knowing what to do.

New FLMs often struggle with conducting performance reviews, interviewing, doing a return to work interview after a period of absence, managing discipline, and filling in the HR and payroll paperwork. They need to be *formally* taught what to do and what is required as understanding processes and developing the necessary knowledge seldom happens by osmosis.

Organizations should provide clear guidance on where new FLMs can find all the relevant paperwork, documents, management guides, and employment policies. In addition, new FLMs should be provided orientation or onboarding as opposed to assuming that because they are not new to the organization they already know what to do, where to go, and who to ask. This means that other FLMs and organizational leaders should talk to new FLMs about all these things and make sure to identify any basics that need to be covered (and constantly review with them how things are going) before moving any further with their development.

New FLM Challenge 4

It's hard to break old habits. Learning how to be in a group, but maintain sufficient distance from the group to be able to supervise or manage the group members is really hard and a constant learning curve. What newly promoted FLMs sometimes feel they have lost is the camaraderie. Any significant job change can result in feelings of losing something, as well as venturing into the unknown. FLMs and other organizational leaders should help a new FLMs' direct reports understand that she or he has moved from familiar territory into unfamiliar territory. It is not unlikely that the new

FLM may well be terrified of what that might mean in the long term, whilst outwardly excited at the opportunity presented.

New FLM Challenge 5

I feel like I'm on an island (all by myself). When you are neither one of the team nor a fully integrated member of management, then it can be pretty lonely. As a new FLM, you're not one of them, but you're not one of us either. How would that make you feel?

What happens when a new FLM feels like they are on an island all by themselves or simply isolated? They often become demotivated, or disengaged at work, they might even resign. Worse still they might just withdraw into themselves, get depressed or visibly stressed. They might then decide that being an FLM is not right for them and step away from the position.

Other FLMs and organizational leaders should take time to make sure the new FLMs don't feel like they are on an island all by themselves or isolated. This entails something as basic as talking to new FLMs, listening to them, giving them moral support and most of all never just leave them alone for days or weeks on end to just figure it out or get on with it.

New FLMs often take a while to speak up in meetings, assert themselves. During this initial period they might feel isolated as a result. So other FLMs and leaders in an organization need to take time to engage them, invite them into discussions and involve them in decisions rather than expect them to simply find their way through the fog on their own. Part of engaging an FLM should include having an FLM developmental plan.

An FLM Developmental Plan

Perhaps one of the best things an organization can do to help FLMs make a smooth transition to their new role is to make sure they have a supervisory development plan. And this plan should begin before they become an FLM.

Preparing for an FLM's Job

The first step required to obtain an FLMs job is to master the basic FLM skills discussed in this book. FLM success requires sound preparation in the FLM basics.

An excellent developmental activity is to attain FLM experience. Development is much more than just taking training courses. In fact, one of the most important developmental activities is new or on-the-job experience, no matter what your learning or career objectives are. Therefore, preparation for an FLM job or managerial career must include those developmental activities that will provide an opportunity to practice knowledge, skills, and abilities you need to develop. In practical terms, for example, shadowing those in FLM positions are excellent proving grounds for managerial development.

You must also learn the art and theory of managing human, financial, and material resources. Just as with any profession, the state of the management art is continually evolving. Moreover, it is a life-long study. In this high tech era, it does not take long to become obsolete. You must be computer literate today, deal effectively with unions, develop partnerships, initiate employee involvement processes, and keep up with your organization's new or evolving human resource management initiatives.

Pursue formal education opportunities whenever possible. Most organizations offer tuition reimbursement for certifications, workshops, evening college courses, and other college training initiative programs or in-house initiatives. The academic experience is vital to the enlightened FLM who is not satisfied with maintaining the status quo and is continually pushing her or his organization to reach above and beyond itself. It provides a perspective that cannot be obtained elsewhere and gives you an opportunity to learn from others outside the government.

Potential or new FLM's development plans should begin with an assessment of the individual's skills as compared to the basic requirement of an FLM (or an effective or ideal FLM) in the organization. For example, an effective FLM directs the work of a group, team or department; is held accountable for the success of specific line or staff programs; monitors the progress of their group, team, or department toward goals and periodically evaluates and makes appropriate adjustments; and typically performs the full range of the following duties and responsibilities:

- Determines goals and develops plans for the group, team, or department independently of or jointly with more senior managers.
- Determines resource needs and allocation of resources, and accounts for their effective use.
- Determines the need and develops plans or changes that have considerable impact, such as those involving a basic structure, operating costs or key positions.
- Considers a broad spectrum of factors when making decisions (or recommendations to more senior managers), including productivity improvements in the form of efficiency and effective-

ness; cost savings; improving employee relations; effect on other
organizational elements; and so forth.

- Coordinates operational efforts with other internal activities or
  with the activities of other organizations (i.e., suppliers, etc.).
- Implements policy for their area of responsibilities such as determining operating guidelines and understanding and communicating organization policies and priorities.
- Deals with general human resource management policy matters
  affecting their direct reports.
- Delegates authority to direct reports and holds them accountable
  for their performance.
- Develops direct reports to their full potential as well as keeping
  their own development on going.
- Negotiates or delegates negotiations as required by HRM or senior managers with unions when impacting HRM's policies, practices, and working conditions. This also applies to FLM positions.

There are a number of steps that should be followed to draft an individual FLM development plan (IFLMDP; see Table 2.1). These steps are:

- Start with a short- and long-term goal.
- Potential or new FLMs should develop a personal goals worksheet
  to capture their short- and long-term goals.
- Decide what KSAs are needed to reach these goals. Focus on your
  short-term goals first. Make them formal, informal, and self-
  developmental.
- Review the FLM's knowledge, skills, and general competencies as
  provided by HRM.
- Determine specific training/details that will provide the KSAs.
- Prepare a draft IFLMDP.

The IFLMDP form records the FLMs specific developmental plans over the
next 1 to 5 years. The employee is responsible for preparing this form with
their FLM or if they are already an FLM with their manager's input and
after the employee and manager have met to discuss the plan.

The final IFLMDP should be submitted for formal approval to the individuals' immediate FLM or manager. The approval will affirm that actions
proposed in the plan are consistent with organization needs and resources,
and, most importantly, that support should be forthcoming to assist in the
implementation of the FLM personalized FLMIDP. The individual or FLM
has the primary responsibility for pursuing career development and for

On Becoming a Front-Line Manager ▪ 53

TABLE 2.1 Individual Front-Line Manager Developmental Plan

Employee Name	Position Title	Work Area	FLM's Name

Section I—Career Goals

Short-Term Goals (1–2 years)	Long-Term Goals (2–5 years)

Section II—Individual FLM Development Plan (Completed by Manager & FLM)

Development Objectives (KSAs) Needed to Reach Goal	Developmental Assignment, etc., Including Target Completion Dates	Other Activities

Section II—Individual FLM Development Plan (Continued)

Developmental Objectives	Developmental Assignments	Other Activities

(continued)

TABLE 2.1 Individual Front-Line Manager Developmental Plan (Continued)

Section III—Formal Training and Accomplishment Schedule

Remarks	Formal & Informal Training (e.g., on-the-job), out-of-organization (e.g., certification, degrees, correspondence, etc.)	Projected Cost	Target Completed Data	Actual Completed Data

FLM's Signature	Date	FLM's Manager's Signature	Date

Department/Division Manager's Signature (optional)	Date

Note: This IDP is subject to change depending on availability of funds, courses, and candidate's requirements.

completing their IFLMDP. The organization should be committed to assisting the employee within the limits of available resources. Individual initiative is the key, along with departmental, divisional, or other higher-level support and organization commitment.

The career planning process should be facilitated by the individual or FLMs' continual monitoring of the IFLMDP. They and their managers should periodically review and examine objectives and assignments, and make modifications and revisions to accommodate personal and organizational changes. The IFLMDP should be reviewed by the manager and the FLM semi-annually. Each FLM participating in the IFLMDP process should complete a progress review with their immediate manager during the semi-annual discussion.

An IFLMDP can go a long way in helping a potential and a new FLM have a smooth transition to the position. It is important to remember that individual development plans, like the IFLMDP, is not a performance evaluation tool or a one-time activity. It should be looked at like a partnership between the FLM and their manager. It involves preparation and continuous feedback. Senior managers and leaders should require IDPs for new FLMs and potential ones to increase their potential for success.

Conclusion

It is important to remember that "no-one" is born with great FLM skills. Many of the skills have to be learned and developed. Organizations must proactively help their FLMs achieve their full potential using their training, mentoring, and buddy systems.

Transitioning from an individual contributor or just "one member of the team" to an FLM may seem like a natural progression. Prior to becoming an FLM you were successful and valued for many years as an individual contributor and the next step is management, right?

Well, not necessarily. Truthfully, there is little that's "natural" at all about this direct transition. Odds are the expertise—the skills that made you a successful and valued individual contributor—are decidedly less valuable at the next level—FLM.

- An individual contributor is the vocal and go to expert in the room. A great FLM is a supportive listener.
- An individual contributor shines by consistently exceeding expectations. An FLM shines by helping others exceed their own.

- A successful individual contributor always surpasses their performance targets and goals. An effective FLM manager spends time ensuring their direct reports or team members can achieve theirs.

Effective FLMs understand inclusivity and how to empower others. They have exemplary listening skills, know how to develop individual performance and roadmap careers. These skills don't come naturally at all for many individual contributors and for most, are developed and fine-tuned over years of experience.

The reality is that as a new FLM, "What got you here won't get you there." As a new or first-time FLM, one of the prominent struggles is letting go of the workplace persona that helped you thrive as an individual contributor.

The rules of the game have changed. A new FLM's very survival is now dependent upon their ability to help others succeed. There is less emphasis on their accomplishments and knowledge and more on their ability to deliver results through others.

Essentially, success is no longer about you. When transitioning into an FLM role, it's an absolute necessity that the person adapt to this new reality. Failure to do so results in widespread problems both for the new FLM and each of their direct reports or team members.

Those FLMs who successfully make the transition from being an individual contributor continue to seek ways to grow throughout their entire career. They realize that they can read all of the books and take all of the courses or development opportunities offered by their organization but there is no substitute for never stopping to look for new ways to improve.

People not in management often think management is easy, but in reality that's far from the truth. In fact, there are many who believe that the move to new FLM may well be one of the hardest transitions in organizations. It involves new responsibilities, new ways of relating to one's former and current co-workers, and new ways of looking at the world. Thus, there is no doubt that the role of the FLM will be even more challenging in the years to come. And clearly, the FLM will continue to play a critical role in every organization's success. However, their organizations must do everything they can to help prepare employees for FLM positions and make the transition to front-line management as smooth as possible. And one thing they can do is to make use of individual FLM development plans.

3

Ethics and Doing the Right Thing

The "Buck Stops With You"

For the past few decades, many front-line managers (FLMs and other managers and leaders), social scientists, and the public-at-large see unethical behavior as a cancer working on the fabric of society in too many of today's organizations and beyond. Many are concerned that we continue to face a crisis of ethics in business that is undermining society. This crisis involves people from all walks of life to include business-people, government officials, customers, and employees. Especially worrisome more and more in recent years is unethical behavior exhibited by senior leaders, FLMs, and employees at all levels of the organization.

FLMs like many others are all too familiar with what we continue to hear about illegal and unethical behavior on and off Wall Street, in small or big organizations, in government, and in different industries domestically and internationally. FLMs see way to many members of the C-suite willing to continue to gamble on risky business ventures with employees' retirement funds, expose their workers to hazardous working conditions, set unrealistic pressure or performance expectations, and blatant favoritism in hiring and

Succeeding as a Frontline Manager in Today's Organizations, pages 57–87
Copyright © 2021 by Information Age Publishing
57

promotion practices. Although such practices have occurred throughout the world in years gone by and today, their presence nonetheless serves to remind us of the challenge facing contemporary organizations and their FLMs.

This challenge is especially difficult for FLMs because in too many instances standards for what constitutes ethical behavior lie in a "gray zone" where clear-cut right versus wrong answers are still allowed to exist. As a result, sometimes a case can be made that unethical behavior is forced on FLMs and their organizations by the environment in which it exists and laws such as the Foreign Corruption Practices Act (FCPA) or Sarbanes-Oxley Act. For instance, one still hears the following as the difficult challenge for those individuals and organizations that are global in nature. "If you were a sales representative for an American company abroad and your foreign competitors used bribes to get business, what would you do?" In the United States such behavior is illegal, yet it is perfectly acceptable in other countries. What is ethical here? Similarly, in many countries women are systematically discriminated against in the workplace; as there are many who still archaically believe that their place is in the home. In the United States, again, this practice is illegal. If you were an FLM in an American company in one of these countries, would you hire women in important positions? If you did, your company might be isolated in the larger business community, and you might lose business. If you did not, you might be violating what most Americans believe to be fair business practices.

Some of the most common ethical issues in international business FLMs and other leaders might be confronted with include outsourcing, working standards and conditions, workplace diversity and equal opportunity, child labor, trust and integrity, FLM oversight, human rights, religion, the political arena, the environment, bribery, and corruption. FLMs and their organizations trading internationally are expected to fully comply with federal and state safety regulations, environmental laws, fiscal and monetary reporting statutes, and civil rights laws.

Cultural considerations can also make or break an organization conducting business globally. Every culture and nation has its own history, customs, traditions, and code of ethics. Cultural barriers include language, which often means FLMs and others may need to rely on translators when speaking to business contacts and customers. As noted above, gender can be an issue in countries where women do not have the same rights as men. Religious holidays and other cultural events can prohibit conducting business at certain times. Acting in accordance with ethical and cultural values is crucial for FLMs in a multinational company to win customers'/clients' support and business and to achieve a competitive advantage in a particular market.

The effective leadership and management of ethical issues in today's and tomorrow's world of work require that FLMs and other organizational leaders ensure their organizational members do not commit unethical acts and are familiar with how to deal with ethical issues in their everyday work lives. These charges are especially important today as governments, consumers, pressure groups, and employees are increasingly demanding organizations to seek out more ethical and ecologically sounder ways of doing business. The media also constantly keeps the spotlight on organizational abuses and malpractices. And more and more organizations are increasingly recognizing that being ethical and socially responsible (or at the very least being seen to be ethical and responsible) may actually be good for organization.

Today as in the past, there is increasing demand for a renewed emphasis on values, morals, and ethics and that the business debate moving forward is but a subset of a larger societal concern. Whether the business community will be able to respond and elevate its ethical or moral reputation to a new plateau remains to be seen. One thing is sure: Like years gone by, the interest in business ethics is not likely to dissipate in the near term. FLMs and other organizational members can more effectively respond to the public's justifiable expectations by first understanding what it means for their organizations to be ethical and social responsibility as discussed below and throughout this book. This chapter begins our discussion of what business ethics is (and is not) before taking a look at operational levels of business ethics, and why business ethics matters in organizations. Next, the chapter takes a look at ethics at the operational level which is where FLMs traditionally fulfill their responsibilities. The chapter then focuses on FLMs and why there is an increased emphasis on ethics. The chapter concludes by discussing what FLMs and others can do to institutionalize ethics in the organization.

What Is Business Ethics?

Almost every year, it seems, more and more organizations are enveloped in an ethics scandal that generates a new tremor of public distrust of large corporations and other organizations. Consider the following list of organizations in the headlines for their unethical actions: Citigroup, Deutsche Bank, EDMC, Navient, FIFA, General Motors, Goldman Sachs, Honda, JPMorgan, Mylan, Takata, Toshiba, Turing Pharmaceuticals, Valeant, and Wells Fargo. As a result of these never ending ethics scandals the word "ethics" along with having various definitions will undoubtedly continue to be a major part of the news today and tomorrow.

Ethics is often associated with the words "right" and "good," along with their opposites "wrong" and "bad." For instance, we might speak of a particular action as being right or wrong, meaning that it is an ethically correct or an ethically incorrect thing to do. Or we might refer to a particular state of affairs as good or bad, meaning that it has some form of intrinsic ethical desirability or undesirability.

As well as referring to certain actions as being ethically right, we also use the word "right" in a different sense when talking about ethics. That is, we talk of "a right" as being something that people have rather than as a quality of an action. To recognize someone's right to something is to acknowledge that they have an ethical claim to that thing. Furthermore, when we speak of people's rights in this way, we also sometimes speak of other people's "responsibility" to respect those rights. If somebody has an ethical claim to a certain thing, we tend to believe that others have an ethical responsibility to let them have that thing, or perhaps even to enable them to have it. And just as we speak of ethical responsibilities, we also assume that words like "obligations" and "duties" mean more or less the same thing. Responsibilities, obligations, and duties, then, refer to things that we have some sort of ethical compulsion to do.

We also talk a lot about "fairness" when we discuss ethics. We tend to think that if a situation is fair then it is ethical, and if it is unfair then there is something unethical about it. Furthermore, ethics-related talk often includes references to virtue: We sometimes refer to a person who behaves ethically as "a virtuous person," or we refer to an ethical act as "a virtuous act."

But perhaps the word that crops up most often in association with ethics is "morality."

Indeed, ethics and morality are often used interchangeably in everyday speech, as are the words ethical and moral. Philosophers frequently make a distinction between morality and ethics though. In philosophical texts, morality often refers to a particular person's beliefs about what is right and wrong, good and bad, and so on; or perhaps it refers to what a particular community thinks about such matters. Meanwhile, ethics is often taken by philosophers to refer to the study of morality. Ethics, then, might be understood as a subject that puts various moralities to the test; as the process of enquiring into the legitimacy of various notions of good, bad, right, wrong, fairness, unfairness, virtue and vice. And when philosophers say that something is ethical, they are usually implying that it has a value against which the morals of a particular person or a particular community can be judged.

Several scholars generally agree that the terms ethics and morality, and ethical and moral are synonymous. The English terms ethics and morality are translations of the same word in Greek and Latin respectively; and as such, each word is translated into English slightly differently. The word ethics derives from the Greek word *ethikos*, and from the root word ethos, referring to character or custom. This definition is germane to effective leadership in organizations in that it connotes an organization code conveying moral integrity and consistent values in service to the public. Ethics involves determining how one should act based on a group's determination of right and wrong. The referenced group may be a profession, a company, an industry, or society. The determination of what is good or right is made in reference to ethical standards.

The word *morality* derives from the Latin word, *moralitas*, based upon the root word, *mores*, referring to character, custom, or habit. Therefore, these interchangeable terms refer to the character or disposition of beliefs, values, and behaviors that shape perceptions of what is right and wrong based upon one's personal, social, cultural, and religious values and the standards by which behavior is deemed acceptable or unacceptable regarding responsibilities, rules, codes of conduct, and/or laws.

One's morals certainly are part of the discussion regarding ethical behavior, but the term morals, generally connotes something different from ethics. Morals are personal principles, associated with one's conscience that guides an individual in determining right and wrong. For some business ethics is the study of business situations, activities, and decisions where issues of right and wrong are addressed. According to this definition, business ethics covers the whole spectrum of interactions between firms, individuals, society, and the state. In other words, business ethics is as complex as business itself. It is not an optional accessory to business life or a mere enthusiasm of the philosophers and moralists; business ethics is how the people conduct their business affairs, from the basest fraud to the highest levels of excellence. Others define ethics as the study and practice of decisions about what is good and right and business ethics as the use of ethics and ethics principles to solve business dilemmas

Ethics has also been defined as the discipline that deals with moral duty and obligation. Ethics is a set of moral principles or values and morality is a doctrine or system of moral conduct. Moral conduct refers to principles of right, wrong, and fairness in behavior. For the most part, many view ethics and morality as being so similar to one another that they use the term interchangeably to refer to the study of fairness, justice, and moral behavior in business.

Ethical behavior is that which is morally accepted as good and right as opposed to bad or wrong in a particular setting. For the individual that means acting in ways consistent with one's personal values and the commonly held values of the organization and society. Is it ethical, for example, to pay a bribe to obtain a business contract in a foreign country? Is it ethical to allow your company to withhold information that might discourage a job candidate from joining your organization? Is it ethical to ask someone to take a job you know will not be good for their career progress? Is it ethical to do personal business on company time?

The list of questions could go on and on. Despite one's initial inclinations in response to these questions, the major point of it all is to remind leaders and other organizational members, that the public-at-large is demanding that government officials, business leaders and managers, workers in general, and the organizations they represent all act according to high ethical and moral standards. There is every indication that the future will see a continued concern with maintaining high standards of ethical behavior in organizational transactions and in the workplace. All FLMs have a general idea of what business ethics means, but it is helpful to see some of the agreement on what ethics is not.

What Ethics Is Not

It has been argued by some social scientists that there is a natural tendency to overlay our wants, needs, and beliefs on an ethical issue, only to obfuscate the facts and undermine an ethical line of reasoning. Perhaps the best way to understand ethics is to understand what it is not.

Two of the biggest challenges to identifying ethical standards relate to questions about what the standards should be based on and how we apply those standards in specific situations. Experts on ethics agree that the identification of ethical standards can be very difficult, but they *have* reached some agreement on what ethics is *not*. At the same time, these areas of agreement suggest why it may be challenging to obtain consensus across countries and regions as to "What is ethical?" The following five-point excerpt from the Markkula Center for Applied Ethics at Santa Clara University offers a look at what ethics is not:

- *Ethics is not the same as feelings.* Feelings provide important information for our ethical choices. Some people have highly developed habits that make them feel bad when they do something wrong, but many people feel good even though they are doing something wrong. And often our feelings will tell us it is uncomfortable to do the right thing if it is hard.

- *Ethics is not religion.* Many people are not religious, but ethics applies to everyone. Most religions do advocate high ethical standards but sometimes do not address all the types of problems we face.
- *Ethics is not following the law.* A good system of law does incorporate many ethical standards, but law can deviate from what is ethical. Law can become ethically corrupt, as some totalitarian regimes have made it. Law can be a function of power alone and designed to serve the interests of narrow groups. Law may have a difficult time designing or enforcing standards in some important areas, and may be slow to address new problems.
- *Ethics is not following culturally accepted norms.* Some cultures are quite ethical, but others become corrupt—or blind to certain ethical concerns (as the United States was to slavery before the Civil War). "When in Rome, do as the Romans do" is not a satisfactory ethical standard.
- *Ethics is not science.* Social and natural science can provide important data to help us make better ethical choices. But science alone does not tell us what we ought to do. Science may provide an explanation for what humans are like. But ethics provides reasons for how humans ought to act. And just because something is scientifically or technologically possible, it may not be ethical to do it.

Now that we have looked at what ethics is and is not, the next section focuses on the relationship between ethics and business. More specifically, the ethical standards of an organization have a major influence on how it conducts business. Business ethics can be viewed as the behavior stands of leaders and other members, and the way in which business is carried out at both a strategic and operational level. As described in the next section business ethics or ethical standards can be classified at three levels.

Operational Levels of Business Ethics

A number of theorists have highlighted the merits of considering the relationship between ethics and business at more than one level. It is important for FLMs to understand that ethical problems are not only an individual or personal matter, therefore, it is useful for FLMs to see the different "levels" at which issues originate and how they often move to other levels. Since today's FLMs and other organizational leaders must interact with a wide range of stakeholders inside and outside their organizations, understanding the levels of issues that stakeholders face facilitates an FLMs understanding of the complex relationships within and among participants involved in addressing ethical problems.

Ethical and moral issues in business can be examined from at several levels: individual or personal, organizational, and macro (i.e., industry, societal, and international).

Individual Level

Since organizations and their various components are run by FLMs and other organizational leaders, the ethical standards day-to-day activities and decisions of individuals in the business are an important consideration. Individuals may well have a very different set of ethical standards from their employer and this can lead to tensions. Factors such as peer pressure, personal financial position, and socio-economic status all may influence individual ethical standards. FLMs should be aware of this to manage potential conflicts.

We all experience individual or personal level ethical challenges. These include situations FLMs face in their personal lives that are generally outside the work context. Questions or dilemmas that we might face at the personal level include:

- Should I tell the cashier that he gave me change for a $20 bill when all I gave him was a $10 bill?
- Should I notify my bank that it credited someone else's $00 to my checking account?
- Should I cheat on my income tax return by overinflating my charitable contributions?
- Should I return the extra merchandise that the store sent me by accident?
- Is it ethically acceptable for an FLM to withhold information from her colleagues about their impending redundancy in order to retain their commitment to the company and thus to avoid a downturn in corporate performance?
- In a supply-contract negotiation, is it OK for a company buyer to give preferential treatment to a supplier with whom he has developed a long-standing business relationship or should supplier arrangements be governed purely by financial considerations?
- And is it all right for a supplier to offer a gift to the buyer of a company with which she does business in order to thank that person for their custom?
- Moreover, is it ethically permissible for a company buyer to accept such gifts from a supplier?

If an ethical issue involves or is limited to an individual's responsibilities, that person may examine her or his own ethical motives and standards before choosing a course of action.

Organizational Level

At an organizational level, ethical standards are embedded in the policies and procedures of the organization, and form an important foundation on which organizational strategy is built. These policies derive from the influences felt at macro level and therefore help a business to respond to changing pressures in the most effective way. There can be a gap between the organization policy on ethical standards and the conduct of those in charge of running the business, especially if they are not the direct owners, which can present an ethical challenge for some employees.

People also confront ethical issues at the organizational level in their roles as leaders or FLMs or employees. Certainly, many of these issues are similar to those we face personally. However, these issues may carry consequences for the company's reputation and success in the community and also for the kind of ethical climate or culture that will prevail on a day-to-day basis at the office.

Some of the issues posed at the organizational level might include:

- Should I overlook the wrongdoings of my peers and direct reports in the interest of company harmony?
- Should I perform an unethical or illegal act to earn a division or work unit profit?
- Should I offer a kickback to ensure I get the client's business to meet my sales quota?
- Should I make this product safer than I'm required by law, because I know the legal standard is grossly inadequate?
- Should I accept this gift or bribe that is being given to me to close a big deal for the company?

It is important for FLMs to understand that at this level they might think about things like right, wrong, good, and bad in relation to the activities of particular firms or specific industry sectors. For example, in addition to the questions above one might ask whether it is ethically acceptable for a firm to structure its accounts in such a way that it avoids paying taxes in the country within which its operations take place, paying them instead in another country that offers more favorable arrangements. Or we might question whether a global commodity-supply corporation is justified in disposing of waste products at low cost in developing nations. And we might ask if it is OK for financial-service firms to establish highly complex derivative trading structures, which offer the possibility of high returns but in which systemic risk is hard to predict or control.

If an ethical issue arises at the organizational level, FLMs should examine the organization's policies and procedures and code of ethics, if one exists before making a decision or taking action.

Macro Level

At the macro level, sometimes called the systemic level, ethics are defined and influenced by the wider operating environment in which the organization exists. At this level we might consider the wider role that business plays, or should play, within society. Additionally, at this level business ethics touches on considerations of national and international economic policy. It also crosses into the realm of political ideology. Factors such as political pressures, economic conditions, societal attitudes to certain businesses, and even business or industry regulation can influence a company's operating standards and policies. Contemporary organizational leaders, FLMs, and other organizational members must be aware of how these pressures affect operations and relationships, and how they may impact markets locally, nationally, and internationally.

The types of questions that occur at a macro level might include whether economic markets alone should be allowed to govern business activity, or whether governments should exercise control over market activity in order to bring about specific social and environmental objectives. Macro-level inquiry might also ask whether corporations have an obligation to consider the impact of their activities on society and the natural environment, or whether they should just do all they can to maximize shareholder returns. And macro-level inquiry might consider whether the benefits and burdens of economic activity are fairly distributed between various communities. Some have suggested the importance of looking at business ethics more specifically from an industry or societal or international perspective.

Industry Level

The industry level is another level at which organizational leaders and others might influence business ethics. The industry might be insurance, stock brokerage, manufactured homes, real estate, automobiles, or a host of others. Related to the industry might be the profession of which an individual is a member—law, medicine, accounting, pharmacy, or engineering.

Some examples of questions that might pose ethical problems or dilemmas at this level include the following:

- Is this standard contract we condominium sellers have adopted really in keeping with the financial disclosure laws that have recently been strengthened?
- Is this practice that we stockbrokers have been using for years with prospective clients really fair and in their best interests?
- Is this safety standard we mechanical engineers have passed really adequate for protecting the consumer in this age of do-it-your-selfers?
- Is this standard we physicians have adopted violating the Hippocratic' oath and the value it places on human life?

At this level conflicts of interest and conscience can arise in such situations. At this level, professionals can refer to their professional association's charter code of ethics for guidelines on conducting business or the set of ethical practices of a particular industry.

Societal and International

At the societal and international levels, laws, norms, customs, and traditions govern the legal and moral acceptability of behaviors. Business activities acceptable in China or Turkey or Russia may be immoral or illegal in the United States, and vice versa. At these levels it becomes very difficult for the individual FLM or other leaders to have any direct effect on business ethics. However, FLMs acting in concert through their companies and trade and professional associations can definitely bring about high standards and constructive changes. The greatest impact of FLMs can be felt through what she or he does personally or as a member of the broader organizational leadership team.

It is also important for FLMs to recognize that as leaders they also have an important role to play as ethical role models for society. To the extent that they successfully convey to the general public that they believe in the importance of integrity in business and throughout society, FLMs may have a significant impact on society's general level of ethics and on the future course of the free enterprise system.

Integrated Approach

Ethical standards (and problems) flow through the entire structure of an organization, shaping how it plans its strategy, deals with customers, and manages its workforce. The standards have a reach far beyond day-to-day operations where FLMs find themselves, and should be considered in all aspects of a business, from the boardroom to the lowest level (i.e., shop floor) and across all functions and areas. Supporting this effort, FLMs and organizations that genuinely understand the value and importance of ethics have appropriate metrics in place to measure achievement and identify problems before they become major issues.

Front Line Managers and the Increased Focus on Ethics

Based on our discussion to this point FLMs should at a minimum understand that ethics are the rules, principles, standards, or beliefs that commonly define right and wrong. Additionally, ethics are involved in all facets of business from decision-making to budgeting, from personnel issues to leadership. Today's FLMs must be able to see the ethical issues in the choices they face, make decisions within an ethical framework, and build and maintain an ethical work environment. FLMs must be particularly sensitive to ethical issues because of their key role as a bridge between upper management and operating employees. For most employees, their FLM is the only contact they have with middle- and top-management. As such, employees interpret the company's ethical standards through the actions and words of their FLMs. If FLMs take company supplies home, cheat on maintenance reports, or engage in other unethical practices, they set a tone for their work groups that is likely to undermine all the efforts by top management to create a corporate climate of high ethical standards. In a sense, therefore, FLMs must be even more ethical than their direct reports.

There are many stakeholders with interests in ethical decision-making: the organization itself, corporate boards, middle and top management, FLMs, operating employees, customers and clients, suppliers, competitors, the industry at large, the community, and the nation or broader society. At one time or another, ethical decisions affect all of these constituencies, and ethical considerations may change based on the particular group of stakeholders affected. When an organization operates ethically, the people who manage that organization evaluate the organization's business practices in light of human values of morality. An ethical dilemma occurs when two or more values or goals (e.g., profit, growth, technological progress, desire to contribute to some basic good) conflict. The best solution to any problem almost always involves a cost of some kind.

The difficulty is that ethical behavior often collides with the bottom line at least in the short-run. However, it seems that things are changing. The word is continuing to get out: That ethical behavior is good business—it contributes to organizational success. A reputation for honesty and integrity attracts and holds customers and it will ultimately show up in the bottom line. Organizations that have strong ethical values and consistently display them in all their activities derive other benefits: improved management control, increased productivity, avoidance of litigation, and an enhanced company image that attracts talent, improves morale, and earns the public's good will. For today's FLMs leading effectively therefore also means leading ethically and morally. While businesses expand over geographic and cultural boundaries, questions concerning the sense of right and wrong within an organization become more complex. It is the responsibility of FLMs to guide the design, implementation, and monitoring of the organization's moral environment and strategies. As organizations put increased pressure on FLMs and employees to cut costs and increase productivity, ethical dilemmas are almost certain to increase. By what they say and do, FLMs contribute toward setting their organization's ethical standards.

The Increased Focus on Ethics

There is a common belief that our society is currently suffering a moral crisis. Actions that were once thought reprehensible—cheating, misrepresenting, lying, and covering up mistakes—have become, in many people's eyes, common business practices. Products that can cause harm to their users still remain on the market. Sexual harassment and discrimination have gone unpunished. A major focus for business in recent years therefore, has been to reassess its ethical behavior. The widely publicized breaches of ethical behavior by business leaders have been a major cause of the renewed interest in business ethics. Over the past two decades, the American public has been bombarded with reports of unethical behavior in different types of organizations to include the more recent ethical scandals involving Citigroup, Volkswagen, and 7-Eleven (Australia), which have rattled the foundations of the business community.

In a less dramatic way, unethical behavior of lower level employees has also had an effect on the bottom line of many businesses in the same period. The loss of traditional family life meant that employees came to work without the ethical standards their parents may have had, due to fewer opportunities to learn them at home. As companies looked to be more efficient (e.g., do more with less) they began to reduce layers of bureaucracy between workers and bosses and employee's productivity became increasingly critical to organizational survival. To compete in the global economy, American businesses continue to have to be more efficient.

A more sophisticated workforce also often leads to a renewed focus on ethical standards in the workplace. FLMs and other managers cannot say one thing and do another without fostering employee mistrust. If FLMs are going to direct the workforce toward a higher ethical standard, they are going to have to improve their own behavior. FLMs' failures to deal candidly with employees increases employee mistrust and organizational disloyalty. Recognition of the need for fair treatment to create loyalty to the organization is an expected result. In some cases, the perception that top-level management takes care of themselves but does not take care of their employees causes high employee turnover and the loss of skilled FLMs to competitors.

For some organizations, increased criminal enforcement of illegal activity causes a resurgence of interest in corporate ethics. Although many might deny this, U.S. sentencing guidelines for federal criminals may have caused companies to implement much needed ethical standards. It has been suggested that an organization with a comprehensive program for ethical behavior including a code of conduct, an ombudsman, a hotline, and mandatory training seminars for FLMs would be treated more leniently should it face criminal charges based on an employee's wrongdoing. It is important that FLMs recognize that despite an organization's best efforts all crimes cannot be prevented, and organizations that at least tried to prevent wrongdoing will most often benefit from their efforts.

Individual Ethics and Potential Pressures

Individual ethics are the things one must do to be considered a person of integrity. As an FLM, consider the following: How would you rate your own standards of ethics? Are you always ethical? Are you ethical except in situations where you can't possibly be found out? Are you ethical except when you are under pressure from your boss or your peers? Are profits or your department's success more important than your personal values? Do your career goals sometimes take precedence over principle? Is it right to bend the rules to your company's advantage whenever you can? Should you always tell the truth? Now, consider a couple of specific cases: Is it wrong to use the company telephone for personal long distance calls? Is it ethical to falsify safety reports? Is it ethical for a member of your team to offer a bribe to an OSHA inspector to ignore safety violations?

Anyone can be ethical when there is no pressure to act otherwise. Pressures to be unethical come from many sources—yourself, your boss, your peers, your employees, your organization—but FLMs today must be able to resist. Personal ambition and self-interest are probably the most common causes of unethical decisions and behaviors. People act in self-serving or unethical ways in order to improve their personal situation or reputation, to gain advancement, to increase income, or to avoid criticism or punishment.

An FLMs peers can also put pressure on them to behave unethically. It is always difficult to turn down a request for help, especially from a colleague; yet if you are asked to support unethical behavior, abandoning your own standards serves neither of you. Unpleasant though it may be, you should decline. Say something like, I appreciate the difficulty of the situation you face, I would like to be able to help you, but I cannot. At some point, FLMs face pressure from their employees to be unethical. People might ask you to conceal absences, to overlook infractions just this time, or to help them cover up a near-accident. As an FLM, you should never give in to such requests. Not only would it be unethical, but it would destroy the employees' respect for you and ruin your power as an FLM and leader. The difficult but right thing to do under these conditions is to get the group together and talk to them along these lines:

"I understand that you're not asking me to do this of self-interest. But I will not tolerate dishonesty. We are going to abide by our code of conduct. We're going to do our job properly."

Pressure to be unethical can also come from an FLM's boss, usually stemming from his or her desire to look good to his or her bosses: "I don't care how you do it, but I want that safety award." Pressure from a boss is extremely difficult, particularly since it is often accompanied by a threat, either direct or implied, of some adverse action, such as a poor performance report or denial of a bonus. But the fact that the pressure comes from an FLM's boss is not an excuse to behave unethically. FLMs should not deceive themselves into believing that they are doing something to make their department look better; recognize that their motivation is self-protection. Although it's difficult, FLMs should refuse to compromise their values.

The culture of the organization is still another source of unethical conduct. Some organizations choose to engage in questionable practices. Other organizations are just as likely to stimulate unethical actions when they place too much emphasis on managerial aggressiveness or on organizational expansion, competitiveness, and profit.

Common Rationalizations for Questionable Conduct

Over the years, people have developed some common rationalizations to justify questionable conduct, such as when they ignore safety issues in order to increase financial returns. These rationalizations provide some insights into why FLMs might make poor ethical choices and feel comfortable doing so. Let's look at some of these rationalizations in greater detail. When you are faced with ethical/unethical choices you are faced with a problem. Ethical concerns then become a part of your decision-making. For instance, one alternative may generate a considerable higher financial return than the others, but it might be ethically questionable because it compromises employee safety. Some individuals will ignore the safety concerns to achieve the financial return and feel very comfortable in defending their actions through various rationalizations.

Since It Helps the Organization, the Organization Will Condone It and Protect Me

This response represents loyalty gone berserk. Some FLMs come to believe that not only do the organization's interests override the laws and values of society, but also that the organization expects its employees to exhibit unqualified loyalty. FLMs who use this rationalization place the organization's good name in jeopardy. For example, this rationalization has motivated FLMs to justify labor mischarges, cost duplications, safety violations, and other abuses. While FLMs should be expected to exhibit loyalty in protecting the organization against competitors and detractors, they shouldn't put the organization above the law, common morality, or society itself.

It's in Our Best Interest

The belief that unethical conduct is in a person's or an organization's best interest nearly always results from a narrow view of what those interests are. For instance, FLMs can come to believe that it's acceptable to bribe officials if the bribe results in a contract award, or to falsify safety records if this improves their unit's performance record. In the long run, these actions are usually counter to the best interests of the organization.

It's Not Really Illegal or Immoral

Where is the line between smart and being shady? Between an ingenious decision and an immoral one? Because this line is often ambiguous, people use it to rationalize their actions, reasoning that whatever isn't prohibited must be OK. This is especially true if there are rich rewards for attaining certain goals, but little evaluation of how those goals are achieved. The practice of accepting a gift from a vendor who was chosen to receive an out-source contract is one example of this behavior.

No One Will Find Out

This final rationalization understands that the behavior is questionable, but assumes that it will never be uncovered. Philosophers ponder:

"If a tree falls in a forest and no one hears it, did it make a noise?" Some FLMs answer the analogous question: "If an unethical act is committed and no one knows it, is it wrong?" in the negative. This rationalization is often stimulated by inadequate controls, strong pressures to perform, large rewards for good that ignore the means by which it is achieved, and the lack of punishment for wrongdoers who are caught.

There is little anyone can do to stop people from rationalizing about their questionable conduct, but companies can try to encourage ethical behavior. The next section presents three different approaches that can be used by FLMs to determine whether a decision is ethical.

Determining Whether a Decision Is Ethical

FLMs often experience an ethical dilemma when they confront a situation that requires them to choose between two courses of action, especially if each of them is likely to serve the opposing interest of different stakeholders. To make an appropriate decision, FLMs might weigh the competing claims or rights of the various groups. Sometimes, making a decision is easy because some obvious standard, value, or norm of behavior applies. In other cases, FLMs have trouble deciding what to do.

In many large companies, FLMs have a code of ethics to guide them as to what constitutes acceptable and unacceptable practices. A code of ethics is a formal document that states an organization's primary values and the ethical rules it expects employees to follow. For instance, a code of ethics might instruct employees to be law-abiding in all activities, truthful and accurate in what they say and write, and to recognize that high integrity sometimes requires the company to forego business opportunities. Codes of ethics do not, however, provide enough guidance for the many difficult dilemmas FLMs face. Philosophers have debated for centuries about the specific criteria that should be used to determine whether decisions are ethical or unethical. The use of different criteria can result in different decisions. Three models of what determines whether a decision is ethical are the utilitarian, moral rights, and justice models. Each model offers a different and complementary way of determining whether a decision or behavior is ethical.

The Utilitarian Approach

The utilitarian approach suggests that FLMs should strive to provide the greatest degree of benefits for the largest number of people at the lowest cost. In other words, FLMs must weigh the costs against the benefits of their actions. In a manner of speaking, you do this whenever you make a decision, as you balance one alternative against another and choose the one that you believe will yield the best results for the lowest cost or less effort. The utilitarian view tends to dominate business decision-making, because it's consistent with goals like efficiency, productivity, and high profits. By maximizing profits, for instance, FLMs can argue that they are securing the greatest good for the greatest number.

The Moral Rights Approach

The moral rights view of ethics is concerned with respecting and protecting the basic rights of individuals, such as, the rights to privacy, free speech, and due process. Even if the decision accomplishes the greatest good for the greatest number of people, it is considered unethical if it denies individual rights. This position would protect employees who report unethical or illegal practices by their organization to the press or government agencies on the grounds of their right of free speech. As an FLM, you can use this approach to assess the implications of your decisions on individuals and not just groups of people. FLMs should not make a decision that compromises individual rights.

The Justice Approach

The justice approach embodies democratic principles and protects the interests of those who might otherwise lack power. It requires FLMs to impose and enforce rules fairly and impartially so there is an equitable distribution of benefits and costs. Union members typically favor this view. It justifies paying people the same wage for a given job, regardless of performance differences, and it uses seniority as the criterion in making layoff decisions. The justice approach is based on two components:

1. The procedural justice component, which requires impartial administration of disciplinary actions.
2. The distributive justice component, which requires people to be judged only in terms of the performance criteria and not on such characteristics as race, gender, or religious preference.

For example, people who vary in job skill should be paid differently, but there should be no differences in pay based on race or gender.

Combining the Approaches

It's difficult to apply a single approach consistently to all situations you encounter. All three approaches can be used as guidelines for helping you to sort out the ethics of a particular course of action. Each of these three models has advantages and disadvantages, however. The utilitarian view promotes efficiency and productivity, but it can ignore the rights of individuals, particularly those with minority representation in the organization. The moral rights view protects individuals from injury and is consistent with freedom and privacy, but it can create an overly legalistic work environment that hinders productivity and efficiency. The justice perspective protects the interests of the under-represented and less powerful, but it can encourage a general sense of entitlement that reduces risk-taking, innovation, and productivity.

Although individuals in business have tended to focus on utilitarianism, times are changing. New trends toward individual rights and social justice mean that FLMs need ethical standards based on nonutilitarian criteria, which are more difficult to evaluate. Criteria such as individual rights and social justice are far more ambiguous than utilitarian criteria such as productivity and profits. An FLM should, therefore, ask themselves what the consequences of their actions will be in terms of each approach. For example, suppose that an FLM, who has been working for a company for about six months, discovers that it is common practice to pour used solvents and cleaning solutions down a storm drain. The FLM isn't sure whether the practice is legal or ethical. In considering such a situation and what to do, the FLM can ask:

1. Does my decision fall within the accepted values or standards that typically apply in the organizational environment?
2. Am I willing to see the decision communicated to all stakeholders affected by it—for example, by having it reported on television?
3. Would the people with whom I have a significant personal relationship, such as family members, friends, or even supervisors in other organizations, approve of the decision?

Questions 4–14 should also be asked by FLMs when making important decisions with obvious ethical implications:

4. How did this problem occur in the first place?
5. Would you define the problem differently if you stood on the other side of the fence?
6. To whom and to what do you give your loyalty as a person and as a member of your organization?
7. What is your intention in making this decision?
8. What is the potential for your intentions to be misunderstood by others in the organization?

9. How do your intentions compare with the probable result?
10. Whom could your decision injure?
11. Can you discuss the problem with the affected parties before you make the decision?
12. Are you confident that your position will be as valid over a long period of time as it seems now?
13. Could you disclose your decision to your boss or your immediate family?
14. How would you feel if your decision was described, in detail, on the front page of your local newspaper?

One way to identify an unethical decision is to ask whether the FLM would prefer to disguise or hide it from other people because it would enable the company or a particular individual to gain at the expense of society or other stakeholders. Consider the following situation Marilyn faces in her role as an FLM.

Marilyn's Dilemma

Marilyn Falcone supervises eight production specialists in a computer manufacturing company. Marilyn has a dilemma. She is being transferred to a new assignment with the company, and her boss has asked her to nominate one of her employees as her replacement. She has to decide whether to recommend Juan Hernandez, a Mexican-American who was obviously the best-qualified employee, or Jerome Thompson, who, though not as well qualified, would be better accepted by the other workers.

Juan is a very intelligent 27-year-old specialist, who has just completed course work to earn his management degree. He has done an excellent job on every assignment Marilyn has given him. Juan has all the qualifications Marilyn feels a good FLM should have: he is punctual, diligent, mature, and intelligent. Jerome, on the other hand, is a 28 year old high school graduate with little other educational experience. He is a hard worker who is well-liked and respected by the others including Juan. Like Juan, he has made it clear that he wants to move into management.

Marilyn also knows that her employees are prejudiced against Mexican-Americans. Therefore, she thinks that if Juan is given the promotion, he will have difficulties, no matter what his qualifications. Marilyn must ask herself, "If Juan were White, would I have any hesitation about recommending him for the job?" The answer was clearly no. Juan is without doubt the better-qualified person. Marilyn also struggled with the question, "How will performance and employee attitudes be affected if Juan is given the job?" Marilyn knows that Juan will not be accepted as the new manager, and that morale and productivity will probably plunge for a time.

As Marilyn labors over the decision, she thinks about how unfair it would be to Juan if he were denied a deserved promotion based on his race. At the same time, Marilyn feels her primary responsibility should be to maintain the productivity of the unit. The existing prejudice is a fact of life that Marilyn cannot eliminate. Marilyn realizes that it would be very easy to rationalize either decision: She could recommend Juan on the basis of fairness or Jerome on the basis of maintaining group morale.

Marilyn knows that the way she handles this promotion issue might substantially affect her future within the company. If her unit falls apart after her departure, it will hurt her reputation. More important, however, Marilyn believes that she will face even more difficult ethical decisions in her new job. If she stands by her principles in this case, she believes it will make those future ethical decisions easier.

At that moment, the phone rings. It is Marilyn's boss, Francis Akers. "Marilyn," he said, "I need to see you. Can you come to my office in a few minutes?" As Marilyn hangs up the phone, she thinks, "I know Francis wants to talk about my replacement." Marilyn is concerned about her reputation within the company, but she must also be at peace with herself. Marilyn will personally benefit in the long run by keeping her actions consistent with her beliefs. Ethical issues like the one confronting Marilyn are a daily and increasingly important component of business.

Marilyn could use the three approaches (utilitarian, moral rights, justice) in deciding whom to promote. She could ask: Would the promotion of either Juan or Jerome result in greater costs or benefits for the company (or society)? (Does this refer to society or just the company?)

If Marilyn promotes Juan, employee discrimination against him may cause productivity and profits to decline, while Jerome could maintain productivity through being better accepted by his co-workers. Giving Jerome the promotion would therefore be beneficial for the company in the short-term. On the other hand, if employees could accept Juan, he should be a better FLM and could improve productivity in the long-term. Furthermore, if he is not promoted, he could leave the company and the company would lose a valuable employee.

Would the promotion of either Juan or Jerome deny any individuals of their rights?

If Marilyn promotes Jerome, it could deny Juan his basic right against discrimination, to be judged on his past performance, and his opportunity to receive a promotion. Would the promotion of either Juan or Jerome give people the justice they deserve?

If Marilyn does not promote Juan, she will be acting unfairly. In order to promote justice within the organization, Marilyn must promote the best person for the job and not respond to pressures to discriminate. If she were to promote Jerome instead, it would not only be unfair to Juan, but would send the wrong signal to all the employees at the company.

Given the answers to these questions, Marilyn should promote Juan. The company will have to provide Juan with the support he will need to maintain productivity, and management should clearly demonstrate its disapproval of discriminatory attitudes. When a company meets the ethical standards established by the federal government, or by its industry or profession (e.g., doesn't discriminate against employees on the basis of race in a promotion decision), the organization is fulfilling its social obligation.

Various laws prohibit employers from putting employees at risk, polluting, or discriminating against certain groups, and this company is abiding by those laws. The story of Marilyn's decision is one example of encountering a dilemma with legal and social ramifications. Meeting social obligations doesn't always involve a question of legality. When a company packages its products in recycled paper or provides health care insurance for an employee's significant other, it is being socially responsive. How so? Although it may be responding to social pressures; it is providing something society desires without having to be told to do so by law!

Contemporary Organization Ethics

An organization has a value system that determines its ethical behavior. Individual and organizational wrongdoing during the past few decades drew and continues to draw attention to the lack of ethical behavior in many organizations. Given the increased focus on ethics in recent years, it has become important for organizations to demonstrate their commitment to ethics and to being socially responsible. FLMs who wish to be a part of an ethical organization have to understand the organization's ethical character or culture. FLMs should be as aware of an employer's ethical character as they are of its economic health. For example, if an organization emphasizes short-term revenues over long-term results, it may be creating an unethical atmosphere. If it expects employees to leave their private ethics at home, thus encouraging unethical behavior or discouraging ethical behavior for financial reasons, it is promoting an unethical work environment. If an organization links its ethical behavior to a code of ethics but will not address the complexity of ethical dilemmas, then the code may merely be window dressing. Proactive organizations do more than adopt a document when they establish a code of ethics. They may establish board-level committees to monitor the ethical behavior of the organization, or develop ethics training courses or other programs.

The treatment of employees can also indicate the ethical nature of an organization. If employees are not treated as well as customers or if performance-appraisal standards are unfair or arbitrary, the organization may be unethical. Additionally, an absence of procedures for handling ethical issues, or the lack of a whistle-blowing mechanism, or even the lack of a basic communication avenue between employees and FLMs can indicate an organization that is ethically at risk.

Finally, an organization may be unethical if it fails to recognize its obligations to the public as well as to its shareholders. Ethical problems are not merely public relations issues, and legal decisions may not be ethical ones.

Organizations Need to Demonstrate Social Responsibility

What responsibility do an organization's leaders have to provide benefits to their stockholders and to adopt courses of action that enhance the well-being of society at large? Social responsibility is an obligation organizations have to society. It means going beyond legal responsibilities and profit-making. Social responsibility tries to align organizational long-term goals with what is good for society. An organization should recognize the impact of its actions on others and be able to predict how those actions would threaten or further its existence. Becoming a "moral actor" can be a fundamental issue of survival for the organization. Social responsibility therefore obligates FLMs to make decisions that nurture, protect, and promote the welfare and well-being of stakeholders and society as a whole.

We can understand social responsibility better if we compare it with two similar concepts: social obligation and social responsiveness. Social obligation is a business' most basic duty to society. An organization has fulfilled its social obligation when it meets its economic and legal responsibilities and no more. It does the minimum that the law requires. In contrast to social obligation, social responsiveness adds a moral obligation to business responsibilities. It requires organization to take actions that make society better and to refrain from actions that could make it worse. Societal norms guide this process.

Why Organizations Should Be Socially Responsible

Several advantages may result from socially responsible behavior. First, employees, and society benefit directly when organizations bear some of the costs of helping workers that would otherwise be borne by the government. Second, if all organizations in a society were socially responsible, the quality of life as a whole would be higher. Some have argued that the way organizations behave toward their employees determines many of a society's values and the ethics of its citizens. It has been suggested that if all organizations adopted a caring approach and agreed to promote the interests of their employees, a climate of caring would pervade to greater society.

Some point to Japan, Sweden, the Netherlands, and Switzerland as countries with very socially responsible organizations and where, as a result, crime and unemployment rates are relatively low, the literacy rate is relatively high, and socio-cultural values promote harmony between different groups of people. Finally, being socially responsible is the right thing to do. Evidence suggests that socially responsible FLMs and other managers are, in the long run, best for all organizational stakeholders. It appears that socially responsible organizations are also sought out by communities, which encourage these organizations to locate in their cities by offering them incentives such as property-tax reductions, new roads, and free utilities for their plants. Additionally, FLMs who promote a proactive approach to social responsibility are also sought out by organizations. There are many reasons to believe that, over time, strong support of social responsibility greatly benefits FLMs, their organizations, organizational stakeholders, and society at large.

Ethics of a Diverse Workforce

One of the most important trends to emerge in organizations over the last 30 years has been the increasing diversity of the workforce. Diversity means differences among people due to age, gender, race, ethnicity, religion, sexual orientation, socioeconomic background, and capabilities/disabilities who make up the employees in an organization.

As the world economy has opened up opportunities for education and jobs, companies find talent in a lot of unique and different areas. This has led to very diverse teams coming from different religious, cultural, ethnic and gender backgrounds. Diversity in the workplace isn't directly an ethical issue, however, diversity raises important issues of ethics and social responsibility for FLMs and organizations. If not handled well, diversity challenges bring an organization to its knees, especially in our increasingly global environment.

Diversity in the workplace isn't directly an ethical issue. As alluded to above, it refers to the different types of people from different backgrounds who make up the staff in the office. As the world economy has opened up opportunities for education and jobs, companies find talent in a lot of unique and different areas. This has led to very diverse teams coming from different religious, cultural, ethnic, and gender backgrounds. There are benefits of a diverse workforce.

When diversity is embraced, it builds stronger teams with better communication. Teams become more innovative, tackling problems from different points of view. When diversity isn't embraced, not only does it have a negative effect on the team but it can become an ethical issue. If a person feels harassed or discriminated against for his background or beliefs, this is an ethical issue. This not only leaves departments feeling strain and anxiety, but it also leads to problems with productivity, added conflict, and potential lawsuits.

Establishing policies and procedures. FLMs and other organizational leaders are responsible for the organization culture and how ethics and diversity issues are viewed. If leadership is complacent, the team will adopt an organic culture that may lead to problems. Every organization as will be highlighted later should establish ethics policies and a code of conduct. These policies should address common concerns about ethics including legal and moral issues. FLMs and other organizational leaders set the tone for how they want to build an ethical culture in the organization. For example, if an organization is driven by high-moral standards, it might adopt a policy of "do the right thing" and take returns, for example, from customers for any reason no questions asked. This becomes part of the culture and brand.

Employee policies must be written and distributed. Employees can't be held accountable to rules, if they don't know or understand the rules. This is why training and review are imperative to integrating ethics rules properly into the organization. On top of the written policies and training, diversity workshops help employees learn which actions are commonly unappreciated. Often, employees think they are being friendly and are just joking around, and they don't realize that their words or actions make others feel bad. By conducting training with role-playing, FLMs and other leaders are able to help employees better understand each other and how to appropriately communicate on different things.

It has been suggested that ethics and diversity share a special bond. That is, one cannot be talked about without including the other. Ethics and diversity share common ground. One way to think about ethics is that it serves as the soil in which the seed of diversity must be planted by FLMs and other organizational leaders and from which members of the organizations' understanding of the relationship grows.

Diversity is about the makeup of an organization and about who is making decisions. It is also about the way decisions are made and how work is done in the organization. Diversity is about inclusiveness in the organization where everyone is valued, treated fair, and have a voice. In conclusion, FLMs must never lose sight of the fact that diversity is an integral part of ethics. And any discussion of ethics would be incomplete without it.

How Front-Line Managers and Organizations Can Institutionalize Ethical Behavior

How should FLMs and organizations decide which social issues are important and to what extent the organizations should trade profits for social gain. First, illegal behavior should not be tolerated, and FLMs should be alert to its occurrence and report it promptly. The term whistleblower is used to refer to a person who reports illegal or unethical behavior and takes a stand against unscrupulous FLMs and stakeholders who are pursuing their own ends. Laws now exist to protect the interest of whistleblowers, who risk their jobs and careers to reveal unethical behavior. In part, these laws were implemented because of the experiences of two engineers at Morton Thiokol who warned that the Challenger space shuttle's O-ring gaskets would be adversely affected by cold weather at launch. Their warnings were ignored by everyone involved in the headlong rush to launch the shuttle. As a result, seven astronauts died when the Challenger exploded shortly after its launch in January 1986. Although the actions of the engineers were applauded by the committee of inquiry, their subsequent careers suffered because managers at Morton Thiokol blamed them for damaging the company's reputation and harming its interests.

Any organization must clarify that ethical considerations are valued by the organization. An organization's mission statement often details its goal of providing the highest quality product at the least cost and recognizes its commitment to all stakeholders. In addition, it needs to include a commitment to an ethical standard for all employee actions.

An organization must communicate its commitment to ethical values to all of its employees and external stakeholders. Codes of conduct or ethics should be adopted and distributed to all employees. Communication cannot be limited to the distribution of the code of ethics, however, because actions speak louder than words. Through their actions, FLMs should foster employee commitment to the organization's goal of ethical behavior in the same way that they foster employee commitment to its goal.

During the promotion and recruitment process, organizations can include in their criteria an interest in ethical decision-making. Several methods can be used to evaluate employees, such as honesty tests, background checks, and an employee's willingness to sign a commitment to the corporate code of ethics. Some leaders look for integrity when hiring and promoting employees in the organization. Integrity includes a personal allegiance to excellence, honesty, a sense of teamwork, and a balanced perspective on long-term goals and short-term profits. Early in an organization's process, a psychological contract is formed between the employer and employee. Psychological contracts typically cover the expectations that the employer and the employee form about each other. The degree to which both parties satisfy these expectations affects the success of the relationship. It is important for FLMs to understand that if the two do not or cannot agree on their fundamental needs, then the relationship will suffer. Furthermore, because ethical behavior cannot be reduced to simple do's and don'ts, both parties' expectations will continually change and thus there must be opportunity and structure to address evolving expectations.

Training employees to make an ethical analysis as part of their decision-making is critical. Training can be formal, focused on the organization's goals and objectives and on decision-making techniques. Training can also be achieved through the normal socialization that occurs during the orientation of a new employee. If the employer is operating ethically then the role models whom the employee emulates will exhibit the proper ethical behavior. The system of rewards and punishment will confirm and reinforce ethical behavior.

Models for Ethical Conduct

Distributive Justice

The principle of distributive justice requires that FLMs not be arbitrary and use only relevant information to determine how to treat people. It demands a fair distribution of pay raises, promotions, job titles, interesting job assignments, office space, and other organizational resources among members of an organization. Fairness means that rewards should be based on the meaningful contributions that individuals have made to the organization, such as time, effort, education, skills, abilities, and performance levels, and not on irrelevant personal characteristics over which individuals have no control, such as gender, race, or age.

FLMs have an obligation to ensure their departments and organizations follow distributive justice principles. This does not mean that all members of a department or organization should be rewarded equally; rather it means that those employees who receive greater rewards than others should have made substantially higher or more significant contributions to the organization. In the scenario presented earlier in this chapter, Marilyn should clearly promote Juan, using these guidelines. In many countries, FLMs and other managers have not only an ethical obligation, but also a legal obligation to strive to achieve distributive justice in their organizations, and they risk being sued by employees who feel that they are not being fairly treated.

Procedural Justice

The principle of procedural justice requires that FLMs clearly state and consistently administer the rules and established procedures of the organization and not bend the rules to serve their own interests or to show favoritism. This principle applies to procedures such as appraising an employee's performance, deciding who should receive a raise or a promotion, and deciding whom to lay off when an organization is forced to downsize. Procedural justice exists, for example, when FLMs

1. carefully appraise the job performance of employees reporting directly to them;
2. take into account any environmental obstacles to high performance beyond the employees' control, such as lack of supplies, machine breakdowns, or dwindling customer demand for a product; and
3. ignore irrelevant personal characteristics such as an employee's age or ethnicity.

Like distributive justice, procedural justice is necessary not only to ensure ethical conduct but also to avoid costly lawsuits.

Institutionalizing ethics means that FLMs and other managers and leaders create and sustain an ethically oriented organization culture, the shared organizational values and behavioral norms—"How we do things around here." FLMs must "walk the talk" when it comes to ethical behavior by continually talking about ethics and role modeling conduct or behavior themselves with integrity; where people are held accountable; and open, two-way communications occur in an environment free of fear.

So, in the end, what difference does institutionalization of ethics make? Those organizations have less misconduct by employees at all levels. They are able to mitigate risk by preventing and detecting problems early, so they can address them before problems escalate. They also enjoy an edge when it comes to attracting and retaining talent. Honest, open communications facilitate their processes and improvement efforts. Their organization's reputation is less at risk.

FLMs who help their organizations institutionalize ethics by doing such things as introducing ethics training programs will have a profound impact.

But as part of that effort, one of the most powerful things organizations can do to influence employee behavior is to focus on FLMs and help them to be ethical leaders. This is especially important since the reality is that in many organizations, FLMs are the only people in leadership positions that employees interact with on a daily basis. As a result, their behavior serves as a proxy for the values and priorities of senior leadership and the organization as a whole.

It has been noted that employees judge three factors most rigorously in FLMs when assessing them as ethical leaders: setting a good example; conducting one's own life in an ethical manner; and being accountable for violations of ethical standards. Employees also are influenced by whether FLMs listen to employees, support employees' efforts to uphold the organization's ethics standards, keep promises and commitments, and define success by how it is achieved—not just by results.

Findings also identify overlapping and consistent lists of FLM attributes that positively impact ethical culture. FLMs who are viewed as ethical leaders treat employees with respect, listen well, hold others accountable, are trustworthy and honest, make fair decisions, and talk about ethics.

There are a number of things an organization can do to strengthen FLMs' roles as ethical leaders and help them positively impact the organization's culture as listed below:

- Communicate and demonstrate in no uncertain terms to FLMs that integrity matters. The "tone from the top" is important but can become diluted as it trickles down. FLMs need to understand that how results are attained is just as important as what is attained, and they must be supported for making decisions accordingly.
- Help FLMs promote a work environment in which questioning and acknowledging problems and mistakes is OK. Employees' good faith efforts to do the right thing for the business must be appreciated. Encourage FLMs to admit their own mistakes; employees will trust and respect them more.
- Give FLMs tools to recognize people who positively impact the organization by encouraging others to behave with integrity or by confronting and helping resolve ethical dilemmas. FLMs should be able to recognize an employee who, for example, helps a co-worker who is feeling pressured to compromise ethical standards or who volunteers to lead a team discussion about ethics.
- Train FLMs how to receive and respond to reports of perceived ethical misconduct.

- Give FLMs tools, such as case studies, to help them communicate with employees and help them and their team gain comfort talking about ethics with "what would you do" scenarios.
- Teach FLMs about retaliation. When they understand what it is—and what it is not—they are better equipped to prevent it.
- Implement train-the-trainer sessions and give trainers tools to conduct training with their own employees about topics such as valuing diversity, treating others with respect, and so on.
- Build ethical leadership measures into FLMs' performance appraisal processes and clarify expectations for them, and recognize supervisors who actively promote and support the company's ethics and compliance program.

Organizational leaders and FLMs should promote an organizational culture that encourages ethical behavior and a commitment to not just compliance with the law but to "doing the right thing" no matter the situation. Having a reputation as an ethical organization can be a competitive advantage in many ways. FLMs and other leaders should make sure the organization is committed to harnessing and supporting the powerful impact FLMs make on the organization's culture of character or integrity when they fulfill their role as ethical leaders.

Conclusion

Business ethics is an important topic today. Business ethics is ethical behavior in the workplace that influences how a business functions, such as individual and corporate ethics. FLMs can apply ethical standards to help themselves decide on the proper way to behave toward organizational stakeholders.

Social responsibility refers to an organization's and FLM's duty to make decisions that nurture, protect, enhance, and promote the welfare and well-being of stakeholders and society as a whole. Promoting ethical and socially responsible behavior is an FLM's major challenge. Organizations can institutionalize ethical behavior by establishing the value, communicating the value, and selecting and training employees with ethical behavior in mind. Three models available to FLMs to determine whether a decision is ethical are: utilitarian, justice, and moral rights.

The issue of diversity (i.e., differences among people due to age, gender, race, ethnicity, religion, sexual orientation, socioeconomic background, and capabilities/disabilities) also poses ethical challenges for today's FLMs. In particular, generational values help decide where employees choose to work, how they approach the work, and how well they work together. Changes in the nature of the employee-employer relationship have come about in U.S. business, in part, because of the changing values of American workers.

Institutionalizing ethics means getting ethics formally and explicitly into daily organization life. It means FLMs and other organizational members getting ethics into organization policy formation at the board, top management, and FLM levels and through a formal code, getting ethics into all daily decision-making and work practices down the line, at all levels of employment.

4

Planning, Organizing, and Controlling

Within every organization structure are managers. No matter the type of organization, a manager's job is essentially the same across the board but there are certain functions or activities of management to consider regardless of the leadership style. In general, management has been described as a social process involving responsibility for economical and effective planning and regulation of operation of an organization in the fulfillment of given purposes. It is a dynamic process consisting of various elements and activities. These activities are different from operative functions like marketing, finance, purchasing, and so on. Rather these activities are common to each and every manager irrespective of her or his level or status.

Understanding the four functions of management can help an FLM become more effective in their management role and be a better leader for their group, team, or department. This can also help an FLM's organization reach goals and objectives more efficiently. Using the four management functions effectively in the workplace takes time and practice. In this chapter, we discuss three of the four different functions of management. More

Succeeding as a Frontline Manager in Today's Organizations, pages 89–116
Copyright © 2021 by Information Age Publishing
89

specifically, after briefly taking a look at the difference between efficiency and effectiveness, this chapter focuses on planning, organizing, and controlling, while Chapter 8 discusses leading.

Getting Things Done, Effectively and Efficiently Through and With People

Organization is the key to succeeding as an FLM. As an FLM, the responsibilities can be overwhelming if the FLM does not effectively plan, schedule, and delegate tasks appropriately. These processes lead to a more controlled environment which, in turn, leads to a less hectic workplace in which FLMs and other managers execute the process of getting things done, effectively and efficiently, through and with other people. Several terms of this execution warrant some discussion: process, efficiently, and effectively.

The term process represents the primary activities that FLMs perform. These are called management functions. Efficiency means doing the task right and refers to the relationship between inputs and outputs. If you get more output for a given input, you have increased efficiency. You also increase efficiency when you get the same output with fewer resources. Because FLMs deal with input resources that are scarce—money, people, and equipment—they are concerned with efficient use of these resources. Consequently, FLMs must be concerned with minimizing resource costs.

Although minimizing resources costs is important, it isn't enough simply to be efficient. An FLM must also be concerned with completing activities. This is called effectiveness. Effectiveness means doing the right task. In an organization, this translates into goal attainment. Figure 4.1 shows how efficiency and effectiveness are interrelated. The need for efficiency has a profound effect on the level of effectiveness. It is easier to be effective if you ignore efficiency. For instance, you could produce more sophisticated and higher-quality products if you disregard labor and material input costs—yet that would more than likely create serious financial problems. Consequently, being a good FLM means being concerned with both attaining goals (effectiveness) and doing so as efficiently as possible.

The management functions of planning, organizing, leading, and controlling are widely considered to be the best means of describing the FLM's job, as well as the best way to classify accumulated knowledge about what contributes to the success of FLMs. Although there continue to be major changes in the environment faced by FLMs and the tools used by them to perform their roles, FLMs still perform these essential functions. Let's take a brief look at each of these.

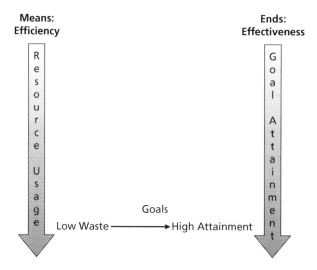

Figure 4.1 Efficiency versus effectiveness.

Because organizations exist to achieve some purpose, someone has to define that purpose and the means for its achievement. An FLM and other managers are that someone. The planning function encompasses defining an organization's goals, establishing an overall strategy for achieving these goals, and developing a comprehensive hierarchy of plans to integrate and coordinate activities. Setting goals keeps the work to be done in its proper focus and helps organizational members keep their attention on what is important.

FLMs and other managers also have to divide work into manageable components and coordinate results to achieve objectives. This is the organizing function. It includes determining which tasks will be done, who will do them, how the tasks will be grouped, who will report to whom, and when decisions will be made.

We know that every organization contains people and that part of an FLM's or other manager's job is to direct and coordinate the activities of these people. Performing this activity is referred to as the leading function in management. When FLMs, for example, motivate employees, direct the activities of others, select the most effective communication channel, or resolve conflicts among members, they are engaging in leading.

The final function FLMs and other managers perform is controlling. After the goals are set, the plans formulated, the structural arrangements determined, and the people hired, trained, and motivated, something may still go amiss. To ensure things are going as they should, an FLM, for example, must monitor their group's, team's, or department's performance. Actual performance must be compared with the previously set goals. If there are any significant deviations, it is the FLM's responsibility to get the group, team, and department back on track. This process of monitoring, comparing, and connecting stakeholders constitutes the controlling function.

Given our brief look at the four management functions FLMs must set a plan, then organize resources according to the plan, lead employees to work towards the plan, and finally, control everything by monitoring and measuring the effectiveness of the plan.

Planning

Planning is the function of management that involves setting objectives and determining a course of action for achieving those objectives. Planning requires that FLMs be aware of environmental conditions facing their organization and forecast future conditions. It also requires that managers be good decision makers.

Planning is a process consisting of several steps. For example, the process begins with environmental scanning which simply means that planners must be aware of the critical contingencies facing their organization in terms of economic conditions, their competitors, and their customers. Planners must then attempt to forecast future conditions. These forecasts form the basis for planning.

Planning is the process of establishing objectives and selecting courses of action, prior to taking action. Planners must establish objectives, which are statements of what needs to be achieved and when. Objectives are the specific desired results such as the goal to "increase energy efficiency by 10%." Planners must then identify alternative courses of action for achieving objectives. Courses of action are the series of steps taken to reach an objective, such as "hire a new maintenance engineer to boost maintenance response time by 20%." After evaluating the various alternatives, planners must make decisions about the best courses of action for achieving objectives. They must then formulate necessary steps and ensure effective implementation of plans. That is, at a minimum, plans should specify what steps will be taken, how the steps will be accomplished, and a deadline for completing the step. Finally, planners must constantly evaluate the success of their plans and take corrective action when necessary.

In most organizations, an FLM must plan for the accomplishment of tasks in his or her own team or department. This planning may include developing goals and identifying the tasks, resources, and responsibilities necessary to accomplish these goals. Through planning, the goals, which become the basis of all other actions, are established. Goals influence who the department hires, what types of incentives are used, and the controls instituted. As Vellice Taylor's experience shows, planning can create a more positive environment for the FLM and her or his employees.

"This past December my manager told me to schedule a major software and hardware update for our IT systems to be done on the 3rd and 4th of January. To get this done, I worked late with my IT staff, on the hardware, updated the checklist, made a test of the new software, and ordered additional items that might be needed. The very next morning I met with my IT team to prepare them for the job. Over the next few days I reviewed the steps for our software and hardware update. I worked with the team to write a schedule of tasks to be done and assigned each task to the team members who were most competent to complete the tasks. I knew that after the systems and hardware were down and the backup was successfully running, and we began the software and hardware update, I would find some unexpected issues and everything wouldn't go exactly as planned. I assigned my best IT person—Marchet—to be in charge of unexpected glitches and to help other team members when needed.

When the team returned from the Christmas holidays, I gave each employee a list of assigned tasks for the software and hardware update project. On January 2, we had a final meeting to prepare for the updates. We all worked some extra hours that weekend, but the updates were completed and the latest defenses like security patches and advances in firmware to keep our organization safe from new and ever-evolving threats were in place and up and running on Monday morning.

As can be seen from this case of an IT FLM for XXX products, planning is a critical part of an FLM's work. In order to do the project, Vellice Taylor first identified what needed to be accomplished and the tasks involved. During December, Vellice continued to plan the software and hardware update, while also making the daily plans for his IT team.

There are many advantages of being an effective planner. Planning makes life easier for the FLM and the employees. Planning creates expectations and strategies for accomplishing the work which lead to more effective outcomes. Good planning also leads to tangible rewards at the team and organization level (e.g., increased productivity) and personally (e.g., pay increases or promotions). Planning keeps FLMs from constantly fighting fires, allowing them to act rather than react.

Planning Skills

Planning is an activity that everyone does to some extent. There are skills which you can develop, however, to make you a more effective planner. Understanding the basics of planning can make the task much easier. First, there are many different types of plans. Plans differ in terms of format (how they are expressed), horizon (the span of time they cover), and time span (how often they will be used). Let's take a look at each of these differences.

Formats

Plans are defined by their content. The content of the plan dictates the format to some extent. Some plans are developed to accomplish a task or a goal. This type of plan is a *descriptive plan*. A descriptive plan is what comes to mind when most people say they have a "plan of action." This type of plan includes a written account of what is to be achieved and how.

Budgets are plans stated in numerical or financial terms. This type of plan typically expresses anticipated results and expenses in dollar terms for a specific time period, such as budgeting $8,000 this year for travel. Budgets may also be calculated in non-dollar terms, including employee hours, capacity utilization, or units of production. Budgets may cover daily, weekly, monthly, quarterly, semi-annual, or annual periods.

Budgets enter into not only the planning process, but are considered control devices as well. The creation of a budget identifies what activities are important and how resources should be allocated to each activity. A budget becomes a control mechanism when it provides standards against which resource consumption can be measured and compared.

Plans which identify the activities to be done, the priorities of those activities, and the individual responsible for each is a *schedule*. The effective FLM continually considers how much work the department or team needs to accomplish in a given period and how the deadlines can be met. Scheduling is basically the process of formulating detailed lists of activities that must be accomplished to attain an objective, determining which activities have priority over others, and deciding who will do what tasks and when. This detailed listing is an integral part of a department's plan.

Plan Horizons

Plans also differ in the spans of time they cover. Some plans are developed to address a short-term need. Other plans target longer time frames. Strategic (or long-term) planning involves analyzing competitive opportunities and threats, as well as the strengths and weaknesses of the organization, and then determining how to position the organization to compete effectively in their environment. Strategic planning has a long time frame, often 3 years or more. Strategic planning generally includes the entire organization and includes formulation of objectives and the major steps it must take to reach them. Strategic planning is often based on the organization's mission statement (that answers fundamental questions about the organization), which is its fundamental reason for existence. An organization's top management most often conducts strategic planning. Traditionally, FLMs will have little effect on the strategic plan or planning process but they should know what it is and be able to communicate it to their employees.

Middle managers typically focus on developing shorter-term *tactical plans* with an intermediate term of 1to 3 years. Tactical plans show how top management's plans are to be carried out at the departmental level. They are subsets of the long-term or strategic plan, addressing many of the same issues within the context of a competitive marketplace. Typical questions asked when preparing a tactical plan are: "What changes are going to occur among our customers, suppliers, and competitors, and how must we change to prepare for this new environment? What skills will our personnel need to compete effectively, and what must we do now so that they will be ready?"

First-line FLMs focus on *shorter-term operational plans* which assume the existence of organization-wide or subunit goals and objectives and specify ways to achieve them. These day-to-day or week-to-week plans are concerned with specific, current issues, such as levels of staffing, project scheduling, vendor reliability, and customer satisfaction, among others. Operational plans might show, for instance, exactly which employees are to be assigned to which tasks or projects or exactly how many repairs will be made on a given day. Operational plans are focused in the moment and such planning is designed to develop specific action steps that support the strategic and tactical plans.

Frequency of Plan Use

Plans may be used only once, or repeatedly. *Single-use plans* are aimed at achieving a specific goal that, once reached, is not likely to recur in the future. One type of single-use plan is a *program.* A program is designed to carry out a one-time event or activity. It usually includes the steps involved, a schedule for their execution, a budget, and a list of affected personnel and their duties. A program may involve the expansion of a facility or the installation of major new technology. Deciding to undertake a program is the responsibility of top management. In well-managed organizations, FLMs who are affected by the program will be asked to contribute information to help develop it and will be involved in its execution in their areas of responsibility. A common example of a program is a management development program, designed to raise FLMs levels of technical skills, conceptual skills, or interpersonal skills. Increasing the skill levels of FLMs is not an end in itself, as the purpose of the program is to produce competent FLMs who are equipped to help achieve organizational success over the long run. Once an FLMs management skills have been raised to a desired level, the program is de-emphasized.

Another type of single-use plan is a *project.* A project is a one-time activity with a well-defined set of results. Other characteristics of a project include a definite start and finish, a time frame for completion, uniqueness, and involvement of people on a temporary basis, a limited set of resources (people, money, and time), and a sequence of activities and phases. A project does not have to be part of a larger program, but may be a separate, self-contained set of activities.

In contrast to single-use programs, *standing plans* are plans made to be used repeatedly, as the need arises. For example, when an FLM has an employee who increasingly fails to show up for work, the problem can be handled more efficiently and consistently if a disciplinary procedure has been established in advance. There are three major categories of standing plans: policies, procedures, and rules.

Policies usually set broad guidelines for the organization. Policies may be written guidelines (e.g., each employee accrues eight hours of sick leave each month) or unwritten practice (e.g., we do whatever it takes to satisfy customers, we promote from within wherever possible). They cover a range of subjects, from how to deal with customer complaints, to the company dress code, to personnel issues, such as vacations, compensation, and promotions. Policies define the limits within which FLMs can make decisions and reduce ambiguity. Policies help FLMs make decisions, but they are not firm rules.

Procedures, as the name implies, specify what to do in a specific situation. For example, a procedure might state: "Before refunding the customer's purchase price, the salesperson should carefully inspect the garment and then obtain approval from the floor manager for the refund." Procedures are more specific than policies. Like policies, they provide consistency. By defining the steps to take and the order in which to take them, procedures provide a standardized way of responding to repetitive problems.

FLMs follow procedures set by higher levels of management. They also create their own standardized procedures for their employees to follow as conditions change and new, recurring problems surface. FLMs should make sure employees know company procedures and that they follow them. It is also important, however, to avoid clinging to ineffectual procedures when there are more efficient ways to do a task.

A *rule* is a highly specific, non-negotiable guide to action. They are formulated to avoid problems that would occur without them. Rules often have to do with issues of health and safety, interaction among employees, and attendance. Some examples of rules are: "Always wear a hard hat on the job site"; "No smoking on the plant floor"; and "Except for emergencies, all absences must be approved by your FLM." Failing to follow rules usually involves a penalty, perhaps even dismissal. It is important to keep rules up-to-date and to enforce them impartially and consistently so that employees will take them seriously. FLMs frequently use rules when they confront a recurring problem because they are simple to follow and ensure consistency.

Why Plans Fail

Now that we have a better understanding of plans and planning, let's take a look at why plans fail. Some plans fail because they are unrealistic. The quickest way to set a plan for failure from the start is to set unrealistic goals or expected outcomes. This ensures failure. This often occurs due to outside pressure to succeed. If you tend to make unrealistic plans, stop committing yourself before you understand what is involved.

Some plans fail because they do not take the team into account. It is difficult to make a successful plan without input from the people who will carry it out. To make success more likely participants must be willing to participate and take responsibility for the work, capable—possessing the skills and time to participate, and willing to make plan success a priority.

Failure to provide performance expectations and feedback can lead to failure of the plan. Desired outcomes must be specified in measurable terms, setting the standards against which performance will be assessed and ultimately improved. Employees should frequently and frankly communicate about their progress in meeting performance objectives, and FLMs should give them frequent feedback.

Characteristics of Good Plans

Good plans are realistic plans. Carefully consider whether the desired outcome is actually an attainable goal. If the success of a delivery service hinges on getting the average order delivered within 35 minutes of the customer's phone call, and the driver's best average has been 42 minutes, the objective may be unrealistic. Simply wanting a change is not enough to make it happen.

If plans require people with special skills or knowledge to carry out the required tasks, training may be needed. It is important to match the skill requirements to the available staff. If the skills aren't readily available from the staff, training should be implemented.

A plan that states specific means to an end is a workable plan. If the FLM does not define the desired outcome and the method to achieve that outcome, the plan may not be seen as attainable. Specificity is a key to successful planning. This leaves less responsibility for the parties carrying out the plan.

Successful plans are specific, but they are also flexible. Every plan should have a "Plan B" just in case the first option goes off track. Some roadblocks to plan success can be seen as detours when the FLM demonstrates flexibility with the plan. The prudent FLM watches carefully for signs of how well the target plan is working and then adjusts accordingly.

Finally, the strategy for successful plan achievement is a strategy that involves *communication*. Communication up and down in the organization's hierarchy must be a priority. If the delivery drivers are to be held accountable for new levels of performance, they must understand the plan to achieve those standards. Senior leadership also cannot be expected to allocate money to buy the drivers' phones if they do not understand or accept the plan.

Defining the Objectives

FLMs must communicate their precise expectations to their employees if they expect to obtain optimal results. FLMs should begin by defining their objectives. Objectives can range from the tasks the FLM intends to accomplish on a certain day to the level of production the department or team should achieve for the year. Good objectives

- state a clear purpose (e.g., increase productivity by 10%);
- are measurable (e.g., assemble 50 additional television sets);
- specify a time frame within which they will be achieved (e.g., every 8-hour shift);
- specify the resources needed (e.g., by operating an additional assembly line for sub-assemblies);

- specify the quality of the output (e.g., without increasing the rate of rejects above 2%);
- are challenging but also attainable (e.g., handle employee grievances within 24 hours); and
- are stated in writing to increase commitment and understanding.

The more specific an objective is, the more likely it is to be accomplished. By quantifying how much will be done, when it will be finished, and who will do it using which resources, the plan leaves less possibility of misunderstanding or error. The following suggests a format for writing clear, workable objectives:

What's the action? (verb)	What's the result? (noun)	When's it due? (time frame)	Who will check? (monitor)	What's the purpose? (reason/purpose)

FLMs should determine, before beginning the project, what will determine progress. This means that indications of progress and deadlines for those expected indications should be included in the objective.

Writing an Action Plan

The process of writing objectives down forces you to think through the steps you will have to take in order to accomplish the objectives. This is more than a mental exercise: by breaking down large tasks into simple actions, the tasks seem easier. If the objectives are precisely stated and quantified, they will provide clear direction to the people actually doing the work. Clear objectives lead to clear work plans, also called activity plans or action plans. Objectives state what must be done; action plans explain how it will be done, specifying all the work details. While an objective is typically no longer than a paragraph, an action plan can be many pages in length.

The best way to write an action plan is to imagine doing the work, step-by-step, and then write down the key details. The following checklist describes an action planning process for a moderately complex project:

- List everything that must be done to accomplish the objective.
- List the tasks to be done in the order they should be finished.
- Identify, by name, who will do which tasks.
- List the resources that will be necessary for the completion of each task.
- Note the time needed for each task, including the estimated delivery time needed for materials not already on hand.

- Consider the constraints that might upset the plan and note the steps that can be taken to avoid them.
- Write the plan on a chart that reflects the passage of time, such as an event calendar or a Gantt chart that shows the beginning and ending points of every activity.
- Identify the control points that will mark the progress of activity.
- Develop a back-up plan just in case you cannot finish the action plan, or if you finish the plan early.
- Update the plan periodically to reflect feedback and the most current data.
- Refer to the plan frequently. Make it a dynamic part of your operations. It is actually easier to write a plan than to follow it!

A plan with clear, measurable objectives supported by well-defined actions is ready to be communicated to the people who will implement.

Management by Objectives

Management by objective (MBO) is a process in which FLMs and employees identify common goals, specify ways employees will contribute to the accomplishment of those goals, and agree to use the measured results to evaluate the employees' performance. Here is how an MBO program works. Imagine you are the FLM of the data processing (DP) department. You must meet with your employees to discuss and set the department's goals, which are changing because so many microcomputers are being purchased for use throughout the company, as well as in your department.

It is reasonable to assume that the role of the DP department will change because many routine reports will soon be generated without DP staff involvement. In essence, your department is becoming less of a batch processing operation and more of a microcomputer support resource. What will your new goals look like? They will probably identify new customer service needs that will require the technical support people to acquire new skills, for example. Communicating the new goals of the department to your employees will probably require several lengthy discussions.

Next, you and your employees must write out the new objectives to help the department fulfill its new role as a support resource for microcomputer users. The current objectives that relate to batch processing assignments probably need to be updated or scrapped. Any necessary new technical training programs should be specified. Together, you and your employees should decide upon the following:

- what the employees will do;
- how soon these tasks will be done;
- what resources, approaches, or training will be used;
- how the employees' performances will be measured; and
- when to meet next so the plan can be evaluated.

A great advantage of the MBO process is that it gives employees low on the corporate ladder access to the decision-making process. This has two distinct benefits. First, it gives employees some control over their individual work plans. Employees' involvement increases their commitment to the objectives and enhances the likelihood that the objectives will be accomplished. Second, the organization receives the benefits of the employees' input, which may be more insightful about how to reach the new objectives than the ideas of management and may offer new suggestions for improving productivity that FLMs might not have considered. The MBO process may also result in a higher morale among the workforce.

There are four main ingredients common to MBO programs. These are:

- *goal specificity*—specific statements of expected accomplishments;
- *participative decision-making*—the FLM and employee choose the goals and agree on how they will be achieved and evaluated;
- *explicit time limits*—each objective has a concise time period in which it is to be completed; and
- *performance feedback*—continuous feedback on progress toward goals.

Time Management

Time management is a tool anyone can use to schedule time and plan activities effectively. There are so many interruptions in the work day that there is little, if any time to do much planning or scheduling. Efficient time management requires that you know what things you need to accomplish and you use the self-discipline necessary to keep your attention focused on accomplishing them. Unfortunately there are no hard and fast rules for managing time that will work in every case; however, there are several time-management techniques that can make you a better time manager. At a minimum, you should learn to take the following steps:

1. identify your objectives,
2. prioritize your objectives,
3. make a "to do" list of the activities that must be accomplished,
4. set priorities for "to do" list tasks,

5. schedule your day, and
6. try to keep to the schedule throughout the day.

Time management is not something that generally comes easily. It takes a dedicated effort to be a good time manager. It requires learning how to set priorities and keep a schedule. Good time managers also know how to minimize disruptions. There are a number of "time wasters" such as interruptions or phone calls that steal a person's time.

FLMs attend many meetings, which can also waste time if the meeting doesn't have a purpose. Efficiently run meetings are time effective. When your presence is requested at a meeting, ask for an agenda and find out why you need to attend. Send a substitute if possible. Try to practice effective time management to maximize your personal productivity. Attempting to work faster or harder is not the answer; learn to work "smarter" instead.

Vellice Taylor works "smart." She ends each day by reviewing the day's accomplishments and identifying work that remains unfinished. She makes a prioritized list of the work to be done the next day, with tentative schedule and job assignments. When she arrives at work the next morning, she only needs to make adjustments to include any new events, such as an emergency software patch or an absent employee, and he is ready to put everyone to work without wasting time.

Scheduling Your Employees

Often there is some confusion between the scheduling and planning functions. Part of the problem is that two functions are frequently consolidated, particularly on smaller jobs. It is important to remember that the FLM's plan lists all of the resources and requirements needed; while the schedule is a list of necessary activities, their order of accomplishment, who is to do each, and the time needed to complete each activity.

Scheduling requires the evaluation of three basic components: the work, the resources, and the customer. First, the FLM must identify and prioritize the work, including the backlog, pending jobs, and emergencies. Second, the FLM must know which workers and contractors are available when, and the skills, experience, and preferences of each. The availability of non-human resources is also essential.

Finally, the FLM can only schedule effectively by taking into account the convenience of the customer. For example, maintenance scheduling in hospitals must wait until it is convenient for the patients and staff, who could be in the operating room. It may mean that work should be scheduled for nights and weekends. Repairs to the HVAC system should be scheduled during the cool of an evening or during the colder months. Student support areas at universities should be scheduled for times when students are away, such as holidays or summers. The point is clear: Every organization has its special maintenance requirements, and they are generally based on the organization's plan for serving customers at the customer's convenience.

To be effective in planning and scheduling work, the FLM must be proactive. That means that work should be scheduled before employees arrive at work, and the materials needed for work should be identified and allocated to each task or project. In addition, the FLM should be sensitive to the need for providing all employees with advance knowledge of the daily plans. Like other parts of the planning process, good scheduling allows the FLM to maximize the department's efforts.

A proactive scheduling program has many advantages. It is efficient: travel, time, special tool usage, and so forth can be optimized. It provides a good customer service in that the production department runs better and the customer knows exactly when a maintenance service will be undertaken. It allows the FLM to build in training opportunities for team members to develop the experience they need. It also builds morale, by providing a constant level of work for all employees.

A reactive program, on the other hand, is driven by equipment failures and rife with deferred plans. It ensures large overtime charges, long lists of backlogs, aesthetic problems, reduced control over plans and budgets, and worst of all, customer dissatisfaction. This situation is easily spotted and does not bode well for the FLM, as customers and team members alike will react negatively to it. For effective scheduling, an FLM

- reviews all tasks not yet performed and any incomplete jobs;
- puts the jobs in priority order;
- lists all of the people available to complete the jobs, with their available hours, skills, and preferences;
- looks for opportunities to increase efficiency such as making multiple assignments based on job location (e.g., two jobs in the same general area) or tools, materials or skill set needed to perform jobs;
- designates assignments to each team member using a schedule, placing high priority jobs first;
- updates the schedule as new information comes in and jobs get completed;

- shuffles resources as needed such as adding people or contractors or approving overtime to assist large efforts such as a repair that is falling behind schedule;
- keeps a list of back-up jobs so those employees can jump to another job if they finish one quickly or get stuck by a lack of parts or tools; and
- communicates with customers about job schedules and pending disruptions.

There are many techniques used to make the scheduling process more effective. Many organizations expect FLMs to use certain scheduling techniques to assist them. Two of the most widely used techniques are the Gantt chart and the PERT chart. These scheduling techniques are methods of putting all of the information down on paper. Any effective scheduling technique requires the scheduler to be specific, be detailed, and document every step.

Organizing

The process of assigning people and allocating resources to accomplish the objectives set forth in the planning process requires organizational skills. Organizing is a step beyond planning and scheduling. Organizing is the process of making the plans and schedules happen. An organization consists of people whose specialized tasks are coordinated to contribute to the entity's goals. During the planning process, FLMs decide what they are going to do; organizing is part of deciding how to do it, along with scheduling and budgeting. Organizing means figuring out how to make the action plan happen within the organization's formal and informal organizations. The skills and capabilities of people must be accurately assessed, and the FLM must establish a flow of work. Plans must be translated into job duties and job responsibilities.

Organizing is the function of management that involves developing an organizational structure and allocating human resources to ensure the accomplishment of objectives. The structure of the organization is the framework within which effort is coordinated. The structure is usually represented by an organization chart, which provides a graphic representation of the chain of command within an organization. Decisions made about the structure of an organization are generally referred to as organizational design decisions.

Every organization has a formal structure that prescribes relationships among people and resources in order to facilitate the accomplishment of the organization's work. It is important for FLMs to know how your organization is organized and understand why it is organized the way it is.

Organizing at the level of the organization involves deciding how best to departmentalize, or cluster, jobs into departments to coordinate effort effectively. There are many different ways to departmentalize, including organizing by function, product, geography, or customer. Many larger organizations use multiple methods of departmentalization.

Organizing at the level of a particular job involves how best to design individual jobs to most effectively use human resources. Traditionally, job design was based on principles of division of labor and specialization, which assumed that the narrower the job content, the more proficient the individual performing the job could become. However, experience has shown that it is possible for jobs to become too narrow and specialized. For example, how would you like to do the same task one day after another, as you might have done many decades ago if you worked in a company that had an assembling line and rote tasks for its employees to complete over and over again? When this happens, negative outcomes result, including decreased job satisfaction and organizational commitment, increased absenteeism, and turnover. FLMs and their organizations have increasingly recognized the importance of attempting to strike a balance between the need for employee specialization and the need for employees to have jobs that entail variety and autonomy. As a result, many jobs are now designed based on such principles as empowerment, job enrichment, and teamwork.

As suggested above, an organization chart shows the formal structure of an organization. It identifies key managerial positions and, by means of connecting lines, shows who is accountable to whom and who is in charge of what areas or departments. The informal organization is not shown on the chart. The organization chart also shows the chain of command or the line of authority between the top of the organization and the lowest positions in the chart. The chain of command represents the path a directive or suggestion should take in traveling from the president to operating employees at the bottom of the organization chart or from the operating employees to the top. Each position on the organization chart has either a line (operating) or a staff relationship with the other positions.

Line positions are directly involved in doing the money-making work of the organization. They accomplish the primary purpose of the organization. Staff positions provide operating departments with advice and assistance in specialized areas like personnel, finance, and research. The staff employees support the FLMs and operating employees at every level of the organization. This structure essentially serves the organization's two types of customers: The operating employees serve the "real" customers outside the organization, while the staff employees serve the internal customers, who happen to be the operating employees.

Centralization Versus Decentralization

When organizations design their optimal organization structure, they usually find that parts of the company are centralized and other parts decentralized. A computer manufacturer, for example, may have a centralized manufacturing facility with a decentralized network of service providers spread throughout the country. This structure reflects the organization's objectives. Centralization and decentralization refer to the manner in which degrees of authority are spread throughout the organization. In a centralized organization, upper management makes most of the important decisions.

Decentralization describes a physical relationship, but it also describes a management style. The degree of decentralization in an organization can be quickly ascertained by asking one question, "Which decisions are made by whom?" If the first-line FLMs are allowed to make decisions involving large sums of money or affecting many employees, the organization is highly decentralized. On the other hand, if even senior managers must check with headquarters for approval on routine matters, the organization is highly centralized.

Authority is the legitimate or rightful power to lead others, the right to order and to act. It is the power by which an FLM or another manager can require employees to do or not to do a certain thing that the FLM deems necessary to achieve objectives. Management authority is not granted to an individual but rather to the position the individual holds at the time.

Authority is a continuum, with decentralized and centralized authority at each end. With the exception of very small companies, which tend to be centralized, most organizations lie somewhere between the two extremes, but can be classified overall. The key to success in today's world of work seems to be having the right balance between the two extremes.

Understanding the Informal Organization

The informal organization surrounds the formal organization. It is a complex and dynamic network of interpersonal relationships between organization members. These relationships cannot easily be diagrammed like the formal organization, yet they are just as important to the smooth operation of any group of people. By their nature, they are different for every company and are continually changing. An FLM's success depends on the recognition and use of the informal organization. The informal organization and its communication channels provide more than just news; they are also important conduits for sharing experiences, fostering innovation and cooperation, generating support for new ideas, reaching consensus, collecting data for planning purposes, and directly or indirectly influencing people, groups, and events.

FLMs must realize that they cannot eliminate an informal organization and they can never completely control it. Even if it were possible to do so, it might not be desirable. Acknowledging the existence of the informal organization is the FLM's first step toward understanding it. An FLM can create an environment that nurtures the informal organization in such a way that it contributes significantly to the realization of the organization's formal objectives. Managing and using the informal organization requires an appreciation of its nature and its benefits. The FLM must learn to live with its vagueness, its spirit, and its strength. Like it or not, FLMs are a part of the informal organization by virtue of being members of the business. Successful FLMs learn to use their personal power to become active and effective participants in the informal organization.

To influence the informal organization to play a positive role FLMs should group employees so that those most likely to work harmoniously together are assigned as a team to the same assignments. FLMs should also avoid activities that would unnecessarily disrupt any informal groups whose interests and behavior patterns support the department's overall objectives. Conversely, if an informal group is influencing employees in a negative direction, causing a serious threat to the department's functioning, the FLM may have to reorganize by redistributing work assignments or adjusting work schedules, for example. One way to organize employees and to empower them is by delegating, which we shall discuss next.

Delegating

Today's successful FLMs need to empower their employees by giving them greater participation in decisions that affect them and by expanding their responsibility for results (see Chapter 9). One way to empower people is to delegate authority to them. Many FLMs find that this is difficult, because they are afraid to give up control. "I like to do things myself," says one FLM, "because then I know it is done and I know it is done right." Another FLM voiced a similar comment: "I have to learn to trust others. Sometimes I am afraid to delegate the more important projects because I like to stay hands on." Unfortunately there are many reasons why FLMs do not delegate.

FLMs who do not want to delegate will focus on all the reasons why they should not; while FLMs who want to delegate will find ways to do so without adverse results. This section will show that, properly planned delegation can actually increase FLMs' effectiveness and allow them to retain some control. Delegation is frequently depicted as a four-step process:

1. *Allocation of duties.* Duties are tasks and activities that need to be done. These duties are allocated to an employee or team.
2. *Delegation of authority.* Once duties have been assigned, the corresponding authority over those duties can be granted. The essence of the delegation process is empowering employees to act for you. It is passing to the employee the formal rights to act on your behalf. Be sure you have given the employee enough authority to get the materials, the equipment, and the support from others necessary to get the job done.
3. *Assignment of responsibility.* When authority is delegated, you must assign responsibility. That is, when you give someone "rights," you must also assign to that person a corresponding "obligation" to perform.
4. *Creation of accountability.* To complete the delegation process, you must hold the employees accountable for properly carrying out their duties. So while responsibility means an employee is obliged to carry out assigned duties, accountability means that the individual has to perform that assignment in a satisfactory manner. Employees are responsible for the completion of tasks assigned to them and are accountable to you for the satisfactory performance of that work.

The FLM's Role in Delegation

There are many FLMs who use delegation as a tool for developing employees through coaching and feedback. FLMs should recognize that they have an important role in providing employees with "stretch assignments," or more challenging opportunities to increase their skills. Delegation can be used to expand an employee's capabilities from a dependent, low-level performer to an independent, highly competent performer. This process takes time and effort by both the FLM and the employee. It not only enhances employees' self-esteem, but also increases their value to the team and organization. Delegation will only work, however, when the FLM is willing to delegate and the employee is willing to take on the responsibility and to develop appropriate skills.

One way FLMs increase their effectiveness through delegating is by careful planning; studying the tasks that need to be done and making appropriate matches between the work assignments and the employees. For each work assignment, the FLM should consider the nature of the responsibility and the readiness of the employee to assume it. The FLM can therefore avoid hovering, smothering, and generally "over-managing" the work of an employee who does not need much supervision, and can avoid "under-managing" an employee who is not ready to be left alone to complete a task through a hands-off, sink or swim policy. After making an assignment, FLMs must mentally prepare to let go of any emotional investment they have in the responsibility for the task.

When FLMs delegate, they must understand that delegation is not the same as participation. In participative decision-making there is a sharing of authority. With delegation, employees and teams make decisions on their own. That is why delegation is such a vital component of empowering employees! Anyone who follows the suggestions below can be an effective delegator.

- Allow the employees to participate in determining what is delegated, how much authority is needed to get the job done, and the standards by which they will be judged, to increase employee motivation, satisfaction, and accountability for performance.
- Give a detailed assignment by providing clear information on what is being delegated, the results you expect, and any time or performance expectations.
- Specify the employees' range of discretion, including the amount and extent of their authority and their degree of responsibility.
- Inform others that the delegation has occurred, specifying the tasks, the amount of authority and employees involved.
- Establish feedback controls to monitor the employees' progress (i.e., specific time of completion of tasks, dates, when the employee will report back on how well they are doing, and any major problems that have surfaced).

Delegation allows FLMs to accomplish more than they could alone, due to the limitations of their own time and abilities. By letting go of tasks that can be and should be done more efficiently by others, FLMs put everyone's talents to better use. Table 4.1 describes FLM actions which lead to effective and ineffective delegation.

TABLE 4.1 Effective Versus Ineffective Delegataion	
Effective Delegation	**Ineffective Delegation**
• Encourage the free flow of information.	• Hoard information.
• Focus on results.	• Emphasize methods.
• Set firm deadlines.	• Fail to set deadlines.
• Provide all necessary resources.	• Fail to provide necessary resources.
• Give advice without interfering.	• Fail to get input or point out pitfalls.
• Build control into the delegation process.	• Relinquish all control.
• Give credit for accomplishments.	• Fail to provide credit to employees.
• Back up employees in legitimate disputes.	• Fail to provide necessary support.

Managing From a Distance

In planning for and organizing work in today's organization, FLMs must also learn how to lead effectively from a distance. This is because more and more employees work in scattered sites rather than one central location. Remember from our discussion in Chapter 1 on telecommuting that no longer do FLMs have to be at the office or job site to manage teams or individuals. Today's adept FLMs can and should be able to accomplish their charge from a distance.

How can an FLM operating at a distance ensure high performance? It all begins with developing and instilling trust and cooperation between the members of the team. FLMs can develop both of these elements by recognizing that a commitment to teamwork, planning, and good constant communication are important. Delegation can also be used. The following is a list of guidelines that can help FLMs become effective in supervising from a distance:

- ▪ Provide opportunities for face-to-face interaction among team members on a regular basis.
- ▪ Plan team meetings in such a way that there is ample time for team members to get to know and learn from one another.
- ▪ Be responsive to the needs of team members working offsite.
- ▪ Bend over backwards to provide all necessary resources, materials, and supplies and remove obstacles for the team.
- ▪ Ensure that work schedules and job assignments are not prejudicial to team members, so that off-site work is scheduled equitably.
- ▪ Go offsite with team members as needed to understand the work environment, and spot check each employee's work on a regular basis.

- Communicate work priorities and timetables at team meetings and in writing when necessary.
- Give clear directions and instructions, set clear standards and expectations, and measure results against them.
- Give frequent performance feedback.
- When appropriate, send team members offsite to work in pairs.
- Trust your team members—do not assume that if they are out of sight they will goof off.

Controlling

Once a plan is established and the FLM has organized a system for accomplishing the plan everything should seemingly lead to success. Unfortunately, when working with humans who make errors, machines that break down, and changing customer demands, plans can fail—even when the FLM has organized their execution. To avoid plan failure and quickly identify and respond to potential failures, the wise FLM will put control processes into place. Control processes assist in the monitoring of resources and serve as guidelines for use of resources and completion of plans.

Controlling involves ensuring that performance does not deviate from standards. Controlling consists of three steps, which include (a) establishing performance standards, (b) comparing actual performance against standards, and (c) taking corrective action when necessary as will be discussed in more detail in Chapter 12. Performance standards are often stated in monetary terms such as revenue, costs, or profits but may also be stated in other terms, such as units produced, number of defective products, or levels of quality or customer service.

The measurement of performance can be done in several ways, depending on the performance standards, including financial statements, sales reports, production results, customer satisfaction, and formal performance appraisals. FLMs at all levels engage in the managerial function of controlling to some degree.

The managerial function of controlling should not be confused with control in the behavioral or manipulative sense. This function does not imply that FLMs should attempt to control or to manipulate the personalities, values, attitudes, or emotions of their subordinates. Instead, this function of management concerns the FLM's role in taking necessary actions to ensure that the work-related activities of subordinates are consistent with and contributing toward the accomplishment of organizational and departmental objectives.

Effective controlling requires the existence of plans as discussed earlier, since planning provides the necessary performance standards or objectives. Controlling also requires a clear understanding of where responsibility for deviations from standards lies. Two traditional control techniques are budget (as discussed later in this chapter) and performance audits. An audit involves an examination and verification of records and supporting documents. A budget audit provides information about where the organization is with respect to what was planned or budgeted for, whereas a performance audit might try to determine whether the figures reported are a reflection of actual performance. Although controlling is often thought of in terms of financial criteria, FLMs in partnership with other organizational leaders and managers must also control production and operations processes, procedures for delivery of services, compliance with company policies, and many other activities within the organization.

The management functions of planning, organizing, leading, and controlling are widely considered to be the best means of describing the FLM's job, as well as the best way to classify accumulated knowledge about the study of management in general. Although there have been tremendous changes in the environment faced by FLMs and the tools used by FLMs to perform their roles, FLMs still perform these essential functions.

Using Budgets in Planning

Almost every FLM gets involved in planning the budget. Most FLMs already know something about budgets, even if they do not think of a budget as a plan. There is one thing FLMs should remember about budgets: A budget is not an independent goal, but is a tool to help you improve procedures and deliver more value and service to customers.

A budget is a type of comprehensive, numerical plan for the allocation of resources to achieve team, departmental or organizational goals and objectives. To put it somewhat differently, a budget is a statement of expected results expressed numerical terms. It may be financially oriented, as in revenues, expenses, cash and capital budgets, or it may be nonfinancial but still numerical, covering direct-labor hours, materials, equipment, number of programs and services, trainee output, and so on.

A budget is also a form of managerial control. It is a means of ensuring that results conform to plans by providing a basis for measuring performance. Budgets are used to identify deviations and shortfalls, and to remedy those deficiencies or to adjust expectations.

The purpose of a budget, therefore, is to make it possible for managers at different levels of the organization to determine what resources should be expended, by whom, and for what (planning), and what resources are being expended, where, by whom, and for what (control). Budgets help FLMs perform better and help improve the company's overall operation. Here's how. Budgets

- focus FLMs' attention and effort on results;
- compel FLMs to contribute to the attainment of organizational objectives, such as profitability, growth, efficiency, and resource development;
- facilitate measuring performance by comparing results with goals and objectives;
- provide a basis for assessing the appropriateness of the organizational structure, goals, and objectives;
- enhance interdepartmental coordination, effectiveness, and teamwork;
- encourage the use of historical reports and records in the planning process; and
- help identify areas where cost controls and hard-dollar savings can be realized.

The Budget Process

Within their own departments, FLMs are the budget officers. They must prepare the department's budget, present and defend it to their managers, and manage its operation throughout the year. All of the departmental budgets provide input into the overall corporate budget.

Developing a budget is a complex process. Two factors make this complex process much simpler: sufficient time, and clear areas of responsibility and authority. There should be various deadlines throughout, and FLMs must be sure to allow enough time for review and discussion at each step along the way.

Seen from the perspective of the organization as a whole, a healthy and effective budgeting process needs five ingredients:

- a clearly defined organizational structure, with explicit functions, and lines of authority and communication;
- a comprehensive and well understood budget planning process, with a budget calendar, and procedures and guidance for budget preparation, internal controls, and review and analysis;

- a fully developed accounting system, including standard costing, break-even analysis, and profit-contribution accounting;
- fixed responsibility for the comprehensive budget program; and
- FLMs who are knowledgeable about financial planning and the budgeting process.

In designing a budget, FLMs should be sure that the process is clearly defined, preferably in writing, identifying exactly who does what, and should make sure all team members understand it. Usually FLMs prepare the budget with help from their managers and contributions from their employees. Budget preparation must be based on continuous scrutiny of the department's initiatives, operating methods, organization structure, and facilities. It must always be based on departmental plans, and it must be applied within a framework of corporate and department or team goals and objectives.

After preparing the department's expense budget, the FLM usually submits it to the managers at the next higher level for review and approval of accuracy, completeness, and adherence to organizational policy. FLMs may also, depending on their needs, create budgets for employee work hours, revenue forecast, or capital expenditures like machinery and equipment. These budgets set specific standards for FLMs and their department or team to achieve.

Preparing the budget is one challenge; getting their managers' and top management's approval is another. FLMs, like all other managers in organizations, compete with one another for their share of limited organizational resources. They must be able to justify their requirements clearly and convincingly or fail to receive the funds they need. The FLM is the only one who has the stature and knowledge to present the department budget to the decision maker authoritatively and persuasively, and win approval.

After a budget has been approved and adopted, it becomes a management tool. FLMs must continuously monitor their budgets throughout the year and ensure those policies and rules are followed. They must also be alert to the need for budget adjustments and reprogramming as conditions change and impact budget allocations. In other words, FLMs should be flexible during budget allocations and use the numbers established during the budgeting process as guidelines for what's reasonable. For example, the FLM may find that the work unit has almost used up its overtime budget. When a new work request comes in that will require more overtime, the FLM must decide whether to spend extra money on labor to take care of the request or stick to the budget regardless of the request. In some organizations, keeping to the budget becomes so important that the latter choice is preferable and provides little budget allocation for the FLM. This should not happen. Budget numbers are not objectives—they provide guidance for achieving objectives at a reasonable cost.

The key steps an FLM can take to assist in effective budgeting include:

- Develop or review the organization's long-range strategy.
- Determine and set your department's objectives and means of attaining them.
- Establish budget procedures and a schedule.
- Gather cost information.
- Prepare the department's draft budget.
- Share your goals and cost estimates with your boss.
- Revise the draft budget into a proposed budget for review by management.
- Be prepared to negotiate for your budget items.
- Monitor your budget, noting areas of savings and unanticipated expenses.
- Take corrective actions when the budget is not being met.
- Keep your boss informed of your progress.

Budget problems exist in many departments. All too often, people within and outside the department play budget games. There are also numerous pitfalls for the unwary FLM. FLMs should take responsibility for their own budgets. Although they should use the expertise of their managers for advice and assistance, they should never rely on others to prepare their budgets.

FLMs have found countless ways to mislead or deceive decision makers into believing that the FLMs are performing well. One favorite approach is to underestimate sales and overestimate costs. These techniques skew the budget and make the process a useless exercise. FLMs may pad the budget or hide extra funds within it due to the budget folklore: "They'll cut it, so inflate it" or "Conceal it for contingencies." These practices occur when FLMs believe they will be rewarded or punished for either spending their total budget allocations or returning funds at the end of a budget period.

Conclusion

Planning establishes the goals which should be the basis of all the other management functions—organizing, leading, and controlling. The people hired, the incentives used, and the controls instituted all relate to what FLMs want to achieve and to the plans, and goals they set. Plans differ in terms of format, horizon, and frequency of use.

FLMs focus on short-term operational plans. Some plans are programs established to lay out in an orderly fashion all the steps in a major one-time project, each in its proper sequence. Programs and projects are single-use plans that are aimed at achieving a single goal. Policies, procedures, and rules are standing plans made to be used repeatedly, as the need arises.

The plans fail most often because they are unrealistic, they do not take the team into account, they lack meaningful checkpoints, and/or they fail to provide performance feedback. Successful plans are specific, but they also are flexible, reflect reality, and reflect the knowledge, skills, abilities, and experiences of the individuals implementing the plans. Successful plans are the result of precisely stated and quantified objectives that provide clear direction to the people actually doing the work. Clear objectives lead to clear work plans or action plans.

Once a plan is established, the FLM must ensure that the plan is followed. Without implementation, the plan is nothing more than an idea about how work should be accomplished. Plan implementation requires that the FLM use organizing and controlling functions. Organizing is the key to carrying out the plan or schedule. Organizing requires the FLM use available resources in performing required tasks. Often, the FLM chooses to delegate tasks to those whom the FLM manages as the most efficient means of accomplishing those tasks.

Planning and organizing assist the FLM in leading to task accomplishment, but without control processes in place, things can become derailed over time. Control processes are important, not only to ensure that processes are maintained, but also to serve as a warning light for FLMs when processes first begin to go awry.

5

Decision-Making

How Front-Line Managers Make Things Happen

O ne of the primary factors that distinguish front-line managers (FLMs) from operating employees is the type of decisions that they must make. By nature of their role, FLMs must make decisions that impact the people they supervise. They must be concerned with how their decisions might affect their employees and the organization. Operating employees, in contrast, are primarily concerned with how decisions affect them individually.

Like all managers, the quality of the decisions that FLMs make is the measure of their effectiveness despite the fact that such decisions can be difficult to make because they are fraught with uncertainty. For FLMs, like other managers, their skills in making decisions is often a key factor considered in his or her evaluations, promotions, raises, and other rewards. A manager's decision-making ability will ultimately contribute to the success or failure of the organization. All human activities involve decision-making. Everyone must solve problems and make decisions at home, at work, and in social groups. When asked to define their major responsibilities, many

Succeeding as a Frontline Manager in Today's Organizations, pages 117–146
Copyright © 2021 by Information Age Publishing
117

managers respond that "solving problems" and "making decisions" are the most important and sometimes most challenging parts of their jobs.

Decision-making is the process of defining problems and choosing a course of action from among alternatives. Decision-making often is associated with problem-solving, since many FLM decisions focus on solving existing or anticipated problems. "Problems" are not limited to difficult or negative situations, but can include opportunities or positive situations that present alternatives.

A main task facing FLMs and other managers is to manage the organizational environment. External forces in the environment give rise to many opportunities and threats for FLMs and their organizations. In addition, inside the organization, FLMs must address many opportunities and threats that may arise as organizational resources are used. To deal with these opportunities and threats, FLMs must make decisions—that is, they must select one solution from a set of alternatives. FLMs make good decisions when they select appropriate goals and courses of action that increase organizational performance; bad decisions lower performance.

Decision-making in response to opportunities occurs when FLMs search for ways to improve individual, team, and organizational performance to benefit customers, employees, and other stakeholder groups. Decision-making in response to threats occurs when events inside or outside the organization adversely affect organizational performance and FLMs efforts to increase performance.

FLMs are always searching for ways to make better decisions to improve organizational performance. At the same time, they do their best to avoid costly mistakes that will hurt organizational performance.

This chapter first discusses decision-making and the FLM and different types of decisions and levels of management. The chapter then outlines the main steps of the decision-making process and decision-making styles before discussing several biases that may cause FLMs to make poor decisions, both as individuals and as members of a group. Next the chapter discusses group decision-making. Before concluding the chapter, some suggestions are offered for increasing employee involvement in decision-making and pitfalls to avoid in decision-making.

Decision-Making and the Front-Line Manager

Since the day Sasha Gujral became a manager at Carrollton Products, she has been concerned about the many tough decisions she has had to make. Just this morning one of her employees, Thad Clemons, requested a change in the vacation schedule. He had received a last-minute invitation to go on a skiing trip as his cousin's guest. Thad considered this "the chance of a lifetime." The problem is that Sarah had already approved vacation for three other members of the department during the same week. Even with Thad on hand, Sasha's department would be operating with a skeleton crew.

FLMs must make decisions whenever they perform any of the four management functions—planning, organizing, leading, and controlling—discussed earlier in this book. For example, in planning, the manager must decide which objectives to seek, which policies to establish, and which rules and regulations to institute. In organizing, managers must determine how to delegate authority and how duties and responsibilities should be grouped. As leaders, managers must decide how best to communicate with and motivate employees. In controlling, managers must decide to make actual performance match planned performance. Clearly, decision-making is a basic part of every task FLMs perform.

Decision-making is at the center of every FLM's job. For example, inside the organization FLMs must continually decide what will be done, who will do it, and how, when, and where it will be done. Although these decisions may appear to be separate, they are often interrelated. Each decision is affected by, and builds upon, previous ones. For example, the goods a department produces or the services it provides determine what types of facilities are needed. Decisions about production, in turn, influence the types of employees needed and the training compensation they should receive. All these decisions affect the amount of money budgeted for the department.

FLMs—even more than managers at other levels—are involved in directing employees' behavior toward achieving both the organizations and the employees' goals. Employees look to their FLMs for more assistance, guidance, and protection than do employees of managers at higher levels. The lower the level of management, the greater the span of control, which is the number of immediate employees a manager can manage effectively.

FLMs must also make decisions more frequently than other managers must, since they are operating on a day-to-day, person-to-person basis. FLMs frequently must make decisions quickly with little information, or even conflicting information. These decisions involve a variety of activities, as the following example illustrates.

It is Monday morning. Sasha has been at work for only 3 hours, but she has already made seven major decisions.

- She signed up to attend a 1-day course on time management.
- She completed performance appraisals for five of her new employees.

- ▪ She approved vacation requests for two employees in her department.
- ▪ She signed one of her team leaders a work order to schedule the completion of an important project.
- ▪ She resolved a dispute between two of her employees.
- ▪ She selected an employee to replace her during her vacation.
- ▪ She requisitioned supplies needed by her department.

In addition, she made a handful of minor decisions. The newest member of her team said, "Are you always this busy, or is it just because it's Monday morning?" Johnson replied, "It's all a normal part of a manager's job."

FLMs can learn how to make more thoughtful decisions and improve the quality of their decisions. Decision-making is a skill that can be developed—just as the skills involved in playing golf are developed—by learning the steps, practicing, and exerting effort. At the same time, FLMs should ensure that their employees learn to make their own decisions more effectively. An FLM cannot make all the decisions necessary to run a department. Many daily decisions are made by the employees who do the work. For example, how a job is to be done, what materials to use, when it is to be done, and how to coordinate with other departments are decisions that employees often have to make without their managers. As we discussed in previous chapters, organizations are giving employees and teams a more active role in decision-making. Therefore, training FLMs and other employees in the decision-making process should be a high priority for all managers.

Types of Decisions and Levels of Management

All FLMs must make decisions. Even when the decision-making process is highly participative in nature, with full employee involvement, it is the FLM who ultimately is responsible for the outcomes. Regardless of whether the FLM makes decisions unilaterally or in consultation with employees, decisions may be classified into two categories: programmed and non-programmed, though most decisions fall somewhere between the two extremes.

Programmed Decision-Making

Programmed decision-making is a routine, virtually automatic process. Programmed decisions are decisions that have been made so many times in the past that FLMs have developed rules or guidelines to be applied when certain situations inevitably occur. As a result, programmed decisions produce solutions to repetitive, well-structured, and routine problems. When making a programmed decision, the guidelines provide a specific procedure, or program, that can be applied to the problem at hand. Many daily problems that FLMs confront are programmed, and they are not difficult to solve because a more or less set answer is available because FLMs and their organizations have already developed procedures and rules to deal with these problems. Decisions like ordering inventory when supplies fall to a certain level are called programmed because the FLM probably orders the same amount of materials or supplies each time. In programmed decisions FLMs do not need to repeatedly make new judgments about what should be done. FLMs can delegate these kinds of decisions to employees and be confident that the decisions will be made in an acceptable and timely manner because they can rely on long-established decision rules.

FLMs can develop rules and guidelines to regulate all routine activities in their areas also because most decision-making that relates to the day-to-day running of the organization is a programmed decision. In addition to how much inventory to hold, programmed decision-making can also, for example, be applied to things like when to pay bills, when to bill customers, and when to order materials and supplies. FLMs make use of programmed decision-making when they have the information they need to create rules that will guide decision-making for themselves and their direct reports.

Non-Programmed Decisions

Suppose that FLMs are not certain that a course of action will lead to a desired outcome. Or in even more ambiguous terms, suppose FLMs are not even sure what they are trying to achieve. Obviously, FLMs cannot develop rules to predict uncertain events.

Non-programmed decisions are made to address non-routine decisions or new, unusual, or unstructured problems that are unlikely to recur. Non-programmed decision-making occurs when there are no ready-made decision rules that FLMs can apply to a situation. Guidelines or rules do not exist because the situation is unexpected or uncertain and FLMs lack the information they would need to develop rules to cover it.

Non-programmed decisions are often caused by changing situations or unusual circumstances. Non-programmed decisions tend to be more important, demanding, and strategic than programmed decisions. There are no set answers or guidelines for making these decisions.

How do FLMs make decisions in the absence of guidelines or decision rules? FLMs can rely on intuition—feelings, beliefs, and hunches that come readily to mind, require little effort and information gathering, and result in on-the-spot decisions. FLMs may also make reasoned judgments—decisions that require time and effort and result from careful information gathering, generation of alternatives, and evaluation of alternatives. FLMs exercise their judgment as a more rational process than going with their intuition.

FLMs can also use intelligence and creativity in attempting to solve these non-routine problems. Intuition, reasoned judgment, intelligence, and creativity are all flawed and can result in poor decision-making. Regardless of the circumstances, making non-programmed decisions can result in effective or ineffective decision-making. FLMs should apply a decision-making process that is consistent and logical, but also adaptable.

The Decision-Making Process

Step 1: Define the Problem

Before seeking answers, the FLM should identify the real problem. Nothing is as useless as the right answer to the wrong question. Defining the problem is not always an easy task. A problem exists when there is a difference between the way things are and the way they should be. Problems that occur frequently and have fairly certain outcomes should be the concern of the lower levels of management, including managers. What appears to be the problem might be merely a symptom of the problem that shows on the surface. It usually is necessary to delve deeper to locate the real problem and define it.

Consider the following scenario: Sasha believes that there is a problem of conflicting personalities within her department. Two employees, Dorian and Alisha, are continually bickering and cannot get along together. Because of this lack of cooperation, the department's work is not being done in a timely manner. Sasha needs to develop a clear, accurate problem statement. The problem statement should be brief, specific, and easily understood by others. A good problem statement should address the following questions:

- What is the problem?
- How do you know there is a problem?
- Where has the problem occurred?
- When has it occurred?
- Who is involved in or affected by the problem?

A careful review of answers to the key questions can lead to a problem statement like Sarah's below, which reveals that the major problem is not that there is a personality conflict, but that the work is not getting done in a timely manner. When checking into this situation, Sasha should focus on why the work is not getting done.

Problem statement: *The bickering between Dorian and Alisha detracts from the completion of work assignments. Last Monday and Tuesday, neither of them completed assigned work. Customers, co-workers, and other departments are all affected.*

Defining a problem can be time-consuming, but it is time well spent. An FLM should not proceed in the decision-making process until the problem relevant to the situation has been specifically identified. The effective FLM will use problem-solving not only to take corrective action but also as a means to make improvements in the organization.

Step 2: Analyze the Problem Using Available Information

After the problem has been defined, the next step is to analyze it. The FLM begins by assembling the facts and other relevant information. This is sometimes viewed as being the first step in decision-making, but until the real problem has been defined, the FLM does not know what information is needed. Only after gaining a clear understanding of the problem can the manager decide which data are important and what additional information to seek. Information is a fuel that drives organizations. Information is vital to the survival of the organization, but to be useful it must be at the right place at the right time and it must be used efficiently and effectively.

A major job of an FLM is to convert information into action through the process of decision-making. The FLM is either helped or hindered by the availability of information. Making decisions without knowing enough about a situation is risky and sometimes even dangerous. Having too much information can also be a problem. Simple decisions do not require exhaustive information; but specific information is necessary to decide how to handle a complex problem. The quality of a decision depends greatly on understanding the circumstances surrounding an issue and selecting the appropriate strategy. The better the information the better the resulting decision is likely to be, because there is less risk and uncertainty about the facts.

FLMs can stay informed by actively keeping up with everything related to their areas of responsibility and paying careful attention to all kinds of communications. Time spent reading equipment manuals and other technical materials may be helpful. Discussing potential problems with employees and getting their input on possible solutions could eventually lead to a stroke or genius when a problem arises.

Many FLMs often complain that they must base their everyday decisions on insufficient or irrelevant information. FLMs complain that they have too much of the wrong kind of information, information is difficult to locate and/or suppressed by employees or other managers, and vital information often arrives long after it is needed. Historically FLMs did not have to deal with an overabundance of information; instead they gathered a bare minimum of information and hoped that their decisions would be reasonably good. By contrast, today's FLMs often feel buried by the deluge of information and data, much of it useless, confronting them on a regular basis. It is essential that FLMs learn to manage this deluge of information.

How information is used depends greatly on its quality (accuracy), presentation (form), and timeliness (available when needed.) Effective use of information is possible only if the right questions are asked by managers to determine information needs and their employees. The goal is to have the right information at the right time. To this end, timeliness may take precedence over accuracy. If information is not available when it is needed, then its accuracy is not important. In most cases, however, both accuracy and timeliness are critical. Additionally, information should be formally catalogued in some manner to ensure its availability. FLMs cannot remember everything. Critical information should be put where it can be found quickly and easily. Personal computers offer a handy way to maintain ready access to a vast body of information.

After gathering information, the FLM needs to analyze the problem. In our example, Sasha needs to find out why the work is not getting done. When she gathers information, she discovers that she never clearly outlined her expectations for each employee—where their duties begin and where they end. What appeared on the surface to be a problem arising from a personality conflict was actually a problem caused by the FLM. The chances are good that once the activities and responsibilities of the two employees are clarified, the friction will end. Sasha needs to monitor the situation closely to ensure that the new definition of duties results in a more timely completion of work.

An FLM will find that personal opinions are likely to creep into decision-making. This is particularly true when employees are involved in the problem. For example, if a problem involves an employee who performs well, the FLM may be inclined to show this person greater consideration than would be afforded a poor performer. The FLM should therefore try to be as objective as possible in gathering and analyzing information.

In the process of analysis the FLM should also try to think of intangible factors that play a significant role in the problem such as reputation, morale, discipline, and personal biases. It is difficult to be specific about these factors; nevertheless, they should be considered. As a general rule, written and objective information is more reliable than opinions and hearsay.

Step 3: Establish Decision Criteria

Decision criteria are the standards used to evaluate alternatives. They typically express what the FLM wants to accomplish with the decision, and can also be used to evaluate whether the implementation of the decision is producing the expected results. To illustrate, suppose Sasha's initial actions do not remedy conflict between Dorian and Alisha. She then needs to establish decision criteria that can be used to evaluate other courses of action. Sasha has identified six criteria for her decision. Her decision

- should result in timely completion of assignments,
- should incur no additional costs,
- must not impede the quality of service to the customer,
- should not put either David's or Sarah's job in jeopardy,
- should not have a negative impact on other employees, and
- must alleviate the problem within one week.

Once the decision criteria are established, the FLM must determine which criteria are absolutely necessary and their order of priority. Because it is likely that no solution will satisfy all the criteria, the FLM needs to know which are most important. The FLM will evaluate alternatives based on which and how many of the important criteria they meet. The FLM may want to consult with upper-level managers, other managers, or employees to assist in prioritizing the decision criteria.

Step 4: Develop Alternative Solutions

After the FLM has defined and analyzed the problem and established decision criteria, the next step is to develop various alternative solutions. By formulating and considering many alternatives, the FLM is less likely to overlook the best course of action. Stating this another way, a decision will only be as good as the best available alternative. Almost all problems have a number of possible solutions, which may not always be obvious. FLMs must work to develop alternatives rather than fall into an "either/or" kind of thinking. They must stretch their minds to develop alternatives even in the most discouraging situations. Although none of the alternatives may be attractive, some should be better than others.

Suppose that Sasha has been ordered to make a 20% reduction in employment because the organization is experiencing financial problems. After careful study, she develops the following five alternatives:

- Lay off employees who have the least seniority, regardless of their job position or performance, until the overall 20% reduction is reached.
- Lay off employees who have the lowest performance ratings until the overall 20% reduction is reached.
- Analyze departmental duties and decide which jobs are essential. Keep the employees who are best qualified to perform those jobs, and lay off the least qualified until the 20% reduction is reached.
- Without laying off anyone, develop a schedule of reduced work hours for every employee that would be equivalent to a 20% overall reduction.
- Develop proactive alternatives to increase the organization's performance so that no employee has to be laid off.

While the last may be the most attractive, it is not realistic, given the economic situation. Although none of the other alternatives may be an ideal solution to this problem, at least Sasha has considered several alternatives before making a decision. This "no-win" situation unfortunately portrays the realities of organizational life.

One problem that FLMs like Sasha is that they may find it difficult to come up with creative alternatives or solutions to specific problems. Perhaps some of them are used to seeing the world from a single perspective—they have a certain "managerial mindset." As a result, FLMs may find it difficult to view problems from a fresh perspective. Generating creative alternatives to solve problems and take advantage of opportunities may require that FLMs like Sasha abandon their existing mindsets and develop new ones—something that usually is difficult to do.

When enough time is available, an FLM should get together with a group of other FLMs or employees to brainstorm alternative solutions to a perplexing problem. *Brainstorming* is a free flow of ideas within a group, with judgement suspended, in order to come up with as many alternatives as possible. Using the technique, the FLM presents the problem and the participants offer as many alternative solutions as they can develop in the time available. It is understood that any idea is acceptable at this point—even those that may at first appear to be wild or unusual. Evaluation of ideas is suspended so that participants can give free rein to their creativity. Creative approaches and brainstorming meetings are particularly adaptable to non-programmed decisions, especially if the problem is new, important, or strategic. One authority on creativity and brainstorming, has suggested the following four major guidelines for effective brainstorming by both individuals and groups:

Defer All Judgement of Ideas

During the brainstorming period, do not allow any criticism by anyone in the group. Although it is natural for people to suppress new ideas both consciously and unconsciously, this tendency must be avoided. Even if an idea seems impractical and useless at first, it should not be rejected by quick initial judgements, because the rejection itself could inhibit the free flow of more ideas. FLMs should understand that how people respond to creative ideas affect individual and group actions:

> *Seek a quantity of ideas.* Idea fluency is the key to creative problem-solving, and fluency means quantity. The greater the number of ideas, the greater the likelihood that some of them will be viable solutions.
>
> *Encourage "free wheeling."* Being creative calls for a free-flowing mental process in which all ideas, no matter how extreme, are welcome. Even the wildest idea may, on further analysis, have a germ of usefulness, and therefore should be encouraged.
>
> *"Hitchhike" on existing ideas.* Combining, adding to, and rearranging ideas often can produce new approaches that are superior to any one original idea. When creative thought processes slow or stop, review some of the ideas already produced and try to combine them, considering additions or revisions.

When a fairly large group of people are brainstorming an unstructured session can become rather long, tedious, and unproductive because many of the ideas are simply not feasible, and conflicts may develop within the group due to individual biases. For this reason, the so-called nominal group technique (NGT) is more useful, as it allows group members to generate ideas more efficiently. Typically under NGT, individual members of the group each develop and write down a list of ideas and alternatives to solve the problem at hand. Afterwards, the group members share their ideas, discussing, evaluating, and refining them. The group's final choice may be made by a series of confidential votes in which the list of ideas is narrowed until a consensus is reached.

Both in the development and the evaluation of alternatives, an FLM should consider only lawful options that fall within the organization's ethical guidelines. As noted in Chapter 3, more organizations are encouraging their FLMs and employees to make ethical decisions because they recognize that good ethics is good business in the long term. Consequently, many organizations have developed handbooks, policies, and official statements that specify the ethical standards and practices expected. The following guidelines or ethical test for decision-making, while not comprehensive, are relevant in addressing the ethical aspects of most problems:

- *Legal-compliance test:* Legal compliance should be only a starting point in most ethical decision-making. Laws, regulations, and policies should be followed, not broken or ignored. The rationale that "everybody's doing it" or "everybody's getting away with it" are poor excuses if you are caught in an illegal or unethical act. If in doubt, ask for guidance from someone who understands the particular law or regulation.
- *Public-knowledge test:* Decisions should be made as if they were going to be publicized. You should ask what would be the consequences if a particular decision became known to the public, your family, the media, or a government agency.
- *Long-term consequences test:* The long-term and short-term consequences of a decision should be weighed against each other. This test helps avoid decisions that are expedient but could have negative long-term effects.
- *Examine-your-motives test:* You should be sure that your decision benefits the company and others. It should not be primarily selfish in nature or designed to harm other people and their interest.
- *Inner-voice test:* This is the test of conscience and moral values that have been instilled in most of us since childhood. If something inside you says that the choice being contemplated may be wrong, it usually is.

It cannot be stressed enough that if an FLM believes that a particular alternative is questionable or might not be acceptable within the organization's ethical policies, the FLM should consult with his or her manager or with a staff specialist who is knowledgeable in that area for guidance in how to proceed.

Step 5: Evaluate the Alternatives and Select the "Best" Solution

The ultimate purpose of decision-making is to choose the specific course of action that will provide the greatest number of desirable and the smallest number of undesirable sequences. After developing alternatives, FLMs can mentally test each of them by imagining that it has already been put into effect. They should try to foresee the probable desirable and undesirable consequences of each alternative. By thinking through the alternatives and appraising their consequences, FLMs will be in a better position to compare their choices.

The usual way to begin is to eliminate alternatives that do not meet previously established decision criteria. The FLM should evaluate each of the remaining alternatives by evaluating the advantages of each one and whether or not the solutions meet the most criteria at the highest priority levels. More often than not, there is no clear choice.

The key to a good assessment of the alternatives is to define the opportunity or threat exactly and then specify the criteria that should influence the selection of alternatives for responding to the problem or opportunity. One reason for bad decisions is that FLMs often fail to specify the criteria that are most important in reaching a decision. In general, successful FLMs can use four criteria to evaluate the pros and cons of alternative courses of action:

1. *Legality.* FLMs must ensure that a possible course of action will not violate any domestic or international laws or government regulations.
2. *Ethicalness.* FLMs must ensure that a possible course of action is ethical and will not unnecessarily harm any stakeholder group. Many decisions FLMs make may help organizational stakeholders and harm others. When examining alternative courses of action, FLMs need to be clear about the potential effects of their decisions.
3. *Economic feasibility.* FLMs must decide whether the alternatives are economically feasible—that is, whether they can be accomplished, given the organization's performance goals. FLMs where possible should perform a cost-benefit analysis of the various alternatives to determine which one will have the best net financial payoff.
4. *Practicality.* FLMs must decide whether they have the capabilities and resources required to implement the alternative, and they must be sure the alternative will not threaten the attainment of other organizational goals. At first glance an alternative might seem economically superior to other alternatives, but if FLMs realize it is likely to threaten other important projects, they might decide it is not practical after all.

In reality, FLMs should consider these criteria simultaneously.

Non-programmed decisions usually require the decision-maker to choose a course of action without complete information about the situation. In making a decision, therefore, also consider the degree of risk and uncertainty involved in each alternative. No decision will be completely without risk; one alternative may simply involve less risk than the others.

The issue of time may make one alternative preferable to another, particularly if there is only a limited amount of time available, and the alternatives vary in how quickly they can be implemented. The FLM should also consider the facilities, records, tools, and other resources that are needed and available for each alternative. It is critically important to judge different alternatives in terms of economy of effort and resources. In other words, FLM should consider which action will give the greatest benefits and results for the least cost and effort.

In making a selection from among various alternatives, the FLM should be guided by experience. Chances are that certain situations will reoccur, allowing FLMs to make wise decisions based on personal experience or the experience of another FLM. Knowledge gained from experience is a helpful guide whose importance should not be underestimated; on the other hand, it is dangerous to follow experience blindly. When examining an earlier decision as a basis for choosing among alternatives, the FLM should examine the situation and the conditions that prevailed at that time. It may be that conditions remain nearly identical, implying that the current decision should be similar to the previous one. More often than not, however, conditions have changed considerably and the underlying assumptions are no longer the same, indicating that the new decision probably should differ from the earlier one.

FLMs admit that at times they base their decisions on intuition, defined as the ability to recognize quickly and instinctively the possibilities of a given situation. Some FLMs appear to have an unusual "intuitive" ability to solve problems satisfactorily by subjective means. A closer look, however, usually reveals that the so-called "intuition" is really experience or knowledge of similar situations that has been stored in the managers' memory.

Intuition may be particularly helpful in situations in which other solutions have not worked. If the risks are not too great, an FLM may choose a new alternative because of an intuitive feeling that a fresh approach might bring positive results. Even if the hunch does not work out well, the FLM benefits from trying something different. The FLM will remember the new approach as part of his or her experience and can draw upon it in reaching future decisions.

Although an FLM cannot shift personal responsibility for making decisions, the burden of decision-making often can be eased by seeking the advice of others. The ideas and suggestions of employees, other managers, staff experts, technical authorities, and the FLM's manager can be of great help in weighing facts and information. Seeking advice does not mean avoiding a decision, however, ultimately the FLM decides what advice to accept and remains responsible for the outcome.

Many people believe that input from others can improve decision-making. The following four guidelines can help FLMs decide whether to include groups in the decision-making process:

- If additional information would increase the quality of the decision, involve those who can provide that information.
- If acceptance of the decision is critical, involve those whose acceptance is important.
- If employees' skills can be developed through participation in decision-making, involve those who need the development opportunity.
- If the situation is not life threatening and does not require immediate action, involve others, because generally their varied perspectives and experiences will enhance the decision-making process.

In the scientific world, laboratory experimentation is essential and accepted. In supervision, however, experimentation to see what happens often is too costly in terms of people, time, and money. Nevertheless, sometimes a limited amount of testing and experimentation is advisable before making a final decision. For example, there are some instances in which testing provides employees with an opportunity to try out new ideas or approaches, perhaps of their own design. While experimentation may be valid from a motivational standpoint, however, it can be a slow and relatively expensive method of reaching a decision.

In cases in which one alternative clearly appears to provide a greater number of desirable consequences and fewer unwanted consequences than any other alternative, the decision is fairly easy. However, the "best" alternative is not always so obvious. When two or more alternatives seem equally desirable, the choice may become a matter of personal preference. When no single alternative seems to be significantly stronger than any other, it might be possible to combine the positive aspects of the better alternatives into a composite solution. Sometimes none of the alternatives is satisfactory; all of them have too many undesirable effects and none will bring about the desired results. In this case, the FLM should begin to think of new alternative solutions or perhaps even start all over again by attempting to redefine the problem.

A situation might arise in which the undesirable consequences of all the alternatives appear to be so overwhelmingly unfavorable that the manager feels that the best available solution is to take no action at all. This solution may be deceptive, however, as the problem will continue to exist if no action is taken. Taking no action is as much a decision as is taking a specific action, even though the FLM may believe that an unpleasant choice has been avoided. The FLM should visualize the consequences that are likely to result from taking an action. Only if the consequences of taking no action are more desirable than the consequences of the other alternatives should it be selected as the best solution.

Selecting the alternative that seems to be the best is known as optimizing. However, sometimes the FLM makes a satisfying decision—selecting an alternative that minimally meets the decision criteria. A famous management theorist, Herbert Simon, once likened the difference to the comparison between finding a needle in a haystack (satisfying) and finding the biggest, sharpest needle in the haystack (optimizing). An FLM will rarely make a decision that is equally pleasing to everyone.

In concluding the discussion on choosing alternatives, it is important for FLMs to think about not only the original problem but also the goals or expected outcomes resulting from the decision by considering questions like: Which goals does each alternative meet and fail to meet? Which alternatives are most acceptable to you and to other important stakeholders? If several alternatives may solve the problem, which can be implemented at the lowest cost or greatest profit? If no alternative achieves all the FLM's goals, perhaps they can combine two or more of the best ones. Before selecting any alternative, it may be helpful for the FLM to ask:

- Is our information about alternatives complete and current? If not, can we get more and better information?
- Does the alternative meet our primary objectives?
- What problems could we have if we implement the alternative?

In the end, an FLM must determine the value or adequacy of the alternatives that were generated. In other words, which solution will be best?

Step 7: Follow Up and Appraise the Consequences of the Decision

After a decision has been made and implemented, FLMs should evaluate the consequences. Follow up and appraisal of the results of a decision are actually part of the decision-making process. You should ask: "Did the decision achieve the desired results? If not, what went wrong? Why?" The answers to these questions can be of great help in similar future situations.

Follow-up and appraisal of a decision can take many forms, depending on the nature of the decision, timing considerations, costs, standards expected, personnel involved, and other factors. For example, a minor project scheduling decision could easily be evaluated through a short written report or by the manager's observation or discussion with employees. A major decision involving the maintenance of complex equipment, however, will require close and time-consuming follow-up by the FLM, technical or other employees, and higher-level managers. This type of decision usually requires the FLM to prepare numerous detailed written reports on equipment performance under varying conditions, which are compared closely with plans or expected standards for equipment maintenance.

The important point to recognize is that the task of decision-making is not complete without some form of follow-up and appraisal of the actions taken. If the manager has established decision criteria or specific objectives that the decision should accomplish, it will be easier to evaluate the effects of the decision. If the results meet the objectives, the FLM can feel reasonably confident that the decision was sound.

If the follow-up indicates that something has gone wrong or that the desired results have not been achieved, then the FLM's decision-making process must begin all over again. This may even mean going back over each of the various steps of the decision-making process in detail. The FLM's definition and analysis of the problem and the development of alternatives may have to be completely revised in view of new circumstances or data collected in the appraisal process. In other words, when follow-up and appraisal indicate that the problem has not been resolved satisfactorily, it is advisable to treat the situation as a new problem and go through the decision-making process from a completely fresh perspective.

In some situations, FLMs may feel they do not have enough time to go through the decision-making process outlined here. Frequently, an FLM, a co-worker, or an employee approaches the manager, says, "Here's the problem," and looks to the FLM for an immediate answer. Most problems do not require an immediate answer, however, and FLMs cannot afford to make decisions without considering the steps outlined here. Many FLMs get themselves into trouble by making hasty decisions.

When an employee brings up a problem, the FLM should usually ask questions such as those listed below:

■ How extensive is the problem? Does it need an immediate response? Is it safety related?

- Who else is affected by the problem? Should they be involved in this discussion?
- Have you (the employee) thought through the problem, and do you have an idea of what the end result should be?
- What do you recommend? Why?

This approach is a form of participative supervision that can help to develop the employee's analytical skills. With the additional information gained from the process, the FLM can either think through the problem, apply the decision-making steps, or make a decision.

A word of caution here: During any stage of the process, FLMs should specify a specific time when they tell other people that they "will get back to them." If an FLM fails to make a decision or give feedback by the specified time, he or she may incur a serious breach of trust.

Step 7: Implement the Chosen Alternative

Once an FLM has made a decision and an alternative has been selected, it must be implemented. Sometimes the FLM involved in making the choice put it into effect. At other times, they delegate the responsibility for implementation, as when more senior managers or leaders change a policy or operating procedure and have the FLMs carry out the change.

It is not unusual that once an alternative is chosen that many subsequent and related decisions must be made. After a course of action has been decided subsequent decisions are necessary to implement it. And, although the need to make subsequent decisions to implement the chosen course of action may seem obvious, many FLMs make a decision and then fail to act on it. This is the same as not making a decision at all. Implementing may fail to occur when talking a lot is mistaken for doing a lot; when people just assume that a decision will "happen"; when people forget that merely making a decision changes nothing; when meetings, plans, and reports are seen as "actions," even if they don't affect what people actually do; and if FLMs don't check to ensure that what was decided was actually done.

Those who implement the decision should understand the choice and why it was made. They also must be committed to its successful implementation. These needs can be met by involving those people in the early stages of the decision process.

FLMs should plan implementation carefully by taking several steps:

1. Determine how things will look when the decision is fully operational.
2. Chronologically order, perhaps with a flow diagram, the steps necessary to achieve a fully operational decision.
3. List the resources and activities required to implement each step.
4. Estimate the time needed for each step.
5. Assign responsibility for each step to specific individuals.

FLMs should presume that implementation will not go smoothly. It is very useful to take a little extra time to identify potential problems and identify potential opportunities associated with implementation. An FLM can take actions to prevent problems and also be ready to seize unexpected opportunities.

To ensure that a decision is implemented, more senior managers and leaders must assign to FLMs the responsibility for making the follow-up decisions necessary to achieve the goal. They must give FLMs sufficient resources to achieve the goal, and they must hold the FLMs accountable for their performance. If the FLMs succeed in implementing the decision, they should be rewarded; if they fail they should be subject to sanctions.

Step 8: Conduct a Retrospective Analysis and Learn From It

The final step in the decision-making process is to do some self-reflection as part of a retrospective analysis and learn from it. A retrospective analysis (or decision evaluation) is useful whether the conclusion is positive or negative. Feedback that suggests the decision is working implies that the decision should be continued and perhaps applied elsewhere in the organization. Negative feedback means one of two things:

1. Implementation will require more time, resources, effort, or thought.
2. The decision was not a good one.

If the decision was inadequate, it's back to the drawing board. Then the process cycles back to the first stage: definition of the problem. The decision-making process begins anew, preferably with more information, new suggestions, and an approach that attempts to eliminate the mistakes made the first time around.

Effective FLMs should always conduct a retrospective analysis to see what they can learn from past successes or failures.

FLMs who do not evaluate the results of their decisions will not learn from experience; instead they will stagnate and are likely to make the same mistakes again and again. To avoid this problem, FLMs must establish a formal procedure with which they can learn from the results of past decisions. The procedure FLMs can follow include these steps:

1. Compare what actually happened to what was expected to happen as a result of the decision.
2. Explore why any expectations for the decision were not met.
3. Derive guidelines that will help in future decision-making.

FLMs who always strive to learn from past mistakes and successes are likely to continuously improve the decisions they make. A significant amount of learning can take place when the outcomes of decisions are evaluated, and this assessment can produce enormous benefits.

Decision-Making Styles

Effective decision-making is not as easy as some may think. When FLMs make a decision, they consider numerous factors before they make one. For example, these factors can be social, economical, and psychological. They can all influence an FLM's decision-making process. Since all FLMs differ from each other—their perceptions, their thinking process, their personal beliefs, and internal/external stimuli—it all works differently.

FLMs can think of decision-making styles as something similar to personality types. There are three basic decision-making styles: reflexive, consistent, and reflective. Let's take a closer look at each of these styles. *Reflexive decision makers* like to make quick decisions—"to shoot from the hip"—without taking the time to get all the information that may be needed and without considering all alternatives. On the positive side, reflexive decision makers are decisive; they do not procrastinate. On the negative side, making quick decisions can be costly and wasteful when a decision is not the best possible alternative. Reflexive decision makers may be viewed by employees as poor FLMs if they consistently make bad decisions. If you use a reflexive style, you may want to slow down and spend more time gathering information and analyzing alternatives. Following the steps in the decision-making process can help FLMs develop those skills.

Reflective decision makers like to take plenty of time to make decisions, taking into account a considerable amount of information and analyzing several alternatives. On the positive side, the reflective types do not make quick decisions that are rushed. On the negative side, they may procrastinate and waste valuable time and other resources. The reflective decision maker may be viewed as wishy-washy and indecisive. If you use a reflective style, you may want to speed up your decision-making.

Consistent decision makers tend to make decisions without rushing or wasting time. They seem to know when they have enough information and alternatives to make a sound decision. Compared to decision makers using other styles, these decision makers tend to have the most consistent record of good decisions. They usually follow the decision-making steps discussed earlier.

Decision-Making Styles and Cognitive Biases

FLMs make decisions throughout the day. However, many of them are unaware of the thoughts, buried beliefs, prejudices, and biases that influence their decisions, and therefore, most FLMs are unconscious of how they impact their decisions. Even when consciously making a decision, these hidden biases influence good decision-making, and like a pebble thrown into a calm lake, there is a ripple effect from that decision that can impact many areas. Because FLMs are in critical management or leadership roles, that ripple effect can result in multiple consequences in an organization.

How can FLMs become aware of the unconscious and hidden biases that affect their management and decision-making? It is these unconscious biases and beliefs that hold them back, and until they identify these areas, they cannot get out of your own way. When they identify their biases, beliefs, and perspectives, FLMs can begin to bring more consciousness and objectivity into their decisions. Here are some of the common cognitive biases:

- *Confirmation bias.* This bias shows up when an FLM only looks at or finds information that supports their beliefs, rejecting information that doesn't confirm them. In organizations, this can fall under the guise of stability bias by an FLM staying in their comfort zone and the status quo. These FLMs live by the mantra of "Don't rock the boat" and change makes them uncomfortable.
- *Anchoring bias.* Also referred to as first impression bias, this often shows up as an FLM being influenced by the first idea presented, being impressed with the idea, and basing their decision on that rather than considering all the other information. These FLMs live by the mantra of "The first piece of information is the best information."
- *Overconfidence bias.* This is the tendency, for example of an FLM having more confidence in their own abilities than is objectively reasonable. FLMs place too much faith in themselves and their

knowledge and viewpoints can be limiting and result in not arriving at the best decision. These FLMs live by the mantra of "I think my input is more valuable than the rest of the team."

▪ *Attribution* error. FLM's have a tendency to attribute another's actions to their character or personality, while attributing their behavior to external situational factors outside of their control. In other words, they tend to cut themselves a break while holding others 100% accountable for their actions. These FLMs live by the mantra of, "blaming others when a problem occurs rather than looking at the situation objectively."

These are some of the biases to be aware of that shape your perspectives and decisions. FLMs should become aware of biases and their effects, and identify their own personal style of making decisions. FLMs should consciously adopt a curious mindset toward themselves and what biases shape their decisions is a start to making better decisions and altering their thought patterns. Taking these steps will help FLMs uncover the biases, beliefs, and perspectives that impact their decisions.

Group Decision-Making

Decisions in organizations are increasingly being made by groups rather than by individuals. And it is not unusual for FLMs and other managers to convene a group to make an important decision. There seem to be at least three primary reasons for this. First, a group is likely to develop more and better alternatives than a single person. Second, organizations are relying less on the historical idea that departments should be separate and independent decision units. To produce the best ideas and to improve their implementation, organizations are increasingly turning to groups or teams that cut across traditional departmental lines. Third, some suggest that in today's complex world of work, significant problems should always be tackled by groups. As a result, FLMs and other managers must understand how groups operate and how to use them to improve decision-making and the use of group decision-making techniques.

Groups and the Advantages of Group Decision-Making

The basic philosophy behind using a group to make decisions is captured by the adage "Two heads are better than one." But is this statement really valid? Yes, it is—potentially. If enough time is available, groups usually make higher-quality decisions than most individuals acting alone. However, groups often are inferior to the best individual.

Individual and group decisions each have their own set of strengths. Neither is ideal for all situations. How well the group performs depends on how effectively it capitalizes on the potential advantages and minimizes the potential problems. The advantages that group decision makers have over individuals are discussed below.

- *More or complete information.* A group brings a range of experience and diverse perspectives to the decision-making process that an individual, acting alone, cannot. If one member doesn't have all the facts or needed expertise, another member might.
- *More alternatives.* Because groups have a greater quantity and diversity of information, they can identify more alternatives or different approaches, for example, to solving the problem, than could an individual. Or the group may need to consider several viewpoints—financial, legal, marketing, human resources, and so on—to achieve an optimal solution.
- *Intellectual stimulation.* Group discussion provides intellectual stimulation that can get people thinking and unleash their creativity to a far greater extent than would be possible with individual decision-making.
- *Acceptance of solution.* Many decisions fail because people do not accept the solution. If the people who will implement or be affected by a certain decision could participate in the decision-making process, they would be more likely to accept the decision and to encourage others to accept it because they will have heard the relevant arguments both for the chosen alternative and against the rejected alternatives.
- *Higher level of commitment.* Group discussion typically leads to a higher level of commitment to the decision. Buying into the proposed solution translates into high motivation to ensure that it is well executed.
- *Legitimacy.* The group decision-making process is consistent with democratic ideals and therefore may be perceived as more legitimate than decision-making by a single person.

Several of the potential advantages of using a group suggest that better-informed, higher-quality decisions result when FLMs and other managers involve people with different backgrounds, perspectives, and access to information. Some of the other advantages imply that decisions will be implemented more successfully when FLMs and other managers involve the people who will implement the decision as early in the deliberations as possible.

Some groups reach a high level of performance. Effective groups like surgical teams and flight crews develop, over time, "transactive memory" in which members learn each other's strengths, weaknesses, and preferences. This shared memory helps the group to work at an expert level with minimal communication. In essence, the group thinks and acts like a unit.

Disadvantages of Group Decision-Making

If groups are so good, where did the phrase, "A camel is a racehorse put together by a committee," originate? The answer, of course, is that group decision-making has drawbacks and like anything things can go wrong when groups make decisions. Most potential problems concern the processes through which group members interact with one another. The major disadvantages are described below:

- *Time consuming.* It takes time to assemble a group. In addition, the interaction that takes place once the group is in place is frequently inefficient. The result is that a group almost always takes more time to make a decision than one individual does.
- *Minority domination.* Members of a group are never perfectly equal. They may differ in terms of rank in the organization, experience, knowledge about the problem, influence with other members, verbal skills, assertiveness, and the like. This creates the opportunity for one or more members to use their advantages to dominate others and impose undue influence on the final decision.

   When one group member dominates the discussion, the result is the same as it would have been if the dominant person had made the decision alone. However, the dominant person does not necessarily have the most valid opinions, and even if that person leads the group to a good decision, the process may have wasted everyone else's time.
- *Satisficing.* Satisficing is more likely with groups. Most people don't like meetings and will do what they can to end them. This may include criticizing members who want to continue exploring new and better alternatives. The result is satisficing, not optimizing or maximizing, a decision.
- *Pressures to conform.* There are social pressures in groups. The desire of group members to be accepted and to be viewed as assets to the group can quash any overt disagreement and encourage

conformity of viewpoints. This tendency of group members to withhold their individual views in order to appear to be in agreement is called groupthink and can result in bad decisions. It is not unusual for people to choose not to disagree or raise objections because they don't want to break up a positive team spirit.

Some groups want to think as one, tolerate no dissension, and strive to remain cordial. Such groups are overconfident, complacent, and perhaps too willing to take risks. Pressure to go along with the group's preferred solution stifles creativity and other behaviors characteristic of vigilant decision-making.

- *Ambiguous responsibility.* Group members share responsibility for making decisions, but no one person is actually responsible for the final outcome. In an individual decision, it is clear who is responsible, but in a group decision, the responsibility of any single member is diluted.

- *Goal displacement.* This occurs often in groups. Group member's goal should be to come up with the best possible solution. With goal displacement, new goals emerge to replace the original ones. When group members have different opinions, attempts at rational persuasion might become a heated disagreement, and then winning the argument becomes the new goal.

When to Use Group Decision-Making

In making decisions, when are groups better than individuals and vice versa? That depends on what you mean by "better." There are four criteria frequently associated with good decisions. First, the evidence indicates that, on average, groups make more *accurate* decisions than individuals. This does not mean, of course, that every group outperforms every individual. Rather, group decisions have been found to be more effective than those of the average member of the group; however, they seldom are as good as those of the best group member. Next, individual decision makers are *faster* than groups. Group decision processes are characterized by give and take, which consumes time.

Groups tend to do better than individuals in reaching *creative* decisions. This requires, however, that groups must avoid groupthink. They must encourage doubts about the group's shared views and challenges to favored arguments; they must avoid an excessive desire to give an appearance of consensus; and they must not assume that silence or abstention by members is a "yes" vote. Finally, group decisions typically result in greater *acceptance.*

Because group decisions are made using input from more people, they are likely to result in solutions that more people will accept.

Effectively Lead Group Decision-Making

To effectively lead group decision-making FLMs must pay attention to the group process and manage it carefully. Effectively leading group decision-making requires:

1. *Appropriate leadership style.* The group leader must try to keep process-related problems to a minimum by ensuring that everyone has a chance to participate, not allowing the group to pressure individuals to conform, and keeping everyone focused on the decision-making objective.

2. *Constructive conflict:* Total consistent agreement among group members can be destructive, leading to groupthink, uncreative solutions, and a waste of the knowledge and diverse viewpoints that individuals bring to the group.

   A certain amount of constructive conflict should exist. Conflict should be task-related, involving differences in ideas and viewpoints, rather than personal. Still, even task-related conflict can hurt performance; disagreement is good when managed properly. FLMs can increase the likelihood of constructive conflict by assembling teams of different types of people, creating frequent interactions and active debates, and encouraging multiple alternatives from a variety of perspectives. Methods for encouraging different views include assigning someone the role of devil's advocate—the job of criticizing ideas. Or the FLM may use a process called dialectic, a structured debate between two conflicting courses of action.

3. *Creativity:* To "get" creativity out of other people, give creative efforts the credit they are due, and don't punish creative failures. Avoid extreme time pressure if possible. FLMs should support some innovative ideas without heeding projected returns. FLMs should put together groups of people with different styles of thinking and behaving and encourage brainstorming by group members to generate as many ideas about a problem as they can.

Increasing Employee Involvement in Decision-Making

The traditional view of decision-making places the FLM or manager in the eminent position of primary decision maker. In today's complex work environment, it is unrealistic to expect one person to know all the answers. In addition, as employees continue to grow and take advantage of educational opportunities, it is smart to draw on their knowledge, creativity, and experience. When employees are involved effectively in decision-making, the quality of decisions can be improved and an increased commitment to the organization can be achieved. This should not interfere with the authority of the FLM, but rather promote teamwork, improve creativity, increase interaction, expand communications, and enhance overall organizational efficiency. Involving employees in decision-making may earn the FLM greater respect. An FLM's decision-making ability can be improved if more employee ideas and suggestions are collected at the outset.

An effective FLM must learn to be a guardian of decisions instead of the maker of decisions. When possible, decisions should be delegated to employees at lower levels. Employees have a right to participate in decisions directly affecting them. The rationale is that employees possess valuable day-to-day knowledge of the job, and therefore, the organization benefits by allowing them to make certain decisions. The FLM oversees decision-making to ensure that the group's decisions are in keeping with departmental goals, and organizational objectives, and company policy. When employees make decisions, the organization gains because the most knowledgeable people make the decisions and the group gains by being included in the process. Individuals grow as a result, increasing their potential and their long-term contributions to the organization.

Many FLMs have implemented *participative decision-making* techniques to boost productivity, improve employee relations, and increase the quality of decisions. Participative approaches invite decision sharing. Employees are made responsible for contributing opinions and information, and they are expected to participate in the decision-making process as much as possible. Participative FLMs do not disguise their power to make the final decisions, particularly when faced with crisis. They do, however, request and expect constant feedback, a practice that provides them with the best available information, ideas, suggestions, talent, and experience. The move toward participation is increasingly popular. Some organizations prefer traditional authoritarian methods for decision-making; however, many organizations find themselves in transition and may wish to consider the many benefits of a participative approach. When employees participate in making decisions that affect them, they support those decisions more enthusiastically and try harder to make them work.

Practical Pitfalls to Avoid When Making Decisions

Many FLMs have a tendency to run into one or more problems when making decisions. Some FLMs make all decisions into big or crisis decisions.

Pitfall 1: Making All Decisions Into Big or Crisis Decisions

Everyone has run into the manager who treats every decision as if it were a life-and-death issue. These FLMs may spend 2 hours deciding whether to order one or two boxes of rubber bands. Some managers seem to delight in turning all decision situations into crisis situations. These approaches keep the employees confused; they have a hard time distinguishing between important and less important issues, crisis and non-crisis situations. As a result of this approach, the really important problems may not receive proper attention because the manager wastes time becoming bogged down in unimportant matters. This type of FLM must learn to allocate an appropriate amount of time to each decision, based on its relative significance. Even when a true crisis does occur, such as the breakdown of a major piece of equipment or an accident, the manager must learn to remain calm and think clearly.

Pitfall 2: Failing to Consult Others

The advantage of consulting others in the decision-making process was discussed earlier in this chapter. Yet some FLMs are reluctant to seek advice, fearing it will make them look incompetent. Many FLMs, especially new ones, are under the impression that they should know all the answers and that to ask someone else for advice would be admitting a weakness. Successful FLMs put good sense and their reasoning ability ahead of their egos.

Pitfall 3: Never Admitting a Mistake

No one makes the best decision every time. If an FLM makes a bad decision, it is best to admit it and do what is necessary to correct the mistake. The worst possible course is to try to force a bad decision into being a good decision.

Pitfall 4: Constantly Regretting Decisions

Some managers always want to change the unchangeable. Once a decision has been made and it is final, don't brood over it. Remember, very few decisions are totally bad; some are just better than others. An FLM who spends all his or her time dreaming about "what if" will not have enough time or energy to implement decisions already made.

Pitfall 5: Failing to Utilize Precedents and Policies

Why reinvent the wheel? If a similar problem has arisen in the past, managers should draw on that experience. If a situation seems to recur constantly, it is usually useful to implement a policy covering it. For example, it is wise to have a policy covering priorities for vacation time. FLMs should also keep abreast of current organizational policies, which can often help solve problems.

Pitfall 6: Failing to Gather and Examine Available Data

Some FLMs often ignore or fail to utilize available factual information. One common reason for this is that some degree of effort is normally required to gather and analyze data—it is easier to utilize only the data already on hand. A related problem is the need to separate the facts from gossip and rumor. The general tendency is to believe only what you want to believe and not to consider the facts.

Pitfall 7: Promising What Cannot Be Delivered

FLMs sometimes make promises they know they can't keep and commitments when they don't have the necessary authority to do so. FLMs may view such commitments and promises as ways of getting employees to go along with decisions. Failed commitments almost always come back to haunt the FLM. The best approach is never to promise more than can be delivered.

Pitfall 8: Delaying Decisions Too Long

Many FLMs tend to put off making a decision "until we have more information." Timeliness is often critical and even good decisions can be ineffective if delayed too long. Managers rarely ever have all the information they would like. Good FLMs know when they have adequate information and then make decisions promptly.

Conclusion

FLMs confront many decision situations, which can vary from the programmed type at one extreme to the non-programmed at the other.

Decisions for routine, repetitive-type problems are usually made easier by the use of policies, procedures, standard practices, and the like. However, non-routine decisions are usually one-time, unusual, or unique problems that require sound judgement and systematic thinking. When making decisions, FLMs should follow specific steps when making.

Better decisions are more likely to occur when FLMs follow the guidelines for making decisions, get input from others and use group decision-making strategies when appropriate, and take steps to avoid decision-making pitfalls.

6

Human Resource Management

People Performance Equals Organizational Success

FLMs are responsible for acquiring, developing, protecting, and utilizing the resources an organization needs to be efficient and effective. One of the most important resources in all organizations is human resources—the people involved in producing and distributing goods and services. Human resources include all members of an organization, ranging from its most senior leaders to entry-level employees. Effective FLMs realize how valuable human resources are and take active steps to make sure their organizations build and fully utilize their human resources to gain a competitive advantage and enhance their effectiveness and overall success.

This chapter examines how FLMs can tailor their human resources management (HRM) responsibilities to their organization's strategy and structure. The chapter also discusses particular major components of HRM: recruitment and selection, training and development, briefly look at performance appraisal/management (which will be discussed in detail in Chapter 12), pay and benefits, and labor relations.

Succeeding as a Frontline Manager in Today's Organizations, pages 147–181
Copyright © 2021 by Information Age Publishing
147

Human Resource Management

HRM refers to the policies, practices, and systems that influence employees' behavior, attitudes, and performance. HRM includes all the activities FLMs engage in to attract and retain employees and to ensure that they perform at a high level and contribute to the accomplishment of organizational goals. These activities make up an organization's HRM system, which has five major components: recruitment and selection, training and development, performance appraisal and feedback, pay and benefits, and labor relations (see Figure 6.1). It is important for FLMs to remember that each component of an HRM system influences the others, and all five must fit together.

Why Is HRM Important to ALL FLMs?

HRM is important to FLMs for several reasons.

Avoid Personnel Mistakes

First, having a command of HRM knowledge will help an FLM avoid personnel mistakes they don't want to make while managing. For example, they don't want

- to have their employees not doing their best;
- to hire the wrong person for the job;
- to experience high turnover;

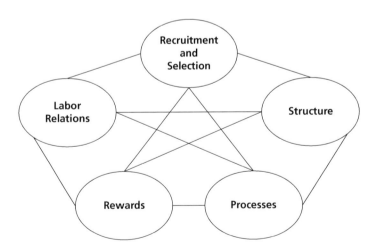

Figure 6.1 Human resource management system components.

- to have their organization in court due to their discriminatory actions;
- to have their company cited for unsafe practices;
- to let a lack of training undermine their team, unit, or department's effectiveness; or
- to commit any unfair labor practices.

Understanding HRM can help an FLM avoid these mistakes.

Improving Profits and Performance

More important, it can help an FLM ensure that they get results—through people. It is important for an FLM to remember that they could do everything else right as a manager—lay brilliant plans, draw clear organization charts, set up modern assembly lines and work processes, and effectively develop and manage budgets—but still fail. On the other hand, many FLMs have been successful even without adequate plans, organizations, or controls. They were successful because they had the knack for hiring the right people for the right jobs and then motivating, appraising, and developing them. An FLM should not lose sight of the fact that getting results is the bottom line of managing and that, as an FLM, they will have to get these results through people. This fact hasn't changed from the dawn of management.

At Some Point, an FLM Will Be Engaged in *All* of the HRM Components

Given all of the things involved in an FLM's job and responsibilities, knowledge of HRM will increase the likelihood of them being more effective. Consider the following FLM's responsibilities and how they overlap with the HRM components:

- managing workflow,
- training new hires,
- creating and managing team schedules,
- reporting to HR and senior management,
- evaluating performance and providing feedback,
- identifying and applying career advancement opportunities, and
- helping to resolve employee issues and disputes.

Let's take a closer look at each of these.

As discussed throughout this book, FLMs assume several roles in the workplace. They are essential in managing an individual, team or department's efficiency and building a positive environment, but while the specifics of these tasks can vary based on the organization, they all require HRM activities.

A supervisor's responsibilities often include:

1. *Managing workflow.* One of an FLM's most important responsibilities is managing a group of individuals, team, unit, or department. This means an FLM will have to establish a workflow—or in other words, a process of how they get stuff done—which will make the work easier. To effectively create and oversee their team's workflow, for example, means that the FLM has to understand the knowledge, skills, abilities, and experiences of the team members as well as the tasks required to complete a job. This means an FLM must define goals, communicate objectives, make sure they have the right employees, and monitor team performance.

2. *Training new hires.* When a new employee joins an FLM's team or unit, the FLM has to help them understand their role and support them during their transition. This might include providing workplace orientation and explaining organization policies or job duties. The FLM may manage all onboarding activities, or they may work with the HRM department to make sure the new hire receives the guidance and information they need.

3. *Creating and managing team schedules.* In some cases, organizations have set hours for their entire workforce, and the FLM won't need to adjust them. However, when direct reports or team members work in shifts, FLMs are usually responsible for creating schedules.

   For example, as an FLM of a retail store, you have to make sure you have an appropriate number of salespeople scheduled for each shift. This usually means scheduling more people during the busiest time of day and balancing shifts so that the salespeople do not feel overworked. Managing employee schedules also means being flexible and prepared when employees need to make changes, such as requesting a day off, calling in sick, or handling a family emergency.

4. *Reporting to HRM and senior management.* As an FLM, you'll often be responsible for reporting team and individual performance to HRM and senior management. You may need to evaluate each member of your team or unit and record employee punctuality, performance on goals, professionalism, disciplinary issues, adherence to company policies, and more. You may also be required to develop and administer performance improvement plans.

5. *Evaluating performance and providing feedback.* An FLM is often tasked with developing or executing employee feedback and recognition programs. This responsibility might include setting employee and team goals and choosing appropriate rewards for

achievements. For example, if a salesperson exceeds their monthly quota, they may be eligible for a bonus. This time should also be used to provide both positive and constructive feedback.

6. *Identifying and applying career advancement opportunities.* Because FLMs work closely with employees, they often help decide who is eligible for promotions. In some cases, FLMs may directly award promotions. However, even when supervisors don't have the authority to directly promote employees, senior management professionals often consult FLMs during the promotion process.

7. *Helping to resolve employee issues and disputes.* When employees are unhappy with their workplace experience, they may approach their FLM before speaking with HRM. FLMs must use active listening skills to understand employee complaints and to work with them to reach a solution. If an employee complains that another employee or member of management has violated organization policies, the FLM will likely need to report the issue to HRM for an investigation. In the case of minor disagreements between employees, FLMs may act as mediators and help the two parties come to a resolution.

There is every indication that the HRM responsibilities of FLMs will continue to increase. And this increase will be a result of more and more organizations moving further and further away from the traditional FLM's duties of monitoring and administration to a set of performance-oriented FLM tasks that require them to identify, assess, and develop the competencies and skills of their employees and align their performance with the organization's strategy and strategic HRM goals.

Strategic Human Resource Management

Strategic HRM is the process by which FLMs, other managers, and senior leaders design the components of an HRM system to be consistent with each other, with other elements of organizational architecture, and with the organization's strategy and goals. The objective of strategic HRM is the development of an HRM system that enhances an organization's efficiency, quality, innovation, and responsiveness to customers—the key building blocks of competitive advantage.

Why Is Strategic HRM Important?

Organizations want to do everything they possibly can to be successful and they are more likely to be successful when all employees are working towards the same objectives. Strategic HRM carries out analysis of employees and determines the actions required to increase their value to the organization. Strategic HRM also uses the results of this analysis to develop HRM techniques to address employee weaknesses. The following are benefits of strategic HRM:

- increased job satisfaction,
- better work culture,
- improved rates of customer satisfaction,
- efficient resource management,
- proactive approach to managing employees, and
- boost productivity.

The Components of HRM

FLMs use recruitment and selection, the first component of an HRM system, to attract, and hire new employees who have the knowledge, skills, abilities, and experiences that will help an organization achieve its goals. An information technology company, for example, might have the goal of becoming one of the to-computing software development organizations in the world. To achieve this goal, FLMs and other managers at the organization must realize the importance of hiring only the best software development engineers: Several hundred qualified candidates are interviewed and rigorously assessed during this phase. The organization has little trouble recruiting top software development engineering talent because candidates know they will be at the forefront of the software development industry if they work at the organization.

After recruiting and selecting employees, FLMs use the second component, training and development, to ensure that organizational members develop the knowledge, skills and abilities that will enable them to perform their jobs effectively in the present and future. Training and development are an ongoing process as changes in technology and the environment, as well as in an organization's goals and strategies, often require that organizational members learn new techniques and ways of working. It is not unusual for newly hired employees at organizations to receive on-the-job training by joining small teams that include experienced employees who serve as mentors. New recruits learn firsthand from colleagues how to complete various tasks and jobs that are responsive to the organization's efforts, for example, to be as efficient and effective as possible.

The third component, performance appraisal and feedback (performance management), serves two purposes in HRM. First, performance appraisal can give FLMs the information they need to make good human resources decisions—decisions about how to train, motivate, and reward organizational members. Thus, the performance appraisal and feedback component is a kind of control system that can be used with management objectives (discussed in Chapter 12). Second, feedback from performance appraisal serves a developmental purpose for the FLM's direct reports and other members of the organization. When FLMs regularly evaluate their direct reports' performance, they can give them valuable information about their strengths and weaknesses and the areas in which they need to concentrate.

On the basis of performance appraisals, FLMs and their organizations distribute pay to employees, which is part of the fourth component of an HRM system. By rewarding high-performing organizational members with pay raises, bonuses, and the like, FLMs increase the likelihood that an organization's most valued human resources will be motivated to continue their high levels of contribution to the organization. Moreover, if pay is linked to performance, high-performing employees are more likely to stay with the organization, and FLMs are more likely to fill positions that become open with highly talented individuals. Benefits such as health insurance are important outcomes that employees receive by virtue of their membership in an organization.

Last but just as important, labor relations encompass the steps FLMs take to develop and maintain good working relationships with the labor unions that may represent employees' interests. For example, an organization's labor relations component can help FLMs establish safe working conditions and fair labor practices in their offices and plants.

FLMs in partnership with other managers and senior leaders must ensure that all five components fit together and complement their organization's structure and control systems. For example, senior leadership decides to decentralize authority and empower employees, they need to invest in training and development to ensure that lower-level employees (and most often FLMs) have the knowledge and expertise they need to make the decisions that other managers would make in a more centralized structure.

Each of the five components of HRM influences the others as mentioned earlier. The kinds of people the organization attracts and hires through recruitment and selection, for example, determine (a) the kinds of training and development that are necessary, (b) the way performance is appraised, and (c) the appropriate levels of pay and benefits. FLMs along with other managers and leaders must ensure that their organizations have highly qualified employees by (a) recruiting and selecting the best candidates; (b) guiding new hires with experienced co-workers or team members; (c) appraising performance in terms of individual contributions and team and department performance; and (d) basing pay, for example, on individual and team performance.

The Legal Environment of HRM

An FLM like other managers and leaders can easily feel swamped by the maze of laws, court rulings, and regulatory-agency pronouncements that organizations must navigate through. However, in order to help their organizations attain goals and gain a competitive advantage FLMs must also understand how the legal environment affects HRM which is the focus of this section.

The local state, and federal or national laws and regulations that FLMs and organizations abide by add to the complexity of HRM. For example, the U.S. government's commitment to equal employment opportunity (EEO) has resulted in the creation and enforcement of a number of laws that FLMs must abide by. The goal of EEO is to ensure that all citizens have an equal opportunity to obtain employment regardless of their gender, race, country of origin, religion, age, or disabilities. Some of the major EEO laws affecting HRM are summarized in Table 6.1.

TABLE 6.1 Major Equal Employment Opportunity Laws Affecting HRM

Year	Law	Description
1963	Equal Pay Act	Requires that men and women be paid equally if they are performing equal work.
1964	Title VII of the Civil Rights Act	Prohibits employment discrimination on the basis of race, religion, sex, color, or national origin; covers a wide range of employment decisions, including hiring, firing, pay, promotion, and working conditions.
1967	Age Discrimination in Employment Act	Prohibits discrimination against workers over the age of 40 and restricts mandatory retirement.
1978	Pregnancy Discrimination Act	Prohibits employment discrimination against women on the basis of pregnancy, childbirth, and related medical decisions.
1990	Americans With Disabilities Act	Prohibits employment discrimination against individuals with disabilities and requires that employers make accommodations for such workers to enable them to perform their jobs.
1991	Civil Rights Act	Prohibits discrimination (as does Title VII) and allows the awarding of punitive and contemporary damages, in addition to back pay, in cases of intentional discrimination.
1993	Family and Medical Leave Act	Requires that employers provide 12 weeks of unpaid leave for medical and family reasons, including paternity and illness of a family member.

Other laws, such as the Occupational Safety and Health Act of 1970, require that FLMs ensure that employees are protected from workplace hazards and that safety hazards are met (see Chapter 14 for a detailed discussion of the OSHA Act and safety and health).

Effectively managing diversity is an ethical and organizational imperative. EEO laws and their enforcement make the effective management of diversity a legal imperative as well. The Equal Employment Opportunity Commission (EEOC) is the division of the Department of Justice that enforces most EEP laws and handles discrimination complaints. In addition, the EEOC issues guidelines for FLMs and other managers to follow to ensure that they are abiding by EEO laws. For example, the Uniform Guidelines on Employee Selection Procedures issued by the EEOC (in conjunction with the Departments of Labor and Justice and the Civil Service Commission) guide FLMs on how to ensure that the recruitment and selection component of HRM complies with Title VII of the Civil Right Act (which prohibits discrimination based on race, gender, color, religion, and national origin).

FLMs face a number of contemporary challenges related to the legal environment to include how to eliminate sexual harassment, how to accommodate employees with disabilities, how to ensure LGBT (lesbian, gay, bisexual, transgender) employees are treated equally, how to address religious rights, how to minimize the wage gap between women and men, how to deal with employees who have substance abuse problems, and how to manage HIV-positive employees and employees with AIDS. HIV-positive employees are infected with the virus that causes AIDS but may show no AIDS symptoms and may not develop AIDS in the near future. Often such employees are able to perform their jobs effectively, and FLMs must take steps to ensure that they are allowed to do so and are not discriminated against.

Recruitment and Selection

Recruitment and selection is an important operation in HRM, designed to maximize employee strength in order to meet the organization's strategic goals and objectives. It is a process of sourcing, screening, shortlisting, and selecting the right candidates for the required vacant positions.

Recruitment includes all the activities FLMs engage in to develop a pool of qualified candidates for open positions. Selection is the process by which FLMs determine the relative qualifications of job applicants and their potential for performing well in a particular job. Before actually recruiting and selecting employees, FLMs need to engage in two important activities: human resource planning and job analysis.

Human Resource Planning

Human resource planning includes all the activities FLMs, other managers, and leaders engage in to forecast their current and future human resource needs. Current human resources are the employees an organization needs today to provide high-quality goods and services to customers or clients. Future human resource needs are the employees the organizations will need at some later date to achieve its longer-term goals.

As part of human resource planning, managers must make both demand forecasts and supply forecasts. Demand forecasts estimate the qualifications and number of employees an organization will need, given its goals and strategies. Supply forecasts estimate the availability and qualifications of current employees now and in the future, as well as the supply of qualified workers in the external labor market.

As a result of their human resource planning, organizations sometimes decide to outsource to fill some of their human resource needs. Instead of recruiting and selecting employees to produce more goods and services, organizations contract with people who are not members of their organization to produce goods and services.

Two reasons human resource planning sometimes leads organizations to outsource are flexibility and cost. First, outsourcing can give organizations increased flexibility, especially when accurately forecasting human resource needs is difficult, human resource needs fluctuate over time, or finding skilled workers in a particular area is difficult. Second, outsourcing can sometimes allow organizations to use human resources at lower costs. When work is outsourced, costs can be lower for a number of reasons: The organization does not have to provide benefits to workers; organizations can contract for work only when the work is needed; and organizations do not have to invest in training. Outsourcing can be used for functional activities such as payroll, bookkeeping and accounting, and the management of information systems.

HR planning is about more than simply numbers of employees. Organizations also have to consider the value that various combinations of human resources can deliver. Effective FLMs and other managers and leaders plan ways to develop and allocate that talent so the value of human resources increases.

Job Analysis

Job analysis is a second important activity that FLMs and others in the organization need to undertake prior to recruitment and selection. Job analysis is the process of identifying (a) tasks, duties, and responsibilities that make up a job (the job description); and (b) the knowledge, skills, and abilities needed to perform the job (the job specifications). For each job in an organization a job analysis needs to be done.

Job analysis can be done in a number of ways, including observing current employees as they perform the job or interviewing them. Often organizations rely on questionnaires compiled by jobholders and their managers. The questionnaires ask about the skills and abilities needed to perform the job, job tasks and the amount of time spent on them, responsibilities, supervisory activities, equipment used, reports prepared, and decisions made.

A trend in some organizations, is toward more flexible jobs in which tasks and responsibilities change and cannot be clearly specified in advance. For these kinds of jobs, job analysis focuses more on determining the skills and knowledge workers need to be effective and less on specific duties.

After FLMs and their organizations have completed human resource planning and job analyses for all jobs in an organization, they will know their human resource needs and the jobs they need to fill. They will also know what knowledge, skills, and abilities potential employees need to perform those jobs. At this point, recruitment and selection can begin.

External and Internal Recruitment

As noted earlier, recruitment is what organizations do to develop a pool of qualified candidates for open positions. There are three fundamental stages of recruitment:

1. Identify and generate applicants.
2. Maintain applicant interest and participation as they continue through the assessment process. During recruitment, the organization is trying both to assess and to attract the best job applicants.
3. Influence job choice so that desired applicants are willing to accept offers made to them.

Regardless of the stages, organizations traditionally have used two main types of recruiting, internal and external, which are not supplemented by recruiting over the Internet.

External Recruitment

External recruitment refers to an organization's actions that are intended to bring a job opening to the attention of potential job candidates outside of the organization and, in turn, influence their intention to pursue the opportunity. A key aspect to external recruitment is to identify the most effective external recruitment sources. Types of external recruitment include external services such as search firms, employment agencies, on-demand recruiting services, alumni employees, job postings on career websites, such as Indeed or Monster; job fairs in the community career fairs at colleges; open houses for students and career counselors at high schools and onsite at the organization; recruitment meetings with groups in the local community; advertising in local newspapers, and military transition services. In addition, some organizations find cultivating an employee pipeline to keep up with anticipated talent demands is useful. Another option is to consider non-U.S. citizens for hard-to-fill positions. This might include offshoring or visa sponsorship issues. Each of these sources has potential benefits and drawbacks that should be considered as part of an organization's recruitment strategy.

External recruiting has both advantages and disadvantages for organizations. Advantages include having access to a potentially large applicant pool; being able to attract people who have the knowledge, skills, and abilities that an organization needs to achieve its goals; and being able to bring in newcomers who may have a fresh approach to problems and are up to date on the latest technology. These advantages have to be weighed against the disadvantages, including the relatively high cost of external recruitment. Employees recruited externally lack knowledge about the inner workings of the organization and may need to receive more training than those recruited internally. Finally, when employees are recruited externally, there is always uncertainty concerning whether they will actually be good performers. Nonetheless, organizations can take steps to reduce some of the uncertainty surrounding external recruitment with methods such as tests, temporary jobs, and internships.

When recruiting external talent, the recruiting function is very similar to the marketing function, in that the organization is promoting both itself and employment opportunities to potential candidates. Adapting marketing principles to employee recruitment is a proven way to bring discipline to the process. For example, organizations can be most effective in recruitment when they identify their potential markets and then create specific messages and activities to reach them.

Targeting passive or active candidates.   Before deciding which recruiting method to use, organizations should first determine whether the ideal candidates are passive or active job seekers. Those who are unemployed or unhappy in their current employment are generally active job seekers, and those who are satisfied and successfully working at another place of business are generally passive job seekers. Most employers, because they are looking for candidates who have a positive record of employment and are satisfied in their work, target passive job seekers.

However, many of the traditional recruitment strategies target active job seekers. For example, posting open positions on an employer's careers website and commercial job boards assumes that interested job seekers are looking for these messages, thus making this strategy appealing to active and not passive job seekers.

Employers must develop strategies that will interest passive job seekers in the employment opportunities they offer. Usually, more assertive strategies will reach passive job seekers, such as direct sourcing (directly approaching potential candidates, often at their places of employment) via telephone and social media, such as LinkedIn.

Job postings/vacancy announcements.   It is important to understand that the job description is not always an effective job posting/vacancy announcement. For the job posting/vacancy announcement to serve as a magnet to attract the right candidates to the job, it should include information about what a prospective candidate may get from the job rather than just the job duties and requirements. Great job postings can be used in communicating the "WIIFM" (what's in it for me?) message and should include why candidates should be interested in the job; detail what's great about the company, such as career paths, benefits, and so forth; and provide candidates a realistic idea of the type of work they'll be doing. It should not be a long list of candidate requirements. A good job posting should compel the right candidates to apply.

Managing employer brand and image.   The organization's reputation as an employer will affect its ability to attract top candidates. When employees are satisfied with the organization, they are likely to tell their friends and contacts about their employer, whether there is a referral program or bonus. Word of mouth and online communications about the organization can either help or hinder formal recruitment strategies.

Employers can also manage their employment image by regulating not only the frequency of recruitment messages (especially within any one recruitment medium) but also the wording used. For example, "We're Hiring" messages can be more effective than "Help Wanted."

Being a good community citizen is another way to enhance the employment brand. Employers can sponsor community events and provide opportunities for employees to donate their work time in community projects.

Managing the "Candidate Experience."   The organization's employer brand is also impacted by the way candidates in the hiring process are treated—whether they get the job they apply for or not. How a candidate is treated from the earliest stages of submitting his or her resume/application through the in-person interviews to the offer/decline process are all considered part of the candidate experience. Employers must develop policies and practices that set guidelines on these elements including:

- Resume/application submission: Is this an easy process that doesn't require providing too much data? Can candidates easily navigate an employer's online or offline application process, including via mobile devices? Can candidates easily find the careers page on the employer's main website—in one or two clicks?
- Candidate communication: Are candidates provided timely and authentic communication on whether their application has been accepted, the status of interviews and answers to questions they may have about where they are in the process?
- Interviewer interactions—Are candidates interviewed by HR and hiring managers who are prepared for the interviews, have reviewed the resume/application in advance, are respectful of candidate responses and questions, and show consideration for the candidate's time?
- Candidate logistics: Are candidates provided clear instructions regarding the logistics for their visits to an employer site, including being provided a schedule of interviews and interviewers in advance; receiving information on how to drive/travel to the employer site and reimbursement procedures for expenses (if applicable); and provided with appropriate meal/restroom breaks, and so on?

Employers can positively affect their employer brand by making their candidate experience a consistent and standardized process that respects the candidate and makes the process simple and even pleasant. Candidates have significant ability to affect external perceptions about a company simply by telling people about how good/bad their experiences were when going through an interview process. Today, due to online employer review sites such as Glassdoor.com or Kununu.com, candidates have even more power to communicate to many people about their experiences during the interview process.

Internal Recruitment

When recruiting is internal, organizations turn existing employees to fill open positions. Employees recruited internally are either seeking lateral moves (job changes that entail no major changes in responsibility or authority levels) or promotions.

The first thing to note about internal recruitment is that organizational culture becomes more important, whereas employer brand and reputation become less important. At the same time, there are key advantages to recruiting internally. One, there is less transition time moving into new jobs. Current employees are already familiar with an employer's products, people, operating procedures, the organization's goals, structure, culture, rules, and norms. Two, there is a greater likelihood of filling a position successfully and particularly because FLMs, for example, already know the candidates—they have considerable information about their skills, abilities, and actual behavior on the job. In contrast to external candidates, an employer has considerably more information about internal candidates (e.g., past performance, temperament, work ethic). Three, filling a higher-level position internally is generally cheaper than filling it from outside. Four, assuming that those promoted from within are seen as deserving, there is a positive impact on the morale and motivation levels of other employees. Those who are not seeking promotion or who may not already be ready for one can see that promotion is a possibility in the future; or a lateral move can alleviate boredom once a job has been fully mastered and can be a useful way to learn new skills. Finally, internal recruiting is normally less time-consuming and expensive than external recruiting.

Internal recruiting typically consists of one or more of the following approaches:

- internal job posting;
- nomination by manager;
- knowledge, skills, and abilities database; and
- succession planning.

Job Posting
Many employers use internal job postings to encourage employees to identify internal promotional opportunities and respond to those openings for which they have skills and interest.

Nominations
Some organizations have a more closed approach to internal recruitment and may ask managers to nominate high-performing individuals as candidates for internal roles. This tends to be an informal system, yet it may be highly effective in smaller organizations in which individuals are familiar with the work of employees in other departments. However, this approach may appear or in fact involve favoritism or unlawful discrimination. The

consequences of either of these may offset any benefits the employer may gain by promoting from within.

Knowledge, Skills, and Abilities Database

Human resource information systems (HRISs) are commonly used to track various personnel-related issues. These may include a database of employees' knowledge, skills, and abilities (KSAs). New hires can create a KSA profile that details their background, experiences, and career goals and update the profile periodically, usually in conjunction with a performance review or career development discussion. This database can be used by HRM to identify individuals for potential promotion or transfer.

Succession Planning

Organizations can use succession planning strategies not only to identify the potential talent in the organization, but also to establish developmental plans to help prepare individuals for promotional roles.

Given the advantages of internal recruiting, why do organizations rely on external recruiting as much as they do? The answer lies in the disadvantages of internal recruiting—among them, a limited pool of candidates and a tendency among those candidates to be set in the organization's ways. Often the organization simply does not have suitable internal candidates. Sometimes even when suitable internal applicants are available, organizations may rely on external recruiting to find the very best candidate or to help bring new ideas and approaches into their organization. When organizations are in trouble and performing poorly, external recruiting is often relied on to bring in talent with a fresh perspective.

Regardless of which approach—or combination of approaches—an organization adopts, it should craft a policy that is fair and equitable to internal applicants, that sets expectations for employees applying for a position, and that is implemented consistently and communicated openly throughout the organization.

The Employee Selection Process

Ideally, the recruiting efforts have been broad enough and equitable enough to meet the standard of equal opportunity and provide a pool of applicants who meet basic qualifications. FLMs and others in the organization then need to find out whether each applicant is qualified for the position and likely to be a good performer. If more than one applicant meets these two conditions, FLMs for example, must further determine which applicants are likely to be better performers than others.

Employee selection is the process of interviewing and evaluating the candidates for a specific job and selecting an individual for employment based on certain criteria (knowledge, skills, abilities [KSAs] and experiences or more simply qualifications and skills and experience). Employee selection can range from a very simple process to a very complicated process depending on the organization and the position. Certain employment laws such as anti-discrimination laws must be obeyed during employee selection.

It is important for FLMs to understand that selection is much more than just choosing the best available person. Selecting the appropriate set KSAs— which come packaged in a human being—is an attempt to get a "fit" between what the applicant can and wants to do, and what the organization needs. Besides needing to obey relevant laws, the task is made more difficult because it is not always possible to tell exactly what the applicant really can and wants to do. Fit between the applicant and the organization affects both the employer's willingness to make a job offer and an applicant's willingness to accept a job. Fitting or matching a person to the right job is called placement.

Good selection and placement decisions are an important part of successful HRM management. Some would argue that these decisions are the most important part. Productivity improvement for an organization may come from changes in incentive pay plans, improved training, or better job design; but unless the employer has the necessary people with the appropriate KSAs in place, those changes may not have much impact. The very best training will not enable someone with little aptitude for a certain job to do that job well and enjoy it. Again, thus the importance of striving for the best fit or match between the applicant and the organization.

How well an employee is matched to a job is very important because it directly affects the amount and quality of employee's work. Any mismatches in this regard can cost an organization a great deal of money, time, and trouble, especially, in terms of training and operating costs. In course of time, the employee may find the job distasteful and leave in frustration. They may even circulate "hot news" and juicy bits of negative information about the organization, causing incalculable harm to the organization in the long run. Effective selection, therefore, demands constant monitoring of the "fit" between people and the job.

There are a variety of selection tools to help increase the likelihood of a fit or match between an applicant and the organization. These selection tools help sort out the relative qualifications of job applicants and appraise their potential for being good performers in a particular job. These tools include background information, interview, paper-and-pencil tests, physical ability test, performance tests, and references.

Background Information

To aid in the selection process, organizations obtain background information from job applications and from resumes. Such information might include the highest levels of education obtained, college majors and minors, type of college or university attended, years and type of work experience, and mastery of foreign languages. Background information can be helpful both to screen out applicants who are lacking key qualifications (such as a college degree) and to determine which qualified applicants are more promising than others.

Interviews

Virtually all organizations use interviews during the selection process. Interviews may be structured or unstructured. In a structured interview, FLMs ask each applicant the same standard questions (such as, "What are your unique qualifications for this position?" and "What characteristics of a job are most important to you?"). Particularly informative questions may be those that prompt an interviewee to demonstrate skills and abilities needed for the job by answering the question. Sometimes called situational interview questions, these often present interviewees with a scenario they would likely encounter on the job and ask them to indicate how they would handle it.

An unstructured interview proceeds more like an ordinary conversation. The interviewer feels free to ask probing questions to discover what the applicant is like and does not ask a fixed set of questions determined in advance. In general, structured interviews are superior to unstructured interviews because they are more likely to yield information that will help identify qualified candidates, are less subjective, and may be less influenced by the interviewer's biases.

Even when structured interviews are used, however, the potential exists for the interviewer's biases to influence his or her judgment. Interviewers must be trained to avoid various biases and sources of inaccurate perceptions as much as possible.

Paper-and-Pencil Tests

The two main kinds of paper-and-pencil tests used for selection purposes are ability tests and personality tests; both kinds of tests can be administered in hard copy or electronic form. Ability tests assess the extent to which applicants possess the skills for job performance, such as verbal comprehension on numerical skills.

Personality tests measure personality traits and characteristics relevant to job performance. Some retail organizations, for example, give job applicants honesty tests to determine how trustworthy they are. The use of personality tests (including honesty tests) for hiring purposes is controversial. Some critics maintain that honesty tests do not really measure honesty (i.e., they are not valid) and can be faked by job applicants. Before using any paper-and-tests for selection purposes, FLMs for example, must have sound evidence that the tests are actually good predictors of performance on the job in question. Organizations who use tests without such evidence may be subject to costly discrimination lawsuits.

Physical Ability Tests

For jobs requiring physical abilities, such as firefighting, garbage collecting, and package delivery, organizations use physical ability tests that measure physical strength and stamina as selection tools. Autoworkers are typically tested for mechanical dexterity because this physical ability is an important skill for high job performance in many auto plants.

Performance Tests

Performance tests measure job applicants' performance on actual job tasks. Applicants for secretarial positions, for example, typically are required to complete a keyboarding test that measures how quickly and accurately they type. Applicants for middle and top management positions are sometimes given short-term projects to complete—projects that mirror the kinds of situations that arise in the job being filled—to assess their knowledge and problem-solving capabilities.

Assessment centers, first used by AT&T, take performance tests one step further. In a typical assessment center, about 10 to 15 candidates for FLM positions participate in a variety of activities over a few days. During this time, they are assessed for the skills an effective manager needs—problem-solving, organizational, communication, and conflict resolution skills. Some of the activities are performed individually; others are performed in groups. Throughout the process, current FLMs and other managers observe candidates' behavior and measure performance. Summary evaluations are then used as a selection tool.

References

Applicants for many jobs are required to provide references from former employers or other knowledgeable sources (such as a college instructor or adviser) who know the applicants' skills, abilities, and other personal characteristics. These individuals are asked to provide candid information about the applicant. References are often used at the end of the selection process to confirm a decision to hire. Yet the fact that many former employers are reluctant to provide negative information in references sometimes make it difficult to interpret what a reference is really saying about an applicant.

Several recent lawsuits filed by applicants who felt that they were unfairly denigrated or had their privacy invaded by unfavorable references from former employers have caused organizations to be increasingly wary of providing any negative information in a reference, even if it is accurate. For jobs in which the job holder is responsible for the safety and lives of other people, however, failing to provide accurate negative information in a reference does not just mean that the wrong person might get hired; it may also mean that other people's lives will be at stake.

An important final takeaway for FLMs is that they and their organizations have an ethical and legal obligation to use reliable and valid selection tools. Yet, reliability and validity are matters of degree rather than all-or-nothing. Thus, FLMs and their organizations should strive to use selection tools in such a way that they can achieve the greatest degree of reliability and validity. For ability tests of a particular skill, organizations should keep up to date on the latest advances in the development of valid paper-and-pencil tests and use the test with the highest reliability and validity ratings for their purposes. Regarding interviews, FLMs can improve reliability by having more than one person interview job candidates.

Training and Development

Training and development helps to ensure that organizational members have the knowledge and skills needed to perform jobs effectively, take on new responsibilities, and adapt to changing conditions. Training and development describes the formal, ongoing efforts that are made within organizations to improve the performance and self-fulfillment of their employees through a variety of educational methods and programs. In the contemporary workplace, these efforts have taken on a broad range of applications—from instruction in highly specific job skills to long-term professional development. Training and development continues to evolve as a formal organization function, an integral element of strategy, and a recognized profession with distinct theories and methodologies. More and more organizations of all sizes increasingly embrace "continual and lifelong learning" and other aspects of training and development as a means of promoting employee growth and acquiring a highly skilled workforce. In fact, the quality of employees and the continual improvement of their skills and productivity through training, are widely recognized as vital factors in ensuring the long-term success and profitability of organizations.

For the most part, the terms "training" and "development" are used together to describe the overall improvement and education of an organization's employees. However, while closely related, there are important differences between the terms that center around the scope of the application. In general, training programs have very specific and quantifiable goals, like operating a particular piece of equipment, understanding a specific process, or performing certain procedures with great precision. Developmental programs, on the other hand, concentrate on broader skills that are applicable to a wider variety of situations, such as decision-making, leadership skills, and goal setting. A basic way for FLMs to distinguish between training and development are as follows:

Training
- Training is mostly short-term with a concrete goal.
- Training focuses on the role.
- Training aims at a specific job or role requirement.
- Training revolves around an immediate or present need.
- Training enhances the knowledge or skills for a particular job or role.
- Training programs are group focused, where more than one individual participates in organized group events.
- The company takes the responsibility of training.

Development
- Development is a long-term activity, with goals that are open-ended and ongoing.
- Development focuses on the person.
- Development is more conceptual and focuses on overall progression of the individuals.
- Development activities are about the future.
- Development is a self-assessment procedure, where individuals are held responsible for creating and owning their development plan and activities.

Training in Today's Organizations

Implementation of formal training and development programs offers several potential advantages to organizations. For example, training helps organizations create pools of qualified replacements for employees who may leave or be promoted to positions of greater responsibility. It also helps ensure that organizations will have the human resources needed to support business growth and expansion. Furthermore, training can enable an organization to make use of advanced technology and to adapt to a rapidly changing competitive environment. Finally, training can improve employees' efficiency and motivation, leading to gains in both productivity and job satisfaction. Today's organizations receive a variety of benefits from effective training and development of employees, including reduced turnover, a decreased need for supervision or management, increased efficiency, and improved employee morale. All of these benefits are likely to contribute directly to an organization's fundamental financial health and vitality.

Effective training and development begins with the overall strategy and objectives of the organization. The entire training process should be planned in advance with specific organization goals in mind. In developing a training strategy, it may be helpful to assess the organization's customers and competitors, strengths and weaknesses, and any relevant industry or societal trends. The next step is to use this information to identify where training is needed by the organization as a whole or by individual employees. It may also be helpful to conduct an internal audit to find general areas that might benefit from training, or to complete a skills inventory to determine the types of skills employees possess and the types they may need in the future. Each different job within the organization should be broken down on a task-by-task basis in order to help determine the content of the training program.

The training program should relate not only to the specific needs identified through the organization and individual assessments, but also to the overall goals of the organization. The objectives of the training should be clearly outlined, specifying what behaviors or skills will be affected and how they relate to the strategic mission of the organization. In addition, the objectives should include several intermediate steps or milestones in order to motivate the trainees and allow the organization to evaluate their progress. Since training employees is expensive, an organization needs to give careful consideration to the question of which employees to train. This decision should be based on the ability of the employee to learn the material and the likelihood that they will be motivated by the training experience. If the chosen employees fail to benefit from the training program or leave the organization soon after receiving training, the organization has wasted its limited training funds.

Organizations tend to use two general types of training methods, on-the-job techniques and off-the-job techniques. On-the-job training describes a variety of methods that are applied while employees are actually performing their jobs. These methods might include orientations, coaching, apprenticeships, internships, job instruction training, and job rotation. The main advantages of on-the-job techniques is that they are highly practical, and employees do not lose working time while they are learning. Off-the-job training, on the other hand, describes a number of training methods that are delivered to employees outside of the regular work environment, though often during working hours. These techniques might include lectures, conferences, case studies, role playing, simulations, film or television presentations, programmed instruction, or special study.

On-the-job training tends to be the responsibility of FLM, HRM professionals, or more experienced co-workers. Consequently, it is important for organizations to educate their seasoned employees in training techniques. In contrast, off-the-job tends to be handled by outside instructors or sources, such as consultants, technical and vocational schools, or continuing education programs. Although outside sources are usually better informed as to effective training techniques than organization FLMs and other managers, they may have a limited knowledge of the organization's products and competitive situation. Another drawback to off-the-job training programs is their cost. These programs can run into the multi thousand dollar per participant level, a cost that may make them prohibitive for many organizations.

Actual administration of the training program involves choosing an appropriate location, providing necessary equipment, and arranging a convenient time. Such operational details, while seemingly minor components of an overall training effort, can have a significant effect on the success of a program. In addition, the training program should be evaluated at regular intervals while it is going on. Employees' skills should be compared to the predetermined goals or milestones of the training program, and any necessary adjustments should be made immediately. This ongoing evaluation process will help ensure that the training program successfully meets its expectations.

Common Training Methods

While new techniques continue to be developed, several common training methods have proven highly effective. Good continuous learning and development initiatives often feature a combination of several different methods that, blended together, produce one effective training program.

Orientations

Orientation training is vital in ensuring the success of new employees. Whether the training is conducted through an employee handbook, a lecture, or a one-on-one meeting with a supervisor, newcomers should receive information on the organization's history and strategic position, the key people in authority at the organization, the structure of their team unit or department and how it contributes to the mission of the organization, and the organization's employment policies, rules, and regulations.

Lectures

A verbal method of presenting information, lectures are particularly useful in situations when the goal is to impart the same information to a large number of people at one time. Since they eliminate the need for individual training, lectures are among the most cost-effective training methods. But the lecture method does have some drawbacks. Since lectures primarily involve one-way communication, they may not provide the most interesting or effective training. In addition, it may be difficult for the trainer to gauge the level of understanding of the material within a large group.

Case study

The case method is a non-directed method of study whereby students are provided with practical case reports to analyze. The case report includes a thorough description of a simulated or real-life situation. By analyzing the problems presented in the case report and developing possible solutions, employees can be encouraged to think independently as opposed to relying upon the direction of the training facilitator or instructor. Independent case analysis can be supplemented with open discussion with a group. The main benefit of the case method is its use of real-life situations. The multiplicity of problems and possible solutions provide the student with a practical learning experience rather than a collection of abstract knowledge and theories that may be difficult to apply to practical situations.

Role Playing

In role playing, students assume a role outside of themselves and play out that role within a group. A facilitator creates a scenario that is to be acted out by the participants under the guidance of the facilitator. While the situation might be contrived, the interpersonal relations are genuine. Furthermore, participants receive immediate feedback from the facilitator and the scenario itself, allowing better understanding of their own behavior. This training method is cost effective and is often applied to marketing and management training.

Simulations

Games and simulations are structured competitions and operational models that emulate real-life scenarios. The benefits of games and simulations include the improvement of problem-solving and decision-making skills, a greater understanding of the organizational whole, the ability to study actual problems, and the power to capture the employee's interest. For example, in a simulation, key aspects of the work situation and job tasks are duplicated as closely as possible in an artificial setting. Consider the fact that air traffic controllers are trained by simulations because of the complicated nature of the work, the extensive amount of learning involved, and the very high costs of air traffic control errors.

Self-Instruction

Self-instruction describes a training method in which the employees assume primary responsibility for their own learning. Unlike instructor-led or facilitator-led instruction, employees retain a greater degree of control regarding topics, the sequence of learning, and the pace of learning. Depending on the structure of the instructional materials, students can achieve a higher degree of customized learning. Forms of self-instruction include programmed learning, individualized instruction, personalized systems of instruction, learner-controlled instruction, and correspondence study. Benefits include a strong support system, immediate feedback, and systematization.

▬▬▬▬
Development

While training programs are organized by the organization to develop employees' knowledge, abilities and skills as per their job requirements, development is not directly related to job requirement, rather it aims at the generic development of the individual employees for the long run. Development is an organized activity in which the employees of the organization learn and grow in their career. Development is future-focused and helps with performance and retention. When an employee has a clear career path at the organization, she or he is likely to seek out other opportunities. FLMs having regular conversations with their employees about their career goals is critical to ensuring they provide the right type of development opportunities.

Besides the training methods above, development often includes additional activities such as varied work experiences and formal education.

Varied Work Experiences

Organizations frequently make sure that employees with high potential have a wide variety of job experiences. Varied work experiences broaden employees' horizons and help them think, for example, beyond their immediate job or work unit or department. Another development approach is mentoring. A mentor is an experienced member of an organization who provides advice and guidance to a less experienced member, called a protégé. Having a mentor can help employees seek out work experiences and assignments that will contribute to their development and can enable them to gain the most possible from varied work experiences. Although some mentors and protégés create relationships informally, many organizations have found that formal mentoring programs can be valuable ways to contribute to the development of all employees.

Formal mentoring programs ensure that mentoring takes place in an organization and structure the process. Participants receive training, efforts are focused on matching mentors and protégés so meaningful developmental relationships ensue, and organizations can track reactions and assess the potential benefits of mentoring. Formal mentoring programs can also ensure that diverse members of an organization receive the benefits of mentoring.

Formal Education

Many organizations reimburse employees for tuition expenses they incur while taking college courses and obtaining advanced degrees. This is not just benevolence on the part of the organization or even a simple reward given to the employee; it is an effective way to develop employees who can take on new responsibilities and more challenging positions.

To save time and travel costs, some organizations also rely on distance learning to formally educate and develop employees. Some employees seek to advance their education through online degree programs.

Transfer of Training and Development

Whenever training and development take place off the job or in the classroom setting, it is vital for organizations to promote the transfer of the knowledge and skills acquired to the actual work situation. Trainees should be encouraged and expected to use their newfound expertise on the job.

Performance Appraisal and Feedback (Performance Management)

The recruitment/selection and training/development component of an HRM system ensures that employees have the knowledge and skills needed to be effective in the future. Performance appraisal and feedback complement recruitment, selection, training, and development. Performance appraisal is the evaluation of employees' job performance and contributions to the organization. Performance feedback is the process through which FLMs, for example, share performance appraisal information with their direct reports, give direct reports an opportunity to reflect on their own performance, and develop, with direct reports, plans for the future. Before performance feedback, performance appraisal must take place. Performance appraisal could take place without providing performance feedback, but wise FLMs are careful to provide feedback because it can contribute to employee motivation and performance.

FLMs need to understand the critical role performance management plays as one of the components in HRM. Chapter 12 provides a detailed discussion of performance management and the role of FLMs in this process.

Employee Compensation (Pay and Benefits)

Employee compensation includes all forms of pay going to employees and arising from their employment. It has two main components, direct financial payments (salaries, pay raises, and bonuses) and is determined by a number of factors such as the characteristics of the organization and the job and levels of performance, and indirect financial payments (financial benefits, like employer-paid medical and life insurance, sick days, and vacations) which are based on membership in an organization.

In turn, organizations can make direct financial payments to employees based on increments of time or based on performance. Time-based pay still predominates. Blue-collar and clerical workers receive hourly or daily wages, for instance. Others like managers or web-designers tend to be salaried and paid weekly, monthly, or yearly.

The second direct payment option is to pay for performance. For example, piece-work ties compensation to the amount of production (or number of "pieces") the employee turns out. Sales commissions tie pay to sales. Many organizations' pay plans combine time-based pay and incentives.

It is important to link pay to behaviors or results that contribute to organizational effectiveness, thus the need for organizations to align total rewards with strategy. Organizations must also establish a pay level and pay structure.

Aligning Total Rewards With Strategy

The compensation plan should first advance the organization's strategic aims—leadership should produce an aligned reward strategy. This means creating a compensation package that produces the employee behaviors the organization needs to achieve its strategy.

Put another way, the rewards should provide a clear pathway between each reward and specific organization goals.

Many organizations formulate a total rewards strategy to support their strategic aims. Total rewards encompass traditional pay, incentives, and benefits but also "rewards" such as more challenging jobs (job design), career development, and recognition.

Pay level. Pay level is a broad comparative concept that refers to how an organization's pay incentives compare, in general, to those other organizations in the same industry employing similar kinds of employees. Organizational leaders must decide if they want to offer relatively high wages, average wages, or relatively low wages. High wages help ensure that an organization is going to be able to recruit, select, and retain high performers, but high wages also raise costs. Low wages give an organization a cost advantage but may undermine the organization's ability to select and recruit high performers and to motivate current employees to perform at a high level. Tither of these situations may lead to inferior quality or inadequate service.

In determining pay levels, senior managers and leaders must take into account their organization's strategy. A high pay level may prohibit organizations from effectively pursuing a low-cost strategy. However, a high pay level may be worth the added costs in an organization whose competitive advantage lies in superior quality and customer service.

Many organizations, particularly smaller ones, simply price their jobs based on what other organizations are paying—they just use a market-based approach. Doing so involves conducting formal or informal salary surveys to determine what others in the relevant labor markets are paying for particular jobs. Then they use these figures to price their own jobs. However, most organizations also base their pay plans on job evaluation methods. Job evaluation methods involve assigning values to each of the organization's jobs. This process helps produce a pay plan (or pay structure) in which each job's pay is equitable based on what other organizations are paying for these jobs and based on each job's value to the organization. After all, organizations want employees' pay to be equitable internally (relative to what their colleagues in the organization are earning), but also competitive externally (relative to what other organizations are paying).

Pay structure. A pay structure clusters jobs into categories, reflecting their relative importance to the organization and its goals, levels of skill required, and other characteristics FLMs and other managers and leaders consider important. Pay ranges are established for each job category. Individual jobholders' pay within job categories is then determined by factors such as performance, seniority, job complexity, and skill levels.

When developing a pay structure, an overarching objective should be to ensure that its resulting policies adhere to the principles of fairness and equity. Specifically, steps should be taken to ensure individual employees are paid equitably relative to other employees in the organization and relative to employees at other organizations. Further, pay structure should abide by prevailing employment laws. In sum, when developing and administering a pay structure and associated policies, an organization should strive for the following goals: (a) internal equity, (b) external equity, (c) individual equity, and (d) legal compliance (see Figure 6.2).

Benefits. "What are your benefits?" is the first thing many applicants ask. Benefits—indirect financial and nonfinancial payments employees receive for continuing their employment with an organization—are an important part of just about everyone's compensation.

Organizations are legally required to provide certain benefits to their employees, including workers' compensation, social security, and unemployment insurance. Workers' compensation helps employees financially if they become unable to work due to work-related injury or illness. Social security provides financial assistance to retirees and disable former employees. Unemployment insurance provides financial assistance to employees

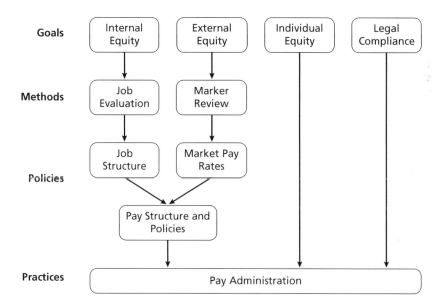

Figure 6.2 The goals, methods, policies, and practices of an effective compensation system.

who lose their jobs due to no fault of their own. The legal system in the United States views these three benefits as ethical requirements for organizations and thus mandates that they be provided.

Other benefits such as health insurance, dental insurance, vacation time, pension plans, life insurance, flexible working hours, organization-provided child-care assistance, and employee assistance and wellness programs have traditionally been provided at the options of employers. The Affordable Care Act signed into law by former President Obama in 2010 now requires employers with 50 or more employees to provide their employees with health care coverage or face fines. Benefits enabling employees to balance the demands of their jobs and of their lives away from the factory or office are of growing importance for many employees who have competing demands on their scarce time and energy.

In some organizations, senior leadership determines which benefits might best suit the employees and the organization and offer the same benefit package to all employees. Other organizations, realizing that employees' needs and desires might differ, offer cafeteria-style benefit plans that let employees choose the benefits they want. Cafeteria-style benefit plans sometimes help organizations deal with employees who feel unfairly treated because they are unable to take advantage of certain benefits available to other employees who, for example, have children. Some organizations have success with cafeteria-style benefit plans; others find them difficult to manage.

As health care costs escalate and overstretched employees find it hard to take time to exercise and take care of their health, more organizations are providing benefits and incentives to promote employee wellness. Wellness programs refer to a wide variety of employer-sponsored initiatives aimed at promoting health behaviors. In most instances, organizations provide some kind of incentive, prize, or reward to employees who take steps to improve their health. Accumulated evidence indicates that, in general, wellness programs are associated with positive employee health and work outcomes, as well as positive organizational financial performance.

For working parents, family-friendly benefits are especially attractive. For example, access to on-site child care, the ability to telecommute and take time off to care for sick children, and provisions for emergency back-up child care can be valued benefits for working parents with young children.

Same-sex domestic partner benefits are also being used to attract and retain valued employees. Gay and lesbian employees are reluctant to work for organizations that do not provide the same kinds of benefits for their partners as those provided for partners of the opposite sex.

FLMs and other managers and leaders in organizations should not underestimate the attractiveness of benefits to potential and current employees. Organizations can leverage benefits strategically to boost their recruitment and retention efforts and improve organizational performance.

Labor Relations

Labor relations are the activities FLMs and other managers engage in to ensure that they have effective working relationships with the labor unions that represent their employees' interests. Much of employee relations is tied to an organization's HRM policies and procedures. In addition, organizations must adhere to formal labor laws such as terms of employment and particularly labor laws relating to unions and collective bargaining (e.g., labor relations). Although the U.S. government has responded to the potential for unethical and unfair treatment of workers by creating and enforcing laws regulating employment (including the EEO laws listed in Table 6.1), some workers believe a union will ensure that their interests are fairly represented in their organizations.

Let's look at some examples of important employment legislation before describing unions in more detail. In 1938 the government passed the Fair Labor Standards Act, which prohibited child labor and provided for minimum wages, overtime pay, and maximum working hours to protect workers' rights. In 1963 the Equal Pay Act mandated that men and women performing equal (work requiring the same levels of skill, responsibility, and effort performed in the same kind of working conditions) receive equal pay. In 1970 the Occupational Safety and Health Act mandated procedures for FLMs and other managers to follow to ensure workplace safety. These are just a few of the U.S. government's efforts to protect workers' rights. State legislatures also have been active in promoting safe, ethical, and fair workplaces.

Unions

Unions exist to represent workers' interest in organizations. Given that managers and other leaders have more power from rank-and-file workers and that organizations have multiple shareholders, there is always the potential for managers to take steps that benefit one set of stakeholders, such as shareholders, while hurting another, such as employees. For example, FLMs and other managers may decide to speed up a production line to lower costs and increase production in the hopes of increasing return to shareholders. Speeding up the line, however, could hurt employees forced to work at a rapid pace and may increase the risk of injuries. Also, employees receive no additional pay for the extra work they are performing. Unions would represent workers' interest in a scenario such as this one.

The history of the labor movement and the growth of labor unions can be traced back to fundamental changes in the workplace. In the early 1900s, factories began to set up procedures to address concerns regarding employee wages and additional labor concerns. However, following the Great Depression in the 1930s and then World War II, a surge in union membership took place through the 1950s. Union membership has been on a steady decline in the United States in recent decades.

The initial rise in unions can be traced to congress acknowledging the role that unions could play in ensuring safe and fair workplaces when it passed the National Labor Relations Act of 1935. This act made it legal for workers to organize into unions to protect their rights and interests and declared certain unfair or unethical organizational practices to be illegal. The act also established the National Labor Relations Board (NLRB) to oversee union activity. Currently, the NLRB conducts certification elections, which are held among the employees of an organization to determine whether they want a union to represent their interests. The NLRB also makes judgments concerning unfair labor practices and specifies practices that FLMs and other managers must refrain from.

Employees might vote to have a union represent them for a variety of reasons. They may think their wages and working conditions need improvement. They may believe, for example, that FLMs are not treating them with respect. They may think their working hours are unfair or they need more job security or a safer work environment. Or they may be dissatisfied with management and leadership and find it difficult to communicate their concerns to their bosses. How engaged employees are at work is also related to whether employees are interested in unionizing. Employees who are not engaged with their work are also more likely to vote yes to a union and to become union members. Regardless of the specific reason, one overriding reason is power: A united group inevitably wields more power than an individual, and this type of power may be especially helpful to employees in some organizations.

Although these would seem to be potent forces for unionization, some employees are reluctant to join unions. Sometimes this reluctance is due to the perception that union leaders are corrupt. Some employees may simply believe that belonging to a union might not do them much good while costing them money in membership dues. Employees also might not want to be forced into doing something they do not want to, such as striking because the union thinks it is in the best interest. Moreover, although unions can be a positive force in organizations, sometimes they also can be a negative force, impairing organizational effectiveness. For example, when union leaders resist needed changes in an organization or are corrupt, organization performance can suffer.

Union membership in the United States has decreased dramatically by nearly half since the 1980s. The global landscape stands in sharp contrast with the trend in the United States. For example, 92% of workers in Iceland belong to a union. Overall, the United States has a relatively low percentage of unionized workers across all workers. Part of the decline in union membership in the United States is due to the changing nature of work. Unions tend to be highly concentrated within certain industries such as transportation and utilities, construction, manufacturing, education and health services, wholesale and retail trade, and public-service employees. However, even in many of those industries, membership has been declining.

Collective Bargaining

Collective bargaining is negotiation between labor unions and managers to resolve conflict and disputes about important issues such as working hours, wages, working conditions, and job security. Sometimes union members go on strike to drive home their concerns to managers. Once an agreement that union members support has been reached (sometimes with the help of a neutral third party called a mediator), union leaders and managers sign a contract spelling out the terms of the collective bargaining agreement.

The signing of a contract, for example, does not finish the collective bargaining process. Disagreement and conflicts can arise over the interpretation of the contract. In such cases, a neutral third party called an arbitrator is usually called in to resolve the conflict. An important component of a collective bargaining agreement is a grievance procedure through which workers who believe they are not being fairly treated are allowed to voice their concerns and have their interests represented by the union. Employees who think they were unjustly fired in violation of a union contract, for example, may file a grievance, have the union represent them, and get their jobs back if an arbitrator agrees with them. Union members sometimes go on strike when FLMs and other managers make decisions that the members think will hurt them and are not in their best interests.

FLMs are an organizations' first line of defense when it comes to labor relations. They are in the best position to sense employee attitude problems, and to discover the first signs of potential conflict or disputes. They can also inadvertently contribute to potential conflict or disputes if they exhibit unfair labor practices. FLMs must understand what to do and not to do to enhance positive relationships with their direct reports and this is key to their successfully fulfilling their role in HRM.

Conclusion: So, What is the FLM's Role in HRM?

FLMs, in most situations, are the first rung on the management or leadership ladder in an organization. They still perform work duties while taking on some of a manager's functions, from both their own department and the HRM. FLMs may perform tasks from all areas of HRM oversight.

Recruiting and Selection

FLMs have HRM duties in job hiring functions, such as identifying the need for additional employees or specific skills to improve team or departmental performance. Organizations using peer-based interviews may use an FLM in the interview group. Though more typically a management function, one-on-one interviews and hiring decisions are delegated to FLM. Selection and paperwork is often assigned to FLMs, particularly in organizations where HRM personnel aren't staffed in specific parts of the organization (e.g., a plant or factory).

Orientation and Training

FLMs may often assist HRM personnel during orientation, onboarding, and training. The handoff of a new recruit from HR to supervisor usually happens during or prior to orientation. The FLM may be responsible for following an orientation checklist, later submitted to HRM. For example, in a manufacturing or plant setting this typically includes practical safety training as well as a tour of the workplace and introductions with other employees. FLMs may perform job training with the new hire, or assign her with another worker in the department.

Development and Retention

FLMs complete performance evaluations on existing employees, or may simply provide data to HRM for evaluation purposes. As the first level of management, FLMs are usually the contact point for employees with vacation requests or other HRM-related communications. Job coaching, while typically a departmental task, may be requested by HRM in cases of poor job performance, and FLMs may be responsible for implementing disciplinary steps in the absence of HRM personnel.

In conclusion, an FLM's role in HRM is that of setting the strategic course for the individual employee, team or department to improve organization performance. The FLM can use HRM to create levers to influence how employees focus their energy and select employees with knowledge, skills, and interests aligned with the organization's goals.

HRM practices are valuable to an organization. Decisions such as whom to hire, what to pay, what training to offer, and how to evaluate employee performance directly affect employees' *motivation* and *ability* to provide goods and services that customers or clients value. By influencing who works and how those people work, HRM contributes to basic measures of success such as quality, profitability, and customer or client satisfaction. So, HRM helps determine the effectiveness and competitiveness of a business or other organization.

7

Change

The Reality for Effective Front-Line Managers

Today's fast-paced business or world of work climate calls for front-line managers who see change as an exciting part of the management process and who anticipate, implement, and manage or lead the change process.

It is a rare FLM who has the luxury to operate in a stable and predictable environment as they are often asked to turn grand strategies into practical initiatives. The reality is that the life or world of FLMs is chaotic as they along with their organizations are confronted with actual realities like—competition among organizations continue to escalate as never before. In addition, with the rise in technological advancements, evolving customer expectations, demographic shifts, globalization, sociopolitical upheaval, and changes in regulatory requirements, to maintain their competitive edge organizations must constantly look for ways to become faster, more responsive, and more efficient at providing quality products and services to their customers.

Succeeding as a Frontline Manager in Today's Organizations, pages 183–210
Copyright © 2021 by Information Age Publishing
183

As organizations search for efficiency expands beyond core operations into other areas change becomes the norm and thus change increases the chaos in the world of FLMs. Take a look at the experience of one FLM, Jamal Fletcher. It has been a stressful couple of weeks for Jamal Fletcher. Things had just begun to settle down after he reorganized his department into five-person work teams. Then, Jamal received word that a new team-based performance appraisal system would soon be introduced throughout the company. Jamal remembered the department's introduction to the computer system 3 years ago. The transition had been traumatic, to say the least. Now everyone would have to adjust to a new performance appraisal system. As he recalled the problems he had experienced during the previous changes in the department, Jamal wondered how to introduce this new change to make the transition less stressful for everyone. In today's work world, change is an everyday occurrence for managers like Jamal. The message is clear: "Change or else!"

It is not unusual to hear FLMs and others say, "The business landscape is not the same as it was just a few years ago. Change is everywhere." The organizations that increasingly FLMs find themselves in are not static, but continually change in response to a variety of influences like those mentioned above which come from both outside and inside. Those organizations that fail to change when required may likely find themselves going the way of the dinosaur. For today's FLM, the challenge is to anticipate and help implement change processes on the front-line so that organizational performance is enhanced.

This chapter begins with a consideration of the nature of the change process to include external and internal forces for change. Next, the chapter discusses planned versus unplanned change. The focus then shifts to a brief discussion of several change models FLMs can use to navigate the change process is then discussed. Then, the chapter examines employee's reactions to change and particularly the importance of understanding and managing resistance, and managing the change process to manage resistance. The job and roles of FLMs during a change initiative are described before concluding the chapter.

The Nature of the Change Process

Organization change is any substantive modification to some part of the organization. It involves movement from the present state of the organization to some future state. The future state may be a new strategy for the organization, changes in the organization's culture, introduction of new technology, and so on. Change can involve virtually any aspect of an organization including from a broad perspective things like strategy, structure, technology, talent management and culture or expressed in another way in work schedules, departmentalization, span of management, equipment or machinery, organizational design and specific work processes, and employee recruitment, selection, training/development and performance appraisal. It is important to keep in mind that any particular change in an organization may have ripple effects. For example, when an organization installed a new computerized production system at one of its plants employees were required to learn to operate the new equipment, the compensation system was adjusted to reflect those newly acquired skills, the manager's span of management was altered, several related jobs were redesigned, the criteria for selecting new employees was changed, and a new quality control system was implemented.

Forces of Change

Organization as a system, depends on many interdependent forces which influence it's day to day functioning, strategic decisions, and future action plans for facing the competitive challenges successfully. Forces for change often differ greatly, and to help make sense of the variety they can be categorized into external and internal forces (see Figure 7.1).

External Forces

Organizations cannot function in a vacuum—they need to be aware of and respond to events and trends in the outside world. External forces for change originate outside the organization. Such forces often apply to an FLMs organization and its competitors or even entire industries. External forces therefore can dramatically affect why an organization exists, as well as which markets it participates in and how. For instance, external changes can either present new opportunities for organizations to realize and group (e.g., smartphones for consumers and Apple's iPhone), or they can cause the ultimate demise or failure of a business (e.g., smartphones for consumers and Blackberry). Several key external forces for change are: demographic characteristics, technological advancements, shareholder, customer and market changes, and social and political pressures.

Demographics Characteristics

FLMs and their organizations need to adapt to demographic changes such as aging and increasing diversified customer populations. To deal with

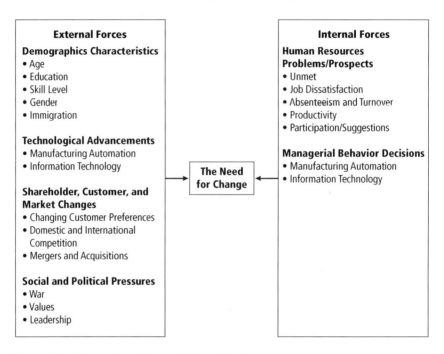

Figure 7.1 External and internal forces for change.

these changes, some organizations are changing their benefits and aspects of the work environment in order to attract, motivate, and retain diverse employees by ensuring fair treatment for people regardless of age, religion, sexual orientations, gender, or race and ethnicity. Many organizations are also changing the way in which they design and market their products and services and design their store layouts based on generational differences to appeal to a variety of different consumers.

Technological Advancements

Technology is not just computer technology, it is any machine or process that enables an organization to gain a competitive advantage in changing materials used to produce a finished product. Technology is a common and often cost-effective tool for improving productivity, competitiveness, and customer service. The rapid rise of and continuous innovation in computer and wireless technology means that organizations must move equally fast to complete.

Technological advancements and innovations in communication and computer technology, have revolutionized the organizational functioning by facilitating newer ways of working and added in newer range of products/services thus creating a need for developing a framework for managing change effectively and proactively responding to the challenges as a result of these changes due to the technological forces. Many organizations now use social networks to market their products, build awareness of their brands, and connect more fully with their consumers. As in the past, advancements in the technological field will continue to greatly contribute to the overall organization's success or failure in the competitive environment.

Shareholder, Customer, and Market Changes

Shareholders have become more involved with pressing for organizational change in response to ethical lapses from senior management and anger over executives' compensation packages. Customers also are increasingly sophisticated and demand organizations with whom they do business to deliver higher value products and services. If they don't get what they want, then they will shop elsewhere.

Social media has given customers a platform for sharing their opinions in ways that organizations have never had to deal with before. This has led more organizations to seek customer feedback about a wide range of issues in order to attract and retain customers because "turning a potential negative into visible positive sentiment is social media's biggest advantage."

Negative feedback from customers that has the potential to reach countless others online can immediately influence sales, and it can also enhance or damage the organization's reputation in the long term. For example, customer comments on review sites like TripAdvisor and Yelp can help or hurt restaurants, tourist attractions, and hotels.

Organizations that listen to their customers and keep up with the evolving market landscape are more likely to succeed than those who don't.

Social and Political Forces

These forces are created by social and political events. Social events can create great pressures and social values are changing. Consumers are interested in buying environmentally safe products that have been manufactured in an ethical manner, and many organizations have adapted their practice to cater to these values. Organizations have gone "green," looking for ways to use less energy themselves and to sell products that consume less energy and are safer to use.

Organizations can also be subject to political pressures, and organizations must often comply with new regulations or adapt to existing ones. Political events, such as wars and unrest in different parts of the world also create substantial change. Governments can apply political pressures that can force or block changes. Government forces can, for example, come in the form of deregulation, foreign exchange, anti-trust laws, and protectionism.

Internal Forces

Although it is essential that organizations respond to external forces, it is just as important to look inside the organization at the internal forces at play. Internal forces for change come from inside the organization. These forces may be subtle such as low job satisfaction, or can manifest in outward signs, such as low productivity, conflict, or strikes. Internal forces for change come from both human resource problems and managerial behavior and decisions.

FLMs and their organizations must address internal problems as soon as they arise and strive to build a positive working environment based on mutual respect, teamwork, and collaboration. Management change (i.e., human resource problems and prospects), organizational restructuring, and intrapreneurship are some examples of the internal forces that affect organizations.

Management Change (i.e., Human Resource Problems or Prospects)

These problems stem from employee perceptions about how they are treated and the match between individual and organization needs and desires. New CEOs or executives can have a significant impact on an organization's culture and strategy. When new CEOs take charge they often bring their own people. It is not unusual for members of the C-suite to be gone within a year of a new chief executive taking the reins. Unusual or high levels of absenteeism and turnover also represent forces for change.

Human Resources Concerns

Is there a gap between employees' needs and desires and the organization's needs and desires? Job dissatisfaction—as expressed through high absenteeism and turnover—can be a major signal of the need for change. Organizations may respond by addressing job design, reducing employees' role conflict, and dealing with work overload, to mention a few matters.

Managers' Behavior

Excessive conflict between managers and employees or between an organization and its customers is another indicator that change is needed.

Perhaps there is a personality conflict, so that an employee transfer may be needed. Or perhaps some interpersonal training required.

Organizational Restructuring

There may be instances when organizations need to change their organization structure as well as its overall design in order to adapt to new strategies, new product lines, or global expansion. Structural changes can be regarded as a strategic move on the part of the organization to improve profitability and for achieving a cost advantage. These changes may take the form of downsizing, job redesign, decentralization, and so on.

Intrapreneurship

Many organizations foster a spirit of intrapreneurship in their employees by encouraging them to come up with new ideas and new ways of doing things. When an employee suggests something innovative, the organization must consider the best way of implementing the idea, which may mean allocating more resources, putting more people to work on the initiative, or coming up with different branding in the case of a new product.

It is hard to adjust to change. We tend to be the willing victims of inertia-comfortable with the status quo because we are used to it. If something threatens to "rock the boat," we often view it with suspicion and distrust. The accelerating rate of change makes change even more difficult to tolerate. Those FLMs who fail to adjust to it are condemning themselves to professional obsolescence. It is important for FLMs to recognize that change is a natural part of life, and that change can be planned or unplanned, encounter resistance and produce progress.

Planned Versus Unplanned Change

Organizational change is either planned well in advance or comes about as a reaction to unexpected events. Planned change is change that is designed and implemented in an orderly, systematic, and timely fashion by managers to move an organization, or a subsystem, to a new state. Planned change includes deliberately changing the organization's design, technology, tasks, people, information systems, and the like. Although FLMs try to follow a plan for change, it does not always move forward smoothly. The plan often hits roadblocks, causing managers to rethink their goal and plan. Unplanned change often results in piecemeal responses to events as they occur. Unplanned change occurs when pressures for change overwhelm efforts to resist the change. Such change may be unexpected by management and can result in uncontrolled, if not chaotic, effects on the organization. There is a greater potential for unplanned change to be poorly conceived and executed. Planned change is therefore almost always preferable to unplanned change.

The importance of approaching change from a planned perspective is reinforced by the frequency of change in well-run organizations. Many companies implement some form of moderate change at least every year and major changes every 4 to 5 years. FLMs and other managers who sit back and respond only when necessary are likely to spend time and money hastily changing and rechanging things. It is more effective to anticipate the forces urging change and plan ahead to deal with them. Responsiveness to unplanned change requires tremendous flexibility and adaptability on the part of the organization. FLMs must be prepared to handle both planned and unplanned forms of change in the organizations.

Types of Change: Another View

As discussed in the previous section one of the ways for an FLM is to view it as either planned or unplanned. There are other ways to distinguish the types of change which is the focus of this section.

Organizational change can also be viewed as administrative or technological, however, in either case it can be adaptive, innovative, or radically innovative, depending on (a) the degree of complexity, cost, and uncertainty; and (b) its potential for generating employee resistance.

Adaptive Change

Adaptive change is the reintroduction of a familiar practice—the implementation of a kind of change that has already been experienced within the same organization. This form of change is lowest in complexity, cost, and uncertainty. Because it is familiar, it is the least threatening to employees and thus will create the least resistance.

Innovative Change

Innovative change is the introduction of a practice that is new to the organization. This form of change is characterized by moderating complexity, cost, and uncertainty. It is therefore apt to trigger some fear and resistance among employees.

Radically Innovative Change

Radically innovative change introduces a practice that is new to the industry. Because it is the most complex, costly, and uncertain, it will be felt as extremely threatening to FLMs confidence and employees' job security and may well tear at the fabric of the organization.

Change Models

As discussed this far, organizational change is part and parcel of any organization. The adoption of new business practices, or promising new technology, represents examples of changes that occur all the time. Models exist that can help FLMs to clarify the steps that can be taken to minimize the task of change management. Two of the most common include Lewin's 3-step model, and Kotter's 8-step model, which will be discussed below. Both models attempt to address the question: "How does successful change happen?"

Lewin's model involves only three steps. These are known as "unfreeze," "transition," and "freeze." The first step is about trying to lessen the forces involved in maintaining the status quo, and changing the current institutional attitude. The status quo can be considered the equilibrium position, which naturally wants to keep things as they are. Unfreezing can be achieved by, for instance, increasing the forces that drive behavior and attitudes away from the status quo. This can be done by helping people realize the need for change, and building trust. The second step involves developing new behaviors, values, and attitudes. This can be accomplished via changes to organizational structure or development techniques. One method that can be used is to convince both individuals and groups that the status quo is not beneficial, and they need to see the problem from a fresh perspective. The final step is concerned with the refreezing of the new state of affairs, after the change has been made. The organization may revert back to the old ways of doing things unless the changes are reinforced, through freezing.

Kotter's 8-step change model is comparatively more complex than the Lewin model, it encourages employees to accept the need for change after being convinced of the urgency by leaders. The steps are briefly as follows:

Establishing a sense of urgency, which serves as a motivator during times of change, is essential to inspire the necessary teamwork, ideas, and eagerness to make sacrifices related to the change.

Once individuals feel that the change is necessary, their energy needs to be directed and guided so that the change process can begin. To do this, an FLM will create the guiding coalition by selecting and recruiting a team of individuals who will be capable of carrying out the change.

Next, an FLM will need to create a change vision to provide employees with a clear understanding of what the change is all about.

Once created, a manager must communicate the vision so that all employees are able to see how the vision for change will affect and benefit them as an individual.

An FLM will then empower broad-based action by removing obstacles that block the change vision or disempower individuals with unrealistic and unattainable goals.

Throughout the change process, planning for and generating short-term wins is needed to maintain enthusiasm and momentum to keep the change initiative going. Because change takes time, Kotter believed that it was important to consolidate gains to produce more change by focusing on the role of early success as an enabler of future success.

Finally, in order to achieve true transformational change, the manager and organization must anchor changes within the organizational culture by monitoring the acceptance of change and how well the organizational culture is adapting to the change.

Lewin's change model has been criticized for over-simplifying the change process and has been defended by others. Kotter's 8-step process actually fits *within* Lewin's foundational model for change.

Both models offer excellent insights into how successful change management happens. FLMs should use both to give their change initiatives the best chance at success. If both are used in tandem, it can help to offset the inherent weakness of either one individually. For example, FLMs can use Kotter's model to flesh out more detail in the steps given by Lewin. When it comes to change management, FLMs can either adopt a rigid approach of many detailed steps, or opt for simplicity. In the former case, Kotter's model is more suited, and in the latter, it is better to use Lewin's model.

A Systems Approach to Change

Change creates additional change—that's the lesson of systems theory. Promoting someone from one group to another, for instance, may change the employee interactions in both (as from cordial to argumentative, or the reverse). Adopting a team-based structure may require changing the compensation system to pay bonuses based on team rather than individual performance. A systems approach to change presupposes that any change, no matter how small, has a rippling effect throughout an organization.

A system is a set of interrelated parts that operate together to achieve a common purpose. The systems approach can be used to diagnose what to change and determine the success of the change effort. The systems model of change consists of three parts: (a) inputs, (b) target elements of change, and (c) outputs.

Inputs: "Why Should We Change, and How Willing and Able Are We to Change?"

"Why change?" A systems approach always begins with the question of why change is needed at all—what the problem is that needs to be solved. (Example: "Why? Change? Because our production department can't produce quality products we can't sell.") Whatever the answer, the systems approach must make sure the desired changes align with the organization's mission statement, vision statement, and strategic plan.

A second question is, "How willing and able are management and employees to make the necessary change?" Readiness for change is defined as the beliefs, attitudes, and intentions of the organization's employees regarding the extent of the changes needed and how willing and able they are to implement them. Readiness has four components: (a) how strongly the company needs the proposed change, (b) how much the senior leaders support the change, (c) how capable employees are of handling it, and (d) how pessimistic or optimistic employees are about the consequences of the result.

Target Elements of Change: "Which Levers Can We Pull That Will Produce the Change We Want?"

The target elements of change represent four levers that managers may use to diagnose problems (such as, "Our R&D scientists are too inbred and have few ideas and are too insular") and identify solutions (such as, "We need new managers and new blood in the R&D group").

Four target elements of change (the four levers) are:

1. *People*—their knowledge, ability, attitudes, motivation, and behavior.
2. *Organizational arrangements*—such as policies and procedures, roles, structure, rewards, and physical setting.
3. *Methods*—processes, workflow, job design, and technology.
4. *Social factors*—culture, group processes, interpersonal interactions, communication, and leadership.

Two things are important to realize:

- Any change made in each and every target element will ripple across the entire organization. For example, if a manager changes a system of rewards (part of the organizational arrangements) to reinforce team rather than individual performance, that change is apt to affect organizational culture (one of the social factors).

▪ All organizational change ultimately affects the people in it and vice versa. Thus, organizational change is more likely to succeed when managers consider the prospective impact of a proposed change on the employees.

Outputs: "What Results Do We Want From the Change?"

Outputs represent the desired goals of a change, which should be consistent with the organization's strategic plan. Results may occur at the organizational group, or individual level (or all three) but will be most difficult to effect at the organizational level because changes will most likely affect a wide variety of target elements.

Feedback: "How Is the Change Working and What Alterations Need to Be Made?"

Not all changes work out well, of course, and organizations need to monitor their success. This is done by comparing the status of an output such as employee or customer satisfaction before the change to the same measurable output sometime after the change has been implemented.

Employee Reactions to Change and Understanding and Managing Resistance

How employees perceive a change greatly affects how they react to it. While many variations are possible, there are only four basic reactions. If employees clearly see that the change is not compatible with their needs and aspirations, they will resist the change. In this situation, the employees are certain that the change will make things worse. If employees cannot foresee how the change will affect them, they will resist the change or be neutral, at best. Most people shy away from the unknown. They often assume that the change may make things worse.

If employees see that the change is going to take place regardless of their objections, they may initially resist the change and then resignedly accept it. Although their first reaction is to resist, once the change appears inevitable, they often see no other choice than to go along with it. If employees see that the change is in their best interests, they will be motivated to accept it.

Obviously, it is critical for employees to feel confident that the change will make things better. It is the FLM's obligation to foster an accepting attitude. Note that three out of the four situations involve some form of resistance to change. Resistance to change is an emotional/behavioral response to real or imagined threats to an established work routine. FLMs must understand resistance to change and learn techniques to overcome it.

Understanding and Managing Resistance to Change

Historically, and still, many FLMs and other managers of change see resistance as employees pursuing their own interests and attempting to undermine the interests of the manager or larger organization. This view suggest that there is a victim, either the FLM of the change who must "fight" or overcome the lack of compliance or commitment by employees, or employees who are victims of uncaring or inconsiderate FLMs or other organizational managers or leaders and employers who serve their interests at the expense of employees. These two perspectives are why resistance is commonly viewed as a negative.

We tend to be creatures of habit. Many people find it difficult to try new ways of doing things. It is precisely because of this basic human characteristic that most employees are not enthusiastic about change in the workplace. This resistance is well documented. As one person once put it, "Most people hate any change that doesn't jingle in their pockets." No matter how technically or administratively perfect a proposed change may be, people make or break it.

Rare is the manager who does not have several stories about carefully cultivated changes that died on the vine because of employee resistance. It is important for FLMs to learn to manage resistance because failed change efforts are costly. These costs may include decreased employee loyalty, a lowered probability of achieving corporate goals, a waste of money and resources, and the difficulty of fixing the failed effort.

People resist change for many reasons. Resisting change does not necessarily mean that they will never accept it. In many cases, the change may be resisted because it was introduced improperly. The manager, by implementing drastic change, could have created feelings of insecurity in the employees. Perhaps the manager did not inform the employees about the change until the last minute. Sometimes the change is introduced properly but is still resisted. The manager may use resistance to change as a means of "taking the pulse" of the department. If minor change meets with resistance, it could indicate that other problems exist, such as problems with morale, commitment, or trust.

Individual and group behavior following an organizational change can take many forms, ranging from extremes of acceptance to active resistance. Resistance can be as subtle as passive resignation or as overt as deliberate sabotage. Resistance can also be immediate, or deferred. It is easiest for managers to deal with resistance when it is overt and immediate. For instance, a company proposes a change, and employees quickly respond by voicing complaints, engaging in a work slowdown, or threatening to go on strike. Although these responses may be damaging, their cause is clearly identifiable.

It is more challenging to manage resistance that is implicit or deferred. Implicit resistance is subtle-such as loss of loyalty to the organization, loss of motivation to work, increased errors or mistakes, or increased absenteeism due to "sickness"—and hence more difficult to recognize. Similarly, deferred resistance clouds the link between the source of the resistance and the reactions to it. For example, a change may produce what appears to be only a minimal reaction at the time it is initiated, but then resistance surfaces weeks, months, or even years later. In another type of deferred resistance, a single change that in and of itself might have had little impact can become the straw that breaks the camel's back. Reactions to change can build up and then explode in a response that seems totally out of proportion to the change it follows. The resistance, or course, has merely been deferred and stockpiled. What surfaces is a response to an accumulation of previous changes.

FLMs need to learn to recognize the manifestations of resistance to change both in themselves and in others if they want to be more effective in creating, supporting, and managing change. So why do people resist change? A number of specific reasons are discussed in the next few paragraphs.

Individual Resistance to Change

Individual sources of resistance towards a change exist in the basic human tenets or characteristics and are influenced by the differences in perception, personal background, needs, or personality-related differences. It is important for FLMs to understand those triggering factors or issues which refrain individuals from endorsing change or extending their support and cooperation towards any change initiatives at an organizational level. When people resist change it can affect their productivity, performance, and relationships. Let's explore some of the individual sources of resistance before briefly focusing on organizational sources of resistance.

Predisposition Against Change

Some people are predisposed to dislike change. This predisposition is highly personal and deeply ingrained. It is an outgrowth of how they learned to handle change and ambiguity as a child. Consider the hypothetical examples of Avis and Felipe. Avis's parents were patient, flexible, and understanding. From the time Avis was weaned from a bottle, she was taught that there were positive compensations for the loss of immediate gratification. She learned that love and approval were associated with making changes. In contrast, Felipe's parents were unreasonable and unyielding. They frequently forced him to comply with their wishes. They required him to take piano lessons even though he hated them. Changes were accompanied by demands for compliance. This taught Felipe to be distrustful and suspicious of change. These learned predispositions ultimately affect how Avis and Felipe handle change as adults.

Habits

Habit is a wonderful thing for human beings. Can you imagine how difficult life would be without habits? Imagine if you had to think consciously about every little movement needed to drive an automobile. Would you ever make it to work in the morning? When we drive by habit our mind can think about other things, secure in the knowledge that our senses will warn us when something is wrong.

We do things by habit: routine household chores, dressing ourselves, greeting one another, sorting our mail, and so forth. Habits are easy and comfortable, freeing our minds to focus on other, more important things. Furthermore, habits are often difficult to change—reflect on a time when you or a friend tried to alter your morning routine or drop a bad habit. One very important reason we resist is because we do not want to change our safe, secure, habitual way of doing things.

Lack of Trust

Trust is a characteristic of high-performance teams, in which team members believe in each other's integrity, character, and ability. FLMs who trust their employees make the change process an open, honest, and participative affair. Employees who trust management are more willing to expend extra effort and take chances with something different. Mutual mistrust, on the other hand, can doom an otherwise well-conceived change or project to failure.

Surprise and Fear of the Unknown

When finding yourself in the presence of an unknown insect, many of us typically choose to kill it by swatting it or stepping on it. We typically rationalize, "Better safe than sorry." It is a natural reaction to fear the unknown. When innovative or radically different changes are introduced without warning, affected employees become fearful of the implications. Grapevine rumors fill the void created by a lack of official announcements and employees often develop negative attitudes toward the change. They may also behave dysfunctionally—complaining, purposely working more slowly, or undermining department morale—if required to go through with the change. In these situations, employees let fear paralyze them into action. FLMs should therefore avoid creating situations in which employees are surprised, and thus fear change. They can do this by keeping all affected employees adequately informed.

Ignoring Change Through Selective Perception

We are bombarded every moment with information pouring into our brains from our sensory organs—our eyes, ears, nose, taste buds, and various touch and balance sensors. We cannot possibly attend to all of the information, so we screen out much of it through a process called "selective perception." This means that we pay attention to those sensations, which we judge to be important, while ignoring the rest. Selective perception is a complex psychological process that occurs both intentionally and unconsciously.

How do we choose those messages to which we pay attention? When faced with messages signaling a change, we frequently attend to those that reinforce our belief in the status quo and maintain our present comfort level. In other words, too often we see only what we want to see, and hear only what we want to hear. Through selective perception, we frequently protect the status quo by filtering out troubling signals that a change is needed, or may be on its way.

Similarly, we often listen only to commentators or others with whom we agree or whose ideas resonate with our own. Dangerous messages, which somehow threaten our comfort level are "tuned out" and ignored. The natural human tendency toward selective perception can harm our ability to deal with change. If we block out all information with which we do not agree, we often miss clear signals that change is on the horizon. Thus when change occurs we are surprised by it, unprepared for it, and afraid of it.

Too Much Dependence on Others

One way to deal with the bombardment of information at work is to specialize. We tend to gravitate to our own spheres of interest and depend on others for information and insights outside our scope of knowledge. For example, when a car needs repairs, you may take it to a trusted mechanic rather than attempt to repair it yourself. The point is that everyone depends on certain people for advice and guidance. This dependence may serve you well, but only if the people on whom you rely are well informed—not if they give you misinformation or poor advice. Although you should not immediately become suspicious of all your advisors, you should recognize that too much dependence on others could become dangerous. FLMs and employees may resist change if they are advised to resist because the change may adversely affect them. Trusting in this advice, they may fail to understand for themselves the true nature of the situation, and may be "blindsided" by the change when it occurs.

Threats to Jobs and Income

Employees often fear that change may reduce their job security or income. New labor saving equipment, for instance, may be interpreted as a signal that layoffs are imminent. When a potential change has the real possibility to cause employees harm, they are likely to resist it with all their might.

Changes in job tasks or established work routines often threaten employees. They worry that they won't be able to perform successfully, particularly where pay is closely tied to productivity. It is therefore important that managers consider any adverse effect employees might experience as a result of a proposed organizational change. If employees perceive that they will lose money, influence, clout, or status as the result of a change, managers can expect strong and active resistance. This resistance is not irrational, but is aimed at protecting employee self-interest.

Organizational Sources of Resistance to Change

In addition to individual sources of resistance to change, organizational factors may prove to be barriers. For example, many organizations are based on stability—people are recruited because they fit in with the organizational culture and are then socialized to behave in certain ways through training, rules, processes, and procedures. However, this uniformity can lead to structural inertia, which makes an organization slow to change after having followed the same rules and procedures for many years.

Organizations can also fall prey to limited focus of change, which arises when only a small number of departments apply the change rather than the whole organization. Confusion often results because the change is not being fully enforced. Another organizational source of resistance to change is group inertia. This means that even if individuals agree with the change, they may be constrained by group norms—a situation that often occurs in unions.

Groups may also feel that organizational changes are a threat to expertise. For example, an information technology department may feel threatened when a new computer program is brought in to perform many of the information or data functions. The group may resist learning the program for fear it will render their roles obsolete. Furthermore, the group may not want to entertain decisions that disrupt cultural traditions or group relationships, which means they will cling to the familiar way of doing things.

Finally, an organization can experience threat to established power relationships, particularly when it is undergoing a reorganization. Organizations moving from an autocratic structure to a participative or self-managed one are likely to experience oppositions from FLMs who may feel their source of power is being threatened.

FLMs' Orientation to Resistance to Change

FLMs can react to resistance to change in two ways. They can treat resistance as a problem to overcome or view it as a signal to get more information about the reasons for resistance. FLMs who view resistance as a problem to overcome may try to forcefully reduce it. Such coercive approaches often increase the resistance.

Alternatively, FLMs may see resistance as a signal that those responsible for the change need more information about the intended change. Those employees who will be affected by the change may have valuable insights about its effects. An alert FLM will involve the employees in diagnosing the reasons for the resistance. In this way, FLMs can use resistance to change as a tool to get needed information.

Should FLMs and other managers see the absence of resistance to change as a stroke of good fortune? Many reasons suggest that they should not. The absence of resistance is also a signal to managers. A change that is automatically accepted can be less effective than one that has been resisted and actively debated. The resisters play an important role by focusing manager's attention on potentially dysfunctional aspects of the proposed change.

Managing the Change Process to Reduce Resistance

Most changes are originated by middle or upper management. The changes are then passed down to the FLM, the link between management and employees, for successful implementation. In this process, the FLM is the person who must cope with employees' anxieties and fears about change. The environment created by the FLM can greatly affect employees' acceptance of change. Several suggestions for creating a positive environment for change are discussed in the following paragraphs.

Build Trust

If employees trust and have confidence in the FLM, they are much more likely to accept changes; otherwise, they are likely to resist change vigorously. Trust cannot be established overnight: It is built over a period of time. The FLM's actions determine the degree of the employee's trust. Employees will trust an FLM they perceive to be fair, honest, and forthright. Employees will not trust a manager who they feel is always trying to take advantage of them. FLMs can go a long way toward building trust if they discuss upcoming changes with their employees, and if they actively involve the employees in the change process.

Openly Communicate and Discuss Changes

Communication about impending change is essential if employees are to adjust effectively. The details of the change should be provided, but equally important is the rationale behind the change. Employees want to know why change is needed. If there is no good reason for it, why should they favor the change? Fear of the unknown, one of the major barriers to change, can be greatly reduced by openly discussing any upcoming or current changes with the affected employees. An FLM should always begin by explaining the five W's and an H to the employees—What the change is? Why is it needed? Whom will it affect? When will it take place? Where will it take place? and How will it take place? During this discussion, the FLM should be as open and honest as possible. The more background and detail the FLM can give, the more likely it is that the employees will accept the changes. The FLM should also outline the impact of the changes on each of the affected employees. People are primarily interested in how change will affect them as individuals.

It is critical that the FLM gives employees an opportunity to ask questions. This is the major advantage of an oral discussion over a written memo. Regardless of how thorough an explanation may be, employees will usually have questions that FLMs should answer to the fullest extent possible. When employees receive all the facts and get their questions answered, their resistance often fades. This explains why, for example, company officials at one organization allow their employees to review company profit and loss statements and answer their questions about the organization's performance. Improved communication is particularly effective in reducing problems resulting from unclear situations. For example, when the grapevine is active with rumors of cutbacks and layoffs, honest and open communication of the true facts can be a calming force. Even if the news is bad, a clear message often wins points and helps employees accept change. When communication is ambiguous and employees feel threatened, they often imagine scenarios that are considerably worse than the actual "bad news."

Involve the Employees

Changes that are "sprung" on employees with little or no warning will likely result in resistance—simply as a knee-jerk reaction—until employees can assess how the change affects them. In contrast, employees who are involved in the change process better understand the need for change, and therefore, are less likely to resist it. Additionally, people who participate in making a decision tend to be more committed to the outcome than those who are not involved. Employee involvement in change can be extremely effective. It is difficult for individuals to resist a change when they participated in the decision and helped implement it. The psychology is simple: No one wants to oppose something that he or she has helped develop. It is useful to solicit employee ideas and input as early as possible in the change process. Don't wait until the last minute to ask the employees what they think about a change. When affected employees have been involved in a change at, or near, its inception, they will usually actively support the change.

Provide Rewards and Incentives

Employers can give employees rewards and incentives to help them see that supporting a change is in their best interests. One rather obvious—and quite successful—mechanism to facilitate change is rewarding people for behaving in the desired fashion. For example, employees who are required to learn to use new equipment should be praised for their successful efforts. In order to make incentives work effectively, employers should analyze the source of the resistance, and what might overcome that resistance. For example, employees may be afraid they won't be able to do a new task. FLMs could provide them with new-skills training, or a short paid leave of absence to allow them to calm down, rethink their fears, and realize that their concerns are unfounded. A difficult change can also have positive aspects. Layoffs can be viewed as opportunities for those who remain, allowing jobs to be redesigned to provide new challenges and responsibilities. Other incentives that can help reduce resistance include a pay increase, a new title, flexible work hours, or increased job autonomy.

Make Sure the Changes Are Reasonable

The FLM should always do whatever is possible to ensure that any proposed changes are reasonable. Proposed changes that originate with upper management are sometimes totally unreasonable. When this is the case, it is usually because upper management is not aware of specific circumstances that make the changes unworkable. It is the FLM's responsibility to intervene in such situations and communicate the problem to upper management.

Educate the Workforce

Sometimes, people are reluctant to change because they fear what the future has in store. For example, fears about economic security may be put to rest by a few reassuring words from management. As part of educating employees about what organizational change means for them, top management must show considerable emotional sensitivity. Doing so makes it possible for people affected by a change to help make it work. Some companies have found that simply answering the question, "What's in it for me?" can help to allay many fears.

Avoid Threats

The FLM who attempts to implement change through the use of threats is taking a negative approach likely to decrease employee trust. A natural reaction is, "This must be bad news if it requires a threat." Most people also dislike being threatened into accepting something. Even though threats may get results in the short term, they may be damaging to employees' morale and attitude over a longer period of time.

Follow a Sensible Time Schedule

As mentioned previously, most changes are passed down from upper management to the FLM for implementation. The FLM often has control or influence over when changes should be implemented, however. Some times are better than others. For example, the week before Christmas or the height of the vacation season would ordinarily not be good times to implement a major change. FLMs should rely on their valuable insights into the department and on their common sense when recommending a time schedule for implementing a change.

Implement the Changes in a Sensible Manner

The FLM often has some choice about where changes will take place. When making these decisions, FLMs should rely on logic and common sense. For example, the FLM usually decides who will get a new piece of equipment. It would be sensible to introduce the equipment through those employees who are naturally more adaptable and flexible than others. If the FLM makes it a point to know their employees, they usually will have a good idea as to which are more flexible. Another consideration in introducing changes is to implement them where possible in a way that minimizes their effects on interpersonal relationships. The FLM should try not to disturb smoothly working groups or teams.

Provide Empathy and Support

Another strategy for overcoming resistance is providing empathy and support to employees who have trouble dealing with the change. Active listening is an excellent tool for identifying the reasons behind resistance and for uncovering fears. An expression of concerns about the change can provide important feedback that FLMs can use to improve the change process. Emotional support and encouragement can help an employee deal with the anxiety that is a natural response to change. Employees who experience severe reactions to change can benefit from talking with a counselor. Some companies provide counseling through their employee assistance plans.

Inevitable Reactions to Change

In spite of attempts to minimize the resistance to change in an organization, some reactions to change are inevitable. Negative reactions may be manifested in overt behavior, or change may be resisted more passively. People show four basic identifiable reactions to change: disengagement, disidentification, disenchantment, and disorientation. FLMs can use interventions to deal with these reactions.

Disengagement is psychological withdrawal from change. An employee appears to lose initiative and interest in the job. Employees who disengage may fear the change but take on the approach of doing nothing and simply hoping for the best. Disengaged employees are physically present but mentally absent. They lack drive and commitment, and they simply comply without real psychological investment in their work. Disengagement can be recognized by behaviors such as being hard to find or doing only the basics to get the job done. Typical disengagement statements include, "No problem" or "This won't affect me."

The basic FLM strategy for dealing with disengaged individuals is to confront them with their reaction and draw them out, identifying concerns that must be addressed. Disengaged employees may not be aware of the change in their behavior, and may need to be assured of the good intentions of the FLM. Helping them air their feelings can lead to productive discussions. Disengaged people seldom become cheerleaders for the change, but they can be brought closer to accepting and working with a change through open communication with an empathetic FLM who is willing to listen.

Another reaction to change is disidentification. Individuals reacting in this way feel that their identity has been threatened by the change, and they feel very vulnerable. Many times they cling to a past procedure because they had a sense of mastery over it, and it gave them a sense of security. "My job is completely changed" and "I used to..." are verbal indications of disidentification. Disidentified employees often display sadness and worry. They may appear to be sulking and dwelling on the past by reminiscing about the old ways of doing things.

Disidentified employees often feel like victims in the change process because they are so vulnerable. FLMs can help them through the transition by encouraging them to explore their feelings and helping them transfer their positive feelings into the new situation. One way to do this is to help them identify what it is they liked in the old situation, as well as to show them how it is possible to have the same positive experience in the new situation. Disidentified employees need to see that work itself and emotion are separable—that is, that they can't let go of old ways and experience positive reactions to new ways of performing their jobs.

Disenchantment is also a common reaction to change. It is usually expressed as negativity or anger. Disenchanted employees realize that the past is gone, and they are mad about it. They may try to enlist the support of other employees by forming coalitions. Destructive behaviors like sabotage and backstabbing may result. Typical verbal signs of disenchantment are, "This will never work" and "I'm getting out of this company as soon as I can." The anger of a disenchanted performer may be directly expressed in organizational cultures where it is permissible to do so. This behavior tends to get the issues out in the open. More often, however, cultures view the expression of emotion at work as improper and unbusinesslike. In these cultures, the anger is suppressed and emerges in more passive-aggressive ways, such as badmouthing and starting rumors. One of the particular dangers of disenchantment is that it is quite contagious in the workplace.

It is often difficult to reason with disenchanted employees. Thus, the first step in managing this reaction is to bring these employees from their highly negative, emotionally charged state to a more neutral state. To neutralize the reaction does not mean to dismiss it; rather, it means to allow the individuals to let off the necessary steam so that they can come to terms with their anger. The second part of the strategy for dealing with disenchanted employees is to acknowledge that their anger is normal and that as their FLM you don't hold it against them. Sometimes disenchantment is a mask for one of the other three reactions, and it must be worked through to get to the core of the employee's reaction. Employees may become cynical about change. They may lose faith in the FLMs and other leaders of change.

A final reaction to change is disorientation. Disoriented employees are lost and confused, and often are unsure of their feelings. They waste energy trying to figure out what to do instead of how to do things. Disoriented individuals ask a lot of questions and become very detail oriented. They may appear to need a good deal of guidance, and may leave their work undone until all of their questions have been answered. "Analysis paralysis" is characteristic of disoriented employees. They feel that they have lost touch with the priorities of the company, and they may want to analyze the change to death before acting on it. Disoriented employees may ask questions like, "Now what do I do?" or "What do I do first?"

Disorientation is a common reaction among people who are used to clear goals and unambiguous directions. When change is introduced, it creates uncertainty and a lack of clarity. The FLM strategy for dealing with this reaction is to explain the change in a way that minimizes the ambiguity that is present. The information about the change needs to be put into a framework or an overall vision so that the disoriented individual can see where he or she fits into the grand scheme of things. Once the disoriented employee sees the broader context of the change, the FLM can plan a series of steps to help this employee adjust. The employee needs a sense of priorities.

FLMs need to be able to diagnose these four reactions to change. No single universal strategy can help all employees adjust because each reaction brings with it significant and different concerns. By recognizing each reaction and applying the appropriate strategy, it is possible to help even strong resisters work through a transition successfully.

The FLM's Job, Roles, and Change

FLMs are a keystone in the success of a change initiative. In times of change, those who lead the teams impacted by change can be both a great ally and a real obstacle for change leaders. FLMs are closest to the employees who must adopt the new processes and behaviors associated with a change initiative. And in many cases the same change also impacts their own work. Getting FLMs on board and prepared to support their direct reports/teams through change is crucial.

The old saying, "The one unchanging principle of life is the principle of change" contains an important element of truth: Change is an inevitable feature in the lives of FLMs and their organizations. For FLMs and their organizations, some facets of change are slow and nearly imperceptible, while others occur quite rapidly. In addition, the impact of change processes can vary from quite minor to truly substantial.

Regardless of the type of change, the FLM is responsible for helping to successfully implement the policies associated with that change. As a result, the FLM must deal with the frustrations and anxieties that usually accompany change and address some difficult questions: "Will the employees resist the change?"; "When should my employees be informed of the change?"; "Am I capable of implementing the change?"; and "What other changes will be necessary as a result of this change?"

Change Roles for FLMs

As emphasized at different points in this book, FLMs are crucial because of the relationship they have with the employees in the organization. They are positioned to coach and influence employees through their own change process. But what do FLMs really need to be doing to drive successful change? Five roles that FLMs must play in times of change are:

- *Communicator.* Communicate with direct reports about the change.
- *Advocate.* Demonstrate support for the change.
- *Coach.* Coach employees through the change process.
- *Liaison.* Engage with and provide support to the project team.
- *Resistance manager.* Identify and manage resistance.

Communicator About the Change

Employees want to hear change messages about how their work and their team will be affected by a change from the person they report to. An employee's FLM is a key conduit of information about the organization, the work that is done and changes to that work resulting from projects and initiatives. The answers to the following questions are best delivered by an employee's FLM:

- What does this change mean to me?
- What's in it for me?
- Why should I get on board?
- Why are we doing this?

The change management team needs to provide talking points and pertinent information, but those messages should ultimately be delivered to employees by their FLM.

Advocate for the Change

Employees look to their FLMs not only for direct communication messages about a change, but also to evaluate their level of support for the change effort. If an FLM only passively supports or even resists a change, then you can expect the same from that person's direct reports. FLMs need to demonstrate their support in active and observable ways. The key is this: FLMs must first be onboard with a change before they can support their employees. A change management team should create targeted and customized tactics for engaging and managing the change first with FLMs, and only then charge this important group with leading change with their direct reports.

Coach for Employees

The role of coach involves supporting employees through the process of change they experience when change and initiatives impact their day-to-day work. The ADKAR mode describes this individual change process as five building blocks of successful change:

- Awareness of the need for change
- Desire to participate and support the change
- Knowledge on how to change
- Ability to implement required skills and behaviors
- Reinforcement to sustain the change

Because of their relationship, managers and supervisors can coach individual employees through this change process and help them address the barrier points that are inhibiting successful change.

Liaison to the Change Team

FLMs liaise between their employees and the change team, providing information from the team to their direct reports. But perhaps more importantly, they provide information about the change from their employees back up to the change team. FLMs are in the best position to provide design input, usability results and employee feedback on particular aspects of the solution back to the change team. They are also positioned to identify and raise valid functionality needs and concerns during the implementation phase of the change.

Resistance Manager

No one is closer to a resistant employee than his or her FLM. In terms of managing resistance, FLMs are in the best place to identify what resistance looks like, where it is coming from, and the source of that resistance. They are also the best suited (when provided with the training and tools to do so) to actively manage that resistance when it occurs. They can use the ADKAR model to hone in on which element of the change process is driving resistance and address it accordingly.

Preparing FLMs to Lead Change

The roles of coach and resistance manager represent a critical part of the FLMs ability to help bring about successful organizational change. Effectively coaching employees through a change and identifying and managing resistance to change require a new set of skills. Oftentimes, good FLMs have difficulty when tasked with becoming great FLMs of change because they have not been adequately prepared to do so. Senior managers and leaders in organizations must recognize that while FLMs are a critical success factor in times of change, they must be adequately prepared and supported to fulfill the roles identified above. Senior managers and leaders should ask themselves these questions:

- Have we told FLMs what we expect from them in times of change?
- Do they fully understand the specific actions and behaviors we need from them to support a change effort?
- Have we provided them with the skills and tools to be successful at leading their direct reports through change?

If they answer "no," then they risk losing the support and benefit that comes from engaging this important cog in the change management system. Senior managers and leaders must always consider how they can build awareness of the need for FLMs to play their important role in times of change, and how they can engage them in learning skills and frameworks or change models for helping themselves and their employees successfully through transitions.

Some Concluding Thoughts on Change

Earlier in this chapter, front-line manager Jamal Fletcher was faced with implementing another change in his unit. Because of uncertainties accompanying this change, he was not sure how the change would be accepted by his employees or how he should introduce the change to make it less stressful than previous changes. In introducing the new changes, Jamal should first concentrate on creating a positive environment. He should discuss the upcoming changes with his employees to solicit their ideas. At this time, Jamal should explain the five W's and H to them: "What the change is," "Why it is needed," "Whom it will affect," "When it will take place," "Where it will take place," and "How it will take place." Jamal should also make sure that the implementation of the change is realistic. He should be aware that the natural reaction of many of his employees will be to resist the change, and he should overcome much of this resistance by carefully explaining what the new changes will do and how they will affect each employee. Finally, it is important that the work climate be conducive to the change being introduced, implemented, and accepted.

8

Leading Through Effective Leadership

Leadership skills are needed at every level of an organization, from creating and communicating an organization's vision, strategies, and goals as well as to executing on these plans and goals at the lowest or front-line managers' level.

In this chapter we first provide an answer to the question, "What is Leadership?" and describe the difference between leadership and management. Next, the chapter focuses on types of leadership and discusses different traditional and contemporary leadership theories along with different leadership styles. The discussion then turns to gender and leadership and then emotional intelligence and leadership effectiveness. The chapter then describes what followers want from leaders, what leaders want from followers, and how to be a good leader by being a good follower. The chapter then identifies the necessary skills to be an effective front-line manager (FLM) and how to build credibility as an FLM. By the end of this chapter, you will gain a greater appreciation of the many factors that FLMs must be aware of in their quest to become effective leaders.

Succeeding as a Frontline Manager in Today's Organizations, pages 211–236
211

What Is Leadership?

The search for what makes a good (or effective) leader has been going on for centuries and, in spite of a myriad of studies, there are no conclusive answers. Although many definitions exist, for our purposes leadership is the process of providing direction from a position of power to influence individuals or groups toward the attainment of common goals. Anyone who exerts influence over others in the pursuit of organizationally relevant matters is a leader.

This definition underscores the broad impact that leaders like FLMs have on organizations. So, what makes an effective leader? The answer to this question is more complicated than you might think because leadership effectiveness as an FLM is more than simply gaining commitment with their influence attempts. In answering the question of what makes an effective leader would you single out CEOs, sports coaches, or presidents as examples of iconic leaders? On what basis do you identify them as leaders? Achievement? Popularity? The way they communicate? Or perhaps its' something intangible, like a leaders' charisma. Societal norms and media influence have much to do with our perceptions about what makes an effective leader, and sometimes they create a false impression of leader emergence, which occurs when someone naturally becomes the leader of a leaderless group. As a result, we fall prey to stereotypes. With so many conflicting impressions and opinions of what makes an effective leader, it is not surprising that endless studies and research continue to fail to agree on the actual constituents of leadership.

It has been suggested that leadership effectiveness entails considerations of the following three issues:

1. *The content of the evaluation: What criteria are being used to assess effectiveness?* Effectiveness depends on what the evaluator wants. For example, the content of effectiveness can entail criteria such as task performance, quality, sales, customer satisfaction, employee job satisfaction, turnover, or an overall evaluation of leadership effectiveness.
2. *The level of the evaluation: At what level are the criteria being measured?* Effectiveness can be measured at the individual, group, or organizational levels. Evaluations at different levels also can produce different conclusions. For example, sales performance may be a good measure of performance for one store location, but not across a geographic region.
3. *The rater's perspective: Who is doing the evaluation?* Assessments of effective leadership can be made by different people or groups, and

their view of leadership may vary and especially when one considers the use of 360 degree evaluations by many of today's organizations. For example, an FLM may be perceived as effective by a direct report, but not by the entire work unit or the boss.

Despite numerous debates regarding the nature of leadership, there is a general view that today's leaders are most likely to be critical thinkers who lead from a position of influence rather than power, and who use their decision-making, motivational, and communication skills to inspire others with their vision in order to generate individual, group, and organizational results. There is agreement that effective leadership can produce astonishing results in terms of increasing an organization's profits, maintaining a successful organization culture, motivating employees through good times and bad, increasing production levels, connecting with the community, and leading the charge on such things as sustainability.

What Is the Difference Between Managing and Leading?

Although management and leadership share some similarities, the two activities are not synonymous. Both managers and leaders work with people, set goals, and influence others in order to achieve those goals, but several distinctions separate the two functions. Managers are mainly a product of industrialization in the 20th century, an era when large-scale production and manufacturing demanded the organizational skills necessary to plan, organize, staff, and control the operations. Of course, as highlighted earlier in this book, these skills are still highly relevant as managers like FLMs are charged with implanting the organization's vision and strategy.

Leadership has been around far longer than management. History records the strategies by military leaders such as Alexander the Great (336–323 BC) and Attila the Hun (406–453 BC). Leadership consists of creating a vision, introducing change and movement, and influencing others to achieve goals, while managers maintain the status quo, promote stability, and ensure the smooth running of operations. There is an overlap between managers and leaders, however. For example, if an FLM is running a project and setting goals for their team, then they are leading their team. Similarly, if an FLM is a leader and they are engaged in the daily operations, then they are fulfilling management functions. In each case, both managers and leaders are leading from a position of influence. Therefore, it could be argued that organizations need strong managers and leaders to be successful. There are several conclusions for FLMs to be drawn from this discussion.

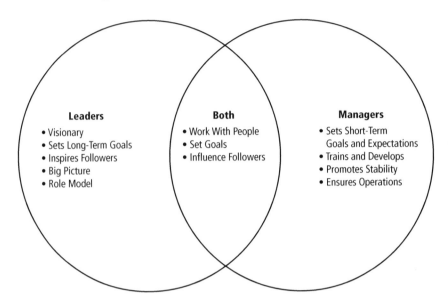

Figure 8.1 Comparison of a leader and a manager.

First, realistically, not all managers are leaders, nor for that matter all leaders managers. For example, FLMs who put their own interests above those of their employer or who fail to motivate, guide, or positively influence their direct reports or teams would not be classified as good leaders. Second, effective leadership requires effective managerial skills at some level. Third, effective managers need to possess some leadership traits in order to optimize the performance of others (see Figure 8.1).

It is important for FLMs to understand that although it is useful for leaders to have managerial skills, it is not essential; certainly, it is advantageous for leaders to understand the disciple of management and have a background in the management functions, but it doesn't mean they need to be managers as well as leaders. Their primary strength lies in the ability to influence the behaviors and work of others in order to realize theirs or the organization's vision and achieve set goals.

What Are Basic Leadership Types?

Four types of leadership behaviors proposed by some scholars are directive leadership, transactional leadership, visionary leadership, and empowering leadership (also known as superleadership; see Figure 8.2).

Directive Leaders	Transactional Leaders
• Implement Guidelines • Provide Expectations • Set Performance Standards • Ensure Rules are Followed	• Set Goals for Followers • Motivate With Rewards
Visionary Leaders	Empowering Leaders
• Create Vision to Motivate Followers • Utilize Charisma to Gain Support • Expect Commitment From Followers	• Develop Followers' Skills • Encourage Followers to Take Ownership of Their Work • Lead Others to Lead Themselves

Figure 8.2   Four basic types of leaders.

Directive leadership behavior consists of implementing guidelines, providing information about what is expected, setting performance standards, and ensuring that individuals follow rules. Directive leaders are sometimes known as production-oriented leaders because they tend to focus more on the technical or task aspects of the job. Directive leaders also tend to rule with an autocratic style, making decisions without asking for suggestions from others. They also rely on power to use their authority to command, reprimand, or intimidate in order to get the desired results from their direct reports.

Transactional leadership assumes employees are motivated by goals and equitable rewards. The transactional leader offers clear and objective goals for followers in order to gain compliance, which occurs when the targets of influence readily agree to carry out the leader's requests.

Visionary leadership, often contrasted with transactional leadership, creates visions to motivate, inspire, and stimulate employees. A visionary leader uses charisma to encourage followers to share in the mission and expects them to commit to her or him and work toward the desired goal. Finally, empowering leadership, or *Superleadership*, shifts the focus from the leader to the follower through the idea of self-leadership. Empowering leaders help to develop the individual skills and abilities of their followers, allowing them to utilize these skills, take ownership of their work, and contribute to organizational performance. Superleadership has been defined as the "process of leading others to lead themselves."

Some Key Leadership Theories

As discussed earlier, there is no set definition or combination of characteristics that describes a good leader or which leadership types are best.

However, in order to support the current understanding of leadership, it is useful to discuss several theories of leadership, which focus on different ways in which a good leader is created.

Great Man Theory

What makes a man or woman rise above others to assume the mantle of leadership? Why are some more drawn to the burdens of the job than others? What set history's great leaders apart from their contemporaries and enabled them to navigate often tumultuous waters, defying the odds to achieve their goals on behalf of themselves and their people?

Some theorists have argued that these questions are answered by the *great man theory*. According to the great man theory (which should perhaps be called the great *person* theory), leaders are born with just the right traits, attributes and abilities necessary for leading. These individuals come into the world possessing certain characteristics and traits not found in all people. These abilities enable them to lead while shaping the very pages of history. Under this theory, prominent leaders throughout the course of history were born to lead and deserved to do so as a result of their natural abilities and talents.

These leaders have the traits, attributes, and abilities (e.g., charisma, intellect, confidence, communication skills, and social skills) necessary to set them apart from those around them and enable them to assume roles of authority and power. Great leaders are heroes who are valiant, mythic, and ordained to rise to leadership when the situation arises, and they accomplish great feats against the odds on behalf of followers. Again, because the ability to lead is inherent—that the best leaders are born, not made—those in power deserve to lead because of the traits they have been endowed with. The term "great man" was adopted at the time because leadership was reserved for males, particularly in military leadership.

Trait Theories

The trait theories are very similar to the great man theory. It was founded on the characteristics of different leaders—both the successful and unsuccessful ones. Thus, trait theories argue that effective leaders share a number of common personality characteristics, or "traits" and qualities (e.g., integrity, empathy, assertiveness, good decision-making skills, and likability that are helpful when leading others). Trait theories are used to predict effective leadership. Usually, the identified characteristics are compared to those of potential leaders to determine their likelihood of leading effectively.

Early trait theories said that leadership is an innate, instinctive quality that you do or don't have. Over the years, the focus has moved on from this idea, as we have learned more about what can be done to develop leadership qualities. While trait theories help us identify traits and qualities, none of these traits, nor any specific combination of them, will guarantee success as a leader. Because traits are external behaviors that emerge from the things going on within our minds—it is these internal beliefs and processes that are important for effective leadership.

The continuing interest in trait theories focuses on trying to identify leadership characteristics from different perspectives. The focus is primarily on the physiological attributes such as appearance, weight, and height; demographics such as age, education, and familial background; and intelligence, which encompasses decisiveness, judgment, and knowledge.

Contingency Theories

The realization that there is no one correct type of leader led to theories that the best leadership style depends on the situation. These theories try to predict which style is best in which circumstance. Therefore, contingency theories emphasize different variables in a specific setting that determine the style of leadership best suited for the said situation. It was founded on the principle that no one leadership style is applicable to all situations and that the best form of leadership is one that finds the perfect balance between behaviors, needs, and context.

According to contingency theories, for example, whether or not an FLM is an effective leader is the result of the interplay among what the FLM is like, what he or she does, and the situation in which leadership takes place. Given the wide variety of situations in which leadership occurs, what makes an FLM an effective leader in one situation such as certain traits or behaviors, is not necessarily what that FLM needs to be equally effective in a different situation. The traits or behaviors that may contribute to an FLM being an effective leader in one situation might actually result in the same FLM being an ineffective leader in another situation.

Good leaders not only possess the right qualities but they are also able to evaluate the needs of their followers and the situation at hand. In summary, contingency theories suggest that effective leadership is a combination of many key variables and is always contingent on the situation or context.

Situational Theories

Situational theories are similar to contingency theories as they also propose that no one leadership style supersedes others. As the name suggests, the theories imply that leadership depends on the situation at hand. Put simply, FLMs should always correspond their leadership to the respective situation by assessing certain variables such as the type of task, nature of followers, and more.

As proposed by several scholars, their situational theory blends two key elements: the leadership style and the followers' maturity levels. Maturity is classified into four different degrees:

- *M1*—Team members do not possess the motivation or tactical skills to complete necessary jobs.
- *M2*—Team members are willing and ambitious to achieve something, but they lack the necessary ability.
- *M3*—Team members possess the skills and capacity to accomplish tasks, but they are not willing to take accountability.
- *M4*—Team members possess all the right talents and are motivated to complete projects.

According to situational theory, a leader exercises a particular form of leadership based on the maturity level of his or her team. When a situation is favorable for leading, it is relatively easy for an FLM to influence direct reports so they perform at a high level and contribute to organizational efficiency and effectiveness. In a situation unfavorable for leading, it is much more difficult for an FLM to exert influence.

Behavioral Theories

Behavioral theories focus on how leaders behave, rather than their traits or characteristics. For instance, do leaders dictate what needs to be done and expect cooperation? Or do they involve their teams in decision-making to encourage acceptance and support?

In a framework based on a leader's behavior it argues that there are three types of leaders:

- *Autocratic leaders* make decisions without consulting their teams. This style of leadership is considered appropriate when decisions need to be made quickly, when there's no need for input, and when team agreement isn't necessary for a successful outcome.

- *Democratic leaders* allow the team to provide input before making a decision, although the degree of input can vary from leader to leader. This style is important when team agreement matters, but it can be difficult to manage when there are lots of different perspectives and ideas.
- *Laissez-faire leaders* don't interfere; they allow people within the team to make many of the decisions. This works well when the team is highly capable, is motivated, and doesn't need close supervision. However, this behavior can arise because the leader is lazy or distracted; and this is where this style of leadership can fail.

Behavioral theories suggest that effective leadership is the result of many learned skills. Thus, FLMs need three primary skills to lead their followers—technical, human, and conceptual skills. Technical skills refer to a leader's knowledge of the process or technique; human skills means that one is able to interact with other individuals; while conceptual skills enable the leader to come up with ideas for running the organization or society smoothly.

Clearly, how leaders behave affects their performance. Researchers have realized, though, that many of these leadership behaviors are appropriate at different times. The best leaders are those who can use many different behavioral styles, and choose the right style for each situation.

Contemporary Leadership Perspectives

The early leadership theories or perspectives discussed to this point can enhance an FLM's understanding of leadership and flower behavior. More recent perspectives leadership have built on these theories to explain how leaders motivate and build relationships with their direct reports to achieve performance beyond expectations. This section takes a brief look at several contemporary perspectives on leadership to include transformational leadership, charismatic leadership, servant leadership, and authentic leadership.

Transformational Leadership

The leadership frameworks discussed so far are all useful in different situations, however, in today's world of work, "transformational leadership" is often the most effective style to use. Transformational leaders inspire their followers to transcend their self-interest for the good of the organization and commit to a shared vision. The four dimensions of transformational leadership are:

- Idealized influence (also referred to as charisma) is behavior that gains the admiration, trust, and respect of followers.
- Inspirational motivation promotes commitment to a shared vision of the future.
- Intellectual stimulation encourages people to view problems from a different perspective and to think about innovative and alternative ways to address them.
- Individual consideration creates mutual respect or trust and a genuine concern for the needs and desires of others.

Transformational leaders have integrity and high emotional intelligence. They motivate people with a shared vision of the future, and they communicate well. They are also typically self-aware, authentic, empathetic, and humble. Transformational leaders inspire their team members because they expect the best from everyone, and they hold themselves accountable for their actions. They set clear goals, and they have good conflict-resolution. This leads to high productivity and engagement. In direct opposition to transformational leadership is laissez-faire leadership, in which a leader fully delegates responsibility to others. This type of leader has little involvement with followers, almost no control over the task, and little interest in making decisions unless forced into it.

The reality is that leadership is not a "one size fits all" thing; often, like other managers and leaders FLMs must adapt their approach to fit the situation. This is why it is useful to develop a thorough understanding of other leadership frameworks and styles; after all, the more approaches an FLM is familiar with, the more flexible they can be.

Charismatic Leadership

Charismatic leadership resembles transformational leadership in that they both use inspirational techniques to energize their followers. They can certainly use their exceptional leadership skills for good. However, though transformational leaders are focused on the best interest of the individuals and the organization, charismatic leaders may place more emphasis on their own needs and interests and become caught up in their own hype. Leaders who follow their own agendas become inflexible, believe they can do no wrong, and tend to dismiss the advice from others if it diverges from their own convictions.

In addition, serious repercussions can occur when charismatic leaders become convinced of their own infallibility—their followers may also buy into this belief and perceive such leaders as invincible. The danger is that followers will relate their own personal job satisfaction and the success of the organization directly to the presence of the leader. In this situation, the departure of a charismatic leader can have a devastating effect on followers. Therefore, the charismatic leader needs to be an appropriate role model for followers.

In summary, the difference between transformational and charismatic leaders lies in their intent. Transformational leaders want to transform their teams and organizations, while leaders who rely on charisma often focus on themselves and their own ambitions, and they may not want to change anything.

Servant Leadership

Servant leadership is a pattern of leadership that places an emphasis on employees and the community rather than on the leader. A "servant leader" is someone, regardless of level, who leads simply by meeting the needs of the team. The term sometimes describes a person without formal recognition as a leader.

Servant leaders share their power and tend to "lead from behind," ensuring the team (not the leader) receives recognition for hard work. They are usually empathic, good listeners, perceptive, and committed to growth in the organization and the community.

Servant leaders often lead by example. They have high integrity and lead with generosity. Their approach can create a positive corporate culture, and it can lead to high morale among team members.

Supporters of the servant leadership model suggest that it is a good way to move ahead in a world where values are increasingly important, and where servant leaders can achieve power because of their values, ideals, and ethics. Servant leadership has been connected with high morale, loyalty, and ethics.

Others believe that people who practice servant leadership can find themselves "left behind" by other leaders, particularly in competitive situations. This style also takes time to apply correctly: it's ill-suited to situations where, for example, an FLM has to make quick decisions or meet tight deadlines.

Authentic Leadership

Authentic leadership is a leadership style in which leaders are honest, self-aware, transparent, and have a reputation for dealing with employees in a straightforward and genuine way. They don't make promises they can't keep, ignore obvious problems, or pretend to be someone they're not. An authentic leader is able to inspire loyalty and trust in their employees by consistently displaying who they really are as a person, and how they feel about their employees' performance.

Employees don't expect leaders to be perfect, of course, but they want them to be genuine people they can have a relationship with. They want to be able to trust their leaders to do the right thing and treat people fairly. When a leader comes across as inauthentic, they will find it more difficult to build trust and influence others.

Support for authentic leadership continues to grow as a reaction to the number of corporate and leader scandals and blunders in recent years. When authentic leaders find their "true north" or moral compass, they are more focused on empowering their direct reports, forming meaningful relationships, and fostering an ethical environment. Authentic leadership has been associated with improved job performance, increased job satisfaction, greater trust in the leader/follower relationship, and organizational commitment. Finally, it has been suggested that authentic leadership is the single strongest predictor of an employee's job satisfaction.

So, including this section, "Why are some leaders successful, while others fail?" The truth is that there is no "magic combination" of characteristics that makes a leader successful, and different characteristics matter in different circumstances. This doesn't mean, however, that FLMs can't learn to be an effective leader. They just need to understand the various approaches to leadership, so that they can use the right approach for their own situations. One way to do this is to be familiar with leadership theories discussed before (while also recognizing that there are many others) that provide the backbone of our current understanding of leadership.

Gender and Leadership

The increasing number of women entering the ranks of management, as well as the problems some women face in their efforts to be hired as managers or promoted into management positions (to include getting equal pay), continues to shine the light on the relationship between gender and leadership. The reality is that despite the fact that there are relatively more women in management positions today than there were a decade ago, there are still relatively few women in top management and, in some organizations, even in middle or frontline management.

Unfortunately, it is a fact that when women, for example, advance to top management positions, special attention often is focused on them and the fact that they are women. A widespread stereotype of women is that they are nurturing, supportive, and concerned with interpersonal relations. Men are stereotypically viewed as being directive and focused on task accomplishment. Such stereotypes suggest that women tend to be more relationship-oriented as managers and engage in more consideration behaviors (e.g., focus on people), whereas men are more task-oriented and engage in more initiating-structure behaviors. Initiating structure is the extent to which a leader defines leader and group member roles, initiates actions, organizes group activities and defines how tasks are to be accomplished by the group. Does the behavior of actual male and female managers bear out these stereotypes? Do women managers lead in different ways than men do? Are male or female managers more effective as leaders?

Research on the similarities and differences in female and male leaders reveals the following four conditions:

1. Men and women were seen as displaying more task and social leadership, respectively.
2. Women used a more democratic or participative style than men, and men used a more autocratic and directive style than women.
3. Men and women were equally assertive.
4. Women executives, when rated by their peers, managers, and direct reports, scored higher than their male counterparts on a variety of effectiveness criteria.

Other research suggests that male and female managers who have leadership positions in organizations behave in similar ways. Women do not engage in more consideration than men, and men do not engage in more initiating structure than women. However, as noted above leadership style may vary between women and men and especially in the area of how participative they are.

There are at least two reasons that female managers may be more participative as leaders than are male managers. First, direct reports may try to resist the influence of female managers more than they do the influence of male managers. Some direct reports may never have reported to a woman before, some may incorrectly see a management role as being more appropriate for a man than for a woman, and some may just resist being led by a woman. To overcome this resistance and encourage direct reports' trust and respect, women managers may adopt a participative approach.

A second reason that female managers may be more participative is that they sometimes have better interpersonal skills than male managers. A participative approach to leadership requires high levels of interaction and involvement between a manager and her or his direct reports' feelings, and the ability to make decisions that may be unpopular with direct reports but necessary for goal attainment. Good interpersonal skills may help female managers have effective interactions with their direct reports that are crucial to a participative approach. To the extent that male managers have more difficulty managing interpersonal relationships, they may shy away from the high levels of interaction with direct reports necessary for true participation.

The key finding from studies on leader behaviors, however, is that male and female managers do not differ significantly in their propensities to perform different leader behaviors. Even though they may be more participative, female managers do not engage in more consideration or less initiating structure than male managers.

While it is important to discuss whether or not male and female managers or leaders differ, perhaps a more important question is whether they differ in effectiveness. Consistent with the results for leader behaviors, research suggests that across different kinds of organizational settings, female and male managers tend to be equally effective as leaders. Thus, there is no logical basis for stereotypes favoring male managers and leaders or for the existence of the "glass ceiling" (an invisible barrier that seems to prevent women from advancing as far as they should in some organizations).

Because women and men are equally effective as leaders, the increasing number of women in the workforce should result in a larger pool of highly qualified candidates for management positions in organizations, ultimately enhancing organizational effectiveness. FLMs and other managers and leaders interested in achieving a balanced gender leadership, should change the overall perception of women in leadership and treat both genders equally.

What Is the Role of Emotional Intelligence and Leadership Effectiveness?

Do the moods and emotions leaders experience on the job influence their behavior and effectiveness as leaders. Some research suggests this is likely to be the case. And, if true, a leader's level of emotional intelligence (EI) may play a particularly important role in leadership effectiveness.

EI is the ability to manage oneself and one's relationship in mature and constructive ways. There are four dimensions of EI:

1. *Self-awareness:* A good understanding of your emotions;
2. *Self-management:* The ability to control and regulate emotions and impulses;
3. *Social awareness:* Skills in perceiving, empathizing with, and reacting appropriately to the emotions of others; and
4. *Relationship management:* The ability to manage the emotions of others to build strong and healthy relationships with them.

Given that leadership is an influence process between leaders and direct reports, it should come as no surprise to FLMs that EI is predicted to be associated with leadership effectiveness. Evidence to date supports two conclusions:

1. *EI is an input to transformational leadership.* In other words, EI helps managers to effectively enact the behaviors associated with transformational leadership discussed earlier in this chapter.
2. *EI has a small, positive, and significant association with leadership effectiveness.* This suggests that EI will help FLMs, for example, to lead more effectively.

EI plays a crucial role in how leaders relate to and deal with their direct reports, particularly when it comes to encouraging direct reports to be creative. Creativity in organizations is an emotion-laden process; it often entails challenging the status quo, being willing to take risks and accept and learn from failures, and doing much hard work to bring creative ideas to fruition in terms of new products, services, or procedures and processes when uncertainty is bound to be high. Leaders who are high on EI are more likely to understand the emotions surrounding creative endeavors, to be able to awaken and support the creative pursuits of their direct reports, and to provide the kind of support that enables creativity to flourish in organizations.

Humility and Leaders

Humility is a relatively stable trait grounded in the belief that "something greater than self exists." Although some think it is a sign of weakness or low self-esteem, nothing could be further from the truth. Humble leaders tend to display five key qualities valued by employees: high self-awareness, openness to feedback, appreciation of others, low self-focus, and appreciation.

FLMs can conclude the following about humility in the context of managing others. First, try to be humble by changing the focus of your accomplishment from "me" to "we." Share credit with others, but by all means be authentic. Don't try to fake humility. Second, try to spend more time asking questions and less time talking about yourself or telling people what to do. Third, an organization's culture can promote humility.

Followers: What Do They Want, How Can They Help?

Is the quality of leadership dependent on the qualities of the followers being led? So it seems. Leaders and followers need each other, and the quality of the relationship determines how we behave as followers.

What Do Followers Want in Their Leaders?

Research shows that followers seek and admire leaders who create feelings of

- *Significance.* Such leaders make followers feel that what they do at work is important and meaningful.
- *Community.* These leaders create a sense of unity that encourages followers to treat others with respect and to work together in pursuit of organizational goals.
- *Excitement.* The leaders make people feel energetic and engaged at work.

What Do Leaders Want in Their Followers?

Followers vary, of course, in their level of compliance with a leader, with helpers (most compliant) showing deference to their leaders, independents (less compliant) distancing themselves, and rebels (least compliant) showing divergence.

Leaders clearly benefit from having helpers (and, to some extent, independents). They want followers who are productive, reliable, honest, cooperative, proactive, and flexible. They do not want followers who are reluctant to take the lead on projects, fail to generate ideas, are willing to collaborate, withhold information, provide inaccurate feedback, or hide the truth.

Leading by Becoming a Good Follower

Effective leaders who work their way up learn about what motivates them and their co-workers. They also learn about what makes a group or team work well together to achieve goals. They also learn what good—and not so good—leadership is, and this allows them to develop empathy and compassion for those they will one day lead. In essence, they learn key "followership" lessons that will serve them well when they become leaders.

Being a good follower does not end when one becomes a leader. FLMs would do well to understand that they must continue to practice good followership in their management roles; they become good followership FLMs. They can be good FLMs by being a good follower and exhibiting these skills:

1. *Understand what motivates people.* Learn about what coworkers, customers, and bosses want, and what drives them to do their best work (or to prevent others from working well). It sounds obvious, but don't overlook the value of asking your manager how you can best communicate with each other and how often.
2. *Choose your battles.* You can't win at everything, but you can choose where to invest your time and energy. Learn how to get along with co-workers, direct reports, and senior managers who are similar to you as well as with those who are different.
3. *Be brave.* Don't be afraid to tell your manager—diplomatically— when you think she or he may be wrong and to offer intelligent alternatives. Helpful feedback is always valuable, and remember to be supportive when things are going well.
4. *Work collaboratively.* Be a good team player, meeting your goals, and letting the team take credit when appropriate can go a long way toward bringing out the best in others, including your manager when you are in a follower role. Ask to keep your manager informed; no one likes being caught by surprise.
5. *Think critically.* Develop your ability to ask the right questions, raise intelligent challenges, and maintain your own competence and motivation.

Frontline Managers Skills and Competencies

The discussion to this point has focused on increasing the FLM's understanding of leadership. As highlighted in different parts of this book, FLMs perform critical management and leadership duties within the organization to sustain quality, service, innovation, employee satisfaction, and financial performance. In order for an FLM to be successful, they need to have the following essential leadership competencies or skills.

Strategic Thinking

FLMs need foundational business skills to understand their organization's strategic priorities and how their own team/unit/department supports those priorities. Equipped with business knowledge, FLMs are able to ensure their work—and the work of their direct reports—is aligned to the objectives of the organization as a whole, as well as show employees how their work contributes to the organization's overall success. Day-to-day decisions are thoughtfully made with the organization's overall success in mind, rather than relying instinct on gut feeling—whether it is increasing throughput, reducing complaints, or other issues that will have the largest impact on the business.

Goal Alignment and Execution

Have to have skills in defining performance standards and creating a limited number of goals aligning to organization priorities so they can ensure their direct reports know what is expected of them and how they will be evaluated. Once goals are established, FLMs need to know how to give direction, set milestones, and monitor progress. They must be able to observe when performance is lagging or goals are at risk in a timely manner so they can put in place corrective measures. Of course, they also need to know how to identify the root causes of lagging performance in order to apply the right corrective measures.

Problem Solving

An FLM needs to have outstanding problem solving skills. Whenever a direct report has a problem, their FLM is often their first port of call; and it's the FLM's job to help them resolve the problem rather than having to refer it further up the chain of command. There will also be problems coming down from higher up regarding the FLM's work unit or team, which the FLM may need to resolve. At the same time, the skill with which you deal with problems on the job has a direct impact on your effectiveness as a supervisor and on your career success. Regardless, FLMs need to know how to take an issue and find the root cause of the problem but also have a structured process for engaging others and solving the problem.

Organizational Savvy

The ability to build relationships and collaborate with other FLMs across the organization is critical—especially when implementing strategic initiatives that are directed from senior leadership. Managing internal stakeholders and navigating organizational politics to achieve goals are key competencies for FLMs since FLMs are the bridge within organizations. Therefore, developing political skills, such as situational awareness and empathy, helps FLMs better fulfill their bridge responsibilities. Being able to network with key stakeholders in the organization and finding out their needs and concerns will help improve the cohesiveness of the organization. Understanding the need for and developing empathy improves collaboration with key members and employees. It also makes the FLM more insightful to the needs of the organization.

Personal Leadership/Self-Awareness

FLMs who understand their own strength and preferences, weaknesses, biases, quirks, working and leadership style, and development needs are better equipped to influence and interact effectively with their own direct reports—and colleagues—who have different working styles and personalities and to make day-to-day decisions and interact effectively with others who have different working and leadership styles and personalities. Also, often developing self-awareness as a leader is the first step in developing emotional intelligence which as discussed has proven particularly valuable in leadership.

The ability of an FLM to be perceptively in tune with her or his self and their emotions, as well as having sound situational awareness can be a powerful tool for leading direct reports or a team. So, not only does self-awareness work to make FLMs more cognizant of their actions, emotions and biases—it helps them develop greater EI in the process. Developing self-awareness as a leader will strengthen not only an FLM's performance but organizational performance as well. Ultimately, the immense amount of understanding, trustworthiness, and wisdom that self-aware FLMs possess equips them with critical skills for success.

Learning Agility

Seeking out diverse experiences, quickly applying lessons learned to new challenges, and being able to integrate experiences and adapt to the environment allows FLMs to swiftly recognize, analyze, and address new problems. FLMs must have an ability to "perform in the future by being comfortable in an unfamiliar situation, while not knowing what to do. FLMs need to be able to use speed and flexibility to successfully exhibit learning agility. Speed is the ability to act quickly, discarding ideas that don't work to accelerate other possibilities. Flexibility is being open to new ideas and proposing new solutions.

Being adept at learning agility allows an FLM to actively engage in experimenting, performance risk taking, interpersonal risk taking, collaborating, information gathering, feedback-seeking, and reflecting. Skill in learning agility allows the FLM to be able to better navigate situations where they have no idea what to do, but they have the wherewithal to try and figure it out. Whenever FLMs can demonstrate a willingness to draw on past experiences and learn new skills to try and navigate a new situation, they are able to prove that they are or can be agile.

Team Building and Leading

One of the main responsibilities of an FLM is to manage their direct reports or the employees in their unit or on their team. The most successful FLMs are able to clearly demonstrate to their direct reports how their work is connected to the larger organization and how that work contributes to the organization's overall success. In addition, there will be times when FLMs must inspire and guide direct reports to exceed expectations or put in extra effort or time—without financial incentives. Effective FLMs are able to accomplish goals by influencing the actions, decisions, and thinking of others.

Whether an FLM works in a private, public, or not-for-profit organization, their ability to generate and sustain a sense of affiliation, peer support, and collaboration may be one of the most important things they do—not only for their direct reports but for themselves. The more direct reports or team members learn to rely on each other and work together to solve problems, the better their leadership skills become, and the less they depend on the FLM to do things for them. In fact, an essential part of team building is an FLM and their direct reports develop their own skills in these areas. To be an effective team builder and leader, FLMs need to use a variety of skills to include—active listening, feedback, conflict resolution, problem solving, and coaching—but instead of applying them one-on-one, they use them with their direct reports.

Communication

Communication skills—whether verbal or written—are core competencies expected in virtually any position within the workplace. A point emphasized throughout this book is that FLMs are in a unique position, serving as the link between more senior management or leadership and the workforce. The organization's vision is articulated by senior leadership, middle management devises the strategy, and the FLM has to ensure that the workforce performs the work. To accomplish this, the FLM has to be able to effectively communicate with the workforce.

FLMs need to be able to communicate well with employees at every level in the organization and especially in efforts to improve team, unit or department operations and the performance and productivity of the employees under them. That might involve giving bad news, enforcing rules they didn't make and saying no to requests—and doing so in a friendly, approachable yet authoritative way.

Because FLMs are the bridge between lower level and those above him or her they must be approachable to improve employee satisfaction, yet authoritative to carry out tasks that come down from the organization. Skilled FLMs can listen, speak, and write clearly and consistently, communicating for maximum impact with people at all levels in the organization, including direct reports, superiors, peers, and others. It's especially important as noted earlier for FLMs to effectively communicate goals and expectations.

Coaching and Emotional Intelligence

Coaching is a process of helping employees grow their own potential by eliminating obstacles that interfere with effective performance. At its core, coaching isn't about teaching, managing, or directing. It's about helping people to learn on their own so that they can perform their best. Shifting into a coaching mindset can be challenging, especially for FLMs.

The role of an FLM isn't to be a commander, but instead a facilitator—one who creates the conditions that will allow their direct reports to thrive. To do this effectively, training and practice is needed. Part of being an effective FLM and coach is providing direct reports with ongoing, meaningful feedback to objectively communicate what they are doing well and what needs to be worked on. Everyone wants to know their work matters, understand what is required of them, be recognized for their efforts, and be treated with understanding and respect.

FLMs who coach employees instead of commanding them are able to build a much more talented and agile workforce, which leads to a healthy and growing business. Emotional intelligence is a critical aspect of coaching employees in a way that builds relationships, boosts engagement, and improves performance. FLMs can see greatly improved coaching skills by taking steps to improve their EI—they go hand in hand!

Motivating Others

The most successful FLMs are able to inspire commitment, recognize and reward the contributions of others, and guide direct reports to complete work, especially when goals are unclear. This may include motivating others to exceed expectations or put in extra effort—without monetary incentives.

A motivated workforce is important, perhaps even essential, to the success of any organization. An FLM's workplace may offer a revolutionary product or a service people desperately need or it may lack real competition and have plenty of working capital on hand, but without employees who care about the organization and take a vested interest in their own performance, the organization's success is far from assured. FLMs must have the skills to foster motivation among employees and can do so simply by understanding the nature of motivation and using tested techniques designed to motivate.

FLMs can make their direct reports day or break their day. Other than the decisions direct reports make on their own about liking their work, FLMs are the most powerful factor in building employee's motivation and positive morale. An FLM's impact on employee motivation is immeasurable. By their words, their body language, and the expression on their face, an FLM telegraphs their opinion of their value to their direct reports. Feeling valued by their supervisor in the workplace is key to building high employee motivation and morale is both challenging and yet supremely simple. It requires skilled FLMs who have the skills and know that paying attention every day to profoundly meaningful aspects of their direct reports has a tremendous impact on their life at work.

Influence Outcomes

Along with motivation, FLMs must have the ability to influence decisions and actions of others. Though supervisors have some authority because of their position, they are constantly faced with the need to influence without authority. FLMs must be able to effectively influence upwards, sideways, and downward.

To achieve greater influence, FLMs should possess necessary communication and negotiation skills. With such skills, FLMs increase their potential effectiveness as they (their direct reports, peers, and senior leadership) will be better able to accomplish goals by affecting the actions, decisions, and thinking of others, persuading them effectively to gain cooperation and get things done to achieve desired outcomes.

FLMs are arguably the most important people in an organization; they manage their direct reports to ensure the smooth running of an organization and are often the voice of upper management to lower level employees. It requires a particular set of skills to become a successful FLM and it can seem a daunting prospect; but with the right mindset, commitment and organizational training and support this can be a most rewarding and uplifting role.

Building Credibility as a New FLM

Whether you are an experienced FLM taking over a new unit, or a high performer moving into your first FLM position, taking over a new management or leadership role is challenging. As an FLM taking over a new unit, for example, your first goal should be to gain personal credibility with your direct reports and your immediate manager or leader. Bear in mind that as a new FLM your earliest actions will have the most impact on how you are perceived by your managers or leaders and your unit for the duration of your tenure. Thus, it is important that you have a well thought out plan for approaching your new FLM challenge. Although there is no "secret sauce" that will ensure you successfully build credibility in a short period of time, there are some characteristics that appear to influence how new FLMs are perceived. New FLMs are perceived as more credible when they:

Are demanding but not unreasonable. New FLMs must establish their authority early on and set challenging, but achievable, goals. FLMs who are demanding and hold their direct reports accountable for high levels of performance earn the respect of their direct reports, peers, and managers.

They communicate an inspiring vision to their direct reports. As an FLM it is not enough to simply be demanding. FLMs must inspire their direct reports to work hard to achieve demanding goals. The best FLMs are capable of creating and communicating a vision that provides the inspiration to achieve results beyond the ordinary. This vision becomes the "why" that the unit focuses on when things get tough, long hours are needed, and sacrifices are required to achieve the goals.

Are seen as willing to take rational risks, but are not reckless. Every new FLM opportunity involves taking risks. Indeed, every management opportunity involves taking risks. FLMs who are overly risk averse may be seen as lacking courage to do what is necessary to succeed, while FLMs who take irrational risks are likely to gain the reputation as being reckless, or poor decision makers. Good FLMs assess risks and weigh potential rewards against potential consequences, and take rational risks.

Are focused on achievable goals, but flexible in how they are achieved. Good FLMs are masters at managing chaos. Stepping into a new FLM role is often chaotic as management/leadership transitions involve significant change, both for the new FLM and for the organization. Thus it is important for the new FLMs to quickly identify key issues and provide focus on their resolution. It is equally important that the new leader align values very quickly to focus the team's behaviors. Chaos in today's organizational leadership arena is unlikely to ever disappear, but good FLMs do not let chaos rule over the team's actions.

Are approachable to not too familiar. As a new FLM you will be a bit of a mystery to your new direct reports. Unless you were promoted from the unit, at best the direct reports will most likely have had a cursory introduction to you through an organizational announcement giving a brief history of your accomplishments. At times the direct reports will have received no information about you whatsoever. In either case, it is important that you realize that there will likely be a bit of uneasiness amongst direct reports at getting a new FLM. As a new FLM you represent uncertainty and change. You must be approachable so that your direct reports may get to know you, your values, your vision, and your personal and management or leadership style. The direct reports must be able to communicate their concerns and ideas, and be comfortable in approaching you. However, you must also avoid becoming too familiar with direct reports so as not to compromise your authority.

Are willing to make tough calls, but keep the unit's (and individual direct report's) well-being in mind. Being a manager/leader by definition means having to make tough decisions. Accountability for your unit's performance rests with you. As such you must hold your unit accountable for their performance. This means enforcing behavioral and performance standards, making tough operational decisions, and taking rational risks. In doing so, good FLMs also retain their humanity and take into consideration the impact their decisions have on the unit and individual direct reports. In order to gain and retain your unit's respect and loyalty, you must also show the unit that you respect and are loyal to them, even when making those tough decisions.

Are able to secure early wins that make an immediate impact on the unit's performance. As a new FLM you must demonstrate your competence and worthiness. While it is unlikely that your actions will make a significant impact on the unit's measurable performance within the first couple of weeks, you should still seek to identify early wins that will bolster your credibility in the short term. Oftentimes these early wins may be related to fixing critical behavioral issues, focusing on obvious process changes, or tackling problems where the solution is already known but has not had real focus. As a new FLM you should seek to identify two or three key problems and focus attention on making substantial, and tangible, gains towards resolving them. These key wins will go a long way to earning the credibility you will need to drive larger, more substantial, programs over the long term.

Gaining personal credibility when stepping into a new management/leadership role is a challenge that typically takes weeks, not days. However, by identifying opportunities for and securing early wins, demonstrating competence and traits that direct reports will want to emulate, you should be able to gain the credibility that will set you, and your unit, up for success much sooner than later.

Conclusion

Leadership is the process of providing direction from a position of power to influence individuals or groups toward the attainment of common goals. Anyone who exerts influence over others in the pursuit of organizationally relevant matters is a leader.

Although management and leadership share some similarities, the two activities are not synonymous. Both managers and leaders work with people, set goals, and influence others in order to achieve those goals, but there are several distinctions that separate the two functions.

There are four basic types of leader behaviors: directive, transactional, visionary, and empowering. Early theories of leadership included: great man theory, trait theories, behavioral theories, contingency theories, and situational theories. Several contemporary perspectives on leadership include transformational leadership, charismatic leadership, servant leadership, and authentic leadership.

Contrary to stereotypes suggesting that women are more relationship-oriented and men more task-oriented, female and male managers do not differ in the leadership behaviors they perform. Sometimes female managers are more participative than male managers. Women and men are equally effective as managers and leaders.

The moods and emotions leaders experience on the job and their ability to effectively manage these feelings, can influence their effectiveness as leaders. Moreover, EI can contribute to leadership effectiveness in multiple ways, including encouraging and supporting creating among direct reports.

To be effective FLMs must develop a variety of skills to successfully manage, and communicate with those above, below, and beside them. And they need to constantly do this while managing or leading direct reports who all have different personalities, skill sets, and who may or may not interact well with each other.

New FLMs, like other new managers or leaders must understand the importance of being a follower and building credibility with their direct reports, peers, and senior managers or leaders. While challenging, there are a number of things FLMS can do to move in the right direction.

9

Motivating Employees

Exceeding Performance Expectations

The world around us constantly presents examples of motivation. Rocky, the prize fighter, down for the count, sees his wife through bleary eyes and rises slowly from the mat, summoning the necessary energy to attack his opponent and win. During halftime, a group of lackluster football players is transformed by the coach into screaming, aggressive, highly motivated players who go on to win the big game. Gymnasts overcome painful injuries to win medals. How does this happen?

Many motivated employees have FLMs with good leadership qualities. It is not easy to be a motivating leader, as so much of motivation is psychological by nature. Although motivation cannot be seen directly, its presence or absence can be recognized by observing employee behavior. When an FLM observes an employee doing a task, the logical assumption is that the employee is motivated. If, on the other hand, an employee is frequently observed wasting time, it can be assumed that the employee is not motivated. When FLMs are effective leaders, the resulting motivated workforce is more likely to achieve organizational goals.

Succeeding as a Frontline Manager in Today's Organizations, pages 237–266
Copyright © 2021 by Information Age Publishing
All rights of reproduction in any form reserved.

Many FLMs do not believe that motivation is part of their job. They think that once an employee is hired, it is the employee's responsibility to ensure that the job is done. Unfortunately, they envision their job as simply making corrections and adjustments when necessary. They erroneously believe that motivation is the responsibility of the individual employee. Today's organizations cannot be successful if they adopt this attitude. FLMs are the movers and shakers whose primary responsibility is to get things done *through others*. In order to motivate effectively, FLMs must understand all aspects of the process and theories of motivation. They must readily recognize the negative consequences of unmotivated employees and how to avoid them.

The chapter first offers a definition of motivation and then explains why employee motivation is important. Next, several theories of motivation are identified before discussing methods used to motivate employees. The focus then shifts to special problems in motivating particular groups: contingent workers, a diversified workforce, employees doing highly repetitive tasks. The next section discusses the challenges motivating different generations in the workplace. The chapter concludes by offering some suggestions on how FLMs can more effectively motivate their direct reports.

What Is Motivation?

In recent weeks, team leader (and FLM) Jackie Ford has noticed that whenever she enters the work area, several of her team members appear to be loafing or chatting. In Jackie's opinion, they just don't seem to be working very hard. A quick review of the human resources records verified another suspicion: absenteeism and tardiness have increased in recent months. Jackie is baffled. Just 2 months ago, everyone received an eight percent pay raise. In addition, the facilities of her department were recently refurbished. What else could the employees possibly want? "Nobody wants to work like they did in the good old days. Half the problems we have around here are due to a lack of personal motivation. Workers just don't seem to care. What *can* I do?"

Jackie's sentiments are often expressed by today's FLMs. Motivating employees is not a new problem. There are examples of motivation problems dating back to biblical times. In the early 20th century, much of the pioneering work in the field of management was concerned with motivation. Motivation is the process of satisfying internal needs through actions and behavior. Motivation is derived from the root of the Latin word meaning "to move." It basically means to impel someone to act. The study of motivation examines why and how people behave as they do. It is concerned with the combination of mental and physical drives and the environment that affects behavior.

FLMs such as Jackie Ford must realize that people behave with a purpose or pattern based on motives. A motive is an internal factor that influences a person's actions. Motives may arise from physiological needs, such as the need for food, water, and air, or from psychological needs such as self-esteem, recognition, achievement, and status. For example, if an employee feels inferior to others and has a need for greater recognition and self-esteem, the employee might be motivated to satisfy this need by returning to school to secure additional training. Employees are individuals by nature, making the total concept of motivation extremely complicated.

Motivation is a word that is tossed around a lot—motivation to lose weight, to accomplish more and to do just about anything! But what is motivation? Motivation is what drives people to success. Think about people who are motivated to lose weight—the more driven they are, the greater success they have. Motivation plays a critical role in employee productivity, quality, and speed of work. FLMs and other managers and leaders are typically held accountable to motivate their team, which is quite challenging.

Why Is Employee Motivation Important?

There are several reasons why employee motivation is important. Mainly because it allows FLMs and other managers and leaders to meet the organization's goals. Without a motivated workplace, organization could be placed in a very risky position.

Motivated employees can lead to increased productivity and allow an organization to achieve higher levels of output. Imagine having an employee who is not motivated at work. They will probably use the time at their desk surfing the internet for personal pleasure or even looking for another job. This is a waste of your time and resources.

Note that this is based on one employee. Try picturing the majority of your employees doing the same thing. This is not a position anybody wants to be in.

Benefits of Motivated Employees

Finding ways to increase motivation is crucial because it allows us to change behavior, develop competencies, be creative, set goals, grow interests, make plans, develop talents, and boost engagement. Employee motivation is highly important for every company due to the benefits that it brings to the company. Benefits include:

- *Increased employee commitment.* When employees are motivated to work, they will generally put their best effort in the tasks that are assigned to them.
- *Improved employee satisfaction.* Employee satisfaction is important for every organization because this can lead towards a positive growth for the organization.
- *Ongoing employee development.* Motivation can facilitate an employee reaching his/her personal goals, and can facilitate the self-development of an individual. Once that employee meets some initial goals, they realize the clear link between effort and results, which will further motivate them to continue at a high level.
- Improved employee efficiency. An employee's efficiency level is not only based on their abilities or qualifications. For the organization to get the very best results, an employee needs to have a good balance between the ability to perform the task given and willingness to want to perform the task. This balance can lead to an increase of productivity and an improvement in efficiency.

Similarly, the benefits of a well-motivated workforce can provide these advantages:

- Better productivity (amount produced per employee). This can lead to lower unit costs of production and so enable an organization to sell its products as a lower price.
- Lower levels of absenteeism as the employees are content with their working lives.
- Lower levels of staff turnover (the number of employees leaving the organization). This can lead to lower training and recruitment costs.
- Improved industrial/employees relations with unions and workers.
- Contented employees give the organization a good reputation as an employer so making it easier to recruit the best workers.
- Motivated employees are likely to improve product quality or the customer service associated with a product, for example.

It is important for FLMs to understand what motivation is, its benefits, and to be familiar with some of the motivation theories which can better help them understand employee's behavior and what motivates them.

Motivation Theories: A Brief Look

Motivation is the state of mind which pushes all human beings to perform things with the highest spirit and with positivity. FLMs will have to ensure that their direct reports are motivated. The various motivation theories help in understanding what will motivate people.

Motivation is a huge field of study. There are many theories of motivation. Some of the famous motivation theories include the following:

1. *Maslow's hierarchy of needs.* Abraham Maslow postulated that a person will be motivated when his needs are fulfilled. The need starts from the lowest level basic needs and keeps moving up as a lower level need is fulfilled. The hierarchy of needs are as follows:
   - *Physiological:* Physical survival necessities such as food, water, and shelter.
   - *Safety:* Protection from threats, deprivation, and other dangers.
   - *Social (belongingness and love):* The need for association, affiliation, friendship, and so on.
   - *Self-esteem:* The need for respect and recognition.
   - *Self-actualization:* The opportunity for personal development, learning, and fun/creative/challenging work. Self-actualization is the highest level need to which a human being can aspire.

   The FLM will have to understand the specific need of each one of their direct reports and accordingly work to help fulfil their needs.
2. *Hertzberg's two factor theory.* Hertzberg classified the needs into two broad categories namely hygiene factors and motivating factors. Hygiene factors are needed to make sure that an employee is not dissatisfied. Motivation factors are needed for ensuring employee's satisfaction and employee's motivation for higher performance. The mere presence of hygiene factors does not guarantee motivation, and presence of motivation factors in the absence of hygiene factors also does not work.
3. *McClelland's theory of needs.* McClelland affirms that we all have three motivating drivers, and it does not depend on our gender or age. One of these drives will be dominant in our behavior. The dominant drive depends on our life experiences. The three motivators are:
   - *Achievement:* a need to accomplish and demonstrate their own competence. People with a high need for achievement prefer tasks that provide for personal responsibility and results based on their own efforts. They also prefer quick acknowledgement of their progress.

- *Affiliation:* a need for love, belonging, and social acceptance. People with a high need for affiliation are motivated by being liked and accepted by others. They tend to participate in social gatherings and may be uncomfortable with conflict.
- *Power:* a need for control of their own work or the work of others. People with a high need for power desire situations in which they exercise power and influence over others. They aspire for positions with status and authority and tend to be more concerned about their level of influence than about effective work performance.

4. *Vroom's theory of expectancy.* Victor Vroom stated that people will be highly productive and motivated if two conditions are met: (a) people believe it is likely that their efforts will lead to successful results and (b) those people also believe they will be rewarded for their success. People will be motivated to exert a high level of effort when they believe there are relationships between the efforts they put forth, the performance they achieve, and the outcomes/rewards they receive.

5. *McGregor's theory X and theory Y.* Douglas McGregor formulated two distinct views of human beings based on participation of workers. The first is basically negative, labelled as Theory X, and the other is basically positive, labelled as Theory Y. Both kinds of people exist. Based on their nature they need to be managed accordingly.
   - *Theory X:* The traditional view of the work force holds that workers are inherently lazy, self-centered, and lacking ambition. Therefore, an appropriate management style is strong, top-down control.
   - *Theory Y:* This view postulates that workers are inherently motivated and eager to accept responsibility. An appropriate management style is to focus on creating a productive work environment coupled with positive rewards and reinforcement.
   - *Hawthorne Effect on Productivity.* The Hawthorne theory is a productivity theory based on the physical conditions employees work in. This includes lighting, shift hours, and breaks. It also includes observation as a key motivator for performance. Hawthorne found that people were more productive based on the idea of being observed rather than changes in their physical working conditions.
   - *Attribution Theory and Response to Success or Failure.* Attribution theory refers to how people respond to success or failure. By looking at the reasons for the end result, employees are able to identify why something succeeded or failed. This is implemented through employee reviews that cover various metrics

and identify root causes. For example, an employee meeting
all sales numbers might be making 50 outbound calls per day
while an employee not meeting standards is only making 10.
The success and failure are attributed to the outbound calls
and can be adjusted for the second employee.

Motivation is very much needed for employees in an organization to be
productive, and an FLM's or other leadership styles have an important role
to play. Motivation is not always based on financial rewards, but non-finan-
cial reward methods can also be used to derive the best out of employees.
Although individuals have their expectations, it is the FLM's responsibility
to develop and align with theories that are suitable to bring job satisfaction to their employees. However, FLMs must understand that there is no
single reliable theory to be used, a mixture of them can be utilized. In terms
of empowering the workforce, as will be highlighted at various points in
the remainder of this chapter, FLMs should encourage employees and give
them a platform to voice out their concerns on how they can be motivated.
Rewards and promotions following performance appraisals may be used to
boost employee morale as well as feedback. All employees should understand the company's vision and goals and work together towards those. In
some organizations, employees perform their duties in an assembly whereby if a certain section of employees is affected it will affect the whole plant.
Employees perform their duties diligently if they are inspired and motivated as the results will always be positive with efficient production. FLMs
and organizations which are results oriented will go all the way to motivate
their employees for them to reach their goals. And, to go all the way it is
important for FLMs to understand the motivation process.

The Motivation Process

In order to understand the motivation process, we need to consider
various job-related factors. These include general factors, such as the organizational environment and the rewards or punishments provided for particular behaviors. It also includes factors that are unique to each employee:
individual perceptions, the personal importance of different needs, personal traits, the ability to perform different types of work, and the amount
of effort the employee is willing to expend.

The following provides a detailed explanation of the motivation process. The process begins with the identification of a need. Money, status,
recognition, and promotion are typical job-related needs. For example,

let's follow an employee who wants to be promoted. The same steps and rationale explored below would apply to many identified needs.

Once the employee wants a promotion, the satisfaction of that desire is subject to Steps 2, 3, and 4. In Step 2, the employee assesses the degree of importance attached to being promoted. Is the employee willing to make the necessary sacrifices to meet this goal? Is the promotion so important that the employee is willing to put aside other activities in favor of seeking it? For example, if promotion is based on superior performance, is the employee willing to commit the extra time and effort necessary to perform in a superior manner? If not, the process terminates at this stage. If the employee is willing to make the commitment, the process proceeds to the third step.

In Step 3, pre-evaluation, the employee attempts to determine the availability of a promotion. The process is likely to terminate at this stage if no higher position is available. However, it is conceivable that the employee will continue with the evaluation although the promotion is not available, with the intention of securing a promotion in another organization. Assuming a promotion is available, the employee must consider any environmental constraints to securing it. The employee might ask: "Have I been here long enough? What does the job require? Do I have the necessary education? Do I have the necessary training and skills? Am I capable? Am I likely to get it? Is the boss's son or daughter standing in my way?" Again, a negative answer to one or more of these questions is likely to end the process.

If the responses to the questions raised in Step 3 are encouraging, Step 4 is initiated. In this step, the employee puts forth the effort necessary to cause the desired outcome. The employee makes a self-assessment to determine if he or she is meeting the employer's standards. In Step 5, the employee evaluates the outcome, asking, "Did I get my reward?" Step 6 analyzes the outcomes of Step 5. Were the employee's efforts justified? If not, the long-term implications (Step 7) could be serious; but if so, the long-term implications could be positive, giving the employee the self-confidence to tackle the process of satisfying new needs.

Just like the employee in our example, FLMs like Jackie Ford must recognize that other employees may be motivated by a bonus or the opportunity for a pay increase and may be willing to work harder to get it. For today's FLM to be successful in motivating employees, it pays to understand the process of motivation.

Methods Commonly Used to Motivate Employees

Experts are saying that today's companies must concentrate on the three R's, recruiting, retraining, and retaining high-quality people. Motivation is involved in all of them, as companies try to appeal to employees' higher-level needs. As industry trends continue to shift toward self-managing teams, employees cannot be expected to turn into motivated self-managers overnight, they need to be given the proper tools through development and training programs.

When employees appear to be unmotivated, FLMs like Jackie Ford will want to size up the situation, identify and understand what is happening, and formulate a response. The description of the motivation process, discussed in the previous section, should help FLMs identify and understand the problems they face. This section describes methods FLMS can use to motivate employees via pay or compensation and nonmonetary ways.

Motivation and Pay/Compensation

Pay for Performance

Frederick Taylor popularized financial incentives—financial rewards paid to workers whose production exceeds some predetermined standard—in the late 1800s. Today's employers use many incentives to motivate employees. All incentive plans are pay-for-performance plans because they tie workers' pay to performance.

Pay for performance is probably the first thing that comes to mind when most people think about motivating employees. Pay for performance refers to any compensation method that ties pay to the quantity or quality of work the person produces. Piecework is the oldest and most popular individual incentive plan. Piecework pay plans are probably the most familiar: Earnings are tied directly to the number of items the worker produces in the form of a "piece rate" for each unit he or she turns out. For example, an employee who gets 40 cents apiece for stamping out circuit boards would make $40 for stamping out 100 a day and $80 for stamping out 200. Sales commissions are another familiar example.

Piecework plans have a firm foundation in motivation theory. Behavior modification theories state that people will continue behavior that is rewarded, and pay for performance plans, of course, tie rewards directly to behavior.

Pay for performance plans of all types—including those that let employees share in profits by paying them with shares of company stock—are becoming more popular because they make sense. Pay-for-performance programs can be designed to reward individuals or groups. In terms of time orientation, they can be attached to short- and long-term goals.

In the United States employees generally prefer individual pay-for-performance programs over group pay-for-performance programs. Pay-for-performance programs aimed at rewarding individuals can be broadly organized and categorized using the categories of merit pay and variable pay.

Companies like IKEA and PepsiCo are successful examples of companies that use pay for performance. For example, at IKEA employee motivation is considered important when an organization is building relationships for better communication with their employees. IKEA once conducted a special bonus for its employees by pledging the entire day's sales revenue for its employees. That day the sales doubled and all the employees received $2,400 each.

Variable Pay Plans and Gainsharing Plans

Variable pay is an umbrella. Under the umbrella you can find any number of bonuses, incentives, commissions, and other cash compensation that is contingent on something happening. Depending on who you talk to, this could be either potential pay ("I can earn this money if I just work hard enough for it") or pay at risk ("This is money I'm not guaranteed, so I don't trust that I'll receive it"). People differ in whether and how much they are amenable to variable pay, depending on their job level, job function, life stage, financial goals, and personal risk versus reward calculus.

- "Bonus" falls under the umbrella. Bonuses may or may not be tied to a plan, they may or may not be connected to performance, and they are typically backwards in orientation. "Dear employee. You did this thing. This thing worked out well; I liked it. Here's some money to say thank you."
- "Incentive" also falls under the umbrella. Incentives are associated with a specific plan, focused on performance and are future-facing. "Dear employee. I'd like to see you do this thing. If you do, I'll give you some money. And in fact, if you do even better, I'll give you even more money." Because they're tied to a plan, incentives tend to have better return on the compensation investment.

Variable pay plans put some portion of the employee's pay at risk, subject to the organization meeting its productivity/financial goals. That is, variable pay plans usually means incentive plans that tie a group's pay to company profitability (although some experts use variable pay to include incentive plans for individual employees); profit-sharing plans are one example. In either case, when both the company succeeds and the employee succeeds, the employer hands out a performance-based check, and the amount depends on how well the company performs during the year and how well the employee performs during an evaluation period. For many companies, employee performance is measured at the end of 12 months.

In one such plan at the DuPont Company for example, employees could voluntarily place up to six percent of their base pay at risk. If they then met the department's earnings projections, they would get that six percent back plus additional percentage, depending on how much the department exceeded its earnings projections.

Other companies have gainsharing plans. These are incentive plans that engage many or all employees in a common effort to achieve a company's productivity goals. Implementing a gain-sharing plan requires several steps. The company establishes specific performance measures, such as the cost per unit produced, and a funding formula, such as "47% of savings go to employees." Management decides how to divide and distribute any cost savings between the employees and the company, and among employees themselves. If employees are then able to achieve the desired cost savings, they share in the resulting gains.

FLMs should understand that variable pay plans can motivate employees, which is one of the pros of this type of incentive. Although some employees aren't motivated by compensation and benefits, a year-end bonus can prod many workers to a higher level of performance. In this case, a variable pay plan is akin to dangling a carrot in front of workers who otherwise would perform just satisfactory work rather than strive for excellent ratings come performance appraisal time. High performance ratings are a boost for employees, but the challenge for FLMs and their organizations is to sustain employees' job performance levels beyond the season when companies disburse performance pay.

The prevalence and use of variable pay has increased over time, and this 2018 data showed that variable pay continues to be a prominent player in the modern compensation landscape. Approximately 71% of all organizations surveyed said that they offer some type of variable pay. That number is even higher among top-performing organizations—where 79% offer variable pay (versus 70% of typical organizations).

Merit Pay

When most employees do a good job, they expect to be rewarded with at least a merit raise at the end of the year. It is different from a bonus in that it provides a continuing pay increase, while a bonus is a one-time payment. Traditional merit raises are gradually being replaced by lump-sum increases that, like bonuses, are awarded in a single payment that does not become part of the employee's continuing pay. The term merit pay is more often used for white-collar employees, particularly professional, office, and clerical employees.

To the extent to which it is actually tied to performance, the prospect of a merit raise may focus the employee's attention on the link between performance and rewards. A year is a long time to wait for a reward, however, so relying too heavily on merit raises as rewards could be dangerous, as the reinforcement benefits of merit pay are somewhat suspect. The motivational basis for the merit plan can also be undermined by inadequate employee evaluations. You may have personally experienced the questionable nature of some performance appraisal systems, including the fact that some FLMs take the easy way out and rate everyone's performance about the same, regardless of actual effort.

Merit pay is the subject of much debate. Advocates argue that just awarding pay raises across the board (without regard to individual merit) may actually detract from performance, by showing employees they'll be rewarded regardless of their performance. Detractors argue, for instance, that because many appraisals are unfair, so too is the merit pay you base them on. Merit pay effectiveness depends on differentiating among employees.

Spot Awards or Rewards

As its name implies, a spot award is a financial award given to an employee literally "on the spot," as soon as superior performance is observed. Programs such as these have been around for some time. Spot awards are designed to recognize special contributions, as they occur, for a specific project or task. Spot awards are generally for a special contribution accomplishment over a relatively short time period. A spot award lets employees know that someone has noticed their noteworthy contribution. At the same time, it recognizes and reinforces the behaviors and values that are important at an organization. For example, in the early 1900s, Thomas J. Watson, Sr., the founder of IBM, reportedly wrote checks on the spot to employees doing an outstanding job.

Spot rewards should not be something expected by employees following the achievement of every goal. In reality, when goals are very difficult, rewarding people only if they reach their goals can actually hurt performance and does not serve as a motivator for employees. This is because people's motivation and self-efficacy decrease once they realize their efforts could be for nothing in a bonus system where there is no reward if you fail to reach the goal. The negative effects disappear when people are rewarded for their effort toward achieving a goal, rather than achievement of a goal itself.

Ultimately, FLMs and their organizations should use spot awards as a sign of recognition and appreciation of the behaviors that they want to encourage from employees in the future. Spot awards are more effective when they are used to recognize and encourage highly effective behaviors, as opposed to being used as a motivator or reward for past accomplishments.

FLMS would do well to remember the rules of reinforcement. That is, the motivational value of spot awards comes from using them as a tool for positive reinforcement. Recognizing and rewarding employees for displaying certain behaviors increases the odds of that behavior occurring again in the future. There are four major factors that influence the value of rewards used for positive reinforcement.

- *Contingency.* To be effective, spot rewards must be tied to demonstration of certain behaviors. FLMs should have clear criteria to use as a guide for when to give employees different types of spot awards. This is also important for ensuring equity by creating consistency across FLMs in their use of awards. Whether an employee receives spot awards should depend on whether they display behaviors that the organization believes are exceptional, and not their manager's attitudes about what constitutes exceptional behavior.
- *Immediacy.* In the case of motivation, immediacy equals effectiveness. When FLMs forget about a reward and push it off to the next week, or worse, wait until the end of the year to distribute rewards to employees, the reward will have less effect on motivation than if it had been awarded immediately following the behavior.
- *Satiation.* When the same type of reward is used over and over again, it can lose its reinforcing value. In other words, there is such a thing as "too much of a good thing" in the context of reinforcement. For example, monetary rewards can reduce intrinsic motivation if they are overused. If an FLM's organization uses nonmonetary rewards in addition to cash bonuses, consider switching up the type of reward given to employees. Keep in mind that reward type should be reflective of the behavior demonstrated, and that not all employees will value the same type of rewards equally. Understanding what motivates each employee can help managers to determine the most appropriate type of reward.
- *Size.* The size or value of spot awards should reflect the behavior demonstrated. It is important that FLMs are thoughtful in this decision and avoid choosing arbitrary values for the rewards given to employees. Employees will use past reward values to create an expectation level against which to judge future rewards. If the

reward does not meet or exceed this expectation level, employees may feel frustrated and unmotivated.

FLMs should also understand the limits of rewards like spot rewards. When determined and distributed the right way, spot rewards can be an effective way for FLMs to encourage and motivate employees. But used incorrectly, spot awards can hurt motivation. Even when used correctly, over reliance on spot awards can undermine their value. The motivation people get from positive reinforcement fades quickly. Receiving a spot reward might increase their motivation and satisfaction for a short time, but eventually, the feelings fade. The best way to ensure that your employees are truly motivated at work is to ensure that they find their work motivating. And this requires FLMs and other managers and leaders engaging employees and truly understanding their unique skills and capabilities at a deeper level.

Skill-Based Pay

Most FLMs are probably aware of the fact that in most organizations pay is determined by the level of the job responsibilities. Thus, CEOs make more than presidents, presidents generally make more than vice presidents, sales managers make more than assistant sales managers, and secretary IVs make more than secretary IIIs because higher-level jobs have more responsibilities.

Skill-based pay is different in that you are paid for the range, depth, and types of skills and knowledge you are capable of using, rather than for the level of responsibility you exercise in the job you currently hold. The difference is important: It is conceivable that in a company with a skill-based pay plan a secretary III could be paid more per hour than a secretary IV, for instance, if it turns out that the person who happened to be the secretary III had more skills than did the person in the secretary IV job.

A skill-based plan was implemented at one organization's manufacturing facility. The organization was trying to boost the flexibility of its factory workforce by implementing a pay plan that would encourage employees to develop a wider range of skills in order to make it easier to find employees able to take over any vacant position in the plant as the plant's needs changed.

In this plan, the employees were paid based on their attained skill levels. For each type of job in the plant, workers could attain one of three levels of skill: limited ability (ability to perform simple tasks without direction), partial proficiency, and full competence (ability to analyze and solve problems associated with that job). After starting a job, employees were tested periodically to see whether they had earned certification at the next higher skill level. If so, they received higher pay even though they continued to hold the same job. This system allowed higher-skilled workers to receive higher pay than others doing the same job. Employees could then switch to other jobs in the plant, again starting at skill level one and working their way up if they so desired. In this way, employees could earn more pay for more skills, particularly as they became skilled at a variety of jobs, and the company ended up with a more highly skilled and, therefore, more flexible workforce.

Skill-based pay makes sense in terms of what we know about motivation. People have a vision of who they can be, and they seek to fulfill their potential. The individual development emphasis of skill-based pay helps employees to do exactly that. Skill-based pay also appeals to an employee's sense of self-efficacy in that the reward is a formal and concrete recognition that the person can do a more challenging job and do it well.

FLMs can use skill-based pay to motivate employees by encouraging them to be in charge of their own development and control their own work lives. In the end, in the skill-based pay plan, employees put their efforts to increase their skill base in order to get higher pay. Skill-based plans are generally more accepted by employees because it is easy for them to see the connection between the plan, the work, and the size of the paycheck. Consequently, the plans provide strong motivation for individuals to increase skills that in the end benefit them and their organizations.

In accordance with most theories of motivations described earlier in this chapter, for pay or incentive plans to work, certain criteria are advisable, as follows.

1. Rewards must be linked to performance and be measurable.
2. The rewards must satisfy individual needs.
3. The rewards must be agreed on by the FLM (or manager) and employees.
4. The rewards must be believable and achievable by employees.

Nonmonetary Ways of Motivating Employees

Employees who can behave autonomously, solve problems, and take the initiative are apt to be the very ones who will leave if they find their own needs are not being met; namely,

1. the need for work–life balance,
2. the need to expand skills,

3. the need for a positive work environment, and
4. the need to matter—to find meaning in their work.

While one of the most effective ways of motivating employees is an age-old, tried and tested one—give them a raise; as evidenced from the needs mentioned above, there are many other nonmonetary ways that an employee might feel motivated to give a 110% to the organization that they are part of. This section discusses some nonmonetary ways FLMs can motivate their direct reports and improve productivity within their group, team, department, and ultimately the organization.

Recognition

Most people like to feel appreciated. In one study, over two-thirds of respondents said they highly valued day-to-day recognition from their FLMs, peers, and team members. If you have ever spent a day cooking a meal for someone who gobbled it up without saying a word, or 2 weeks doing a report for a boss who did not even say, "Thanks," let alone, "Good job," you know the importance of having your work recognized and appreciated.

The motivating power of being recognized—and not necessarily just financially—for a job well-done makes sense in terms of motivation theory. Immediate recognition can be a powerful reinforcer of good performance. Recognition also helps to satisfy people's need for a sense of achievement.

Many companies therefore formalize the common sense process of saying, "Thank you for a job well done." For example, one organization gives what it calls bell-ringer awards for good work: a bell is rung in the corridor while the person is formally recognized by his or her boss. At ShackNation, the CEO recognizes teams on work anniversaries and birthdays by writing a hand-written note thanking them for the hard work they put in each day and highlighting some of their recent achievements. O. C. Tanner works to keep recognition fresh and unique with reward initiatives ranging from custom trophies, to social buttons, merchandise, gift cards, and emblematic and symbolic awards. More importantly, they work hard on building a culture that has employees recognizing great work of other employees. In turn, this helps employees build better relationships and a teamwork mentality.

The tech giant, Google, wants their employees to feel valued when they walk into work. As such, Google has created a "gThanks" program where employees can give recognition to their coworkers for a job well done. Besides giving thanks, employees can also nominate each other with the peer bonuses program where coworkers can receive a bonus of $175. Another aspect of this employee participation culture is a designated area developed from one Google department called "Wall of Happy" where workers can place thank you notes and emails that recognize hard work and achievements to display and motivate others. Lastly, other Google recognition awards range from spot bonuses to personalized awards.

FLMs must identify which kinds of behaviors they reward. "The things that get rewarded get done" is what one author calls, "the greatest management principle in the world." With this in mind the author describes ten types of behavior that should be recognized to motivate high performance. Organizations and individual FLMs should reward the following:

- solid solutions instead of quick fixes,
- risk taking instead of risk avoiding,
- applied creativity instead of mindless conformity,
- decisive action instead of paralysis by analysis,
- smart work instead of busywork,
- simplification instead of needless complication,
- quietly effective workers instead of self-promoting talkers,
- quality work instead of fast work,
- loyalty instead of turnover,
- working together instead of working against each other, and
- lack of absenteeism and tardiness.

Job Redesign

FLMs have long been concerned about the unmotivating qualities of highly specialized, short-cycle, assembly-line jobs that are monotonous and boring. In an effort to respond to this problem, many employers set up programs to redesign those jobs. The term job design refers to the number and nature of activities in a job. The basic issue in job redesign is whether jobs should be more specialized or, at the other extreme, more "enriched" and less routine.

An important aspect of job redesign FLMs can make use of is job rotation, or cross-training. Job rotation involves moving task responsibilities from one employee to another. Those in jobs that require monotonous tasks can benefit from this practice.

Job redesign can help increase not only job satisfaction, but also the employee's individual commitment to the organization. A reduction in boredom and increase in motivation benefits both the employee and the company. Thus, by taking the components of job design and introducing job redesign, FLMs can help motivate employees in a different way and better address employees being bored, possibly looking elsewhere, or actually leaving the organization.

Empowering Employees

Empowering employees has become a popular approach to work organizations. It means giving employees the authority, tools, and information they need to do their jobs with greater autonomy, as well as the self-confidence required to perform their new duties effectively. Empowering is inherently a motivational approach. It boosts employees' feelings of self-efficacy and enables them to meet their potential, satisfying high-level needs for achievement, recognition, and self-actualization. Empowerment results in changes in employees' outlook: from feeling powerless to believing strongly in their own personal effectiveness. The result is that employees become willing to take more initiative and persevere in achieving their goals and their organization's vision even in the face of obstacles. Additionally, studies show that empowered employees are more satisfied with their jobs, and it's one of the biggest factors in creating a great customer experience. Instead of waiting for results, issues can be solved immediately in the way that best meets customers' needs.

Today, organizations often empower their employees. Airlines are notorious for requiring customers to go through an arduous process to get some kind of service recovery if there is an issue with their flights. However, American Airlines recently started a new program that allows flight attendants to give customers complimentary miles on the spot. The goal is to avoid customers filing complaints and to make sure everyone gets off the plane feeling good about their experience.

Costco, the bulk warehouse store is famous for its no-risk return policy, which means customers don't need a receipt to make a return and there isn't a time limit on when things can be brought back. Instead of having to turn away customers who are not satisfied with their purchases, employees have the power to take back items, make exchanges, and ensure issues get resolved.

More than two decades ago, organizations like Saturn began to empower their work teams. At Saturn Corporation, for example, empowered, self-managing work teams were responsible for a variety of duties. For each team, these duties include planning the team's work and schedule; designing and determining team member job assignments; resolving internal conflicts; selecting new members of the work unit; replacing any absentee members; working directly with suppliers, customers, and other partners maintaining and repairing the equipment it uses; seeking improvements in quality, cost, and the work environment; and performing within its budget.

Empowering does not just mean assigning broader job responsibilities. Teams also need the training, skills, and tools to allow them to do their jobs, such as knowing how to make consensus decisions. Firms like Saturn also made sure their FLMs actually let their people do their jobs as assigned.

In virtually all cases of empowering employees, employees find empowerment exciting, while employers find it helps workers to enjoy using their potential to achieve new goals, thereby boosting motivation and employee commitment. The guidelines below can make FLMs more successful in empowering their employees:

- Make sure people understand their responsibilities.
- Give them authority equal to the responsibilities assigned to them
- Set standards of excellence that will require employees to strive to do *all* work "right the first time."
- Provide them with training that will enable them to meet the standards.
- Give them information they need to do their job well.
- Trust them.
- Give them permission to fail.
- Treat them with dignity and respect.
- Provide them with feedback on their performance.
- Recognize them for their achievements.

Goal Setting

Have you ever set your sights on a goal—becoming an FLM or earning enough money for a trip abroad, for instance? What effect did setting the goal have on you? Setting specific goals with your employees can be one of the simplest yet most powerful ways of motivating them.

There are many ideas on how to set goals that motivate employees. Chapter 4 provides a more extensive description of goal setting for the purpose of planning. Here is a summary:

- *Be clear and specific.* Employees who are given specific goals usually perform better than those who are not.
- *Make goals measurable and verifiable.* Whenever possible, goals should be stated in quantitative terms and should include target dates or deadlines for accomplishment.
- *Make goals challenging but realistic.* Goals should be challenging but not so difficult that they appear impossible or unrealistic.

- *Set goals together.* If employees participate in setting their goals, they will usually perform better.

Lifelong Learning

Many employers today face a tremendous dilemma. On the one hand, in order to be competitive, a company needs highly-committed employees who exercise self-discipline and basically do their jobs as if they owned the company. On the other hand, competitive pressures have forced many companies to downsize, which decreases employee motivation and commitment. They may question whether it pays for them to work their hearts out for the company.

Organizations are increasingly using lifelong learning to address both of these issues simultaneously. Lifelong learning provides extensive and career-long training, from basic remedial skills to advanced decision-making techniques. Implemented properly, lifelong learning programs can achieve three things. First, the training, development, and education provide employees with the decision-making and other knowledge, skills, and abilities they need to work competently in a demanding, team-based job. Second, the opportunity for lifelong learning is inherently motivational: It gives employees the ability to fulfill their potential, it boosts their sense of self-efficacy, and it helps them gain the sense of achievement that motivation theorists argue is so important. Third, lifelong learning can help alleviate the potential negative effects of downsizing by giving employees useful and marketable new skills.

It is never easy to evaluate the success of lifelong learning initiatives because not all employees choose to participate, and many other factors affect productivity and employee motivation. The evidence suggests, however, that lifelong learning programs improve commitment, skills, motivation, and possibly productivity too.

FLMs can help their organizations make use of lifelong learning as a motivator by working to build a company culture that supports lifelong learning. This means that their organizations will need to establish cultures focused on personal growth.

One of the ways to cultivate a learning culture at work is to tie learning into performance. At each review (annual, or more frequent one-on-ones), it is worth establishing learning and development goals for employees. FLMs and their organizations must make sure these goals are documented and can be measured. They can be as simple as cross-training in another department or as ambitious as attaining an advanced degree.

Most people learn at work through their peers. By identifying subject matter experts, organizations can integrate them into the learning environment. This can be done through peer-led training or simple on the job shadowing.

Linking learning activities with core competencies through subject matter experts helps foster growth as well as increases institutional knowledge. Additionally, it also encourages mentorship and cross-generational collaboration, and helps to future-proof the FLM's organization. As FLMs and subject matter experts move on or retire, their organizations don't want that knowledge to go away with them.

In sum, nonmonetary ways of motivating employees do not involve money payments. These are also important in motivating employees as they bring in psychological and emotional satisfaction to them. These include so many techniques. People do work for money—but they work even more for meaning in their lives. FLMs should understand that regardless of which theory of employee motivation they may prefer, the best way to motivate their direct reports is to focus on things like providing them with interesting work, appreciation, pay, good working conditions, and job security.

Special Problems in Motivating Particular Groups of Employees

FLMs today face specific challenges in motivating special groups of employees. This concluding section looks at some of the unique problems FLMs face in trying to motivate contingent workers, groups of diverse and cross-cultural employees, low-skilled workers who perform repetitive tasks, and baby busters. We also address how to motivate yourself.

Contingent Workers

Contingent workers are a group of people who do not have a contract that explicitly defines any long-term employment with a company. Their work is exclusively based on short-term engagements.

Employees who do not want to work in a certain company for a long period of time also fall under the category of contingent workers. Such employees may be defined as freelancers, consultants, or independent contractors. They can either work in the company's offices or remotely. They are highly skilled and experts in their areas of specialization.

Contingent workers are not considered employees of a company. They work as freelancers under a contract or on a temporary basis. Unlike permanent employees, their retention depends on the continued existence of the job at hand.

Contingent workers do not receive salaries. Instead, they receive payments or commissions for the work done. They are not liable for benefits like contracted employees and are responsible for their own taxes. As such, they do not identify with the organization in the same way or display the same commitment as permanent employees.

Contingent workers cannot be told how to complete a project, as they work for themselves. The organization's main focus when dealing with them is on the results of the project, not how it is being done.

What will motivate involuntarily temporary employees? An obvious answer is the opportunity for permanent status. In those cases where permanent employees are selected from a pool of temporaries, the temporaries will often work hard in hopes of becoming permanent. A less obvious answer is the opportunity for training. The ability of temporary employees to find new jobs is largely dependent on their skills. If employees see that their current jobs can help develop useful skills, then their motivation will increase.

There are a number of things FLMs (and their organization) can do to keep contingent workers engaged and motivated. Here are some tips:

- *Ensure the entire experience is seamless and enjoyable.* If you want to hire the very best contingent workers in your industry, then you need to nail the entire contingent work experience. This will include everything from the hiring process, onboarding, payments, all the way to the exit process.
- *Share information and processes with contingent workers.* Where possible, include contingent workers in some of the processes that are usually reserved for permanent workers—such as onboarding, organizational learning, and expertise sharing—this will make non-permanent workers feel like a valued member of your group or team. A contingent worker that feels engaged with your organization will work with increased efficiency, passion, and effectiveness towards achieving your organization's overall vision and goals.
- *Frequent communication.* One of the main reasons that a large number of workers choose freelance work is the opportunity to be able to choose where they work and when they work. This means that it is likely that many of your contingent workers will be remote, rarely (if at all) coming to your organization. Thus, it is important that you communicate with them regularly, either by video or voice communication. Not only will this make them feel like a valuable member of your group or team, but it is also a

great tool to clearly communicate KPI's and current objectives to your contract workers.

From an equity standpoint, FLMs should also consider the motivation problems that result from mixing permanent and temporary workers who earn significantly different amounts. When temps work alongside permanent employees who earn more and get benefits for doing the same job, the performance of temps is likely to suffer. Separating such employees or converting all employees to a variable-pay or skill-based pay plan might help lessen this problem.

Diversified Workforce

Many people think diversity in the workplace refers mainly to gender and race, but diversity also refers to differences in age, culture, religion, sexual orientation, and physical ability. The contemporary perspective on workplace diversity also recognizes individual differences in temperament and other personal qualities. All this creates quite the challenge for FLMs who must motivate their direct reports.

As evidenced by the changing demographics of the United States workforce there are many cultural groups represented. On any given day an FLM may have groups of employees who are Asians with ties to Japan, China, and Thailand, Spanish speakers from Mexico, El Salvador, Cuba, and Spain; African-Americans with ties to Africa, and an array of Russian immigrants, Middle Eastern immigrants, and many other culturally diverse individuals. Each of these groups may present the FLM with unique motivation problems. Do the motivation strategies presented above work the same way for all of these culturally diverse individuals? The answer to this question is important for today's FLMs who wish to create an optimal motivational climate for their employees, whether it be in a domestic or a foreign-based organization.

Managing Diversity

Understanding motivation requires understanding how to manage diversity. Every employee has his own background, beliefs, attitudes, values, and way of thinking. One might be motivated by financial rewards, another by perks, still another by job quality. To further complicate matters, motivations change as employees' age or change roles. Rather than treat everyone the same or apply broad assumptions, FLMs must understand what makes each employee unique and build on those strengths.

As noted earlier, today's FLMs must realize that not everyone is motivated by money. Not everyone wants a challenging job. The needs of women, singles, immigrants, the physically and mentally challenged, senior citizens, and others may differ from those of a White American male with three dependents. Several examples can make this point clearer. Employees who are attending college or training classes typically place a high value on flexible work schedules. They may be attracted to organizations that offer flexible work hours, job sharing, or temporary assignments. Parents also have special needs. A father may prefer to work the midnight to 8:00 a.m. shift in order to spend time with his children after school when his wife is at work.

Assessing employees' needs, preferred rewards, work patterns, and sensitivities to workplace practices has become an important part of FLM responsibilities. If FLMs are going to maximize their employees' motivation, they must understand and respond to a variety of concerns. How? The key is flexibility. Be ready to design work schedules, compensation plans, benefits, physical work settings, and the like to reflect your employees' diverse needs. This might include offering child and elder care, flexible work hours, and job sharing for employees with family responsibilities. It also might include offering flexible leave policies for immigrants who occasionally want to make extensive return trips to their homelands, creating work teams for employees who come from countries with a strong collectivist orientation, or allowing employees who are taking courses to vary their work schedules from semester to semester or course to course.

Employees Doing Highly Repetitive Tasks

We next consider the motivation problems of employees who do standardized, repetitive jobs. For instance, working on an assembly line or transcribing court reports are jobs that workers often find boring and stressful. Motivating individuals in these jobs will be easier if they are selected carefully. People vary in their tolerance for ambiguity. Many people prefer jobs that have a minimal amount of discretion and variety. These people are obviously a better match for standardized jobs than individuals with strong needs for growth and autonomy. Standardized jobs should also be the first considered for automation, which would remove the problem.

Many standardized jobs, especially in the manufacturing sector, pay well. This makes it relatively easy to fill vacancies. While high pay can ease recruitment problems and reduce turnover, it does not necessarily create highly motivated workers.

Unfortunately, some jobs have little else to offer. This includes jobs that cannot realistically be redesigned. Some tasks, for instance, are far more efficiently done on assembly lines than in teams. This leaves limited options.

An FLM may not be able to do much more than try to make a bad situation tolerable by being empathetic and creating a pleasant work climate. This might include providing clean and attractive work surroundings, ample work breaks, and the opportunity to socialize with colleagues.

Motivating Different Generations of Workers: Boomers, Gen X, Millennials, and Gen Z

For the first time in the nation's history, four to five generations are working side by side in the workplace. As FLMs and others work beyond retirement age, many organizations are trying to manage a generation gap of more than 50 years among their oldest and youngest employees.

Although there is no official consensus of the exact birth dates that define each generation, they are generally broken into five distinct groups:

- Traditionalists (born 1926 to 1945),
- Baby Boomers (born between 1946 to 1964),
- Generation X (born between 1965 to 1980),
- Generation Y/Millennials (born in 1981 to 2000), and
- Generation Z (born 2000 to 2020).

The diverse perspectives, motivations, attitudes, and needs of these generations have changed the dynamics of workplace setting. A little insight into the differences among the generations can help explain the needs and expectations of an age-diverse workforce. By learning the motivations and generational footprint of each segment, FLMs can leverage their own talents and capitalize on the diversity of their direct reports.

Clearly, there's something interesting going on in the workplace right now given that it is composed of multiple generations working side-by-side for the first time that in modern history. That can be a challenge for FLMs who are trying to bring their direct reports or team together in accomplishing a shared goal. But, that can be accomplished once they understand how each generation wants to be motivated.

Traditionalists

Since this generation was born between 1926 and 1945, you don't see many of them in the workplace. However, they still impressively make up around three percent of the workforce.

This is the generation who firmly believes in an "honest day's pay for an honest day's work." They are extremely loyal and enjoy being respected for that. Since they're conformists, they value most job titles and money.

Baby Boomers

Born between 1946 and 1964, this group is also referred to as the "me" generation. They are predominately in their 40s and 50s and are well-established in their careers. As such, they hold positions of power and authority in many organizations.

Boomers are often ambitious, loyal, work-centric, and cynical. They prefer monetary rewards, but also enjoy nonmonetary rewards like flexible retirement planning and peer recognition. They also don't require constant feedback and have "all is well unless you say something" mindset.

Since Boomers are so goal-oriented generation they can be motivated by promotions, professional development, and having their expertise valued and acknowledged. Prestigious job titles and recognition like office size and parking spaces are also important to Boomers.

They can also be motivated through high levels of responsibility, perks, praise, and challenge.

It's expected that around 70 million Boomers will be retired by 2020. So, they're also paying attention to 401(k) matching funds, sabbaticals, and catch-up retirement funding.

Gen X

Generation X has around 44 to 50 million Americans who were born between 1965 and 1980. They are smaller than the previous and succeeding generations, but they're often credited for bringing work-life balance. This is because they saw first-hand how their hardworking parents became so burnout.

Members of the generation spent a lot of time alone as children. This created an entrepreneurial spirit with them. In fact, Gen Xers make up the highest percentage of startup founders.

Even if they're not starting their own businesses, Gen Xers prefer to work independently with minimal supervision. They also value opportunities to grow and make choices, as well as having relationships with mentors. They also believe that promotions should be based on competence and not by rank, age, or seniority. Gen Xers can be motivated by flexible schedules, benefits like telecommuting, recognition from the boss, and bonuses, stock, and gift cards as monetary rewards

Millennials (Generation Y)

Born after 1980, the tech-savvy generation is currently the largest age group in the country. They have more recently come into their own in the workforce. They're the fastest growing segment of today's workforce.

For some Millennials, they're content with selling their skills to the highest bidder. That means unlike Boomers, they're not as loyal. In most cases, they have no problem jumping from one organization to another.

That is not to say that you can't motivate this generation because you can by offering skills training, mentoring, and feedback. Culture is also extremely important for Millennials.

They want to work in an environment where they can collaborate with others. Flexible schedules, time off, and embracing the latest technology to communicate are also important for Gen Y. Millennials also thrive when there's structure, stability, continued learning opportunities, and immediate feedback. If you do offer monetary rewards, they prefer stock options.

Gen Z

This generation is right on the heels of Millennials. And, they are starting to enter the workplace. Even more interesting, they make-up one-quarter of America's population, making this generation larger than Baby Boomers or Millennials.

This generation is motivated by social rewards, mentorship, and constant feedback. They also want to be meaningful and be given responsibility. Like their predecessors, they also demand flexible schedules.

Other ways to motivate this generation is through experiential rewards and badges such as those earned in gaming and opportunities for personal growth. They also expect structure, clear directions, and transparency. What's most intriguing about Gen Zers is that more than 50% prefer face-to-face communication.

Motivating a Multigenerational Workforce

To manage across the generations FLMs have to learn to be mindful of each other and treat each other as individuals. No matter what generation we are from, it's too easy to keep doing what we are doing now and acting like each generation is (or should be), motivated by the same things we are.

Even if an FLM's professional–management instincts say, "No—of course they don't do this," FLMs have to be careful that their actions don't demonstrate that they do. FLMs always have to be mindful of their and others actions and stay open to listening to others.

FLMs should use everyone's ability and goals. However, it's still their responsibility to make every employee, regardless of their generation, feel engaged. FLMs also need to integrate them into the organization's culture and make them feel valued. That may sound like a tall order to fill, but FLMs can achieve that by first making sure that they have hired the right person for the job. They also have to make sure that they are a good fit within their organization's culture.

FLMs also need to ensure that each employee believes and can see that there is purpose and meaning behind their work. Creating and sharing a mission or vision should help them understand why their job exists.

Finally, FLMs and their organizations should not forget to encourage work–life balance, offer health and welfare benefits, and provide rewards that *their* employees would care about.

Motivating Yourself

Throughout this chapter we have addressed practical ways FLMs can motivate employees. In concluding this chapter, this section suggests ways for FLMs to keep themselves motivated. As a current or future FLM, you may find that you concentrate so much on motivating your employees that you forget to motivate yourself. Zig Ziglar, author of *See You at the Top*, offers some suggestions FLMs should find useful for motivating themselves:

- *Give yourself a pep talk.* If you expect your employees to believe in you, you have to believe in yourself.
- *Set goals.* Be specific about the goals you want to achieve. Create a "wild idea sheet" listing "everything you want to be, do, or have."
- *Think positive and have reasons to support your outlook.* It is important to be enthusiastic about what you are doing, but you also need to *know* what you are doing. Get the training you need to support a positive attitude.
- *If necessary get professional counseling* from the Human Resource Management Department. There may be times in your career

when you need help. Do not be afraid to ask for it from someone who has the wisdom and necessary knowledge to assist you.

- *Control your environment.* Control as many elements of your environment as you can. Exercise and eat well. Listen to music with positive messages, especially in the morning.
- *Use positive words to convey your message.* Learn to phrase your communications in a positive manner. This will give you better results and make you feel good about yourself and your co-workers.
- *Leave every encounter on a positive note.* Try to end every challenging situation with another person on a good note. This may be difficult sometimes, but doing so will make you feel better, and will make the other person feel good as well. The other person will remember you favorably for it.

So, How Can FLMs Increase Employee Motivation?

Here are three immediate actionable tips for FLMs to increase employee motivation in your workplace.

- Improve communication. The easiest way to increase employee motivation is by having positive communication at the workplace. Not relying only on emails but by making sure they talk to their employees in person and even on a personal level, if possible.

  Try setting aside some time each day to talk with employees or you can join them during coffee breaks instead of sitting at your desk. By doing so, you actually make employees feel as though you are part of the team; a leader instead of just the boss. Experts agree that team communication is super valuable.

  Employees also want to see the organization that they are working for succeed. Many have excellent ideas, ranging from money saving to operational improvements. FLMs must make an effort to take some time to ask and listen to suggestions. Nothing is more worthwhile than feeling valued.
- Value individual contributions. FLMs should assure their employees that their individual efforts and contribution plays an important part of the organization's overall goals and direction. Employees will take pride and be engaged in their work if they are aware how their efforts create an impact on the organization; regardless of how big or small their contributions are.

  FLMs do not have to reward their employees with gifts every single time they do a good job at a task. At times, a simple,

"Thank you" or "Great job" will suffice. These meaningful words acknowledge effort, build loyalty, and encourage people to work even harder.

- Positive workplace environment. Sometimes, the employees lack motivation because their workplace does not have a positive work environment. To fix this, FLMs and their organizations could send out surveys and get feedback from employees in order to solve the issues that they may face.

    FLMs could also post a positive quote or picture by the copier, coffee machine, or somewhere else that is visible and that receives high foot traffic so that others can see. Flora and fauna also help create a serene workplace environment for your employees, so why not add a couple of plants around the office. FLMs could also find creative ways in which to consistently keep their employees motivated as much as possible.

Conclusion

Motivation is a complex, yet important topic for the FLM to understand. Unfortunately, some FLMs do not believe that motivation is a part of their job, believing instead that motivation is the responsibility of the individual employee. Effective FLMs realize that they must understand that general patterns of individual behavior contribute to motivation.

Motivation is the process of satisfying internal needs through actions and behaviors. It involves a composite of mental and physical aspects, combined with the environment and other factors that aid in explaining why people behave the way they do. Motivation theories offer valuable insight on what motivates various individuals. For example, one model suggests that a need or motive leads to action or behavior that, in turn, results in the satisfaction of the need.

There are a number of methods FLMs and organizations can use to motivate employees. The methods based on motivational approaches include pay for performance, spot awards, merit pay, recognition awards, job redesign, empowerment, goal-setting, positive reinforcement, and lifelong learning.

Different groups provide specific motivational challenges in today's organizations. FLMs must recognize the unique motivational problems they will face in working with contingent workers, a diversified workforce, employees doing highly repetitive tasks, and multiple generations who make up the workforce.

10

Building and Leading Effective Groups and Teams

It is almost assumed that today's progressive organization must employ teams in some capacity to achieve its objectives. The drive to use teams has come from many organizational pressures such as increased competition, downsizing, and the trend toward a flatter, more flexible organization. Much of the work that involves front-line managers (FLMs) in today's organizations takes place in groups or teams. As an FLM, a manager may serve as a team member on some teams and as a team leader or supervisor of other groups. As a part of these teams, the FLM must see that groups of employees work together to accomplish objectives.

This chapter addresses ways in which the FLM can work effectively as a leader and member of a group or other team. The chapter first discusses groups and particularly focuses on the differences between formal and informal groups before taking a brief look at the benefits of formal and informal organizations. Then, the discussion turns to the group development process. The final section of the chapter describes the FLM as a team leader, what they can do to build a team and create a team of team players.

Succeeding as a Frontline Manager in Today's Organizations, pages 267–299
Copyright © 2021 by Information Age Publishing
267

Groups

A group is two or more freely interacting individuals who share norms and goals and have a common identity. A group is also defined as a collection of individuals who interact with each other such that one person's actions have an impact on the others. In other words, a group is defined as two or more individuals, interacting and interdependent, who have come together to achieve particular objectives. People for groups for many reasons. Most fundamental among these reasons is that groups routinely outperform the average of their individual members.

Types of Groups

Within most organizations different groups are formed at different levels. There are two types of groups: formal and informal. Groups may be classified according to many dimensions, including function, the degree of personal involvement, and degree of organization.

Formal and Informal Groups

A formal group is assigned by organizations or their FLMs to accomplish specific goals. Such groups often have labels: work group, team, committee, or task force. An informal group exists when the members' overriding purpose of getting together is friendship or a common interest. Formal and informal groups often overlap, such as when a team of accountants heads for the bowling alley after work. Friendships forged on the job can be so strong as to outlive the job itself in an ear of job hopping, reorganizations, and mass layoffs.

The desirability of overlapping formal and informal groups is debatable. Some managers firmly believe personal friendship fosters productive teamwork on the job, while others view such relationships as a serious threat to productivity. Both situations are common, and it is the FLM's job to strike a workable balance based on the maturity and goals of the people involved.

Difference Between Formal and Informal Groups

Functions of Formal Groups.   Formal groups fulfill two basic functions. Organizational and individual.

Organizational functions include:

1. Accomplish complex, interdependent tasks that are beyond the capabilities of individuals.
2. Generate new or creative ideas and solutions.

3. Coordinate interdepartmental efforts.
4. Provide a problem-solving mechanism for complex problems requiring varied information and assessments.
5. Implement complex decisions.
6. Socialize and train newcomers.

Informal functions include:

1. Satisfy the individual's need for affiliation.
2. Develop, enhance, and confirm the individual's self-esteem and sense of identity.
3. Give individuals an opportunity to test and share their perceptions of social reality.
4. Reduce the individual's anxieties and feelings of insecurity and powerlessness.
5. Provide a problem-solving mechanism for personal and interpersonal problems.

Difference Between Formal and Informal Groups

Formation of Formal and Informal Groups. As noted earlier, one of the main differences between formal and informal groups is the process through which some groups are formed.

The leadership of an organization to achieve specific tasks deliberately forms formal groups. This means that some rules and regulations guide the formation of a formal group. One cannot leave the group without the authority of the management and leadership. On the other hand, an informal group is voluntarily formed by members coming together to satisfy their personal and psychological needs. One can join and leave the group when he or she decides.

Structure of Formal and Informal Groups. Structures of a formal group are defined where the hierarchy and flow of information from one member of the group to the other member is communicated. This means that there is a chain of command through which instructions are administered.

Most of the time an informal group does not have structures, but when it does exist it is mostly not defined. This means that there is no chain of command and the flow of information from one member to the other. Additionally, communication in a formal group flows from top to bottom while conversation in an informal group moves sideways without a defined path.

Relationship of Formal and Informal Groups. In a formal group, the relationship between members is professional because the group is created to achieve a specific task or goal that is controlled by the management and leadership of the organization. Moreover, the professional relationship between members is brought about by the fact that some members are senior in the organization.

In an informal group, the relationship between members is personal. Members of an informal group know each other at a personal level thus making their relationship to be guided by personal aspects. Additionally, there is no seniority in the group, which means that any member can assume a leadership position.

Size of Formal and Informal Groups. Formal groups are usually large because they are formed with the purpose of ensuring they can achieve goals that measure the success of the organization. Members of a formal group have skills and competencies to handle official activities on behalf of the organization.

Informal groups are comparatively small because close friends or people who know one another on a personal level form them. This makes it challenging to assemble many members since not all persons in the organization know one another at a personal level.

Nature/Level of Formal and Informal Groups. Formal groups are usually stable and are likely to exist for a lengthy period. Additionally, the task allocated to a formal group may last for a long duration hence making the formal group exist until the task allocated is completed.

Informal groups are not stable because they are governed by the feelings between the members. In case the sentiments between members become volatile, the group is likely to be dissolved. Unlike formal groups, whose existence is determined by the nature of the activity, the length of life of an informal group is dependent on the members.

Behavior and Leadership of Formal and Informal Groups. The practice of members of a formal group is governed by specific rules and regulations, which are usually formulated at the inception of the group. All members of the group are supposed to adhere to the rules and guidelines that define the group. Moreover, formal groups have a defined leadership structure where there is an official leader who ensures that the group is in line to achieve its goals while at the same time enforcing rules among members.

The behavior of an informal group is governed by the expression of members, norms, beliefs, and the values that members hold dear. There is no official leader of the group to enforce nonexistence rules and regulations as members do what is necessary to them instead of what is imposed.

In summary, the basic distinguishing feature between formal and informal groups is that formal groups are always formed with an objective,

TABLE 10.1 Differences Between Formal Group and Informal Group		
Basis for Comparison	**Formal Group**	**Informal Group**
Meaning	Groups created by the organization, to accomplish a specific task, are known as formal groups.	Groups created by the employees themselves, for their own sake are known as informal groups
Formation	Deliberately	Voluntarily
Size	Large	Comparatively small
Nature/Life	It depends on the type of group	It depends on the members
Structure	Well defined	Not well defined
The Importance is Given To	Position	Person
Relationship	Professional	Personal

but when an informal group is created, there is no such kind of attention at all. Table 10.1 offers a summary view of the differences between formal and informal groups.

The Benefits of Informal and Formal Organizations

It is important for FLMs to recognize that there are benefits to formal and informal organizations. Formal organizations are useful for reaching defined goals. The structure of a formal organization makes it effective for realizing profit or conducting business. The components and structure of a formal organization are necessary in order to efficiently meet stated objectives.

Informal organizations can be more responsive to change due to the lack of rigid structure. They are inherently more oriented around people rather than outcomes. An example would be a company softball team that allows employees to interact socially away from the formal hierarchies in order to build morale.

Both formal and informal organizations serve human needs and meet goals ranging from financial to values-based. They allow people to build communities and achieve goals that would not be possible alone.

A summary of formal versus informal groups are as follows:

- Formal groups are formulated when two or more members of an organization are assembled by the management with the purpose of achieving a specific goal.
- Informal groups are formed by two or more members with the purpose of satisfying their personal and psychological needs.

- There exist rules and regulations within a formal group with an official leader who is supposed to enforce the laws and regulations while at the same time offering direction and guidance to the group.
- An informal group does not follow a defined pattern, rules, or guidelines and no official leader controls the group. Any person can assume leadership at any given time.
- Other differences between formal and informal groups include some members, behavior, relationship between members, and structure among others.

Skills for a Healthy Group Climate

To work together successfully, group members must demonstrate a sense of cohesion. Cohesion emerges as group members exhibit the following skills:

- openness,
- trust and self-disclosure,
- support,
- respect,
- individual responsibility and accountability, and
- constructive feedback.

Let's take a closer look at each one of these.

Openness

Group members are willing to get to know one another, particularly those with different interests and backgrounds. They are open to new ideas, diverse viewpoints, and the variety of individuals present within the group. They listen to others and elicit their ideas. They know how to balance the need for cohesion within a group with the need for individual expression.

Trust and Self-Disclosure

Group members trust one another enough to share their ideas and feelings. A sense of mutual trust develops only to the extent that everyone is willing to self-disclose and be honest yet respectful. Trust also grows as a group the members demonstrate personal accountability for the tasks they have been assigned.

Support

Group members demonstrate support for one another as they accomplish their goals. They exemplify a sense of team loyalty and both cheer on the group as a whole and help members who are experiencing difficulties. They view one another not as competitors (which is common within a typically individualistic educational system) but as collaborators.

Respect

Group members communicate their opinions in a way that respects others, focusing on "What can we learn?" rather than "Who is to blame?"

Individual responsibility and accountability. All group members agree on what needs to be done and by whom. Each member determines what he or she needs to do and takes responsibility to complete the task(s). They can be held accountable for their tasks, and they hold others accountable for theirs.

Constructive Feedback

Group members can give and receive feedback about group ideas. Giving constructive feedback requires focusing on ideas and behaviors, instead of individuals, being as positive as possible and offering suggestions for improvement. Receiving feedback requires listening well, asking for clarification if the comment is unclear, and being open to change and other ideas.

The Group Development Process

Groups and teams go through a maturation process. Their development is much like the life-cycle processes found in many disciplines—products in marketing and human development in biology. All of these processes are described in terms of stages that differ in terms of number, sequence, length, and nature. Bruce Tuckman formulated perhaps the most popular group development process that includes five stages: forming, storming, norming, performing, and adjourning. Let's look at each stage in more detail.

Forming

In this stage, most team members are positive and polite. Some are uncertain and anxious, as they haven't fully understood what work the team will do. Mutual trust is low and there is a good deal of holding back to see who takes charge and how. Others are simply excited about the task ahead. As manager or leader, FLMs play a dominant role at this stage, because team members' roles and responsibilities aren't clear. This stage can last for some time, as people start to work together, and as they make an effort to get to know their new colleagues. If an FLM does not assert his or her authority, an emergent leader will often step in to fulfill the group's need for leadership and direction.

Storming

Next, the team moves into the storming phase, where people start to push against the boundaries established in the forming stage. This is a time of testing. This is the stage where many teams stall or fail because of power and politics. Subgroups take shape, and subtle forms of rebellion, such as procrastination, occur. Storming often starts where there is a conflict between team members' natural working styles. People may work in different ways for all sorts of reasons but, if different working styles cause unforeseen problems, they may become frustrated. Storming can also happen in other situations. For example, team members may challenge an FLM's authority, or jockey for position as their roles are clarified. Or, if FLMs haven't defined clearly how the team will work, people may feel overwhelmed by their workload, or they could be uncomfortable with the approach you're using.

Some may question the worth of the team's goal, and they may resist taking on tasks.

Team members who stick with the task at hand may experience stress, particularly as they don't have the support of established processes or strong relationships with their colleagues.

Norming

Gradually, the team moves into the norming stage. This is when people start to resolve their differences, appreciate colleagues' strengths, and respect your authority as a leader.

Now that your team members know one another better, they may socialize together, and they are able to ask one another for help and provide constructive feedback. People develop a stronger commitment to the team goal, and an FLM will start to see good progress towards it. A feeling of team spirit is sometimes experienced during this stage because members believe they have found their proper roles. Group cohesiveness, defined as the "we feeling" that binds members of a group together, is the principal by-product of this stage. There is often a prolonged overlap between storming and norming, because, as new tasks come up, the team may lapse back into behavior from the storming stage.

Performing

The team reaches the performing stage, when hard work leads, without friction, to the achievement of the team's goal. Activity during this vital stage is focused on solving task problems, as contributors get their work done without hampering others. This stage is often characterized by a climate of open communication, strong cooperation, and lots of helping behavior. Cohesiveness and personal commitment to groups' goals help the group achieve more than could anyone individually acting alone. The structures and processes that an FLM has set up support this well. As leader, the FLM can delegate much of their work, and they can concentrate on developing team members. It feels easy to be part of the team at this stage, and people who join or leave won't disrupt performance.

Adjourning

The work is done; it is time to move on to other things. The return to independence can be eased by rituals celebrating "the end" and "new beginnings." Parties, award ceremonies, and graduations can punctuate the end. Many teams will reach this stage eventually. For example, project teams exist for only a fixed period, and even permanent teams may be disbanded through organizational restructuring. Team members who like routine, or who have developed close working relationships with colleagues, may find this stage difficult, particularly if their future now looks uncertain. FLMs need to emphasize valuable lessons learned during the adjourning stage.

Teams

The most successful FLMs and their organizations value and understand the nature of teams and create a productive environment in which teams flourish. In reality, one of an FLM's most important responsibilities is managing a team. Consider the experience of Jacquelyn Foster.

Jacquelyn Foster, production FLM at a company in the Southwest, has experience working with teams. "Teams have worked well in our company. We made the transition to teams about a year ago. I moved from supervisor to team leader. I once spent all of my time telling people what to do. Since we've gone to the team approach, occasionally they will come to me with this or that problem, and I will go out and see if I can help them, and they will go from there. On a normal day, I lay out the schedule for them, post it on the board, and they come and look at it, and that pretty much takes care of it. It's getting now so most of them can handle most maintenance problems, unless there is a major crisis with some equipment breaking down or whatever; then they want to let me know about it. I know that before we had teams—when I was just their boss instead of their team leader—people would be afraid to tell me anything because they were afraid somebody was going to get fired. Now we just sit down and discuss it, and everything comes out in the open, and they know nobody's going to get in trouble. I think a team strategy has been really positive for my organization. Even though the transition process was somewhat difficult in the beginning, I'm glad we made the change. The employees seem happier also."

What Is a Team?

To guide the use of teams effectively, FLMs must understand what characteristics define a team. A team is a small number of people with complementary skills who are committed to a common purpose, set of performance goals, and approach for which they hold themselves mutually accountable. Shared accountability and commitment to a common goal make the use of teams particularly appropriate when coordination of various activities or skills sets of multiple individuals is necessary. Tasks that do not require coordination are better left to individual contributors.

In today's team-focused work environment, organizations need FLMs who are adept at teamwork themselves and can cultivate the level of trust necessary to foster constructive teamwork. Employees tend to admire FLMs that exhibit trust in them, honesty/authenticity, and have great team-building skills. FLMs can be more effective in the team context by clearly understanding the distinction between groups and teams.

Teams Are More Than Just a Group

Some have suggested that it is a mistake to use the terms group and team interchangeably. A group becomes a team when the following criteria are met:

1. Leadership becomes a shared activity.
2. Accountability shifts from strictly individuals to both individual and collective.
3. The group develops its own purpose or mission.
4. Problem-solving becomes a way of life, not a part-time activity.
5. Effectiveness is measured by the group's collective outcomes and products.

It is important for FLMs to understand that well-functioning groups or teams can be incredibly effective in achieving goals and quite fulfilling for members. However, they can also be a tremendous amount of time. It is thus important for FLMs to be able to distinguish the former from the latter.

Teams in Terms of Group Development Stage

Compared to our discussion of groups and group development in the previous sections, teams are task groups that have matured to the *performing* stage. Because of conflicts due to power, authority, and unstable interpersonal relations, many work groups never qualify as a real team. FLMs can make the distinction this way: "The essence of a team is common commitment. Without it, groups perform as individuals. With it, they become a powerful unit of collective performance." This underscores two other important distinctions between teams and groups: Teams assemble to accomplish a common task and require collaboration.

Types of Teams

Once an FLM has determined that a team approach is conducive to the organization in question, the FLM must determine how to use teams. There are many types of teams that can be useful in a variety of organizational settings. An FLM must determine which team type most closely matches their organization's needs. There are a variety of choices, because teams can be structured differently and be used to meet different needs.

Problem-Solving Teams

If we look back 20 years or so, teams were just beginning to grow in popularity. At that time teams were typically composed of five to twelve hourly employees from the same department who met for a few hours each week to discuss ways of improving quality, efficiency, and the work environment. We call these problem-solving teams. In problem-solving teams, members share ideas or offer suggestions on how to improve work procedures and methods. These teams are rarely given the authority to unilaterally implement any of their suggested actions. One of the most popular applications of this type of team was quality circles, widely used in the 1980s.

Self-Managed Teams

While problem-solving teams were on the right track, they did not involve employees in work-related decisions and processes. A desire for greater employee participation led to experimentation with truly autonomous teams that could not only solve problems, but also implement solutions and take full responsibility for outcomes. These employee groups are self-managed teams and are also commonly referred to as self-directed work teams, autonomous work groups, high-commitment teams, or empowered employees.

Movement toward self-managed teams represented a complete change in organizational structure. The traditional hierarchy of managers, FLMs, and operating employees was replaced by these teams, which are entirely responsible for their own operations. The real change is that the first level of management has been eliminated and replaced by self-managing teams. The team members become individually and jointly accountable for performance and results. To build this accountability, team membership is a full-time, mandatory part of the job.

In this "FLM free," more personally rewarding environment, employees are exposed to all of the team's operations and skills. This exposure forces employees to learn the work procedures in order to find more productive ways to work. While the benefits of using self-managed teams is evident, today's FLMs should realize that using self-managed teams does not eliminate the need for all managerial control. Instead self-managed teams should represent a balance between management and group control.

As in any team-based environment, simply imposing a team structure doesn't ensure an effective process. First, management must help employees develop the skills they will need to work together as a team. Implementation of teamwork training is perhaps the most important thing FLMs and organizations can do to increase the likelihood of success of self-managed teams. Additionally, FLMs and organizations would be wise to debunk some of the myths FLMs and other managers hold about self-managed teams and how they work. The following presents some of common misconceptions and corresponding truths about self-managed teams:

- *"Self-managed teams do not need leaders."* Teams definitely need some type of leader to transfer traditional leadership responsibilities to team members. The role of the leader varies from team to team (e.g., coach, facilitator), but leaders are necessary in every team.
- *"Leaders lose power in the transition to teams."* In fact, leaders retain power but use it differently. Instead of exercising power within the group to control people, team leaders use their power to break down organizational barriers that can prevent team effectiveness.
- *"Newly formed teams are automatically self-managing."* Team development takes time. Describing new teams as self-managed may establish unrealistic expectations.

- *"Employees are eager to be empowered."* Although this may be true for many employees, it is not true for all. Some consultants estimate that 25% to 30% of working Americans—regardless of their position in the organization—don't want to be empowered. Team work must be learned, but also accepted.
- *"If you group employees in a team structure, they will function as a team, and the organization will reap the benefits of teamwork."* Unfortunately, it doesn't always work that way. Groups must go through a developmental process before they can function successfully in teams.

Cross-Functional Teams

A team concept that has recently become popular is the cross-functional team. This is a team made up of employees from about the same hierarchical level, but from different work areas, who come together to accomplish a task. Cross-functional teams are an effective means for allowing people from different areas within an organization, or between organizations, to exchange information, develop new ideas, solve problems, and coordinate complex projects. An example of a commonly used cross-functional team is the task force. There are particular difficulties managing cross-functional teams. Later in this chapter, we shall discuss ways FLMs can help facilitate this type of team building.

Virtual Teams

With continuing developments in information technology, a new type of group has entered the workplace. This is the virtual team, whose members connect and collaborate entirely through virtual channels, like video conferencing, texting, WebEx, Skype, GoToMeeting, Google Hangout, and many others. In this new age of the Internet, intranets, and continued advances in technology, there is no doubt that more and more virtual teams will operate in all types of organizations as some have lauded them as modeling the workplace of the future.

Members of virtual teams typically do the same things as members of face-to-face teams, but the team members communicate in a different environment. They share information, make decisions, and complete tasks. Virtual teams are an everyday phenomenon at Google where two in five of its teams include Googlers in more than one location; 30% of its meetings involve two or more time zones.

Although technology can make communication possible among a group of people separated by great distances which has the advantage of focusing group interactions and decision-making on facts and objective information rather than on emotional considerations, the limited social context can also be a disadvantage to decision makers. The lack of social rapport and direct interaction among members of virtual teams may make it more challenging to work on these teams possibly because it is more difficult to understand other team members' perspectives and biases. The high cost of supporting technology and training to bring virtual teams on-line can also be a drawback.

Response Teams

Some organizations have developed teams organized solely for the purpose of responding to specific situations in the organization. Emergency-response teams are designed to respond to emergency situations. These response teams often require mandatory participation by all employees in such efforts as incipient fire-fighting, spill-response teams, and bomb threat-search teams. Some organizations use a type of emergency-response team to address maintenance problems that may occur in the evenings and on weekends when the regular maintenance crew is not on duty. The members of these teams have the same responsibilities, backgrounds, and experience as regular team members although they primarily handle maintenance issues that occur outside regular hours.

In an effort to reduce workplace violence, some organizations have formed violence-response teams. These teams, composed of both hourly and managerial employees, conduct initial risk assessment surveys, develop action plans to respond to violent situations, and perform crisis intervention during violent, or potentially violent encounters. There is every indication that more and more organizations will develop violence-response teams given the rise in violence at work. The Occupational Safety and Health Administration (OSHA) has developed voluntary guidelines that some organizations are following to prevent and deal with workforce violence.

It should be evident by the above discussion that there are a variety of teams in place in organizations. Today's FLMs must understand the purposes of these teams and do what is necessary to develop successful teams in their particular work areas.

The Benefits of Using Teams

More than three decades ago, when companies like General Foods, Volvo, and Toyota introduced teams into their production processes, they made news because no one else was doing it. Today, it is just the opposite. Pick up almost any business magazine, and you will read that teams have become an essential part of the way business is being done in organizations like General Electric, AT&T, Motorola, Lululemon Athletica, Johnson & Johnson, Green Solar Technologies, and others.

Why the continued popularity of teams? The evidence suggests that teams typically outperform individuals when the tasks being done require multiple skills, complex judgments, and a range of experience. As organizations have restructured themselves to compete more effectively and efficiently, they have turned to teams as a better way to utilize employee talents. Teams are more flexible and responsive to changing events than are traditional departments. Teams can be quickly assembled, deployed, refocused, or disbanded.

In addition the use of teams can indirectly help with worker motivation and skill development. The team experience can be motivating to team members in that team participation can promote employee involvement in operating decisions. For instance, some assembly-line workers at John Deere are part of sales teams that call on customers. These workers know the products better than any traditional salesperson; and by traveling and speaking with farmers, they develop marketing skills and a greater connection to the company.

Teams are just like any other tool, however. They can be very powerful if used correctly, and they can be useless or even detrimental if used inappropriately. There is no doubt that teams have the potential to improve performance dramatically. The success of team proponents such as Ford and General Electric cannot be disputed. Yet teams alone are not enough. Strong supervision and organizational vision, mission, and goals must guide the use of teams.

Why Some Teams Don't Work/Fail

FLMs and organizations should understand that while advocates of the team approach to management paint a very optimistic picture, there is still a dark side to teams. While exact statistics are not available, teams can and often do fail.

If teams are to be effective, FLMs and other managers must make a concerted effort to avoid common management mistakes. Likewise, team members must be aware, be prepared for, and able to recognize common pitfalls as well. After all, working on a team is demanding. Not everyone may be ready to be a team member. Analysis of failed attempts at introducing teams into the workplace identify several obstacles to team success. These pitfalls, described below, can be avoided with a little work.

Common Management Mistakes With Teams

When management is to blame for the failure of a team, it is usually because the FLMs failed to create a supportive environment in which a team can function. For instance, reward plans that encourage individuals to compete with one another erode teamwork. Teams need a good, long-term organization life-support system. Teams also cannot be used as a quick fix to any organizational problem—they require a sustained commitment over time. Some FLMs are unwilling to relinquish control to the team. In the past, good FLMs worked their way up from the plant floor by giving orders and having them followed, and they may find it difficult to change that approach.

One FLM, Thad Boston, has experienced the difficulty of implementing teams in the workplace:

> We had a real struggle in the beginning of the transition to teams. The organization just wasn't set up for the team environment. We were still giving people bonuses based on the number of contacts they personally made. This certainly didn't encourage employees to give up their time to work with others on a team. Once we recognized the problem, some of us managing the teams approached upper management suggesting a system to reward the teams. They went along with it and I think it has been very successful. Once the team members understood that management was in this for the duration and the team wasn't just a trial solution, they were more comfortable with this method of operation.

Common Problems for Team Members

FLMs must recognize that team members frequently experience common problems. Contrary to those who contend that teams fail because employees lack the motivation and creativity for real teamwork, teams frequently don't succeed because they take on too much too quickly and drive themselves too hard for fast results. Nurturing important group dynamics and developing strong team skills get lost in the rush toward the goal.

Failure is part of the learning process with teams, as it is elsewhere in life. Comprehensive training in interpersonal skills can prevent many common teamwork problems as well, which may arise from conflicts in personalities, work styles, and approaches to communication. Teams fail when their members are unwilling to cooperate with each other and with other teams. In expectation that setbacks and small failures may occur, teams need to be counseled against quitting when they run into an unanticipated obstacle.

FLMs should recognize that merely requiring several people to work together does not necessarily make them into a team, much less a high-performing one. This section outlines symptoms of low-performing teams that indicate intervention may be necessary to keep them from failing. It also notes the common characteristics of high-performing teams.

Symptoms of Low-Performing Teams

Obviously, many problems can lead to low-performing teams. The absence of the basic conditions for a cohesive team—trust, complementary goals, and a clear mission usually will result in low productivity. Various symptoms, outlined below, should help you to recognize low-performing teams:

- *Cautious or guarded communication:* Low performing teams may have members who ridicule or respond negatively to other team members. They may also say nothing or act guarded in what they do say.
- *Participative leadership:* Creating interdependency by empowering, freeing up, and serving others.
- *Lack of disagreement:* Lack of disagreement among team members may reflect poor team interaction indicating that members are unwilling to share their true feelings and ideas.
- *Use of personal criticism:* Personal criticism such as, "If you can't come up with a better idea than that, you better keep quiet," is a sign of unhealthy team member relations.
- *Ineffective meetings:* Low-performing teams often have ineffective meetings characterized by boredom, unenthusiastic participation, failure to reach decisions, and dominance by one or two people.
- *Unclear goals:* Low-performing teams often do not have a clear sense of the team mission or objectives.
- *Low commitment:* Without a clear sense of purpose, low-performing teams tend to have low commitment.
- *Destructive conflict within the team:* Low-performing teams are often characterized by a suspicious, combative environment and by conflict among team members.

Characteristic of High-Performing Teams

Remember, a team is "a small number of people with complementary skills who are committed to a common purpose, set of performance goals, and approach for which they hold themselves mutually accountable."

Specifically, high-performing teams have six characteristics. First, the very essence of a team is a *common commitment to a shared goal*. Without it, groups perform as individuals; with it, they become a powerful collective unit. Teams must, therefore, have a clear mission to which they are committed.

High-performing teams translate their common purpose into *specific performance goals*. In fact transforming broad directives into specific and measurable performance goals is the surest first step for a team trying to shape a purpose meaningful to its members.

It is important to create teams that are the *right size* made up of the *right mix* of individuals. Best-performing teams generally have between seven and fourteen members, the skills of whom should complement each other. For example, a team usually needs people strong in technical expertise, as well as those skilled in problem-solving, decision-making, and interpersonal relationships.

High-performing teams agree on the system by which they will work together to accomplish their mission. They must adopt a *common approach*. Team members determine who will do particular jobs, how schedules will be set and followed, what skills need to be developed, what members will have to do to remain a part of the team, and how decisions will be made.

The most productive teams also develop a sense that, as team members, they must all hold themselves accountable for doing whatever is needed to help the team achieve its mission. Such *mutual accountability* cannot be coerced. Instead, it emerges from the commitment and trust that comes from working together toward a common purpose.

The following eight attributes offer another way for FLMs to think about high-performance teams:

1. *Participative leadership.* Creating interdependency by empowering, freeing up, and serving others.
2. *Shared responsibility.* Establishing an environment in which all team members feel as responsible as the FLM for the performance of the work unit.
3. *Aligned on purpose.* Having a sense of common purpose about why the team exists and the function it serves.
4. *High communication.* Creating a climate of trust and open, honest communication.
5. *Future focused.* Seeing change as an opportunity for growth.
6. *Focus on task.* Keeping meetings focused on results.
7. *Creative talents.* Applying individual talents and creativity.
8. *Rapid response.* Identifying and acting on opportunities.

Teamwork

All teams need members who are motivated to work well with others to accomplish important tasks. Whether those tasks involve recommending things, making or doing things, or running things, teamwork is required. A commitment to teamwork is demonstrated by the willingness of every member to listen and respond constructively to views expressed by others, give others the benefit of the doubt, provide support, and recognize the interests and achievements of others. Teamwork can lead to greater

- goal commitment,
- self-confidence,
- sense of well-being,
- motivation and enthusiasm,
- job satisfaction,
- problem-solving skills,
- emotional support within team,
- endurance and energy levels,
- sharing of individual skills,
- productivity,
- quality and quantity of output, and
- loyalty to goals and objectives.

Becoming a Team Leader

Besides having a good understanding of how to create a team, FLMs need to understand how to act as a team leader. They need to know and understand the team leader's role, typical transition problems they will face as they move into the position of team leader, and principles of an effective leader. Grace Green, FLM at a health care facility expresses the difficulty of her transition, "It took some doing on my part, as well as on theirs. It was not an instant thing. It probably took nine months for me to let loose and let them do what they thought was best. And there are still guidelines. You just don't turn the ship over and say, 'Here you are.' But on normal day-to-day activities, it's turned over to them. Most of the time now they can solve problems themselves."

The FLM's Role as a Team Leader

The FLM is ultimately responsible for the functioning of the team, even though this responsibility obviously is shared by the team itself. In addition to removing organizational barriers for the team, the FLM must supply resources and support when needed.

An important role for FLMs is to ask questions to identify potential team problems. FLMs have the responsibility of helping the team diagnose problems. FLMs must also assess the degree to which they, as team leader, feel comfortable working in teams, the knowledge they have about team building, and whether or not they might be a major source of a team's difficulty. FLMs need to analyze the extent to which they, as the manager, their employees, and the organization are open to teams and team development.

Transition to Team Leader

Like the transition from an individual contributor to an FLM, moving from being a traditional authoritative FLM to being a facilitating team leader is not easy. Why is it so difficult for some individuals to make the transition to team leader? There are at least four problems that can make the transition process less than smooth. First, many FLMs experience a perceived loss of power or status. One day you are the boss; the next day you are merely a facilitator, trying to make sure your team members have what they need to do their jobs—to a large extent, without you. You may not control, direct, or make all of the decisions anymore. FLM Terry Fletcher felt like his authority was threatened in the beginning. "At first, when we made the transition to teams, I felt like I was losing control of my own people. I wasn't making the decisions any longer—they were. Everything was decided as a group. The immediate loss of power and control took some getting used to."

The FLM whose job was once clear as supervisor is now undefined. The change to team leader can be difficult for many FLMs. When you move to a team leader role, companies can make the mistake of overemphasizing what you are not, without clearly defining what you are. While the role of the team may be somewhat clearly defined, the role of the team leader is not. A team is created with a task of "make it happen." Without a good understanding of their role as team leader, the FLM can fail. Donovan Declan, an FLM in a small production firm, had difficulty defining his place in the new system:

> I guess the most confusing thing about moving to teams was figuring out my role in all of it. I still had to guide the group—especially at first, but I wasn't supposed to *tell*. This was really an adjustment for me. I was no longer the problem-solver. The group did it together. That meant that I wasn't making all of the decisions, yet I was still responsible for them as group leader. I had to figure how to get the group to move in the right direction.

It's not uncommon for FLMs to experience job security concerns during the transition to team leader. Telling new team leaders that they are no longer in charge understandably undermines their sense of job security. After all, it is not unreasonable for someone to ask, "Just how secure is the job of supervising or managing a self-managing team?" Team leaders may feel like creating an effective team is essentially a means of working themselves out of a job.

The movement to teams often seems to be a positive, enriching, and empowering move for employees, yet defeating for the FLM. Some organizations make the mistake of forgetting the FLM in the transition to teams, providing him or her with little or no attention, training, or clarification of the new role. The employee gains power and input while the FLM may seem to lose these things. One FLM, Gillian West expresses her initial frustration during the implementation of teams:

> I have to admit that it was particularly difficult in the beginning. The employees received all of this training to be an effective team. I guess they just expected me to know what to do as a team leader. I had never done that before. I wasn't sure what to do. I finally found some information on teamwork and managing teams. I talked to my supervisor about sending me to a conference on managing teams. He admitted that management hadn't ever discussed the impact the move to teams might have on the front-line managers.

This type of treatment can obviously make FLMs annoyed and resistant to the use of teams. Organizations should instead create and implement a transition plan which includes FLMs. The plan should clarify their new team leadership duties, outline how their security will be ensured, and identify training they can expect to receive as they make the transition from to team leader.

Principles of an Effective Team-Leader

Not everyone is cut out to be an effective leader of self-managing teams. Not every leader is psychologically or philosophically prepared to stop "being a boss" and instead oversee a team that is empowered to work with a minimum of supervision.

A leader of a self-managing team should have a set of personal principles that supports the empowered nature of teams. What personal principles are consistent with building self-confidence, sharing authority, and ensuring the team has the tools and information it requires? Important team-leader principles focus on the needs of the team. A team leader should put the team members first and trust that they will do their best. In order to help team members reach their potential team leaders must enhance team members' capabilities through training and development. Team leaders must demonstrate that they believe in the team and value the team members. In order to do this they must use delegation and let the team members make decisions and take action. The leaders should eliminate barriers that may hinder decision-making processes or team actions.

Perhaps the biggest difference between successful and unsuccessful team leaders is that those who are successful believe their primary responsibility is to make sure their teams have the means to get their jobs done. They give the team the support it needs.

How Team Leaders Can Create a Team of Successful Team Members

In addition to understanding what affects their role as team leaders, FLMs must also understand how to

- develop team players,
- build the team,
- coach the members,
- motivate team members,
- reduce social loafing,
- help manage conflict, and
- communicate effectively.

Developing Team Players

Forming teams and urging employees to be team players are good starting points for FLMs on the road to leading and building effective teams. But they are not enough. Teamwork competencies need to be role modeled and taught. These include group problem-solving, mentoring, conflict management skills, and emotional intelligence. Research suggests that teams collaborate most effectively when organizations develop and encourage teamwork competencies. This means that teamwork competencies should be measured and rewarded, too. If teamwork is important, then how can FLMs and their organizations measure it? There are five common teamwork competencies (see Table 10.2).

Evaluating Teamwork Competencies

There are at least two ways FLMs can use Table 10.2 and knowledge of teamwork competencies. The first is as a tool to enhance your own

TABLE 10.2 Common Teamwork Competencies	
Competency	Examples of Member Behaviors
1. Contributes to the team's work	• Completed work in a timely manner • Came to meetings prepared • Did complete and accurate work
2. Constructively interacts with team members	• Communicated effectively • Listened to teammates • Accepted feedback
3. Keeps team on track	• Helped team plan and organize work • Stayed aware of team members' progress • Provided constructive feedback
4. Expect quality work	• Expected team to succeed • Cared that the team produce quality work
5. Possesses relevant knowledge, skills, and abilities (KSAs) for team's responsibilities	• Possessed necessary KSAs to contribute meaningfully to the team • Applied knowledge and skill to fill in as needed for other members' roles

self-awareness. The second is to use these competencies as a way to measure your performance and the performance of other members of your team.

Barrier to Teamwork

One substantial barrier to the success of teams in organizations is individual resistance. To perform well as team members, individuals must be able to communicate openly and honestly, to confront differences and resolve conflicts, and to make personal sacrifices for the good of the team.

Many people are not inherently team players. Some are loners by nature. Others want to be recognized for their individual achievements. These people have often worked in an organization that has historically nurtured individual accomplishments and created competitive work environments where only the strong survive. If these organizations adopt teams, what do they do about the selfish, "I've-got-to-look-out-for-me" employees that they have created?

The primary approaches used by FLMs and organizations to identify and develop individuals into team players are selecting good team members, training them, and rewarding them based on team—not only individual—performance.

Some people already possess the interpersonal skills to be effective team players. When hiring new employees who will work as team members, care should be taken to ensure that candidates can fulfill their team roles as well as the technical requirements of the job. Many job candidates, particularly those who have previously worked as an individual contributor, lack team skills. When faced with such candidates, FLMs can train them, use them elsewhere in the organizations, or refuse to hire them.

Most people can be trained to become team players. Training specialists conduct exercises that allow employees to experience the satisfaction that teamwork can provide. Workshops can help employees improve their problem-solving, communication, negotiation, conflict-management, and coaching skills. At Bell Atlantic, for example, trainers focus on how a team goes through various stages before it finally works well together. Employees are reminded of the importance of patience—because it often takes teams longer to make decisions than one employee acting alone.

In established organizations that redesign jobs around teams, it should be expected that some employees will resist being team players and may be untrainable. Unfortunately, such people typically become casualties of the team approach, and will lose their jobs or be transferred to another part of the organization without teams.

The reward system must be one that encourages cooperative rather than competitive efforts. Promotions, pay raises, and other forms of recognition should be given to individuals for how effective they are as collaborative team members. Recognition of team effectiveness does not mean individual contribution is ignored; rather, it is balanced with selfless contributions to the team. Trigon Blue Cross Blue Shield changed its system to reward individual and team achievements equally. Examples of behaviors that should be rewarded include training new colleagues, sharing information with teammates, helping to resolve team conflicts, and mastering new skills that the team needs but in which it is deficient. Additionally, teamwork provides the intrinsic reward of camaraderie. It is exciting and satisfying to be an integral part of a successful team. The opportunity to engage in personal development and to help teammates grow can be a very rewarding experience for employees.

Team Building

Team building is a catch-all term for many different techniques aimed at improving the internal functioning of work groups. Some authorities have suggested that the primary purposes of team building are to set goals and priorities, to analyze or allocate the way work is performed, to examine the way a group is working and its processes, and to examine relations among the people doing the work. Trainers achieve these objectives by allowing team members to wrestle with simulated or real-life problems. The group analyzes its results to determine what group processes need improvement. Learning occurs by recognizing and addressing faulty group dynamics. With cross-cultural teams becoming commonplace in today's global economy, team building is more important than ever to help alleviate misunderstandings and improve communication.

Whether conducted by company trainers or outside consultants, team-building workshops are designed to promote greater cooperation, better communication, and less dysfunctional conflict. Learning tools such as interpersonal trust exercises, conflict-handling role-play sessions, and interactive games are commonly used to build teamwork skills.

Team building is participative and data based. Whether the data are gathered by questionnaires, interviews, nominal group meetings, or other creative methods, the goal is for team members to give good answers to such questions as, "How well are we doing in terms of task accomplishment?"; "How satisfied am I as a group member?"; and "How effectively does the group operate?" There are a variety of ways for such questions to be asked and answered in a collaborative and motivating manner.

Towards Being a Team Player
Besides what just discussed one place for FLMs and other team members to start to develop or become a team place is to understand and exhibit the competencies noted earlier. While there are clearly different views on what is important as a team player, it is likely that most FLM's and others' views include the three Cs of team players:

committed,
collaborative, and
competent.

Put another way, the three Cs are the "cover charge" or the bare minimum to be considered a team player. FLMs should think of a team on which they either are or were a member. It would be difficult to consider any individual member a team player if she or he didn't possess and exhibit all three. Effective team players therefore don't just feel the three Cs—they display them. To make the point, FLMs should think of somebody on one of their teams who clearly displays the three Cs, and somebody who does not. How do the differences affect them as an FLM? The team?

How to Build Teams—Quickly

Like goal setting, creating and communicating performance expectations for teams is extremely important. However, the reality is that today teams are often put together in a hurry; they are assemblies of people who do not routinely work together but must get results—quickly. It therefore is necessary for effective teams to be built and start performing in real time. Knowing how to do this is a real advantage for FLMs. Today's dynamic workplace often requires FLMs to bring different people together across boundaries (e.g., departments, experience levels, knowledge, and age). FLMs and their organizations sometimes need to build effective teams fast. These six actions can help FLMs accelerate the development of their teams and get them performing sooner rather than later.

1. *Break the ice.* Have each team member share relevant details about her or his experience. Doing so helps everybody learn what types of skills and abilities the team possesses, and it also facilitates cooperation because team members can use each other's experiences as a shared history, which substitutes for the history that they don't actually have together. Sample questions FLMs might consider are—"Please tell us about the types of teams in which you've participated?"; and "What are some of the biggest challenges and how were they dealt with?"

2. *Don't reinvent the wheel.* Ask team members what has worked in the past. This can help signal respect for their competence and judgment and lead to greater engagement and commitment.

3. *Communicate a purpose and a plan.* Clearly explain the team's purpose and how they will work together. Do more than simply hand out assignments, but instead explain why the team was created, the problem to be solved, and the benefits of success. Describe milestones, or key dates, and the main deliverables.

4. *Play to strengths.* Set individuals and the larger team up to win. This means match individual members' skills to responsibilities and goals of the team. Fit is likely to lead to higher performance and shows that you were listening to individuals and care about their success.

5. *Clarify decision-making.* Think about and explain how you approach decision-making in dealing with conflicts. Decisions that will affect the team's final product, for example, are often handled by the FLM (or team leader or boss). Beware, however, not to interfere in decisions that should be made within the team.

6. *Information is essential—make it flow.* Establish clear processes and expectations for sharing information within the team—emails, face-to-face meetings, voicemail, Sharepoint, Skype, Dropbox, and

so on. FLMs should explicitly include their expectations for giving and receiving feedback.

The Three Cs of Highly Effective Teams

There are three additional and important factors FLMs should consider when building effective teams. The three Cs are at the team level, which contrasts with the three Cs of effective team players discussed earlier that focus on the individual or member level:

charters and strategies,
composition, and
capacity.

Charters and Strategies

Groups and teams should plan before tackling their tasks, early in the group development process (e.g., storming stage). These plans should include team charters that outline why a team exists, what its goals are, and how members are expected to behave to achieve said goals. Charters also establish norms that govern individual behavior, provide criteria for measuring team outcomes, and develop guidelines for assessing member behavior. Charters are helpful to FLMs and teams because they really focus on describing how the team will operate, such as processes for sharing information and decision-making (teamwork). Teams should also create and implement team performance strategies, which are deliberate plans that outline what exactly the team is to do, such as goal setting and defining particular member roles, tasks, and responsibilities.

Composition

Team composition is a term that describes the collection of jobs, personalities, knowledge, skills, abilities, and experience of team members. Defined in this way, it should be no surprise to FLMs that team composition can and does affect team performance. It is important that team member characteristics fit the responsibilities of the team for the team to be effective. Fit facilitates team effectiveness and misfit impedes it—FLMs need the right people on their team.

Capacity

Team adaptive capacity (i.e., adaptability) is important to meet changing demands and to effectively transition members in and out. It is fostered by employees who are motivated to achieve an accurate view of the world (versus an ethnocentric or self-centered view) and to work effectively with others to achieve outcomes.

Using Effective Coaching Skills

Coaching is a big part of what team leaders do. Like coaching, team building involves assessing the team's skills and helping the team use them to the fullest. Employees tend to contribute more effectively when they are coached to make optimal use of all their strengths and resources.

What is required to coach employees? Experts agree that coaches must first know their people. As a coach you should assess each employee's skills so you can help team members use them to the fullest. Good coaches guide—not control—employees. If you tell them what to do, they will not develop the independence necessary to operate as a team. It is important that coaches provide the emotional support necessary for the team to work together. You should ensure that a supportive environment exists in which employees believe they have the freedom to make contributions and provide their input. Coaches provide specific feedback. You should explain what and why improvements are required from your point of view. Coaches let team members generate answers. You should ask questions that will lead your employees to find the answers for themselves. Finally, good coaches communicate high expectations for the team and its members.

Motivating Teams to Achieve Goals

When work is difficult, tedious, or requires a high level of commitment and energy, FLMs cannot assume that team members will always be motivated to work toward the achievement of organizational goals. Consider the case of a group of house painters who paint new homes for a construction company and are paid on an hourly basis. Why should they strive to complete painting jobs quickly and efficiently? Doing so will just make them feel more tired at the end of the day and they will not receive any tangible benefits. It makes more sense for the painters to adopt a relaxed approach, working at a leisurely pace. This relaxed approach, however, impairs the construction company's ability to gain a competitive advantage because it raises costs and increases the time needed to complete a new home.

FLMs can motivate members of teams to achieve organizational goals by making sure that the members themselves benefit when the team performs well. If members of a self-managed team know that they will receive a percentage of any cost savings discovered and implemented by the team, they probably would strive to cut costs. If the house painters were paid based on the amount of surface area they actually painted, or if they were to receive a bonus for each house completed in a timely, efficient manner, it is likely that they would work more quickly.

FLMs often rely on some combination of individual and group-based incentives to motivate team members to work toward the achievement of organizational goals and a competitive advantage. When individual performance within a group can be assessed, pay is often determined by that individual performance or by both individual and group performance. When individual performance within a group cannot be accurately assessed, then group performance should determine pay levels. A major challenge for FLMs is to develop a fair pay system that will lead to both high individual motivation and high group or team performance.

Reducing Social Loafing in Teams

So far the focus has been on the steps that FLMs can take to encourage high levels of team performance. FLMs, however, need to be aware of an important downside to teamwork: the potential for social loafing. Social loafing is the tendency of individuals to put forth less effort when they work in groups or teams than when they work alone. Have you ever worked on a group project in which one or two group members never seemed to be pulling their weight? If you have, you have witnessed social loafing.

Social loafing is problematic because it typically involves more than simply "slacking off." Free riders (i.e., "loafers") produce not only low-quality work, which causes others to work harder to compensate, but they often also distract or disrupt the work of other team members.

Social loafing can occur in all kinds of groups and teams and in all kinds of organizations. It can result in lower group performance and may prevent a group from attaining its goals. Social loafing can be reduced or completely eliminated if the FLM will make individual contributions to a group identifiable, emphasize why each member's skills are important to the team's success, and form teams with no more members than are needed to accomplish team goals. Organizations can stop social loafing by keeping the team small and making sure they have challenging work tasks.

FLMs should guard against loafing. Consistent with the definition above, social loafing generally increases as group size increases and work is more widely dispersed. What makes this worse is that loafers expect others to pick up the slack even as they receive the same rewards. To combat such problems

1. limit group size;
2. assure equity of effort to mitigate the possibility that a member can say, "Everyone else is goofing off, so why shouldn't I?"; and
3. hold people accountable—don't allow members to feel that they are lost in the crowd and think "who cares?"

Building Team Trust

Trust is a reciprocal belief that another person will consider how his or her intentions and behaviors will affect you. A crucial factor in developing an outstanding team is the team leader's ability to create a trusting and supportive climate in which the team can work together. The team leader should be supportive, maintaining each individual's sense of personal worth and importance. The relationship between a team leader and employees should be one of reciprocal support and joint commitment to success.

High performance teams are characterized by high mutual trust among members. But as you know from personal relationships, trust takes a long time to build, can be easily destroyed, and is hard to regain. FLMs have a significant impact on a team's climate of trust. As a team leader, FLMs should keep people informed, be candid, explain your decisions, act in a consistent manner, and fully disclose relevant information. To build trust, as the team leader, FLMs must evaluate team members objectively, demonstrate they are working for others' interests as well as their own, and give credit where it is due. Trust needs to be earned; it cannot be demanded. FLMs must take the time to build team members' trust—the foundation of a high-performance team.

FLMs can benefit by practicing the following behaviors for building and maintaining trust:

- *Communication.* Keep team members and employees informed by explaining policies and decisions and providing accurate feedback. Be candid about one's own problems and limitations. Tell the truth.
- *Support.* Be available and approachable. Provide help, advice, coaching, and support for team members' ideas.
- *Respect.* Delegation, in the form of real decision-making authority, is the most important expression of managerial respect. Delegat-

ing meaningful responsibilities to somebody shows trust in her or
him. Actively listening to the ideas of others is a close second.

- ▪ *Fairness.* Be quick to give credit and recognition to those who
  deserve it. Make sure all performance appraisals and evaluations
  are objective and impartial.
- ▪ *Predictability.* Be consistent and predictable in your daily affairs.
  Keep both expressed and implied promises.
- ▪ *Competence.* Enhance your credibility by demonstrating good business sense, technical ability, and professionalism.

Facilitating Communication in the Team Environment

The way the FLM communicates with the other team members will influence the success of the team. Successful teamwork requires open and
positive communication among team members. In order to benefit from
diverse viewpoints, all team members need to feel welcome to express their
ideas constructively. In general, the team leader should build on a climate
of trust and openness, and encourage team members to collaborate. The
team leader should acknowledge disagreement, not squelch it. Practically
all groups and teams experience conflict either within the group or with
other groups at some point. FLMs can help groups manage conflict and
disagreements.

Problems Unique to Leading Teams

To lead a team, a leader must have not only basic leadership characteristics, but also special team building skills and the ability to meet challenges
unique to the team structure. In this section we shall turn briefly to a few of
those uniquely team-related challenges of being a leader.

New Team Member Entry Problems

Given the nature of group dynamics, team building is not a "one-time"
task that you accomplish and put aside. Something is always happening that
creates the need for further efforts to help improve teamwork and group
effectiveness. Special difficulties are likely to occur when team members
first get together in a new work group or when new members join an existing one. Problems often arise as a new member tries to understand what is
expected of them while dealing with the anxiety and discomfort of a new
social setting. New members, for example, may worry about the level of

participation expected of new team members by the group, whether the group's goals mesh well with their own, individual level of control and influence, team member relationships, and group processes such as conflicts within the group.

Workforce Diversity and Teams

Managing diversity on teams is a balancing act. Diversity typically provides new approaches and fresh perspectives on issues, but differences can make it more difficult to unify team members and reach agreement. Diversity among group members obviously brings with it certain advantages such as multiple perspectives; greater openness of the group to new ideas; multiple interpretations; and increased creativity, flexibility, and problem-solving. Unfortunately the advantages of a diverse group of individuals can sometimes be accompanied by the disadvantages of complexity, confusion, miscommunication, and difficulties in reaching agreement or taking action.

Diversity on work teams is most productive for problem-solving and decision-making tasks. Team members bring multiple perspectives to discussions, thus increasing the likelihood that the team will identify creative or unique solutions. The lack of a common perspective usually means diverse teams spend more time discussing issues, which decreases the chances that a poor decision will be made. As diverse groups work together more, two things tend to happen. The team tends to become less creative, offering fewer suggestions as team members become more familiar with perspectives of other team members. In turn, however, as members become more familiar with one another, it is likely that initial working conflicts will dissipate.

Inspiring Mature Teams

Just because a team is performing well at a given point in time is no assurance that it will continue to do so. Effective teams can become stagnant. Initial enthusiasm can give way to apathy and less openness to novel ideas and innovation. Team members believe they know what other team members are thinking. As a result, team members become reluctant to express their thoughts and less likely to challenge each other.

Another source of problems for mature teams is that success may not come as easily as the group matures. Early successes are often due partially to the easy tasks taken on during the early life of the team. Later, the team must confront more difficult issues at the point that it has developed entrenched processes and routines. Internal team processes no longer work smoothly. Communication bogs down. Conflicts increase because problems are less likely to have obvious solutions, and team performance can drop dramatically.

What can FLMs do to re-energize mature teams? The solution involves preparation and encouragement. FLMs should prepare members to deal with the problems of maturity through discussions and training. It is important for team members to understand that all successful teams have to confront maturity issues. Providing team members with training or refresher courses in communication, conflict resolution, problem-solving, and technical skills can serve to vitalize the team. Finally, team members can avoid a negative reaction to problems of maturity if the FLM simply encourages them to see these issues as part of the team's development—a constant learning experience in which they look for ways to improve, to confront member fears and frustrations, and to use conflict as a tool of growth.

Conclusion

Many different types of teams are successfully and commonly used by today's organizations. Creating and developing teams involves four steps: prework, setting performance conditions, forming and building a team, and providing on-going assistance. While teams can be very productive and promote organizational success, there is also evidence that some teams fail due to problems which include lack of cooperation among team members and with other teams, no support from management, and a failure of FLMs and other managers to relinquish control. To make sure that teams perform at the highest possible level, FLMs need to motivate members to work toward the achievement of organizational goals, reduce social loafing, effectively manage conflict, build trust within the team, and understand how to re-energize mature teams.

11

Communication

Successfully Bridging the Exchange of Information

Communication is not an easy word to define, nor is it an easy skill to master; however, it is essential for the functioning of every part of an organization. Although marketing, production, finance, human resources management (HRM), and other departments may receive direction from corporate goals and objectives, communication links them together and facilitates organizational success.

The importance of effective communication for FLMs cannot be overemphasized for one specific reason: Everything an FLM does involves communicating. Not some things, but everything! Planning, leading, organizing, and controlling all require communication. FLMs cannot make a decision without information, and that information has to be communicated. Once a decision is made, it must be communicated to others, or no one will know about it. The best idea, the most creative suggestion, or the finest plan cannot take form without communication. Indeed, it would be safe to say that FLMs spend approximately 85% of their time engaged in some form of communication.

Succeeding as a Frontline Manager in Today's Organizations, pages 301–328
Copyright © 2021 by Information Age Publishing
All rights of reproduction in any form reserved.

The successful FLM, therefore, needs effective communication skills. This does not mean that good communication skills alone make a successful FLM. One can say, however, that ineffective communication skills can lead to a continuous stream of problems.

Communication and Management

Grant Weatherly and Justine Flowers were two FLMs in a large regional company. The company had suffered a major layoff in 2017, and senior leadership had now decided to change from a departmental structure to one based on cross-functional teams. While the details of the proposed reorganization were being finalized, Weatherly and Flowers needed to keep their employees informed about the changes. Weatherly and Flowers each took a different approach to communicating this important news.

Weatherly wrote a short memo that said: "As some of you may have already heard, our department will be undergoing a major change in structure within the next 6 months. Right now, the details haven't been worked out, so I don't have any more information than this to share with you. The effects of the change should be clearer next month, and I will keep you informed." Flowers held a meeting with her direct reports in which she announced the change and described in general terms what would be happening and why. She then spent considerable time answering his employees' questions and listening to their concerns. When Weatherly heard about Flowers' meeting, he said to himself, "There she goes again, wasting everyone's time in unnecessary meetings when a simple memo would do."

Was Flowers' meeting a waste of time? Not if the reactions of Weatherly and Flowers' employees are taken into account. All of Weatherly's employees feared another round of layoffs was coming, and their performance consequently suffered. Flowers' employees, in contrast, felt the organization was concerned about them and were looking forward to learning more about the planned change. One of their first questions at the meeting concerned potential layoffs, and Flowers truthfully assured them that no layoffs would occur. Knowing their jobs were secure, the employees spent the rest of the meeting discussing the pros and cons of the change, inadvertently providing Flowers with useful points to bring up with his FLM. Instead of being a waste of time, Flowers' approach was highly effective and contributed to the successful implementation of the new structure. In contrast, Weatherly's ineffective communication unnecessarily raised the stress levels of his employees and made them wary of the upcoming change.

In this chapter, we define communication and the communication process and describe ways an FLM can be an effective communicator. The latter part of the chapter discusses written and oral communication in detail and offers guidelines for developing these two very important skills.

What Is Communication?

Communication is the sharing of information between two or more individuals or groups to reach a common understanding. The most important part of this definition is that, to be successful, the information or ideas conveyed must be understood. To see what the definition means in practice, return to the opening case. Weatherly and Flowers shared information with their employees, but Flowers' approach was much more effective than Weatherly's for at least two reasons. First, the information Weatherly shared was incomplete; Weatherly never even communicated the nature of the organizational restructuring. Second, Weatherly made no attempt to ensure that a common understanding was reached. Not surprisingly, therefore, his employees jumped to the wrong conclusion that there would be more layoffs. Flowers made sure a common understanding was reached by providing an appropriate level of information, through a face-to-face meeting with her employees and by giving them the opportunity to ask questions. FLMs like Flowers who are able to communicate with their employees so that a common understanding is reached are more effective than FLMs like Weatherly who do not.

Good communication is often incorrectly defined by the communicator as "agreement" instead of "clarity of understanding." If someone disagrees with us, we may often assume the person just did not fully understand our position; but a person can clearly understand us and simply not agree. In fact, when an FLM concludes that a lack of communication must exist because a conflict between two employees has continued for a long time, a closer look often reveals that the two are communicating, they just don't agree.

To function effectively within the organization, FLMs like Grant Weatherly have to be able to effectively communicate horizontally as well as vertically (see Figure 11.1). It would not be unusual for today's FLMs like Grant to spend over three-quarters of their time in some form of interpersonal situation. Poor communication skills carry a great deal of liability. FLMs who do not communicate effectively are at a disadvantage and do not thrive in organizations.

The Communication Process

The communication process consists of two phases. In the transmission phase, information is sent from one individual or group, the sender,

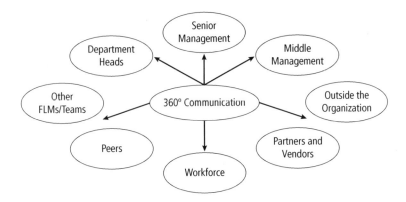

Figure 11.1 FLMs and communication flow.

to another individual or group, the receiver. During this phase the sender first decides what message to communicate and then decides what method or channel to use to communicate that message. In our earlier example, Weatherly and Flowers both sent a message, but they chose different ways to send the message.

In the feedback phase a receiver responds to the message that has been sent. This response might include confirmation that the original message was clear or a request for additional information. For example, when Flowers met with her employees, their responses to her message included questions about the proposed change. If the sender does not receive feedback regarding the message, it is possible that the message will be misinterpreted. In the case of Weatherly, he chose to communicate about the organizational changes through a memo, which left little opportunity for her employees to give his feedback about the message, and resulted in their misunderstanding the message. Flowers, however, made sure that she received feedback from her employees and was able to correct misconceptions, thereby reaching a common understanding with them.

The Role of Perception in Communication

The way that people perceive others or a situation can influence both the way they communicate information, and the way they interpret information from others. Perception is inherently subjective and influenced by people's personalities, values, attitudes, moods, experience, and knowledge. Whenever two people attempt to communicate with each other, their subjective perceptions influence how messages are sent, received, and interpreted. Grant Weatherly perceived that his employees would understand the message about the restructuring if he communicated it in a short memo; this inaccurate perception about his employees led them to interpret his message (via their perceptual filters) incorrectly as an announcement of another round of layoffs.

Perceptual filters play an important role, particularly affecting our decoding. This can involve, for example, a readiness or predisposition to hear, or not to hear, particular kinds of information. Preoccupations that are diverting our attention can also filter information. Past experience affects the way in which we see things today, and can influence what we transmit and how, and what we receive. In any organizational setting, people may have time to reflect, or they may be under time pressure, or experience "communication overload," which again means that some content may be filtered out.

In addition, perceptual biases can hamper effective communication. Biases about individuals or stereotypes about groups of people may result in FLMs communicating less effectively with some individuals and groups or failing to communicate key information for fear of others' reactions. For example, suppose an FLM stereotypes older workers as being fearful of change. When communicating about an upcoming change in the organization to James, an older worker, an FLM downplays the change in order to keep John from "worrying excessively." James, however, has no more fear of change than his coworkers. However, because of what he has been told, interprets his FLM's message to mean there will be little change, and thus he does not prepare for change. As a result, his performance suffers when the change does happen because he has failed to prepare. Clearly, the ineffective communication was due to the FLM's inaccurate assumptions about older workers. Instead of relying on stereotypes, effective FLMs try to perceive other people accurately by focusing on their actual behaviors, knowledge, skills, and abilities. Accurate perceptions contribute to effective communication.

The physical, social, and cultural context in which communication takes place is also significant. In organizations where employees are widely dispersed across a number of locations, the ability to share and compare views is more difficult than when everyone is in the one place. The logistics of communicating with a large number of dispersed employees can be complex and costly. The casual remark by a colleague across a lunch table ("We could be laid off by the end of the year") could be dismissed with a laugh. The same remark made by an FLM in a formal planning meeting could be a source of alarm. If an organization's culture emphasizes openness and transparency, employees may become suspicious if communication is less informative than expected. However, employees may also become suspicious if FLMs (without a good explanation) suddenly start to share large amounts of information openly in a culture that has in the past been less transparent.

Nonverbal Communication

In addition to what we actually say when we communicate, much of what people interpret from our messages is the result of our "nonverbal" communication. Nonverbal communication shares information by means of facial expressions, body language, and even style of dress. Suppose, for example, Jennifer Davis, an FLM, is talking to her team about working together more effectively. She schedules a meeting with the team in her office. At the meeting she says, "Helping you work together effectively is the most important thing I do. I am committed to helping you work through this." While she is verbally expressing their importance, Jennifer is fumbling through papers. She then stops to answer the phone. Further, her voice shows little enthusiasm and she looks out the window while she is speaking to the team. The team hears Jennifer's words, "the most important thing I do," but the message they receive is that they really aren't that important after all.

FLMs need to pay close attention to nonverbal behaviors when communicating. They need to recognize that how they communicate is as important as what they communicate. Nonverbal messages can undermine contrary messages. A message can be given meaning only in a context, and cues or signals are important. You should change your own communication style if you discover that it is interpreted negatively or incorrectly. Table 11.1 presents common nonverbal behaviors exhibited by FLMs and how employees may interpret them negatively.

FLMs also can benefit from watching the nonverbal communication of others who are receiving their messages. If, for example, an FLM is speaking and most of her employees are staring at her with their arms crossed, this may signal that they are frustrated or upset by the message. Thus, by reading others' nonverbal communication, you can often find out their feelings and attitudes toward the communication and toward you.

Communication Media

To be effective communicators, FLMs (and other members of an organization) need to select an appropriate communication medium for each message they send. Should a change in procedures be communicated to direct reports in a memo sent through e-mail? Should a congratulatory message

TABLE 11.1 Common Nonverbal Cues From FLMs to Employee		
Nonverbal Communication	**Signal Received**	**Reaction From Receiver**
FLM looks away when talking to the employee.	Divided attention	My FLM is too busy to listen to my problem or simply does not care.
FLM fails to acknowledge greeting from fellow employee.	Unfriendliness	The person is unapproachable.
FLM glares ominously (i.e., gives the evil eye).	Anger	Reciprocal anger, fear, or avoidance, depending on who is sending the signal in the organization.
FLM rolls the eyes.	Not taking person seriously	This person thinks he or she is smarter or better than I am.
FLM sighs deeply.	Disgust or displeasure	My opinions do not count. I must be stupid or boring this person.
FLM uses heavy breathing (sometimes accompanied by hand waving).	Anger or heavy stress	Avoid this person at all costs.
FLM does not maintain eye contact when communicating.	Suspicion or uncertainty	What does this person have to hide?
FLM crosses arms and leans away.	Apathy and closed-mindedness	This person already has made up her or his mind; my opinions are not important.
FLM peers over glasses.	Skepticism or distrust	He or she does not believe what I am saying.
FLM continues to read a report when employee is speaking.	Lack of interest	My opinions are not important enough to get the FLM's undivided attention.

about a major accomplishment be communicated in a letter, in a phone call or over lunch? Should a layoff announcement be made in a memo or at a general meeting? FLMs deal with these questions day in and day out.

Media Richness

One of the main characteristics on which communication media vary is "information richness." Richness concerns the amount and the kind of information that can be transmitted. The three characteristics of a communication medium that affect richness are (a) the ability to handle many items of information at the same time, (b) the availability of rapid feedback, and (c) the ability to establish a personal focus. Based on these characteristics, media can be classified on a "hierarchy of richness."

Face-to-face communication is the richest because it meets all three criteria: multiple information cues, immediate feedback, and personal focus.

Moving down the hierarchy, telephone allows quick feedback, but the information cues that are available from nonverbal behavior in face-to-face communication are absent; body language such as eye contact, posture, gesture, and head movements. Written communications can be directed at individuals, but carry limited information, and feedback is likely to be delayed. At the bottom of the hierarchy, interpersonal bulletins and computer reports are limited on all three criteria and are therefore "information poor" or "lean."

FLMs should understand that this is not an argument in favor of rich communications. On the contrary, the degree of richness that is appropriate depends on the nature and content of what is being communicated, and in particular on where the issue lies on a continuum from routine to nonroutine. Routine issues are commonplace, simple, rational, straightforward, and contain no surprises. Nonroutine issues, in contrast, concern novel, complex, unexpected events and are often characterized by time pressure, ambiguity, and surprise. The potential fit for misunderstanding is thus greater with nonroutine issues, and a richer exchange of information is therefore necessary in order to establish a common frame of reference. FLMs should consider the following six rules for "matching" media richness to the message:

> Rule 1: Send nonroutine, difficult communications through a rich medium—preferably face-to-face.
> Rule 2: Send routine, simple communications through a lean medium.
> Rule 3: Use rich media to extend your personal presence throughout the organization.
> Rule 4: Use rich media for implementing company strategy.
> Rule 5: Don't let the media use "censor" information about critical issues; formal written reports simplify multidimensional issues and mask the nonroutine.
> Rule 6: Evaluate new communication technology as a single channel in the media spectrum.

Most of an FLM's communication time is spent one-on-one, face-to-face with employees and other members of the organization. Face-to-face communication provides opportunities for immediate feedback from recipients and is the richest information medium because the recipient hears the message and sees all of the nonverbal cues that you are communicating. It is the appropriate medium for delegating tasks, coaching, disciplining, instructing, sharing information, answering questions, checking progress toward objectives, and developing and maintaining interpersonal relations.

While communication that occurs face-to-face can be misinterpreted because of nonverbal cues, other forms of communication such as telephone, e-mail, or letters also have limitations. Overall, you may receive less feedback from the recipient using these forms of communication which may result in a breakdown of communication. For example, in a telephone conversation, you can hear the enthusiasm or frustration in someone's voice, but you cannot tell whether they are paying attention. Further, in written communication, receivers may over interpret or over emphasize some of the words or phrases used by the sender.

Thus, an FLM should think carefully about what form to use for important communications to ensure that the information is provided efficiently and effectively. For example, if a message has a great potential for being misunderstood or is ambiguous, then a face-to-face interaction providing opportunities for immediate feedback enables FLMs to exchange information and ideas rapidly until a common understanding is reached. On the other hand, when the message is clear, well defined, and everyone involved has a similar understanding of the background of the issue, then written memos are appropriate.

How Technology Affects Communication

Exciting advances in information technology have dramatically increased the speed of communication. FLMs can now more easily communicate with their teams and can more quickly access information to make decisions. Further, it is possible to send and receive information from many different locations. In order for FLMs to be successful in today's workplaces, they need to keep up-to-date on advances in information technology.

In order for FLMs to be successful, they also should understand the uses of technology such as groupware (computer software that enables members of groups to share information with each other), Intranets (company-wide systems of computer networks), and the Internet (a global system of computer networks). But FLMs should not adopt these or other advances (e.g., social media) without first considering carefully whether the advance will truly be useful for their situation.

Social Media

Facebook's social networking service launched in 2004 is one of the new communication tools available to FLMs. Internet-mediated tools like Facebook allows FLMs to create, share, and exchange information, ideas, pictures, and videos. Unlike previous "flat" Internet applications, these social media tools allow two-way, real-time communication, interaction, collaboration, and co-creation. To use social media, FLMs need some form of Internet access, which used to mean a computer. The development of mobile technology has made social media independent of traditional computing FLMs now have to access the Internet with a laptop, tablet, smartphone, or ebook reader. Social media and mobile technologies are also "low friction" tools: They are ubiquitous, easy to use, flexible, and do not require specialized equipment. Another feature is their rapid development which will continue to result in more and more technologies that can be used by FLMs as communication tools. As will be discussed later in this chapter related, information richness, social media is "information rich" and close to the top of the hierarchy.

Understanding Communication Networks

Communication in organizations tends to flow in certain patterns. The pathways along which information flows throughout an organization are called communication networks. The type of communication network that exists in a group depends on the nature of the group's tasks and the extent to which group members need to communicate with each other in order to achieve group goals.

Formal and Informal Communication Networks Within Organizations

An organization chart may seem to be a good summary of an organization's communication network, but often it is not. An organization chart summarizes formal reporting relationships in an organization and the formal pathways along which communication takes place. Communication occurs across departments, groups, and teams along these formal pathways. Often, however, communication of information flows around issues, goals, projects, and ideas instead of moving up and down the organizational hierarchy in an orderly fashion. An organization's communication network, therefore, includes not only the formal communication pathways summarized in an organizational chart, but also informal communication pathways along which a great deal of communication takes place.

The Grapevine

One informal organizational communication network along which information flows quickly, if not always accurately, is the grapevine. Every organization has its grapevine, and an amazing amount of information may be transmitted through the grapevine. Employees often know about major decisions such as changes in organizational structure or incentive packages before FLMs have been officially notified.

Unfortunately, information passed through the grapevine often gets exaggerated as it travels from employee to employee. This is particularly true when FLMs or organizations fail to distribute information openly. Given the absence of open and honest information from management, employees try to fill the vacuum by providing bits of information to each other, which may be based on speculation rather than facts, thus starting rumors.

The best prescription for dealing with a rumor is to expose its untruthfulness and to state the facts openly and honestly. If FLMs do not have all the necessary information available, they should frankly admit it and then try to gather the facts by consulting a higher-level manager, asking what information may be told, and when, and then reporting to employees. Otherwise, employees will make up their own, often incorrect, explanations. Further, if your employees trust you, they will be willing to let you know what they hear on the grapevine, thus giving you the opportunity to dispel rumors and provide accurate information. You can also use the grapevine as a way of taking the pulse of your organization. It can help you learn about the basic attitudes and thoughts of employees, and whether they regard the company in a positive or negative light. This may help you better understand and address motivational issues of your work group.

Building Communication Skills

This section will discuss various kinds of barriers to effective communication in organizations and what FLMs can do to overcome them. Some of these barriers have their origin in actions of senders and receivers. Others are based on differences in personal communication styles. FLMs can build their own communication skills to overcome these barriers. First we shall discuss FLMs as senders and receivers.

FLMs as Senders

Organizational effectiveness depends on FLMs being able to send messages to people both inside and outside the organization. There are certain communication skills that help ensure that messages sent by FLMs are properly understood. Let's see what each skill entails.

Send Clear and Complete Messages

FLMs need to learn how to send messages that are clear and complete. A message is clear when it is easy for the receiver to understand and interpret, and it is complete when it contains all the information that the sender and receiver need to reach a common understanding. In striving to send messages that are both clear and complete, FLMs must learn to anticipate how receivers will interpret messages and to adjust messages to eliminate sources of misunderstanding or confusion. Recall from the earlier scenario that Grant Weatherly's message to his direct reports about an upcoming restructuring was unclear, incomplete, and misinterpreted. Weatherly did not anticipate that his employees would interpret the message as a warning of further layoffs, and therefore he did not adjust the message to eliminate this source of misunderstanding.

Encode Messages in Symbols the Receiver Understand

FLMs need to appreciate that when they encode messages, they should use symbols or language that the receiver understands. If, for example, the recipient does not speak English as a native language, the FLM should use simple terms and avoid using high level vocabulary. Further, when speaking with outside groups or individuals, the FLM should avoid jargon (e.g., technical or slang terms that only those in the workgroup understand) that will not be understood by others.

Select a Medium Appropriate for the Message

As you have learned, FLMs can choose from a variety of communication media, including face-to-face discussions, letters, memos, newsletters, phone conversations, e-mail, voice mail, faxes, and video conferences. A primary concern in choosing an appropriate medium is the nature of the message. Jennifer Flowers' superior communication skills led her to just this conclusion in the opening scenario; Weatherly probably never considered this option.

Select a Medium That the Receiver Monitors of Is Able to Understand

Another factor that FLMs need to take into account when selecting a communication medium is whether the medium is one that the receiver monitors. People differ in the amount of attention they pay to different communication media. FLMs should learn which employees like things in writing and which prefer face-to-face interactions and should then choose the most appropriate media for them.

Avoid Filtering and Information Distortion

Filtering occurs when the sender withholds part of a message because he or she mistakenly thinks that the receiver does not need the information or will not want to receive it. In the opening scenario, Weatherly filtered the information he gave his employees. He told them nothing about the nature of the change or its implications for their job security. As a result of his mistake, they misinterpreted his message.

Information distortion occurs when the meaning of a message changes as the message passes through a series of senders and receivers. Some information distortion is accidental—due to faulty encoding and decoding or to lack of feedback. Other information distortion is deliberate. Senders may alter a message to make themselves or their groups look good and to receive special treatment.

FLMs themselves should avoid filtering and distorting information. They should also create an atmosphere of trust to minimize incentives to distort messages. Employees who trust their FLMs believe that they will not be blamed for things beyond their control and will be treated fairly. FLMs who trust their employees provide them with clear and complete information and do not hold things back.

Build a Feedback Mechanism Into Messages

Feedback is essential for effective communication. FLMs should build a feedback mechanism into the messages they send—either including a request for feedback or indicating when and how they will follow up on a message to make sure that it was understood. When FLMs send written messages, they can request that the receiver respond in a letter, memo, or fax; can schedule a meeting to discuss the issue; or can follow up with a phone call. By building feedback mechanisms such as these into their messages, FLMs ensure that they are heard and understood.

FLMs as Receivers

FLMs receive as many messages as they send. Thus, FLMs must possess or develop communication skills that allow them to be effective message receivers. In particular, they must pay attention, be good listeners, and be empathetic. These skills are examined in greater detail below.

Pay Attention

Because of their multiple roles and tasks, FLMs often are overloaded and forced to think about several things at once. Torn in many different directions, they sometimes do not pay sufficient attention to the messages they receive. To be effective, however, FLMs should pay attention to all messages, regardless of their workload.

Listen and Be Empathic

Like most people, FLMs often like to hear themselves talk. Part of being a good communicator, however, is being a good listener. To listen effectively, FLMs should avoid interrupting and maintain eye contact when others are speaking. Once the sender is finished, the FLM should ask questions if necessary or summarize important points so that it is clear that the message is understood. Finally, FLMs should be empathetic and try to interpret a message from the sender's point of view, rather than from only their own point of view. This should increase the likelihood that they will interpret the message in the way it was intended. By displaying empathy, FLMs establish the groundwork for creating an atmosphere of trust and understanding which is important to effective communication.

Communication Styles

As you know from experience, different people tend to communicate differently, and their diverse approaches to saying the same thing may have different effects on their audiences. Some people tend to give more information than you need, while others are vague. Further, some are loud and forceful in their communications while others are quiet and reflective. A successful FLM must understand all of these differences and how they can create barriers to effective communication.

Personal Communication Styles

Keith and Samuel are two FLMs in the same company. Their employee, Findlay, approaches them to discuss the possibility of receiving a salary increase. They both have supervised Findlay during the past year and do not believe he deserves a raise. Keith and Samuel each go about communicating their feelings to Findlay quite differently, however. Samuel couldn't have been more direct. "I'll be blunt," he said, "a raise is out of the question." Keith's approach was far more analytical: "Well, Findlay, let's look at the big picture. I see here in your file that we just gave you a raise two months ago, and that you're not scheduled for another salary review for 4 months. Let me share with you some of the numbers and thoroughly explain why the company will have to stick with that schedule."

Although the message was the same in both cases, Keith and Samuel presented it quite differently. In other words, they differ with respect to their personal communication styles. FLMs will tend to prefer a specific style of communicating with all of their employees. Some may say whatever comes to mind and cut right to the bottom line. Others may want to carefully discuss every issue before making a decision. Still others may focus on interpersonal relationships when communicating. Thus, it is important for FLMs to recognize their own personal style and to attempt to adapt this style to individual employees.

Group Based Communication Differences

Differences in backgrounds or cultures may also increase the likelihood that communication difficulties will occur in a group. Consider the following scenarios: An FLM from New York is having a conversation with an FLM from North Dakota. The FLM never seems to get a chance to talk. He keeps waiting for a pause to signal his turn to talk, but the New York FLM never pauses long enough. The New York FLM wonders why the North Dakotian FLM does not say much. He feels uncomfortable when he pauses and the North Dakotian FLM says nothing, so he starts talking again.

Karla compliments Jefferson on his presentation to upper management and asks John what he thought of her presentation. Jefferson launches into a lengthy critique of Karla's presentation and describes how he would have handled it differently. This is hardly the response Karla expected.

Sue thinks of a new way to cut costs, which she shares with fellow members of her self-managed work team. Mason, another team member, thinks her idea is a good one and encourages the rest of the team to support it. Sarah is quietly pleased by Mason's support. The group then implements "Mason's" suggestion, and it is written up as such in the company newsletter, giving no credit to Sarah.

Each of the individuals in these scenarios has a comfortable, or characteristic way of speaking, called a "linguistic style," that is making communication difficult between them. The scenarios are based on the work of linguist Deborah Tannen, who describes linguistic style as a person's characteristic way of speaking which includes tone of voice, speed, volume, use of pauses, directness or indirectness, choice of words, credit-taking, and use of questions, jokes, and other types of speech. These linguistic style differences may occur because of cultural or regional differences between people. When people's linguistic styles differ and these differences are not taken into account and understood, ineffective communication is likely to occur.

Regional Differences

The first scenarios illustrate regional differences in linguistic style. The North Dakotian FLM expects the pauses that signal turn taking in conversations to be longer than the pauses made by his colleagues in New York. This difference causes communication problems. The North Dakotian thinks that his eastern colleague never lets him get a word in edgewise, and the easterner cannot figure out why his colleague from the Midwest does not get more actively involved in conversations.

Cross-Cultural Differences

It is important to recognize that communication is conducted in different ways around the world. For example, compare countries like the United States that place a high value on individualism with countries like Japan that emphasize collectivism. American FLMs rely heavily on memoranda, announcements, position papers, and other formal forms of communication to stake out their positions in an organization. Japanese FLMs, in contrast to American FLMs, will engage in extensive verbal consultation over an issue before making an announcement.

Today's FLMs must make themselves familiar with cross-cultural communication differences. FLMs and managers communicate with people from abroad, they should try to find out as much as they can about cultural differences and the aspects of communication styles that are specific to the country or culture in question.

Gender-Based Differences

Referring back to the three scenarios that open this section, you may be wondering why Jefferson launched into a lengthy critique of Karla's presentation after she paid him a routine compliment, or why Mason got the credit for Sue's idea in the self-managed work team.

Gender differences also affect the communication process. Here are two examples:

- Asking questions. Women are more likely to ask questions than men; the downside is that male FLMs may interpret women as knowing less than their male peers.
- Confidence and boasting. Women tend to emphasize their doubts and uncertainty, but men tend to express greater confidence and play down their doubts.

An assessment by a male FLM of how well a woman is coping with change, for example, compared with male colleagues may thus conclude: "She seems very uncertain since she is always asking questions." However, this assessment may have more to do with gender differences related to a willingness to question, for example, about change than to real differences in attitude toward the change itself.

Research conducted by Deborah Tannen and other linguists has found that the linguistic styles of men and women differ in practically every culture or language. These differences which are described in this section are demonstrated for men and women in general, and are not indicative of ALL women or ALL men.

In the United States, many women tend to downplay differences between people, are not overly concerned about receiving credit for their own accomplishments, and want to make everyone feel that they are more or less on an equal footing, so that even poor performers or low-status individuals feel valued. Many men, in contrast, tend to emphasize their own superiority, take credit for accomplishments whenever possible, and are not reluctant to acknowledge differences in status. These differences in linguistic style led Karla to give Jefferson a routine compliment on his presentation even though she thought that he had not done a particularly good job. She asked him how her presentation was so that he could reciprocate, complimenting her and thereby putting them on an equal footing. Jefferson and Karla's compliment and question about her own presentation as an opportunity to confirm his superiority, never realizing that she was only expecting a routine compliment. Similarly, Mason's enthusiastic support for Sue's cost-cutting idea and her apparent surrender of ownership of the idea after she described it led team members to assume incorrectly that the idea was Malik's.

Power

The use of language can also reflect underlying power and gender relationships—factors that can also interfere with the communication process. For example, the manner in which FLMs seek employee comments on projects or proposals can reinforce power differentials. Telling employees to provide input may result in responses different from those obtained when the request conveys respect for their opinions. Power differences are normally a barrier to communication. Those who are more powerful may not wish to disclose information that could make them appear to be less powerful or that could weaken their power base. Those who are less powerful may not wish to disclose information that could potentially be used against them.

The term "power tells" describes various signs and clues that indicate how powerful someone is—or how powerful they want to be. The power tells of dominant individuals include:

- sitting and standing with legs apart (men);
- appropriating the territory around them by placing their hands on their hips;
- using open postures;
- using invasive hand gestures;
- smiling less, because a smile is an appeasement gesture;
- establishing visual dominance by looking away from the other person while speaking, implying that they do not need to be attentive;
- speaking first, and dominating the conversation thereafter;
- using a lower vocal register, and speaking more slowly; and
- being more likely to interrupt others, more likely to resist interruption by others.

The power tells of submissive individuals include:

- modifying speech style to sound more like the person they are talking to;
- more frequently hesitating, using lots of "ums" and "ers";
- adopting closed postures;
- clasping hands, touching face and hair (self-comfort gestures); and
- blushing, coughing, dry mouth, heavy breathing, heavy swallowing, increased heart rate, lip biting, rapid blinking, and sweating are "leakage tells" which reveal stress and anxiety.

FLMs can thus "read" the power signals of others. More importantly, however, FLMs may need to control their own "tells" in order to appear less dominant and less powerful, particularly when communicating in a manner that will encourage employee feedback, engagement, and support.

Emotion

Communication models have been criticized for ignoring the role of emotions in organizational communications, focusing instead on the rational and cognitive dimensions of communication. Nevertheless, FLMs need to be aware of, to understand, and where appropriate to respond to emotional responses in organizational communications. Emotions can interfere with the communication process, but emotions can also be a positive

TABLE 11.2 Main Barriers to Successful Communication	
Language	Choice of words and tone of message can lead to misunderstandings and misinterpretations.
Gender Differences	Men and women use different communication styles, which can lead to misunderstanding; men tend to talk more; women tend to listen, and ask more questions.
Power Differences	Employees distort upward communication, and that FLMs/and other superiors often have a limited understanding of direct reports' roles, experiences, and problems.
Context	Organization culture and history, as well as physical setting, can color the way in which communications are transmitted and interpreted.
Cultural Diversity	Different cultures have different expectations concerning formal and informal communication; lack of awareness of those norms creates misunderstanding.
Emotion	Emotional arousal interferes with message transmission and receipt, and emotional response to communication can be negative (anxiety, anger) or positive (exciting, stimulating).

resource, contributing to employee willingness, commitment and support in various situations. In reality, not all FLMs have the skills or the credibility to manage the emotional responses employees may present in given situations, and to achieve positive emotional responses. Table 11.2 summarizes the main barriers to successful communication.

The communication process appears to be simple, but it is prone to errors arising on both sides of the exchange. FLMs cannot confidently assume that receivers will always decode their messages in a way that gives them the meaning that they intended to transmit. Communication is central to FLM and organizational success, but this claim has practical implications. It seems that organizations function better where:

- communications are open,
- relationships are based on mutual understanding and trust,
- interactions are based on cooperation rather than competition,
- people work together in terms, and
- decisions are reached in a participative way.

These features are not universal, and are not present in all countries, cultures—or organizations.

Managing Differences in Communication and Linguistic Styles

FLMs should not expect to change people's communication or linguistic styles and should not try to, but should simply understand them. For example, FLMs should ensure that women have a chance to talk if they know that they are reluctant to speak up in meetings, not because they have nothing to contribute, but because of their linguistic style. FLMs should be extra careful to give credit where it is deserved.

Developing Your Written and Speaking Skills

While understanding differences in communication styles is critical to success as an FLM, it is also important for FLMs to hone the fundamental skills of writing and speaking. The remainder of this chapter discusses the importance of writing and speaking and offers suggestions and guidelines for developing and using these two important skills.

The Writing Process

FLMs can use written communication for various types of messages, including memos, letters, regulations, policies, newsworthy information, and announcements of changes in procedures or personnel. Written instructions can explain how to use equipment or how to process work orders or customer requests in a permanent form. Because the ability to communicate effectively plays an important part in an FLM's success on the job, more and more employers look for prospective FLMs who have skills in written communication.

What Is Good Writing?

Effective writing includes the appropriate content for the readers. It is concise, clear, coherent, well-organized, and free from errors. The information you provide should be accurate and relevant. Further, you should attempt to be concise; write as simply as possible using words and phrases with which the reader is familiar.

Effecting writing is a process. The steps of the process include identifying your purpose and audience, gathering information, generating and organizing ideas, drafting, revising, and proofreading. The remainder of this section shows how an FLM can apply this process to ensure they communicate with others effectively.

Getting Started: Identifying Your Purpose

The first stage in the writing process is to analyze the purpose of your document, or what you want to accomplish. The purpose of most FLMs' writing falls generally into one or more of the three categories: to give information about something, to propose a course of action, or to solve a problem. A report on injuries, for example, could have numerous purposes. Should the report simply compare and contrast injury information? Should it recommend a particular response to the injury information in a given situation? The purpose should determine what to include in the document.

Analyzing Your Readers

Another important consideration in planning a writing project is the audience. A memo on a highly technical topic would be written one way for someone with technical expertise, but another way for a customer or individual with only limited knowledge of your particular job or procedures and terminology.

Getting Your Ideas Together

Once you have evaluated the purpose of the writing and the needs of the readers, you are ready for the next stage in the writing process: gathering information and organizing the ideas you want to present. This step may be easy. For a short letter, you may not need to do research, and you may have only a short list of topics to organize.

For much of the writing an FLM does, however, gathering information and organizing it may be a more complicated process. It may involve a great deal of thought, and perhaps some research as well. Let's look at some techniques you can use.

Gathering Information

Before you begin to write the document, be sure you have all the information you need and that your information is accurate. You may want to check existing files or books on a topic, or interview people who are up-to-date on the issues.

Generating Ideas

Once you have gathered the information you need, you're ready to decide exactly what to say. Try to break up the purpose into several subtopics. Suppose the purpose of your letter is to recommend to the building owner the value of a new computerized-maintenance management system (CMMS) to increase budgeting and preventive maintenance efforts by your unit. The statement of purpose for this letter could specify the different types of systems available and the major advantages and disadvantages of each.

Arranging Ideas/Organization

Once you've decided what you want to say, it's important to consider how best to arrange your ideas so that the reader will find them easy to follow. You could arrange ideas in logical order or in a list according to their importance, beginning with the ideas that are most important to the reader. Before writing, you may want to begin with an outline of the document. Ultimately, most documents will include:

1. *Introduction:* Identifies the subject of the document and tells why it was written.
2. *Concise statement of the main ideas.* Summarizes main ideas, conclusions, or recommendations. This part of a document may be part of the statement of purpose or as long as a three-page executive summary.
3. *Development of the main ideas.* Includes further description of the main ideas, using explanations, examples, analyses, steps, reasons, and factual details. This part is often called the body of the document.
4. *Conclusion.* Brings the document to an effective close. The conclusion may restate the main idea in a fresh way, suggest further work, or summarize recommendations, but an effective conclusion avoids unnecessary repetition.

Writing the Document

The next steps in writing involve drafting, revising, and finalizing the document. Using your outline, you will begin by filling in each section. Don't worry at this point about spelling and punctuation, or finding just the right word. Focus on getting your ideas out.

Second, you will revise the draft, polishing your style and ensuring your ideas are effectively and completely presented. At this point, read the document from the recipient's point of view, ensuring you have included all key information. Finally, after you have polished the style and organization of the document, you will be ready to put it in its final form. Consider questions of document design, such as the use of headings, white space, and other elements of the document's appearance. After the entire document is written, be sure to carefully proofread it for errors, preferably after you have been away from the document for a while.

Listed below is a summary of tips for improving your writing skills. This can serve as an easy reference for you in writing documents in the future.

1. Analyze the purpose of the writing and the needs and expectations of the readers.
2. Organize your ideas so that readers will find them easy to follow.
3. Write the draft and then revise it to make the writing polished and correct.
4. Make the writing unified. All sentences should relate to the main idea, either directly or indirectly. Eliminate digressions and irrelevant detail.
5. Use summary sentences and transitions to make your writing coherent.
6. Write in short paragraphs that begin with clear topic sentences.
7. Be concise—make every word count.
8. Keep it simple—use simple vocabulary and short sentences.
9. Use jargon only when your readers understand it. Define technical terms when necessary.
10. Be precise—avoid ambiguous and unclear writing.
11. Proofread for grammar, punctuation, spelling, and typographical errors.

The next section presents techniques for giving, preparing and evaluating speeches and highlights the importance of oral communication skills.

FLMs as Good Public Speakers

Effective oral presentation skills are also important to management success. FLMs who can impress others with their speech-making abilities are admired, and they frequently become the leaders in their organizations as well as in their communities. Today's FLM can become a successful public speaker by mastering the principles for preparing and making a speech or presentation.

Preparing a Speech

In this section we shall discuss specific steps for preparing an effective oral presentation. These steps include knowing your audience, determining your purpose, choosing and limiting your topic, collecting and organizing information, preparing an outline and finally, planning your speech.

Know Your Audience

If you understand your audience, you will be able to prepare a speech that will be of interest and benefit to them. For example, when making a formal speech to your superiors you should make sure to address their concerns and interests, such as budgeting issues or personnel planning.

Determine Your Purpose

Ask yourself, why was I asked to give this speech? Is this talk for a special occasion, such as an annual management budget presentation? Should the speech be entertaining, persuasive, or informative? Your answers to these questions will help you identify your purpose and select appropriate materials.

Choose and Limit Your Topic

If you have not already been assigned a topic, you must choose your topic carefully. You need to meet the needs and interests of the audience, fulfill the purpose of your talk, and be able to present the topic in the time allotted. You should be careful to limit your subject so that you don't lose the attention of the audience.

Collect Your Information

In order to prepare for your speech, talk to well-informed people and read reliable and up-to-date books and magazines on your topic. You also should recall personal experiences related to the topic to be able to personalize your presentation. Take accurate notes, distinguishing between facts and opinions.

Prepare a Detailed Outline and Organize Your Information

Using the preliminary outline and the information collected, you should prepare a detailed outline from which to develop your speech. The main points in your preliminary outline should guide you in organizing your information. Considering your audience and the purpose of your talk, select the most important points to include in your final outline. You may discover that some topics need to be rearranged, or irrelevant topics need to be omitted. Your organization of information may reveal the need for audio and visual aids, or other materials to help make your speech more interesting and understandable. These could include overhead transparencies, slides, hangouts, pictures, posters, and charts, to help make your speech more interesting and understandable.

Write your speech. Use the outline as the basis for logically presenting your ideas.

Introduction.   Introductory remarks should arouse audience interest in the speaker and the subject. Establish rapport with the audience by making comments that are appropriate for the occasion and that orient the audience to your speech. There are several possible approaches to introducing your speech. You might state the subject and purpose of the talk, tell a humorous story or anecdote, make an unusual or startling statement, quote from familiar or strongly-worded material, use an illustration, or ask a question.

Body.   One way to make a logical transition from the introduction to the discussion is to state the main points. In the body of the speech, you can review them again, supporting them with adequate explanations and illustrations, using transitions to move from point to point. Techniques for explaining and illustrating include:

1. citing examples,
2. quoting recognized authorities,
3. making comparisons,
4. using descriptive language,
5. relating a story,
6. giving pertinent facts and figures, and
7. using audio and visual aids.

Conclusion.   Every presentation needs a conclusion. Give as much thought to concluding your presentation as you do to introducing it. Keep your conclusions brief by summarizing the main ideas, without being too redundant. You might use any of these suggestions that seem appropriate:

1. Tell a story that emphasizes the purpose of the presentation or speech.
2. Request that a specific action be taken.
3. Stress the importance and timeliness of your subject.
4. Make a logical deduction from the information presented.
5. Ask the audience to adopt certain attitudes and beliefs.

Practice your speech.   Rehearsing your speech a number of times in a room similar to the one in which you will give it should help you to speak spontaneously and within the time limit. You may want to tape yourself or ask someone to watch you and provide feedback.

Giving Your Presentation or Speech

A well-written speech may fall flat if the delivery is poor. You can probably cite many examples of times when you have had to sit through an excruciatingly boring speech. Perhaps the person spoke in monotone or rambled on for far too long. To avoid these pitfalls, consider the following suggestions:

Develop Your Own Style

Don't try to imitate someone else. Being yourself will project who and what you are in the most effective way possible.

Maintain Self-Confidence

Your audience will be at ease and more receptive if you are confident and poised. Some nervousness is normal and good for you because it keeps you alert and sparks your delivery. Arrive a few minutes early to talk with the people who will introduce you, arrange the room and equipment, make sure the microphone is working, and give yourself an opportunity to relax.

Makes a Favorable First Impression

Good grooming and proper dress cannot be overemphasized. The audience's first impression is based on your appearance, and a good appearance should improve self-confidence. An energetic talk, good posture, and pleasant facial expressions should cause your audience to respond favorably.

Avoid Objectionable Mannerisms

Some mannerisms or verbal expressions may distract the audience from concentrating on your speech. You should avoid mannerisms such as twisting your hair, tapping your fingers on the podium, clicking a ball point pen, or shifting from one foot to the other. Avoid verbal expressions such as "ah," "anda," "you know," and "like." Practicing your speech and asking others to watch you will help you identify and eliminate these distracting mannerisms or expressions.

Use Appropriate Gestures

Enhance your speech by using gestures that are natural and well timed. Gestures are important because they emphasize your main points, help your audience visualize your ideas, keep the audience interested in your comments, help relieve your nervousness, and help you to use nonverbal communication effectively as you speak. A list of gesture "do's and don'ts" are provided in Table 11.3.

Speak Clearly

Project your voice by keeping your chin up so that each person in the audience can readily understand you. Proper enunciation is critical, especially if you are to be understood by a diverse audience.

TABLE 11.3 Gesture Do's and Don'ts	
Do's	**Don'ts**
• Use gestures to embrace the audience	• Overuse gestures
• Gesture naturally	• Keep hands out of pockets
• Relax hands by your side when not gesturing	• Grasp/touch podium or lectern
• Use both arms/hands	• Lock hands/arms in front/back of you
• Free your arms to gesture emphatically	• Gesture with one arm/hand only
• Keep your feet still to promote gestures	• Avoid rhythmic gestures (looking mechanical)
• Observe yourself gesturing	• Don't point excessively

Vary Your Speaking Rate and Pitch

Vary the pitch of your voice and rate of speaking, incorporating well-timed pauses so the audience will not be lulled to sleep.

Speak Correctly

Speakers who use incorrect grammar may lose the respect of the audience. Many speakers are ineffective simply because of shoddy grammar or inappropriate slang.

Involve the Audience

Maintaining good eye contact and reacting to body language helps you adapt your delivery for optimum audience involvement. Personal eye contact with individuals in all sections of the room gives your audience the feeling that you recognize them as individuals. If individuals look alert, are smiling, and are nodding their heads in approval, you can assume your talk interests them. If listeners are becoming restless or sleepy, however, you will realize that your talk is receiving a negative reaction and can try to alter your style.

Conclusion

Good communication is necessary for an FLM and organization to be successful. To be successful communicators, FLMs must understand that communication occurs in a cyclical process that entails two phases: transmission and feedback.

Communication by FLMs and organizations is impacted by information richness (i.e., the amount of information a communication medium can carry and the extent to which the medium enables the sender and receiver to reach a common understanding) and advances in technology, like the Internet, Intranets, groupware software, and social media continue to allow

FLMs and their organizations to improve communication, performance, and customer service.

There are various barriers to effective communication in organizations. To overcome these barriers and effectively communicate with others, FLMs must possess or develop communication skills as senders and receivers of messages. For example, FLMs should send messages that are clear and complete, use words that the receiver understands, choose a medium appropriate for the message and monitored by the receiver, avoid filtering and information distortion, include a feedback mechanism in the message, provide accurate information to ensure that misleading rumors are not spread, pay attention, be a good listener, and be empathetic. Understanding gender, power and cross-cultural differences, and linguistic styles is also an essential communication skill for FLMs.

Finally, without good written and oral communication skills FLMs cannot expect to build successful personal and business relationships. To do this, they should understand the writing process from beginning to end and the techniques for preparing, giving, and evaluating a speech.

12

Performance Management

Getting the Most Out of Your People

The major purpose of management controls is to ensure that work is progressing according to the FLM's plans. Controls should, therefore, be designed to alert FLMs to problems or potential problems before they become critical, and to give FLMs time to take corrective actions. Controlling is similar to planning in many ways. The major difference between controlling and planning is that planning takes place before work is done, and controlling usually takes place while work is ongoing.

In Chapter 4, we shall first outline the control process, and briefly discuss benchmarking as a contemporary tool for monitoring and measuring performance. The chapter will then provide an in-depth discussion of performance appraisals as an FLM tool for monitoring and improving employee performance and will conclude with a discussion of discipline.

Succeeding as a Frontline Manager in Today's Organizations, pages 329–360
Copyright © 2021 by Information Age Publishing
All rights of reproduction in any form reserved.

The Control Process

As described in Chapter 4, controlling is the management function concerned with monitoring performance to ensure that it conforms to plans and if significant deviations exist, getting the organization back on track. For FLMs, this means following a process of monitoring, comparing, and correcting which constitutes the controlling function. FLMs carry out this process in many ways. Consider the following fictional examples.

- Samuel Johnson told his crew, "I expect the production area to be clean when you leave each day. That means the work area should be clear of all tools and everything should be put away."
- Once or twice each day, Dangaia Weiner took time to check the project documents produced by the design teams she managed. Dangaia would look over a few documents each team had produced that day. If one of the teams seemed to be having trouble with a task—Dangaia would discuss the problem with that team lead.
- Sieya Cammayo learned that customers calling her department complained that they were spending an excessive amount of time on hold. She held a meeting at which the employees discussed how they could handle calls more quickly.

As shown in these examples, FLMs need to know what is going on in the area they manage. Do employees understand what they are supposed to do and are they able to do it? Is all the computers, machinery, and equipment operating properly? Is work being done correctly and on time?

To answer these questions, an FLM could theoretically sit back and wait for disaster to strike, assuming that where there is no problem, there is no need for correction. However, FLMs have a responsibility to correct problems as soon as possible, which means that they need some way to detect problems quickly. Detection and correction of problems is at the heart of the control function.

By controlling, the FLM can take steps to ensure quality and manage costs. By setting standards for a clean workplace, Samuel Johnson reduced the costs related to spending time looking for tools or slipping on a messy floor. By visiting the work area and checking on performance, Dangaia Weiner made sure that her employees were producing satisfactory work and correcting problems before they became severe. By engaging her employees in improving work processes, Sieya Cammayo responded effectively to customer concerns. In many similar ways, FLMs can benefit the organization through the control process.

Steps in the Control Process

Control is accomplished by comparing actual performance with pre-determined standards or objectives and then taking action to correct any deviations from the standards. The control process has three basic steps:

1. Establishing performance standards;
2. Monitoring performance and comparing it with those standards; and
3. Taking necessary corrective actions.

The first step is part of the planning process while the other two are unique to the control process.

Establishing Performance Standards

Once organizational objectives have been set, they generally are used as standards that outline expectations for performance. Standards are used to set expected performance levels for machines, tasks, individuals, groups, or the organization as a whole. Usually standards are expressed in terms of quantity, quality, or time limitations. For example, standards may cover production output per hour; product quality as reflected by the level of customer satisfaction, or production schedule deadlines.

Performance standards attempt to answer the question, "What is a fair day's work?" or "How good is good enough?" Standards take many factors into account that may impact outcomes such as inevitable delays and time for equipment maintenance. Several types of performance standards are described below.

- *Productivity standards*—designed to reflect the output per unit of time. Example: numbers of units produced per work hour.
- *Material standards*—designed to reflect the efficiency of material usage. Examples: amount of raw materials used per unit, or average amount of scrap produced per unit.
- *Resource usage standards*—designed to reflect how efficiently organizational resources are being used. Examples: return on investment, percent of capacity, asset usage.
- *Revenue standards*—designed to reflect the level of sales activity. Examples: dollar sales, average revenue per customer, per capita sales (i.e., sales per person).
- *Cost standards*—designed to reflect the level of costs. Examples: dollar cost of operation, cost per unit produced, cost per unit sold.

Many methods for setting standards are available. The choice of the most appropriate method depends on the type of standard in question. A common approach is to use the judgement of the FLM or other recognized experts to set the standard, but this approach can be very subjective. A variation is for the FLM and the persons performing the job to set the standard together, thus allowing the employees who actually perform the job to provide input. Another approach is to set standards based on an analysis of historical data discussed in Chapter 4, while accounting for any circumstances that may have changed since the data was collected. One objective approach is to use industrial engineering methods, which usually involve a detailed and scientific analysis of the work to be done.

With the above as a backdrop, while the list of major duties of a job tells the employee *what* is to be done, performance standards provide the employee with specific performance expectations for each major duty. They are the observable behaviors and actions which explain *how* the job is to be done, plus the results that are expected for satisfactory job performance. They tell the employee what a good job looks like. For the FLM, the purpose of performance standards is to communicate expectations. Some FLMs prefer to make them as specific as possible, and some prefer to use them as talking points with the specificity defined in the discussion. FLMS should keep in mind that good performance typically involves more than technical expertise. FLMs and their organizations also expect certain behaviors (e.g., friendliness, helpfulness, courteousness, punctuality, etc.). It is often these behaviors that determine whether performance is acceptable. So, performance standards are:

- based on the position, not the individual;
- observable, specific indicators of success;
- meaningful, reasonable, and attainable;
- described as "fully satisfactory" performance once trained;
- expressed in terms of quantity, quality, timeliness, cost, safety, or outcomes;

In determining performance standards, consider the following:

- What does a good job look like?
- How many or how much is needed?
- How long should it take?
- When are the results needed?
- How accurate or how good is acceptable?
- Are there budget considerations?

- Are there safety considerations?
- Are there legislative or regulatory requirements that require strict adherence?
- Are there behaviors that are expected in your department to promote teamwork, leadership, creativity, and customer service?
- What results would be considered satisfactory?
- What condition will exist when the duty is well performed?
- What is the difference between good and poor performance?

Monitoring Performance

The primary purpose of monitoring performance is to provide information on what is actually happening in the organization. Monitoring should be preventive and not punitive. In this light, the reasons for monitoring should always be fully explained to employees.

The major problem in monitoring performance is deciding when, where, and how often to monitor. Timing is important. For example, raw materials or parts like those that took 4 days to be delivered to an FLM's unit must be reordered before they run out so as to allow for delivery time. Monitoring must, therefore, be done often enough to provide adequate information. If it is overdone, however, it can become expensive and can annoy employees. The key is to view monitoring as a means of providing needed information and not as a means of checking up on employees.

There are several tools and techniques FLMs can use to monitor performance. Budgets, reports, audits, and personal observations are the methods most commonly used for this purpose.

Budgets express plans, objectives, and programs of the organization in numerical terms. The administration of the budget is an important controlling function for an FLM. However, excessive reliance on a budget can result in inflexibility or inefficiency. Take, for example, Nandi Sims, a manager in a high tech computer company. Nandi has determined that adherence to his budget is his most important goal. When Jeff, her direct report, comes to her with a new technology in which he thinks they should invest, Nandi says it is not in this year's budget. Despite Jeff's information that this technology will speed up the manufacturing process and ultimately reduce overhead, Nandi still insists they can't afford it this year. Nandi meets her budget goals, but quickly falls behind her competitors in terms of efficiency. In the long run, Nandi's decision hurt the company. Thus, budgets should be used as a standard guideline and not as a fixed goal.

Reports are designed to provide important summary information as a second means of monitoring organizational or unit performance. Written reports can be prepared on a periodic or an as-needed basis. These reports may summarize information or interpret the data provided and make recommendations. Reports should be simple and provide information in the most useful way (e.g., by using tables or graphics when appropriate). FLMs should continually monitor a report's usefulness in terms of its timeliness, cost-effectiveness, acceptability, and flexibility among other factors.

Personal observation is sometimes the only way for an FLM to get an accurate picture of what is really happening in an organization, particularly with respect to individual employees. One type of personal observation is management by walking around (MBWA). When this method is used, FLMs are encouraged to walk around and mingle with one another and with the employees. If used appropriately (and not too much!) observations not only provide information to the FLM, but also communicate to employees the FLM's interest in them. However, FLMs should remember that what they are observing may be employees on their "best" behavior. It is important also to consider how employees work when the FLM is not watching.

In addition to personal observation, many organizations collect performance information electronically. Examples include electronic cash registers that keep a record of what items are sold and when, video cameras that record employee and customer movements, and phones that record how long each customer is engaged. FLMs then can establish appropriate goals for the unit's performance on these measures such as the average number of minutes for processing an insurance claim. While a number of organizations have successfully used these types of monitoring systems, FLMs also should note that there are legal risks associated with hidden surveillance, and that this type of system may be perceived as overly controlling by employees. Further, focusing too heavily on electronic monitoring may encourage employees to focus more on quantity than quality.

Management by Objectives

Management by objectives (MBO) was discussed in Chapter 4 as a means for setting objectives. The development of an MBO system is part of the planning function. Once such a system has been developed, however, it can be used for control purposes. MBO requires the FLM to set specific, measurable, organizationally relevant goals with each employee and then periodically discuss the latter's progress toward these goals. The steps in MBO are:

1. *Set the organization's goals.* Establish an organization-wide plan for next year, and set goals.
2. *Set team/departmental goals.* FLMs/team/department heads and their superiors jointly set goals for their teams/departments.
3. *Discuss team/departmental goals.* FLMs/team/department heads discuss the team's/department's goals with direct reports and ask them to develop their own individual goals. They should ask, "How could each employee help the team/department attain its goals?
4. *Define expected results (set individual goals).* FLMs/team/department heads and their direct reports set short-term performance targets for each employee.
5. *Conduct performance reviews.* After a period, FLMs/team/department heads compare each employee's actual and expected results.
6. *Provide feedback.* FLMs/team/department heads hold periodic performance review meetings with direct reports. Here they discuss the direct reports' performance and make any plans for rectifying or continuing the persons' performance.

Taking Corrective Action

Only after the actual performance has been assessed and compared with the performance standards can FLMs take proper corrective action. All too often, however, FLMs set standards and monitor performance, but do not follow up well. A major problem is determining when and why a deviation from the standard is occurring. How many mistakes should be allowed? Have the standards been set correctly? Is the poor performance due to the employee or some other factor such as a lack of proper equipment or training? The key here is the FLM's timely intervention. An FLM should not allow an unacceptable situation to exist for long, but should promptly determine the cause and take action.

Individual Performance Appraisals

Kani Taylor has just been informed by the human resources management (HRM) department that it is time to conduct performance appraisals of his employees. Prior to becoming an FLM, Kani had always felt uncomfortable during his own performance appraisal; he had always felt on the defensive. His manager never seemed to reward his good performance or give him enough specifics to know how to improve. Now that he is an FLM, he does not want his employees to feel the same way. Kani knows that some of his employees deserve an unfavorable appraisal, however, and he certainly is not looking forward to discussing their appraisals with them.

Kani's attitude about performance appraisals is all too common among FLMs. The need to evaluate individual, maintenance team, or departmental performance effectively is as important as ever in today's organizations. FLMs like Kani should think of appraising performance as a kind of compass—one that indicates an individual's or team's actual direction compared to the desired direction. Like a compass, the job of Kani and other FLMs is to indicate where the individual or team is now and to help focus attention and effort on the desired direction.

Unfortunately, many FLMs view performance appraisal as a once a year event when as a supervisor, he or she completes the company appraisal form for each employee. This approach is a mistake. Appraising employee performance should be part of a continuous improvement process that demands daily, not annual, attention. Think of it this way: Why are weekend golfers willing to pay handsomely for private lessons? So that a professional who understands and can demonstrate good performance will observe their performance, evaluate it, and then provide feedback to build sound habits and eliminate unsound ones. Subsequent lessons focus on the overall objective, such as a smooth, accurate swing, while recalling information about performance given in earlier lessons. This type of golf instruction is similar to supervising for maximum performance. While understanding the steps in the control process, like individual performance appraisals, it is most important for FLMs to focus on performance management.

Performance Management

Performance management is a collaborative, on-going process between an FLM and an employee to plan for, develop, and evaluate an employee's work. It focuses on what employees do and how they do it; it aligns individual, departmental, and organization goals; it identifies areas for employee learning; and, at best practice or benchmark organizations, performance management includes opportunities to discuss and plan for an employee's individual (career) development.

What's the Importance of Performance Management?

Effective performance management supports the organization's commitment to recruit, develop, and competitively compensate an outstanding workforce and to better prepare the organization to meet its future needs. It facilitates on-going conversations between employees and their FLMs that benefit all. Performance management drives consistency and openness across the organization in how it defines and evaluates work. It allows employees to enrich their knowledge in their current jobs and gain skills for future positions. And, performance management helps employees succeed, which helps FLMs succeed.

Effective communication between employees and FLMs is the key to successful performance management. Regular feedback helps employees focus their work activities so the employees, the team, the department, and the organization can achieve their goals. It builds accountability, since employees and FLMs participate in developing goals, identifying competencies, and discussing individual/career development.

The performance management process allows employees to understand

- what their goals and/or duties are and what is expected of them,
- the criteria for success and how well they are doing,
- how their responsibilities help achieve organizational goals,
- how they can improve job performance,
- the proficiency with which employees are achieving goals and/or carrying out duties,
- having a basis for coaching for improvement,
- fairly determining pay for performance,
- fairly recognizing and motivating high performers,
- identifying training and development needs, and
- supporting individual/career development opportunities.

The performance management process complements the organization's mission and leadership characteristics by:

- making explicit the relationship between individual, unit, and organization goals which allows employees to be effective and enjoy a sense of shared purpose;
- requiring that employees be evaluated based on clear and agreed upon goals, competencies, and development plans;
- giving employees specific expectations that they understand, and helping them to achieve high performance; and
- for employees, relating pay to performance by rewarding significant achievement.

Six basic elements of performance management are as follows:

- Direction sharing means communicating the organization's goals throughout the organization and then translating these into do-able individual, team, and departmental goals.
- Goal alignment means having a method that enables FLMs and employees to see the link between the employees' goals and those of their team, department, and organization.
- Ongoing performance monitoring usually includes using computerized systems that measure and then email progress and exception reports based on the person's progress toward meeting her or his performance goals.
- Ongoing feedback includes both face-to-face and computerized feedback regarding progress toward goals.
- Coaching and developmental support should be an integral part of the feedback process.
- Recognition and rewards provide the consequences needed to keep the employee's goal-directed performance on track.

Regular subjective feedback is at the heart of performance management, but such efforts suffer from one potentially calamitous weakness; at the end of the day, FLMs and their organizations need some way to differentiate among employees to make difficult pay raise and promotional decisions. Any performance management process that can't do that is not very practical. And, in the end, FLMs and their organization must strive to make sure performance management and appraisals are indeed practical.

The Purpose of Employee Performance Appraisals

In days gone by, the typical FLM would sit down annually with individual employees and critique their job performances. The purpose of these appraisals was to review how well the employees were progressing towards achieving their goals. The employees found that the performance appraisals gave them little more than a documented list of their shortcomings. Of course, since the performance appraisal is a key determinant in pay adjustments and promotion decisions, anything to do with appraising job performance struck fear into the hearts of employees. Not surprisingly, in this climate FLMs often wanted to avoid the whole appraisal process and in many instances formal appraisal programs yielded disappointing results. Their failure was often due to a lack of top-management information and support, unclear performance standards, lack of important skills for FLMs, too many forms to complete, or the use of appraisals for conflicting purposes.

Today, effective FLMs treat performance appraisals as an evaluation and development tool, as well as a formal legal document. Appraisals review past performance—emphasizing positive accomplishments as well as deficiencies and drafting detailed plans for development. By emphasizing the future as well as the past, documenting performance effectively, and providing feedback in a constructive manner, employees are less likely to respond defensively to feedback, and the appraisal process is more likely to motivate employees to improve where necessary. The performance evaluation also serves as a vital organizational need by providing the documentation necessary for any personnel action that might be taken against an employee.

Few things FLMs do are fraught with more peril than appraising direct reports' performance. Employees tend to be overly optimistic about what their ratings will be, and they know that their raises, careers, and peace of mind may hinge on how FLMs rate them. As if that's not enough, few appraisal processes are as fair as employers think. Numerous problems (such as bias and rating everyone "average") undermine the process. However, the perils notwithstanding, performance appraisal plays a central role in the FLMs efforts to manage human resources. The challenge for FLMs is to do the appraisal the right way.

Again, Why Appraise Performance?

As alluded to earlier, there are several reasons for FLMs to appraise direct reports' performance. First, most employers still determine pay, promotion, and retention decisions on the employee's appraisal. Second, performance appraisals play a central role in performance management (e.g., ensuring that each employee's performance makes sense in terms of the organization's goals). Third, the performance appraisal let the FLM and the direct report develop a plan for correcting any deficiencies and to reinforce the things she or he docs right. Fourth, performance appraisals should provide an opportunity to review and recalibrate the employee's career plans in light of her or his exhibited strengths and weaknesses. Finally, FLMs use appraisals to identify employees' training and development needs.

Performance Appraisal Steps

There are three steps in the performance appraisal process: (1) setting work standards, (2) assessing the employee's actual performance relative to those standards as discussed earlier, and (3) providing feedback to the employee regarding her or his performance. These steps can also be referred to as the performance appraisal cycle, to recognize that the feedback (Step 3) should in turn lead to setting new goals (Step 1).

When Should Appraisals Occur?

Ideally, performance appraisals should occur both formally and informally. Formal performance reviews should be conducted once a year at minimum, but twice a year is better. Informal performance appraisals and feedback should complement the formal appraisal system. The ultimate goal is to establish an effective "performance management system" where performance is monitored and managed overall, not just appraised in a once a year session.

Continuous feedback is primarily important in letting employees know how they are doing. Without constructive feedback, employees tend to assume that their performance is acceptable, and problems may continue. Without positive feedback or praise, employees begin to feel that their hard work is unappreciated and may decide to stop putting forth so much effort. Employees need and expect frequent communication and feedback about their performance—not just during the formal appraisal interview session. They make it a habit to get out among their employees throughout the day or week and do not wait for their employees to come to them. This type of frequent interaction also tells employees that their FLM thinks they are important.

Responsibility for Formal Performance Appraisals

An immediate FLM, who is usually in the best position to observe the employees and evaluate how well they perform their jobs, should complete a performance appraisal. When FLMs do the appraising they must be familiar with basic appraisal techniques, understand and avoid problems that can cripple an appraisal, and conduct the appraisal fairly. There are some situations in which a "consensus" or "pooled" type of appraisal may be done by a group of FLMs, such as when an employee works for several FLMs. In organizations that have implemented a work team concept or large spans of management control, it is important to consider how information can be gathered so that the performance appraisal ratings are based on observation of job performance and are fair to all employees.

The human resources department usually serves a policy-making and advisory role. For example, they might provide advice and assistance regarding the appraisal tool to use but leave final decision on appraisal procedures to the organization's operating division heads. In other organizations, they will prepare detailed forms and procedures that all departments will be expected to use.

Components of an Effective Performance Management System

One key component of a performance management system as briefly mentioned above is the form used to document and appraise performance. There are numerous types of performance appraisal forms that organizations use. Some organizations use graphic rating scales that describe competencies that are important for success (e.g., teamwork) and ask FLMs to rate an employee's level of proficiency or effectiveness (e.g., on a 5-point scale) on each competency. Similarly, behaviorally anchored rating scales (BARS) outline competencies of performance and provide behavioral descriptors of key anchors on the rating scale FLMs use to evaluate performance (e.g., behavior representing a "1"; behavior representing a "5"; etc.). Forms also may ask FLMs to rank order or compare employees in a workgroup or to mark statements that are most or least characteristic of an employee. Essay forms ask FLMs to write a narrative description of an employee's performance. Critical incident appraisal, on the other hand, asks FLMs to record specific instances of very effective or very ineffective performance for an employee. Finally, several approaches to appraisal such as the work standards approach and management by objectives ask FLMs to set specific standards for performance such as quality or timeliness of work produced and to measure employees against these standards.

In most cases, the human resources department in an organization will dictate the performance appraisal form that must be used by the FLM. Further, each type of appraisal format has its advantages and disadvantages. However, there are principles for conducting effective appraisals that can help FLMs, regardless of the appraisal form they have been provided. Further, even with a good form, FLMs can do a poor job of implementing the system. Consider the following example:

Kani sits down to complete a yearly review on Taylor Carter. Taylor has been a good worker in the past, but lately his work has been a bit sloppy. When Taylor arrives, Kani begins the session and the dialogue goes something like this:

Kani: Taylor, as you know it is time to conduct your yearly review. Here are your ratings on the appraisal form. You will see that your work has been unacceptable. If this doesn't improve I am going to have to take drastic action.

Taylor: (startled) This is news to me. I have always worked hard for this organization. I don't know what you mean.

Kani: Well, I have heard there are problems. Last Tuesday you were late to work.

Taylor: I was late to work because of traffic and that is the only day I have been late in years.

Kani: Well, you don't seem to have your heart in work. Your attitude is a problem.

Taylor: (agitated) My attitude is a problem!!?? I have given 10 years to this company and worked hard every single day. I think this whole thing is about personalities, not performance.

Unfortunately, interactions like these are not uncommon in performance appraisal sessions. Kani is willing to give Taylor feedback, but fails to document performance effectively or give Taylor feedback that he can actually use to improve. As a result, Taylor is defensive and attributes everything to a personality conflict. Clearly this is not how an FLM would like the interaction to happen. A good performance appraisal form, coupled with proper implementation, can help avoid disastrous appraisal sessions like this. A good performance management system should include:

Job and Organization Relevant Dimensions: FLMs should be rating job-relevant dimensions or items that are clearly observable and defined in terms of behavior (i.e., How does the organization define teamwork in terms of what you expect people to do?).

Clearly Defined Rating System: The system should have a clearly defined rating scale for FLMs to rate performance.

Integration With Other Systems: The appraisal system should be integrated with other performance monitoring systems such as overall units produced or quality indices the FLM has established for the unit overall. Employees need to be evaluated on their contributions to these overall objectives.

Developmental Focus: Effective performance management includes not only appraising performance, but also establishing specific development plans for employees which include outlining how an employee can improve (e.g., what specific steps he/she will take, what training or resources the FLM will provide, etc.).

Documentation: Effective FLMs will document instances of performance throughout a rating period so that when they complete an appraisal form, they have specific information to provide to an employee. Further, this enables the FLM to ensure he/she is considering performance throughout a rating period, not just what happened (good or bad) this week.

Rater Training: FLMs should receive training on the appraisal system (e.g., how to document and rate performance, complete the forms, and comply with the requirements of the appraisal system). This training also may include sources of bias in appraisal which will be discussed later in this chapter.

Clear Expectations: Regardless of the appraisal form or system in place in an organization, the expectations for performance should be clearly defined and communicated to employees.

Ongoing Feedback: As has been mentioned previously, managing performance occurs every day, not just once a year. Regardless of the appraisal system in place, FLMs should continually provide feedback to employees about both their successes and the things they need to do to improve.

Assessments by Someone Other Than the FLM

FLMs cannot know how an employee behaves at all times or in all situations. Nor can FLMs always appreciate the full impact of an employee's behavior on others, inside and outside the organization. To gain more insight into an employee, FLMs may supplement their appraisals with self-assessments by the employee or with appraisals by peers, rating committees, and customers. Their employees may also evaluate FLMs and other managers. Combining several sources of appraisals is called *360-degree feedback.*

360-degree feedback. With 360-degree feedback, the organization collects performance information all around an employee—from her or his FLMs, direct reports, peers, and internal or external customers—generally for developmental rather than pay purposes. The usual process is to have the raters complete online appraisal surveys on the rate. Computerized systems then compile all this feedback into individualized reports to rates. The person may then meet with the FLM to develop a self-improvement plan.

To use self-assessments or evaluations, an FLM can ask each employee to complete an assessment form. Asking an employee to evaluate himself is often a solid method to obtain an accurate evaluation, when used with an FLM's evaluation. Self-assessments give the FLM/organization a glimpse of what the employee thinks they need to improve on and in which areas they excel. A self-evaluation allows the FLM to see what an employee believes is important and whether the employee is misguided about those priorities.

During the appraisal interview, the FLM and employee would then compare the employee's evaluation or his or her behavior with the FLM's assessment. This can stimulate discussion and insights in areas where the two are in disagreement.

The following are examples of questions employees might ask themselves and their FLMs when completing a self-assessment:

- On a scale of 1 to 10, how does my performance rate?
- What are the strongest elements of my work?
- What are the weakest elements of my work?
- Where can I go in my job or career in the next 18 months to 4 years?
- What skills, training, or education do I need to get to that point?

Appraisals by peers—often called *peer reviews*—are becoming more common, especially in team-based environments. Peers often have a valuable perspective on the performance of their coworkers and may witness things (good or bad) that the FLM does not. They may be in the best position to rate some dimensions such as attendance and timeliness, teamwork and cooperation, or planning and coordination. Peer evaluations may be done in meetings, in which the team discusses each team members' strengths and areas needing improvement. They may also be collected in an anonymous survey which an external source such as human resources summarizes (e.g., provides an average rating for a person from all of his/her peers). Employees often find the information from peers credible because it comes from multiple people who work with them every day.

Rating Committees

Some organizations use rating committees. A rating committee is usually composed of the employee's immediate supervisor or FLM and three or four other supervisors or FLMs. Using multiple raters can help neutralize bias on the part of individual raters. Different raters also often see different facets of an employee's performance, so ratings by committees let you include these different facets of an employee's performance, so ratings by committees let you include these different facets of an employee's performance. It is usually advisable to at least obtain ratings from the FLM, his or her boss, and perhaps another FLM who is familiar with the employee's work. At a minimum, most organizations require that the FLM's boss sign off on any appraisals the FLM does.

Customer Evaluations of Employees

The drive to please customers in a highly competitive market, coupled with a desire for practical information on performance, has encouraged some organizations to institute programs in which customers appraise employees' performance. Asking a customer to evaluate their experience—by way of a survey—allows the organization to gauge, for example, how the customer feels about the employee's customer service skills. The survey can be in the form of a short questionnaire or a "rate your experience" survey with numbers one to ten. Customers are asked to write down the name of the employee they talked to so they can evaluate the correct employee. Feedback from customers, like other performance feedback, should result in actionable steps where appropriate that the FLM sees the employee implement to improve or maintain customer relations.

Combining several sources of performance evaluations can correct for some of the appraisal biases described in the next section. It also can provide information that is more useful for problem solving and employee development than the results of a traditional supervisor only appraisal.

Sources of Bias in Performance Appraisals

Ideally, FLMs should be completely objective in their appraisals of employees. Each appraisal should reflect only an employee's performance, and not any biases of the FLM. Of course, this is impossible to do perfectly. We all have biases that affect our evaluations of other people. FLMs need to be aware of these biases and limit their effects on appraisals. This section discusses some sources of bias that commonly influence performance appraisals.

Some FLMs are prone to a *harshness bias*, that is, rating all employees more severely than their performance merits. New FLMs are especially susceptible to this error, because they may feel a need to be taken seriously. Unfortunately, the harshness bias also tends to frustrate and discourage employees, who resent the unfair assessment of their performance. Further, if ratings are tied to pay, employees in one department may feel, justifiably, that they are being penalized unfairly because their FLM is a more harsh rater than others.

At the other extreme is the *leniency bias*. FLMs with this bias rate all of their employees more favorably than their performance merits. An FLM who does this may want credit for developing a department full of "excellent" employees, or may simply be uncomfortable confronting employees with their shortcomings. The leniency bias may feel like an advantage to the employees who receive the favorable ratings, but it actually cheats them and their department. By not recognizing the benefits of developing and coaching employees, a lenient FLM may actually hinder the employees' progress.

A bias that characterizes the responses of some FLMs is *central tendency*, which is the tendency to select ratings in the middle of the scale. Some people seem more comfortable on middle ground than taking a strong stand at either extreme. This bias also causes an FLM to miss important opportunities to praise or correct employees.

The *similarity bias* refers to our tendency to judge others more positively when they are like us. Thus, FLMs may tend to look more favorably on people who share their interests, tastes, background, or other characteristics. For example, an FLM may view a person's performance in a favorable light because the employee shares his or her interest in sports. On the other hand, an FLM might give a negative assessment of the performance of an employee who is much more shy than the FLM.

The *recency syndrome* refers to the human tendency to place the most weight on events that have occurred most recently. In a performance appraisal, an FLM might give particular weight to a problem the employee caused last week or to an award the employee just won, whereas the FLM should be careful to consider events and behavior that occurred throughout the entire review period. The most accurate way to make a complete evaluation is to document events as they happen (e.g., keep a running log of good and poor incidents of performance) and keep these records throughout the year.

The *halo effect* refers to the tendency of an FLM to generalize one positive or negative aspect of a person to the person's entire performance. Thus, if FLM Christian Jones thinks that a pleasant telephone manner makes a good customer service representative, he is apt to give high marks on everything to Nandi Rebeccah, who has an extremely pleasant voice, no matter what she actually says to the customers or how reliable her performance.

Finally, the FLM's *prejudices* about various types of people can unfairly influence a performance appraisal. An FLM needs to remember that each employee is an individual, not merely a representative of a group. An FLM who believes that one group of employees generally has poor skills in using standard English needs to recognize that this is a prejudice about a group, not a fact to use when evaluating actual employees.

Performance Appraisals and the Law

It may seem unnecessary to emphasize that performance appraisals must be job-related, because appraisals are supposed to measure how well employees are doing their jobs. Yet in numerous cases, courts have ruled that performance appraisals were discriminatory and not job related.

The elements of a performance appraisal system that can survive court tests can be determined from existing case law. A legally defensible performance appraisal includes:

- performance appraisal criteria based on an analysis of the job,
- measuring relevant job performance,
- formal evaluation criteria that limit management discretion,
- formal rating instruments,
- personal knowledge of and contact with the employee being evaluated,
- training of FLMs in conducting appraisals,
- a review process that prevents one FLM acting alone from controlling an employee's career, and
- counseling to help poor performers improve.

How to Conduct a Formal Appraisal

Clearly, conducting performance appraisals is one of the FLM's most important and difficult functions. The first thing an FLM can do to conduct an effective formal performance appraisal is to make sure that there are no surprises in store for employees. This means that, as discussed previously, FLMs should communicate with their employees on a regular basis about how they are doing with their assignments and how well they are collaborating with others. FLMs also should be using the techniques discussed in the chapters on leadership, communication, motivation, teams, and planning.

The formal appraisal session, therefore, should be primarily a way to summarize and continue the informal interaction that has previously taken place between the FLM and the employee. It should also be a time to look at how the FLM and the employee can continue to work well together in the future. The FLM's job in this session is not to tell the employee all the things the employee did wrong over the past year. One reason employees dread these sessions is that FLMs feel they have to find something to criticize as well as praise. The FLM might then mention a negative comment the employee made or similar trivial points. This hypercritical approach will merely increase the employee's resentment and defensiveness and will make employees feel as though they are powerless to improve.

To make sure the session goes as well as possible and to avoid making it uncomfortable for both the FLM and the employee, five general steps should be followed:

1. Refer to past feedback and documented observations of performance.
2. Describe the current performance.
3. Describe the desired performance.
4. Get a commitment to any needed change.
5. Follow up.

Specific guidelines for conducting performance appraisals are described below.

Preparing for the Appraisal Interview Session

Today's FLM must recognize that failure to plan for the performance appraisal is planning to fail. Being prepared is key to making sure the discussion with each employee goes smoothly. Before the meeting, the FLM needs to do some documentation and planning. The FLM should:

- Create and maintain logs or notes, on each employee that include observations of the employee's behavior and the results of his or her work. Write down incidents with date, and whether there were problems or successes at the time you noticed them. Don't rely on memory to recreate what you saw.
- If a rule infraction occurs, describe it in writing and have the employee sign the written record at the time of the infraction. Keep a record of all discussions that deal with problems that are directly attributable to the employee's performance.
- Review your documentation before the formal appraisal session and highlight important points.
- List the points you want to make, focusing on both strengths and areas for improvement. Be prepared to discuss problems in a manner that focuses on the behavior that caused the problem and on solutions, not on the person. Be sure to distinguish between problems that are related to the system (e.g., too many assignments) and those that are attributable to the individual.
- Consider the follow-up actions you think might be appropriate to help the employee improve, but be prepared to take the employee's feelings into consideration.
- Think about how you have interacted with the employee and how these interactions might have affected his or her performance. Be prepared to discuss how you and the employee might improve your interactions.
- Set up an appointment with the employee about a week before the performance appraisal session.

- If the employee needs to fill out a self-assessment form, give it to him or her at the time you set up the appointment to meet.

During the Appraisal Interview Session

Here are some ways FLMs can make the appraisal session go smoothly:

- Put the employees at ease at the start of the session. Acknowledge that these sessions can be a little nerve-wracking, but that their purpose is to help everyone in the team or workgroup improve and to gather information on how to help these improvement efforts.
- Ask employees what they think of their total performance—not just their strong or weak areas.
- Question employees about what they think are their personal strengths. This gives employees a chance to describe what they do best, which helps them feel positive about the appraisal.
- Tell employees what you believe are their strengths. This demonstrates that you are paying attention to their performance and appreciating their good qualities.
- Describe those areas that you think employees might improve and use documentation to demonstrate why you are making these observations. Then ask employees what they think of your assessment and listen silently to what they have to say. Consider their reasons for poor performance (e.g., lack of equipment, lack of training) in determining appropriate actions to take.
- Assuming that you identify the cause of poor performance, ask employees what you can do together to take care of it.
- Regardless of whether or not an employee receives an average or a good rating, explain why he or she did not get a higher rating. The employee should understand what needs to be done during the next performance period to get a higher rating.
- Set new goals for performance for the next appraisal period.
- Keep a record of the meeting, including a timetable for performance improvement and what each of you will do to work toward your goals.
- Be open and honest, yet considerate of the employee's feelings. The goal is to facilitate improvement, not to make the employee feel bad.
- Be sure to give positive reinforcement to the employee during the discussion, preferably near the end. Being positive helps to motivate the employee to make any necessary change.

After the Appraisal Interview Session

It is vital to follow up on any agreements made during the appraisal sessions. Follow up indicates that the FLM and the organization are serious about improvement. The FLM should

- make appointments to meet with employees individually to review their progress;
- set up development opportunities as needed to address skill deficiencies;
- arrange for the employee to get counseling, when available, if a personal problem is involved;
- provide positive feedback when you see improvements in performance; and
- make him or her aware of the consequences, such as demotion or dismissal, if the employee continues to perform poorly.

Follow up means more than just working with employees. FLMs also have to follow up on themselves. An effective appraisal process requires an ongoing and candid self-assessment by the FLM of his or her performance and its effect on employees. FLMs can use the following questions to evaluate themselves:

- Do your employees know specifically what you expect?
- Do your employees have written goals and results?
- Have you tracked your employees' performance to see if the trend is up, down, or about the same?
- Have you updated your employees recently about your own work and how it affects them?
- Are you maintaining performance documentation?
- Have you scheduled interim reviews with all of your employees?
- Do you frequently—even daily—discuss employee performance?
- Do you frequently "catch" your employees doing something right—and tell them about it?

Performance Problems Due to Special Causes

Individual performance problems can harm the productivity of an organization. Some of these performance problems are due to special causes, and they arise through specific actions of the individual employees. Rather than blaming the individual for these problems, which usually does nothing to improve performance and can lower employee morale and motivation, the FLM needs to deal with the underlying causes. If an FLM deals effectively with performance problems due to these special causes, there is a good chance the FLM will eliminate the problems and help assure that the organization operates effectively. These performance problems may include absenteeism and tardiness, disrespect or lack of cooperation, substance abuse, theft, unsafe practices, or personality problems. An effective FLM will recognize these potential problems, take steps to identify the cause, and take actions toward resolving problems. In some cases this may mean referring an employee to a company's employee assistance program, or taking disciplinary action if things do not improve.

Disciplining Employees

"I can't stand Anya's surly attitude any longer!" fumed Kani Taylor, her FLM. "If she doesn't cut it out, she's going to be sorry." This FLM is eager for the employee to experience the consequences of her behavior. Despite his anger and frustration, however, Kani needs to apply discipline in constructive ways. In many cases, effective discipline can quickly bring about a change in an employee's behavior.

Administering Discipline

FLMs must exercise discretion when recommending or imposing penalties on employees. In dealing with mistakes, FLMs must consider what the mistakes were and under what circumstances they were made. Mistakes resulting from continued carelessness call for disciplinary action. Honest mistakes should be corrected by counseling and positive discipline, not by punishment. These corrections should help the employee learn from the mistakes and become more proficient and valuable to the organization.

The specific ways in which an FLM disciplines employees may be dictated by organization policies or the union contract, if any. An FLM must, therefore, be familiar with all applicable policies and rules, which include respecting the rights of employees in the discipline process. Employees' rights include the following:

- the right to know job expectations and the consequences of not fulfilling those expectations;
- the right to receive consistent and predictable responses to violations of the rules;
- the right to receive fair discipline based on facts;

- ▪ the right to question management's statement of the facts and to present a defense;
- ▪ the right to receive progressive discipline; and
- ▪ the right to appeal a disciplinary action.

The Discipline Process

Before administering discipline in response to problem behavior, FLMs need to have a clear picture of the situation. Usually FLMs become aware of a problem either through their own observations or from another employee. In either case, FLMs need to collect the facts before taking further action. Often this will result in a resolution to the problem. For example, Kani Taylor believes that one of his employees is using the office telephone for personal business. The employee has a girlfriend in another state, and Kani suspects the company is paying for the employee's long-distance calls. To solve the problem, Kani should not make hasty accusations or issue a general memo about company policy. Kani should instead ask the employee directly and privately about his telephone conversations. In getting the employee's version of the problem, Kani should use good listening practices and resist the temptation to get angry.

When an FLM observes and understands the facts behind problem behavior, the discipline process takes place in four steps: verbal or written warning, suspension, demotion, and dismissal. These steps can be used one after the other in a "progressive" pattern of discipline, indicating that the steps progress from the least to the most severe action an FLM can take.

In following steps in the discipline process, an FLM should keep in mind that the objective is to end the problem behavior. The FLM should take only as many steps as are necessary to bring about a change in that behavior: The ultimate goal is to solve the problem without dismissing the employee.

Pillars of Fair Discipline

The FLM builds a fair discipline process on three pillars: rules and regulations, a system of progressive penalties, and an appeals process.

Rules and Regulations

An acceptable disciplinary process begins with a set of clear disciplinary rules and regulations. The rules should cover issues such as theft, destruction of organization property, drinking on the job, and insubordination. Examples of rules include the following:

- Poor performance is not acceptable.
- Each employee is expected to perform her or his work properly and efficiently and to meet established standards of quality.
- Alcohol and drugs do not mix with work. The use of either during working hours and reporting for work under the influence are both strictly prohibited.

The purpose of the rules is to inform employees ahead of time what is and is not acceptable behavior. Tell employees, preferably in writing, what is not permitted. The employee orientation handbook should contain the rules and regulations.

Penalties

A system of progressive penalties is the second pillar of effective discipline. The severity of the penalty should depend on the offense and the number of times it has occurred. For example, most organizations issue warnings for the first unexcused lateness. However, for a fourth offense, discharge is usual.

Appeals Process

Third, an appeals process should be part of the disciplinary process. The aim is to ensure that FLMs mete out discipline fairly.

An appeals process is essential but is no panacea. The employer can sometimes mitigate the effects of unfair discipline by catching it during an appeal. However, some FLM behavior may be impossible to overcome. For example, actions that attack the employee's personal identity are difficult to remedy.

Guidelines for Effective Discipline

The guidelines for effective discipline are:

- Act immediately.
- Focus on solving the problem.
- Keep emotions in check.

- Administer discipline in private.
- Be consistent.

These are described further below.

Act Immediately

When an employee is causing a problem—from tardiness to theft to lack of cooperation—the FLM needs to act immediately. This is not always easy to do. Pointing out poor behavior and administering discipline are unpleasant tasks, but FLMs who ignore problem situations are effectively signaling that the problem is not serious. As a result, the problem often gets worse.

Focus on Solving the Problem

When discussing a problem with an employee, an FLM should focus on learning about and resolving the issue at hand. This meeting is no time for name-calling or for dredging up instances of past misbehavior. Nor is it generally useful for an FLM to dwell on how patient or compassionate he or she has been. Instead, an FLM should listen to the employee and be sure he or she understands the problem, and then begin discussing how to correct it in the future. Talking about behavior instead of personalities helps the employee understand what is expected.

Keep Emotions in Check

An FLM should avoid becoming emotional. Although it is appropriate to convey sincere concern about a problem, an FLM's other feelings are largely irrelevant and can even stand in the way of a constructive discussion. Being calm and relaxed when administering discipline tells an employee that the FLM is confident of what he or she is doing.

Administer Discipline in Private

Discipline should be a private matter. The FLM should not humiliate an employee by issuing a reprimand in front of other employees. Humiliation only breeds resentment and may actually increase problem behavior in the future.

Be Consistent

An FLM also should be consistent in administering discipline. One way to do this is to follow the four steps of the progressive discipline process. An FLM should also respond to all instances of misbehavior equitably rather than, for example, ignoring a longstanding employee's misdeeds while punishing a newcomer.

Documentation of Disciplinary Actions

Employees who are disciplined sometimes respond by filing a grievance or suing the employer. To be able to justify their actions, therefore, FLMs must have a record of the disciplinary actions taken and the basis for the discipline. These records may be needed to show that the actions were not discriminatory or against company policy.

While documentation is important for any disciplinary action, it is especially important when an FLM must dismiss an employee. Because the experience is so emotional, some former employees respond with a lawsuit against the employer. The employee's file should show the steps the FLM took leading up to the termination and a record of the specific behaviors that led the FLM to dismiss the employee to protect the organization against this type of legal action. The performance appraisal ratings should correspond to other documentation about problematic performance.

Positive Discipline

Ideally, discipline should not only end problem behavior, but should also prevent problems from occurring. Discipline designed to prevent problem behavior from starting is known as positive discipline, or preventive discipline. One important part of positive discipline is making sure employees know and understand the rules they must follow, and the consequences of violating those rules.

Employees may engage in problem behavior when they feel frustrated or unhappy. Therefore, an FLM also can administer positive discipline by working to create positive working conditions under which employees will be unlikely to cause problems. This includes setting realistic goals, being aware of and responsive to employees' needs and ideas, and making sure employees feel that they are important to the organization.

Establishing Performance Plans: One Key to Succeeding as an FLM

In this final section, it is important to emphasize that one key to succeeding as an FLM is to establish clear performance plans. In doing so, FLMs minimize the likelihood of having problems or issues in the performance management or appraisal process and minimizing the need for employee discipline resulting from performance issues.

It is important for FLMs to recognize that goals should comprise 50% of each employee's evaluation and competencies should make up the other 50%. Clearly, goals can be developed in a number of ways. They can be drafted by the employee, written by the FLM, written jointly, cascaded or aligned and in any case they should be directly tied to the job analysis and job description. It is the FLM's responsibility to provide general guidance on the nature and number of employee goals. Therefore, before an employee can enter goals, a conversation between the employee and FLM *must* take place. During this conversation, the FLM should broadly outline the goals for the year and should then ask the employee to develop and enter more specific performance goals.

The Importance of Aligned Goals

Aligned goals are those individual goals which support an FLM's, team's, department's, or organization's goals. Employee aligned goals are related, but not identical to the FLM's, team's, department's, or organization's goals. Having a clear alignment of goals allows everyone to work in support of a larger goal, and helps employees see how their day-to-day activities contribute to the success of the organization.

Writing S.M.A.R.T. Goals

Developing sound goals is critical to managing employees' performance. Each year FLMs should ask employees to set goals for the upcoming year/evaluation period. Goals should be S.M.A.R.T—specific, measurable, achievable, results-focused, and time-bound. Below is a definition of each of the S.M.A.R.T. goal criteria.

Specific: Goals should be simplistically written and clearly define what will be accomplished.
Specific is the What, Why, and How of the S.M.A.R.T. model.

Measurable: Goals should be measurable so employees have tangible evidence that they have accomplished the goal. Usually, the entire goal statement is a measure for the project, but there are usually several short-term or smaller measurements built into the goal.

Achievable: Goals should be achievable; they should stretch the employee slightly so they feel challenged, but defined well enough so they can achieve them. Employees must possess the appropriate knowledge, skills, and abilities needed to achieve the goal.

Employees can meet most any goal when the goal is thoughtfully planned and a timeframe is established that allows the employee to carry out those steps. As the employee carries out the steps, they can achieve goals that may have seemed impossible when they started. On the other hand, if a goal is impossible to achieve, the employee may not even try to accomplish it. Achievable goals motivate employees. Impossible goals de-motivate them.

Results-focused: Goals should measure outcomes, not activities.

Time-bound: Goals should be linked to a timeframe that creates a practical sense of urgency, or results in tension between the current status of the goal and the vision of the goal. Without such tension, the goal is unlikely to produce a relevant outcome.

The concept of writing S.M.A.R.T. goals is very important for accomplishing individual goals, which in turn are linked to team, department, division, and organization goals. It is also critical for ensuring good communication between employees and supervisors so there are no surprises during annual performance evaluations.

The S.M.A.R.T. Goal Questionnaire and Checklist (see Figure 12.1) that follows assists FLMs and employees in creating S.M.A.R.T. goals. Employees should begin by writing their goal as clearly and concisely as possible. Then they should answer the related questions and conclude by revising their goal, in the space allotted.

In conclusion, most organizations have some sort of performance management/appraisal system in place to evaluate decisions related promotions, pay increases, and professional development. To execute that, a set of expectations is established against which employee's performance is measured. That's where the importance of establishing performance plans and writing SMART performance evaluation goals comes in to play in helping FLMs succeed.

Goal:

1. **S**pecific. What will the goal accomplish? How and why will it be accomplished?

2. **M**easurable. How will you measure the goal (list at least two indicators)?

3. **A**chievable. Is it possible? Have others done it successfully? Do you have the necessary knowledge, skills, abilities, and resources to accomplish the goal? Will meeting the goal challenge you without defeating you?

4. **R**esults-focused. What is the reason, purpose, or benefit of accomplishing the goal? What is the result (not activities leading up to the result) of the goal?

5. **T**ime-bound. What is the established completion date and does that completion date create a practical sense of urgency?

Revised Goal:

S.M.A.R.T. Goal Checklist

____(S) Does the goal focus on a specific area?

____(S) Is the goal written using concrete language?

____(S) Does the goal begin with an action verb? (to + verb)

____(M) Can progress be measured for the goal? Is the progress:
- Numeric or Descriptive?
- Quantitative?
- Qualitative?
- Financial?
- Constrained by Time?

____(A) Is the goal a "stretch," yet still within my control?

____(A) Is the goal sufficiently and reasonably limited in scope?

____(R) Does the goal measure actual outputs or results, not activities?

____(R) Do the results include products, deliverables, or accomplishments?

____(T) Has a reasonable timeframe been identified?

____(T) Is it necessary to identify interim steps or have a plan to monitor progress?

____(R) Is the goal supportive of and directly relevent to the organization and the team/departments mission and goals?

Figure 12.1   S.M.A.R.T. goal questionnaire.

Conclusion

Control is accomplished by comparing actual performance with predetermined standards or objectives and then taking corrective action to correct any deviations from the standards. The control process has three basic steps:

1. establishing performance standards,
2. monitoring performance and comparing it with standards, and
3. taking necessary action.

Among the tools and techniques most frequently used by FLMs to exercise control are budgets, written reports, personal observation, electronic monitors, and management by objectives. Benchmarking is a control tool that organizations use to improve different types of performance.

Performance management is a collaborative, on-going or continuous process between an FLM and an employee to plan for, develop, and evaluate an employee's work. It focuses on what employees do and how they do it; it aligns individual, team, departmental, and organization goals; it identifies areas for employee learning; and includes opportunities to discuss and plan for an employee's individual or career development.

Performance appraisal is a process that involves determining and communicating to an employee how well he or she is performing the job and also establishing a plan for improvement. While there are many types of appraisal forms, effective management of performance involves continually monitoring performance and giving feedback to employees. Further, when conducting performance appraisals, FLMs must avoid the following biases: harshness bias, leniency bias, central tendency, similarity bias, recency syndrome, and the halo effect.

Problems that an FLM can attribute to individuals are special cause problems and include absence and tardiness, disrespect and lack of cooperation, substance abuse, use of unsafe practices, and theft. One way of dealing with special cause performance problems is discipline. Discipline is action taken by an FLM to prevent employees from breaking rules.

Effective ways of administering discipline require the FLM to meet with the employee(s) involved and ask for his or her version of what has happened after collecting the facts of the situation. The FLM should use good listening techniques and, if necessary, let the employee experience the consequences of unsatisfactory behavior through suspension, demotion, and ultimate dismissal. The FLM takes as many steps as are necessary to resolve the problem behavior.

Positive discipline focuses on preventing problem behavior from ever beginning. It can include making sure employees know and understand the rules, creating conditions under which employees are least likely to cause problems, using decision-making strategies when problems occur, and rewarding desirable behavior. Effective positive discipline results in self-discipline among employees; that is, employees voluntarily follow the rules and try to meet performance standards.

SMART goals which stand for specific, measurable, achievable, relevant and timely, should be used by FLMs in establishing performance plans and evaluating employees as a way to enhance performance management. SMART goals are a step-by-step process to help FLMs effectively formulate and achieve goals and can be used in conjunction with evaluations and performance reviews of employees.

13

Conflict, Negotiation, and Organizational Politics

Critical Survival Skills

Organizations are complex, and there are several issues that front line managers (FLMs) and other managers and leaders in organizations have to address in managing them well. Conflict, negotiation, and organizational politics are three such interrelated issues. Organizations and people have goals and hence conflict is inevitable, and FLMs, managers, and other leaders have to implement strategies to manage them and negotiate where required. In addition, because there are power differences in organizations, organizational members attempt to influence others. While doing this, many employees, for example, will try to influence others at work because it is best for the organization, while others will attempt to gain influence through unfair and selfish means. This is called politics.

Conflict, negotiation, and organizational politics are all part of the workplace. As a result effective FLMs need to develop an understanding of and skills in each one of those areas. This section of this chapter discusses

Succeeding as a Frontline Manager in Today's Organizations, pages 361–390
Copyright © 2021 by Information Age Publishing

conflict and some of the reasons it arises in organizations, and identifies types and sources of conflict along with conflict management strategies FLMs can use to resolve conflict effectively. The second section focuses on negotiation, explains why integrative bargaining is more effective than distributive negotiation, and how FLMs can promote integrative bargaining in their negotiating efforts. The final section explains the reason why FLMs need to understand organizational politics and discusses several political strategies that FLMs can use to become more politically skilled.

Understanding and Managing Conflict

This section considers another important tool for the FLM toolkit: an understanding of conflict and methods for handling it, including how to stimulate positive, or functional, conflict. We identify types and sources of conflict, describe major conflict resolution approaches, and discuss workplace violence and aggression. The chapter concludes with an introduction to the related topics of negotiation and mediation.

Conflict: A Definition

Jane Carroll, a new FLM, approaches her mentor in the organization with a concern. She says her team is having difficulty getting along. During meetings, they argue about how to proceed with the work. There also seem to be some interpersonal problems between several team members that have resulted in their not speaking to one another unless absolutely necessary. Jane thinks that her group should just, "get along." Her idea of the perfect team is one where team members don't argue, and these interpersonal situations don't occur.

What Jane fails to recognize is that conflict, defined as a difference of opinion between two or more individuals or groups, is a natural, and sometimes necessary, part of working with others. These differences of opinion, if managed well, can lead to better workgroup decisions and actions because those actions have been thoroughly discussed (or debated). It also can, however, result in workgroups that are unproductive because of their inability to get along and their tendency to personalize disagreements.

Organizational Conflict

Organizational conflict is the discord that arises when the goals, interests, or values of different individuals or groups are incompatible and those individuals or groups block or thwart one another's attempts to achieve objectives. Conflict is an inevitable part of organizational life because the goals of different stakeholders such as FLMs and employees are often incompatible. Organizational conflict also can exist between departments, and divisions that compete for resources or even between FLMs who may be competing for promotion to the next level in the organizational hierarchy.

Not surprisingly, the current business environment, for example, continues to evolve at a rapid pace, which intensifies the existence of conflict throughout various parts of any organization. Factors often cited for why finely tuned conflict resolution skills are essential for today's FLMs and other managers include (a) increased pressure on organizations to change and adapt quickly to maintain competitive advantage; (b) increased diversity due to global business expansion, which may cause more conflict; (c) intense use of technology and flexible working arrangements that have reduced face-to-face communications among FLMs, employees, senior management, and business colleagues, which may increase the opportunity for misunderstanding and communication gaps; and (d) increase conflict among members of self-managed teams, who are now making decisions previously the responsibility of other FLMS and managers in the organization. All of these factors, among others, require greater conflict resolution and negotiation skills at all levels of the organization.

It is important for FLMs to develop the skills necessary to manage conflict effectively. In addition, the level of conflict present in an organization has important implications for organizational performance. It is important for FLMs to understand that conflict is a force that needs to be managed rather than eliminated. FLMs should never try to eliminate all conflict, but rather, should try to keep conflict at a moderate and functional level to promote change efforts that benefit the organization. Additionally, FLMs should strive to keep conflict focused on substantive, task-based issues and minimize conflict based on personal disagreements and animosities. To manage conflict, FLMs must understand the types and sources of conflict and be familiar with strategies that can be effective in dealing with it.

Functional and Dysfunctional Conflict

Conflict can be *functional*, in that it can improve an individual's or group's performance, or *dysfunctional* even destructive, with negative effects on the people or organizations involved. In these situations, people often feel comfortable disagreeing and presenting opposing views which typically brings about a greater awareness of problems, enhance the search for solutions, and motivate employees to change and adapt when advisable. Each of these elements is lacking or even worse in cases of dysfunctional conflict, which threatens an organization's interests by creating distorted perceptions, negative stereotyping, poor communication, decreased productivity, and can even result in sabotage.

Conflict can be viewed as a bell curve. A moderate level of healthy conflict can enhance achievement. Too much or too little conflict, on the other hand, can lead to negative and even destructive behaviors, especially if unreasonable pressures and tensions are present. One responsibility of an FLM is to decide how much functional conflict is needed to create, enhance, and sustain the productivity of employees and to make sure it does not degenerate into dysfunctional conflict.

Research that examined the perceived positive and negative effects of conflict and the conditions under which those effects were likely to result identified seven negative effects of conflict and three positive effects. On the negative side, conflict

- interferes with communication,
- leads to or intensifies grudges and feuds,
- interferes with cooperation and coordination,
- diverts energies from major tasks or goals,
- leads groups to stereotype each other,
- leads to an increase in politics (i.e., individual efforts to acquire power to advance their own efforts), and
- reduces the organization's capacity to compete in the marketplace.

On the positive side, conflict

- brings important problems out into the open;
- encourages innovation, change, and consideration of new approaches and ideas; and
- increases loyalty and performance within each of the groups in conflict.

Sources and Types of Conflict

Before FLMs can respond effectively to a particular conflict, they need to understand it. They need to ask, "Who is involved?"; "What is the source of the conflict?" FLMs are likely to respond differently to a conflict that results from a clash of opinions than to one stemming from frustration over limited resources. Conflict may occur between or within organizations, within departments, and even between an individual and the organization. There are several types of conflict in organizations: interpersonal, intragroup, intergroup, and interorganizational.

Interpersonal Conflict

Interpersonal conflict occurs between two or more individuals. Interpersonal conflicts may arise from differing opinions, misunderstandings of a situation, or differences in value or beliefs. Sometimes two people just rub each other the wrong way. Interpersonal conflict is conflict between individual members of an organization, occurring because of differences in their goals or values. Two FLMs may experience interpersonal when their values concerning protection of the environment differ. One FLM may argue that the organization should do only what is required by law. The other FLM may counter that the organization should invest in equipment to reduce emissions, even though the organization's current level of emissions is below the legal limit.

FLMs may be involved in interpersonal conflicts with a manager, an employee, a peer, or even a customer. In addition, FLMs like Jane Carroll may have to manage conflicts between two or more of their employees.

Intragroup Conflict

Intragroup conflict arises within a group, team, or department. When members of the marketing department in a clothing company disagree about how they should spend budgeted advertising dollars for a new line of designer jeans, they are experiencing intragroup conflict. Some of the members want to spend all the money or advertisements in magazines; others want to devote half of the money to ads on social media platforms like Facebook and Twitter.

Intergroup Conflict

Intergroup conflict occurs between groups, teams, or departments. R&D departments, for example, sometimes experience intergroup conflict with production departments. Members of the R&D department may develop a new product that they think production can make inexpensively by using existing manufacturing capabilities. Members of the production department, however, may disagree and believe that the costs of making the product will be much higher. FLMs and other managers of departments usually play a key role in managing intergroup conflicts such as this.

Interorganizational Conflict

Interorganizational conflict arises across organizations. Sometimes interorganizational conflict occurs when FLMs and other managers in one organization feel that another organization is not behaving ethically and is threatening the well-being of certain stakeholder groups. Interorganizational conflict also can occur between government agencies and corporations.

Sources of Conflict

Certain situations in organizations produce more conflict that others. By knowing these sources of conflict, FLMs are better able to anticipate conflict and take steps to resolve it if it becomes dysfunctional. The ones we examine here are different goals and time horizons, overlapping authority, task interdependencies, different evaluation or reward systems, scarce resources, and status inconsistencies (see Figure 13.1).

Different Goals and Time Horizons

Remember from our earlier discussion that an important managerial activity is organizing people and tasks into teams, departments, and divisions

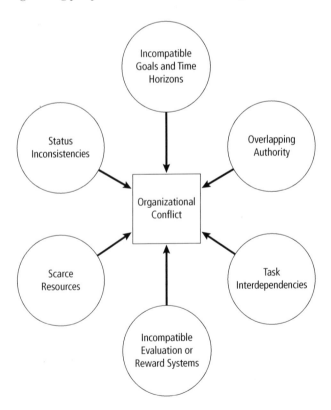

Figure 13.1 Sources of conflict in organizations.

to accomplish an organization's goals. Almost inevitably, this grouping creates teams, departments, and divisions that have different goals and time horizons, and the result can be conflict. For example, those in production usually concentrate on efficiency and cost cutting; they have a relatively short time horizon and focus on producing quality goods or services in a timely and efficient manner. In contrast, those in marketing focus on sales and responsiveness to customers. Their time horizon is longer than that of production because they are trying to be responsive not only to customers' needs today, but also to their changing needs in the future to build long-term customer loyalty. These fundamental differences between marketing and production often breed conflict.

Consider the following: Suppose production is behind schedule in its plan to produce a specialized product for a key customer. Those in marketing believe the delay will reduce sales of the product and therefore insist that the product be delivered on time even if saving the production schedule means increasing costs by paying production workers overtime. Production says that they will happily schedule overtime if marketing will pay for it. Both positions are reasonable from the perspective of their own departments, and conflict is likely.

Overlapping Authority

When two or more FLMs, teams, departments, or functions claim authority for the same activities or tasks, conflict is likely. For example, in a hotel where receptionists and billing cashiers are both assigned the task of collecting money from guests, there would undoubtedly be situations in which conflict could occur. The situation can also cause conflict with their FLMs if neither group did the work while assuming the other was responsible.

Task Interdependencies

It is not unusual for employees to be assigned to a group or team project and have one member who consistently fails to get things done on time, if at all. This most often creates some conflict in the team because other team members are dependent on the late member's contributions to complete the project. Whenever individuals, groups, teams, or departments are interdependent, the potential for conflict exists. With differing goals and time horizons, the FLMs and others in marketing and production come into conflict precisely because the teams and departments are interdependent. Marketing is dependent on production for goods it markets and sells, and production is dependent on marketing to create demand for the things it makes.

Different Evaluation or Reward Systems

How interdependent groups, teams, or departments are evaluated and rewarded can be another source of conflict. Those in production are evaluated and rewarded for their success in staying within budget or lowering costs while maintaining quality. So they are reluctant to take any steps that will increase costs, such as paying workers high overtime rates to finish a late order for an important customer. In contrast, those in marketing are evaluated and rewarded for their success in generating sales and satisfying customers. So, they think overtime pay is a small price to pay for responsiveness to customers. Thus, conflict between production and marketing is rarely unexpected.

Scarce Resources

Management is the process of acquiring, developing, protecting, and using the resources that allow an organization to be efficient and effective. When resources are scarce, an FLMs job is more difficult and conflict is likely. Two or more FLMs, their groups or teams who are competing for the same resources at times engage in argument, disagreement and eventually move to conflict if the different views are not well reconciled. Their energy and attention will be channeled toward gaining a larger share of the resources instead of being directed to the fulfillment of their primary purpose of doing the work.

Status Inconsistencies

The fact that some individuals, groups, teams, or departments within an organization are more highly regarded than others in the organization can also create conflict. In some restaurants, for example chefs have relatively higher status than the people who wait on tables. Nevertheless, the chefs receive customers' orders from the waitstaff, and the waitstaff can return to the chefs food that their customers or they think is not acceptable. This status inconsistency—high status chefs taking orders from low-status waitstaff—can be the source of considerable conflict between chefs and the waitstaff. For this reason, many restaurants require the waitstaff to input food orders directly into an electronic system via iPad or another type of mobile table, thereby reducing the amount of direct ordering from the waitstaff to the chefs.

Diagnosing Sources of Conflicts

A checklist can help employees and FLMs diagnose the sources and types of conflict. Key questions about conflict are listed below.

- Where is the conflict in the system? Is it at the leadership, individual, group/team, intergroup, organizational, or organization-environment level?

- What is the nature of the conflict?
- Is the conflict "functional" or "dysfunctional"? For whom?
- How is the individual, team, or department that is experiencing the conflict related to other parts of the organization?
- How high up and how far down the organizational chart does the conflict extend?
- Which people experiencing the conflict are ready for change?
- Do we have an approved conflict resolution method for solving the problem?

Understanding the sources of conflict in and between organizations is a first step toward resolution. Effective conflict-resolution techniques that can be used by FLMs and organizations as well as individuals and teams, are discussed later in the chapter.

Managing Conflict and Encouraging Resolution

The goal of conflict management is primarily to prevent negative or dysfunctional conflict from occurring, while at the same time encouraging healthy conflict that stimulates individual and team innovation and performance. If dysfunctional conflict cannot be prevented, then the goal is to eliminate it, or at least minimize or decrease it. This section will provide the FLM with a better understanding of available conflict management strategies to encourage functional conflict and discourage dysfunctional conflict in addition to taking a closer look at one specific method of promoting programmed conflict.

If an organization is to achieve its goals, FLMs and other managers and leaders must be able to resolve conflict in a functional manner. Functional conflict resolution means that the conflict is settled, for example, by compromise or by collaboration between the parties in conflict. Thus the importance of conflict management.

Conflict management is one of the most difficult, yet important jobs for FLMs as they cannot do without it. In practice, there are many ways through which FLMs can handle conflict situations and if diligently done, can transform what seems to appear as a negative conflict to a positive contribution that will enhance the welfare of both the employees and the organization. Some of these conflict management strategies available to FLMs are explained below.

1. *Suppression.* Under this method, what FLMs usually do is to use their authority to order the conflicting parties to cease their con-

flict and go back to normal behavior. Although the method is quick in providing solutions to minor conflicts, it does not work very well in organizations where FLMs do not possess authority commensurate with their responsibility.

2. *Smoothing.* FLMs that use this technique attempt to defuse the conflict by consoling the conflicting parties. They use supportive and effective language in restoring peaceful relations among the parties. By smoothing the conflict, FLMs hope to decrease the intensity of the conflict and avoid an escalation of open hostility. Like forcing a solution, smoothing is generally ineffective because it does not address the key points of the conflict which are likely to keep resurfacing. However, smoothing can sometimes be effective as a stop-gap measure to let workers cool down and regain perspective. In the heat of disagreement, employees are likely to make statements that escalate, rather than de-escalate the conflict, and smoothing can bring the disagreement back to a manageable level.

3. *Avoidance.* This is another technique of dealing with conflict. Here, FLMs play the role of mothers or fathers in organizations and in doing that ignore or overlook certain things in order to manage conflict situations. For instance, an FLM that sees a direct doing certain acts though not too detrimental to the success of the organization or receives a report of a minor disagreement between some workers can decide to overlook such things in order to avoid conflict.

   Quite often, executives who adopt this strategy disregard the causes of the conflict, and, as a result, the conflict situation frequently continues or gets worse over time. Some notable situations where avoidance is recommended in practice are where the conflict issue is trivial and where the issue seems symptomatic of other more basic conflicts.

4. *Bargaining/Compromise.* Here, FLMs seek to establish a middle ground that yields somewhat from the original position that generated the conflict. If both parties can move to a middle position, conflict can be controlled. Typically, what happens in bargaining is that each side begins by demanding more than it really expects to get. Both sides realize that some concessions will be necessary in order to reach a solution, but neither side wants to make the first concession because it will be seen as a sign of weakness. A lot of what happens in bargaining is tacit communication. The practice here is that each party signals a willingness to be flexible in exchanging concessions without actually making an explicit offer or promise. This approach decreases the danger of appearing weak since tacit proposal can later be denied if it fails to elicit a positive

response from the other party. Bargaining continues until some sort of mutually satisfactory agreement is reached.

It is also important to note that bargaining at times may result in a compromise agreement that fails to deal with the underlying problem in a rational manner and that is not in the long-term interest of the parties. However, for bargaining to be feasible at all as a conflict resolution strategy, both parties should be of relatively equal power. If not so, one group could simply impose its will upon the other and the solution would not be mutually acceptable as the weaker group would have no recourse in obtaining its concessions from the more powerful group. Again, bargaining is more likely to work if there are several acceptable alternatives that both parties would be willing to consider. If each party has only one acceptable settlement, bargaining will likely end in deadlock.

5. *Third Party Intervention.* Under this method, one or more people who are not a party to the conflict are brought in to find a means to resolve the conflict issue. For instance, in industrial disputes, arbitrators as third parties to the dispute are often effective in resolving labor-management disputes.

6. *Cooptation.* Cooptation as a technique of conflict management occurs when one group takes over or subsumes another group. A typical example of this technique is when teams or departments are part of a reorganization or there is a corporate merger. For example, often the merger is brought about only after a bitter and sometimes drawn-out proxy of fights among the stockholders of the organizations. Once the merger is completed, the means for peaceful resolution can then exist.

7. *Job Rotation.* This involves posting of employees from the group, team, or department of their primary assignment to other groups, teams, or departments. It is an interchange of employees. This method as a technique of conflict management works on the assumption that when members of an organization work together with other groups, they can come to appreciate others tasks, attitudes, and orientations. An idea about the worth of others will possibly remove some conditions that might cause unhealthy competition which often result in conflict.

8. *Confrontation.* This method relies heavily on facts and objectives in its process of solving organization conflict. Confrontation does not suggest that emotions should be ignored completely in conflict management. It only suggests that objectivity and facts should be emphasized rather than emotions. It simply attempts to minimize the role of emotions in conflict management and stresses the importance of facts and objectivity.

9. *Structuring the Interaction between Groups/Teams.* Structuring entails many dimensional approaches to problem-solving. The most frequently and effective strategies in this area include: (a) decreasing the amount of direction interaction between groups in the early stages of conflict resolution, (b) decreasing the amount of time between problem-solving meetings, (c) decreasing the formality of the presentation of issues, and (d) limiting the application of historical precedents. Structuring the interaction between groups, for example, as a means of intergroup conflict resolution is seen most frequently in governmental relations such as diplomatic talks in union-management relations. Two common situations where structuring the interaction can rightly be used as conflict resolution strategies are: (a) when previous attempts to openly discuss the conflict issues led to conflict escalation rather than to problem solution, and (b) when a respected third party is available to provide and maintain some structure to the interaction between the groups and to serve as a mediator.

10. *Integrative Problem Solving/Collaboration.* This strategy involves the two opposing groups working together to define the problem and to identify mutually satisfactory solutions. In order to implement this strategy, organizations generally bring in an outside consultant. The consultant tries to establish some initial trust between the conflicting groups, and to set up ground rules for further discussions. The consultant also helps the groups identify their most important problems and assist them in designing the solutions.

There are two preconditions for integrative or collaborative problem solving to work: (a) There must be a minimal level of trust between the groups—without the trust, each group will unlikely reveal its true preferences and will equally suspect that the other group will give it inaccurate information in return; and (b) There must be enough time and less pressure for quick solutions—integrative/collaborative problem-solving takes a lot of time and can only really succeed in the absence of excessive pressure for quick settlement.

Promoting Programmed Conflict

Practically every FLM has been a part of or managed a group or team that got so bogged down in details and procedures that nothing was accomplished. Such experiences are both a waste of time and frustrating. One way to break out of such unproductive ruts is to generate and monitor functional conflict. When done effectively, collaboration, creativity, and results soar. It has been said that conflict is oxygen and brings issues into the open. The challenge for FLMs is to do it in a functional rather than dysfunctional manner. To do this, FLMs essentially have two options.

1. *Fan the fire and get more of the same.* FLMs can urge everyone to hunker down and slog through—simply persist. While this may work, this approach can be unreliable (conflict can escalate) and slow.
2. *Program conflict.* Alternatively, FLMs can resort to programmed conflict. Programmed conflict is conflict that allows the expression of different opinions in a structured setting, so that personal feelings are not involved. It encourages open dialogue and constructive debate among potentially conflicting parties. The challenge for FLMs is to get contributors to either defend or criticize ideas based on relevant facts rather than on the basis of personal preference or political interests. Two programmed conflict techniques with proven track records are the devil's advocacy and the dialectic method which both require participants to submit proposals for debate, engage in structured role-playing, and effective leadership. Let's explore these two ways of stimulating functional conflict.

The devil's advocate decision program includes the following steps:

1. A proposed course of action is generated.
2. A devil's advocate (individual or group) is assigned to criticize the proposal.
3. The critique is presented to key decision makers and additional information is gathered.
4. The decision to adopt, modify, or discontinue the proposed course of action is taken and the decision is monitored.

The dialectic decision method includes the following steps:

1. A proposed course of action is generated.
2. Assumptions underlying the proposal are identified.
3. A conflicting counterproposal is generated based on different assumptions.
4. Advocates of each position present and debate the merits of their proposals before key decision makers.
5. The decision to adopt either position, or some other position, for example, a compromise, is taken.
6. The decision is monitored.

The primary difference in the two processes is the fact that with the devil's advocate approach, one proposal is being critiqued, while with the dialectic model two competing proposals are considered.

While it is vital that FLMs encourage functional conflict, or disagreement with the "status quo," it can be a real challenge for FLMs to hear unwelcome news. The news may make their blood boil or their hopes collapse, but they can't show it. They have to learn to take bad news without flinching: no tirades, no tight-lipped sarcasm, no rolling eyes, no gritted teeth. FLMs should instead ask calm, even-tempered questions: "Can you tell me more about what happened? What do you think we ought to do?" A sincere, "Thank you for bringing this to my attention," will increase the probability of similar communications in the future.

Other Approaches to Managing Conflict

FLMs have a variety of approaches they can use to address conflict. They may have to intervene as the person to resolve conflict among the work group as well. Some of these are described below. FLMs can

- divide up the conflict by reducing a large conflict into smaller parts and working on each part separately;
- contain the conflict, by limiting discussion to the present problem, not the past; refraining from labeling the conflict as the "fault" of one party; and describing the problem in objective terms;
- allow the griping to set the agenda for problem solving, and cooperate to solve those problems; and
- look for areas of "common ground" where both parties might agree.

FLMs should prepare for conflict resolution by understanding the reasons for the conflict. They should focus on behavior, which people can change, and not on personalities, which they cannot change. It is also important to determine what actions cause the problem, and how that action affects the FLM and others. For example, if you are receiving weekly reports late from another FLM, you can describe the problem and why it is difficult for you. You might say, "I haven't been getting the weekly production reports until late Friday afternoon. That means I have to give up precious family time to review them over the weekend, or else I embarrass myself by being unprepared at the Monday morning production team meetings."

After you have stated the problem, listen to how the other person responds and attempt to understand their point of view. If the other person does not acknowledge there is a problem, restate your concern until the other person understands it or until it is clear that you cannot make any progress on your own. Often a conflict exists simply because the other person has not understood your point of view or your situation. Or, you may not understand their point of view. When you have begun communicating about the problem, the two of you can work together to find a solution. Restate your solution to be sure that you both agree on what you are going to do next.

Whether formal or informal, the essence of the FLM's role and responsibilities in an organization is to mold, modify, direct, and influence the behavior of employees toward the achievement of organizational objectives. In the process of directing and influencing the behavior of employees, conflicts are bound to occur. As the employees work together, conflicts can occur between the employees. Conflicts can equally happen within groups, teams, or departments of employees or between groups, teams, or departments in the organization. This conflict is natural and important in organization life. FLMs should provide for it instead of trying to eliminate it. This is because its benefits outweigh its side effects in organization. What is important is how to productively manage it to bring positive change to the organization and not how to suppress it with managerial fiat.

Negotiation

Negotiation is a part of our everyday lives and our history—from trading cards as kids to asking our boss for a salary raise, or bargaining a purchase as adults. Negotiation is a particularly important conflict resolution technique for FLMs and other organizational members in situations where the parties to a conflict have approximately equal levels of power. During negotiation parties to a conflict try to come up with a solution acceptable to themselves by considering various alternative ways to, for example, allocate resources to each other. The ultimate goal in negotiation is for the various parties is to settle differences, hopefully by compromise or agreement while avoiding argument and dispute. In any disagreement, FLMs or others understandably aim to achieve the best possible outcome for their position (or perhaps an organization they represent). However, the principles of fairness, seeking mutual benefit, and maintaining a relationship are the keys to a successful outcome.

Sometimes the sides involved in a conflict negotiate directly with each other. Other times a third-party negotiator is relied on. Third-party negotiators are impartial individuals who are not directly involved in the conflict and have special expertise in handling conflicts and negotiations; they are relied on to help the two negotiating parties reach an acceptable resolution of their conflict. When a third-party negotiator acts as a mediator, her or his role in the negotiation process is to facilitate an effective negotiation between the two parties; mediators do not force either party to make concessions, nor can they force an agreement to resolve a conflict. Arbitrators, on the other hand, are third-party negotiators who can impose what they believe is a fair solution to a dispute, which both parties are obligated to abide by.

Specific forms of negotiation are used in many situations: international affairs, the legal system, government, industrial disputes, or domestic relationships as examples. However, general negotiation skills can be learned and applied in a wide range of activities. Negotiation skills can be of great benefit to FLMs in resolving any differences that arise between them and others.

Distributive Negotiation and Integrative Bargaining

There are two major types of negotiation—distributive negotiation and integrative negotiation. In distributive negotiation, the two parties perceive that they have a "fixed pie" of resources they need to divide—that is, slicing up the pie. So, this type of negotiation is often referred to as "the fixed pie." There is only so much to go around, and the proportion to be distributed is limited and variable.

In distributive negotiation, the parties take a competitive, adversarial stance. Each party realizes that he or she must concede something but is out to get the lion's share of the resources. The parties see no need to interact with each other in the future and do not care if their interpersonal relationship is damaged or destroyed by their competitive negotiation. In distributive negotiations, conflicts are handled by competition. In a distributive negotiation, for example, one issue at stake might be price. When you are negotiating with a merchant in a flea market, or over a used car closer to home, you are generally involved in a distributive negotiation, as it may be difficult to add issues other than price to the mix.

By comparison, in integrative bargaining, the parties perceive that they might be able to increase the resource pie by trying to come up with a creative solution to the conflict. They do not view the conflict competitively as a win or lose situation; instead, they view it cooperatively, as a win–win situation in which both parties can gain. Trust, information sharing, and the desire of both parties to achieve a good resolution of the conflict characterize integrative bargaining. In integrative bargaining, conflicts are handled through collaboration and/or compromise. Whenever multiple issues are present—such as salary, benefits, and start date, in the case of a job negotiation—negotiators have the potential to make tradeoffs across issues and create value. Often, what looks like a distributive negotiation is, in fact, an integrative negotiation, as there may be additional issues you can add to the discussion.

Strategies to Promote Integrative Bargaining

FLMs in all kinds of organizations can rely on the following strategies to facilitate integrative bargaining and avoid distributive negotiation: emphasizing superordinate goals; focusing on the problem, not the people; focusing on interests, not demands; creating new options for joint gain; and focusing on what is fair.

Emphasizing superordinate goals. Superordinate goals are goals that both parties agree to, regardless of the source of their conflict. Increasing organizational effectiveness, increasing responsiveness to customers, and gaining a competitive advantage are just a few of the many superordinate goals that members of an organization can emphasize during integrative bargaining. Superordinate goals help parties in conflict to keep in mind the big picture and the fact that they are working together to survive and prosper.

Focusing on the problem, not people. People who are in conflict may not be able to resist the temptation to focus on the other party's shortcomings and weaknesses, thereby personalizing the conflict. Instead of attacking the problem, the parties to the conflict attack each other. This approach is inconsistent with integrative bargaining and can easily lead both parties into a distributive negotiation mode. All parties to a conflict need to keep focused on the problem or on the source of the conflict and avoid the temptation to discredit one another.

Focusing on interests, not demands. Demands are what a person wants; interests are why the person wants them. When two people are in conflict, it is unlikely that the demands of both can be met. Their underlying interests, however, can be met, and meeting them is what integrative bargaining is all about.

Creating new options for joint gain. Once two parties to a conflict focus on their interests, they are on the road to achieving creative solutions to the conflict that will benefit them both. This win–win scenario means that rather than having a fixed set of alternatives from which to choose, the two parties can come up with new alternatives that might even expand the resource pie.

Focusing on what is fair. Focusing on what is fair is consistent with the principle of distributive justice, which emphasizes the fair distribution of outcomes based on meaningful contributions that people make to organizations. It is likely that two parties in conflict will disagree on certain points and prefer different alternatives that each party believes may better serve his or her own interests or maximize his or her outcomes. Emphasizing fairness and distributive justice will help the two parties come to a mutual agreement about what the best solution is to the problem.

When FLMs pursue these strategies and encourage other organizational members to do so, they are more likely to be able to effectively resolve their conflicts through integrative bargaining. These skills result in outcomes that benefit the individual participants and the organization as a whole. Furthermore, FLMs who learn these skills are well prepared for many practical career challenges, including the negotiation for pay raises, promotions, and other development and career opportunities. In addition, throughout the negotiation process, FLMs and other organizational members need to be aware of, and on their guard against the biases that can lead to faulty decision-making.

Added-Value Negotiation

One practical application of the integrative approach is added-value negotiation (AVN). During AVN, the negotiating parties cooperatively develop multiple deal packages while building a productive long-term relationship. AVN consists of five steps:

1. *Clarify interests.* After each party identifies tangible and intangible needs, the two parties meet to discuss their respective needs and find common ground for negotiation.
2. *Identify options.* A marketplace of value is created when the negotiating parties discuss desired elements of value (such as property, money, behavior, rights, and risk reduction).
3. *Design alternative deal packages.* While aiming for multiple deals, each party mixes and matches elements of value from both parties in workable combinations.
4. *Select a deal.* Each party analyzes deal packages proposed by the other party. Jointly, the parties discuss and select from feasible deal packages, with a spirit of creative agreement.
5. *Perfect the deal.* Together the parties discuss unresolved issues, develop a written agreement, and build relationships for future negotiations.

Prior to the negotiating process, it is helpful for FLMs to give some thought to the stages of negotiation. The next section takes a brief look at the possible stages of negotiation and informal negotiation.

Stages of Negotiation

In order to achieve a desirable outcome, it may be useful to understand a structured approach to negotiation. For example, in a work situation a meeting may need to be arranged in which all parties involved can come together. The process of negotiation includes the following stages:

- preparation,
- discussion,
- clarification of goals,
- negotiate towards a Win–Win outcome,
- agreement, and
- implementation of a course of action.

Preparation

Before any negotiation takes place, a decision has to be made as to when and where a meeting will take place to discuss the problem and who will attend. Setting a limited time-scale can also be helpful to prevent the disagreement continuing. This stage involves ensuring all the pertinent facts of the situation are known in order to clarify your own position. For FLMs, this includes knowing the "rules" of your organization, to whom help is given, when help is not felt appropriate and the grounds for such refusals. Your organization may well have policies to which you can refer in preparation for the negotiation. Undertaking preparation before discussing the disagreement will help to avoid further conflict and unnecessarily wasting time during the meeting.

Discussion

During this stage, individuals or members of each side put forward the case as they see it (i.e., their understanding of the situation). Key skills during this stage include questioning, listening, and clarifying. Sometimes it is helpful to take notes during the discussion stage to record all points put forward in case there is need for further clarification. It is extremely important to listen, as when disagreement takes place it is easy to make the mistake of saying too much and listening too little. Each side should have an equal opportunity to present their case.

Clarifying Goals

From the discussion, the goals, interests, and viewpoints of both sides of the disagreement need to be clarified. It is helpful to list these factors in order of priority. Through this clarification it is often possible to identify or establish some common ground. Clarification is an essential part of the negotiation process, without it misunderstandings are likely to occur which may cause problems and barriers to reaching a beneficial outcome.

Negotiate Towards a Win–Win Outcome

This stage focuses on what is termed a "win–win" outcome where both sides feel they have gained something positive through the process of negotiation and both sides feel their point of view has been taken into consideration. As discussed earlier, a win–win outcome is usually the best result. Although this may not always be possible, through negotiation, it should be the ultimate goal. Suggestions of alternative strategies and compromises need to be considered at this point. Compromises are often positive alternatives which can often achieve greater benefit for all concerned compared to holding to the original positions.

Agreement

Agreement can be achieved once understanding of both sides' viewpoints and interests have been considered. It is essential for everybody involved to keep an open mind in order to achieve an acceptable solution. Any agreement needs to be made perfectly clear so that both sides know what has been decided.

Implementing a Course of Action

From the agreement, a course of action has to be implemented to carry through the decision.

Failure to Agree

If the process of negotiation breaks down and agreement cannot be reached, then rescheduling a further meeting is called for. This avoids all parties becoming embroiled in heated discussion or argument, which not only wastes time but can also damage future relationships. At the subsequent meeting, the stages of negotiation should be repeated. Any new ideas or interests should be taken into account and the situation looked at afresh At this stage, it may also be helpful to look at other alternative solutions and/or bring in another person to mediate.

Informal Negotiation

There are times when there is a need to negotiate more informally. At such times, when a difference of opinion arises, it might not be possible or appropriate to go through the stages set out above in a formal manner. Nevertheless, remembering the key points in the stages of formal negotiation may be very helpful in a variety of informal situations.

In any negotiation, the following three elements are important and likely to affect the ultimate outcome of the negotiation:

- attitudes,
- knowledge, and
- interpersonal skills.

Attitudes

All negotiation is strongly influenced by underlying attitudes to the process itself, for example attitudes to the issues and personalities involved in the particular case or attitudes linked to personal needs for recognition.

Knowledge

The more knowledge you possess of the issues in question, the greater your participation in the process of negotiation. In other words, good preparation is essential. Do your homework and gather as much information about the issues as you can. Furthermore, the way issues are negotiated must be understood as negotiating will require different methods in different situations.

Interpersonal Skills

Good interpersonal skills are essential for effective negotiations, both in formal situations and in less formal or one-to-one negotiations. These skills include:

- effective verbal communication,
- listening,
- reducing misunderstandings is a key part of effective negotiation,
- rapport building,
- problem-solving,
- decision-making,
- assertiveness, and
- dealing with difficult situations.

Organizational Politics

FLMs must develop the skills necessary to manage organizational conflict for an organization to be effective. Suppose, however, that senior leaders are in conflict over the best strategy for an organization to pursue or the best structure to adopt to use organizational resources efficiently. In such situations, resolving conflict is often difficult, and the parties to the conflict resort to organizational politics and political strategies to try to resolve the conflict in their favor.

Organizational politics are the activities that FLMs (and other members of the organization) engage in to increase their power and to use power effectively to achieve their goals and overcome resistance or opposition. FLMs often engage in organizational politics to resolve conflicts in their favor.

Political strategies are the specific tactics that FLMs (and other members of an organization) use to increase their power and use power effectively to influence and gain the support of other people while overcoming resistance or opposition. Political strategies are especially important when FLMs are planning and implementing major changes in their teams, departments, or those that are happening in the broader organization. FLMs not only need to gain support for their change initiatives and influence organizational members to behave in new ways (or in most situations to sign off on or support their proposed changes), but also need to overcome often strong opposition from people who feel threatened by the change and prefer the status quo. By increasing their power, FLMs are better able to make needed changes. In addition to increasing their power, FLMs also must make sure they use their power in a way that actually enables them to influence others.

Why Organizational Politics Are Important

The word politics often elicits more negative than positive connotations for many people. Some think FLMs and other managers who are political have risen to where they are not because of their own merit and capabilities but because of whom they know. Or people think that political FLMs are self-interested and wield power to benefit themselves, not their groups, teams, departments, or organizations. There is a grain of truth to this negative connotation. Some FLMs do appear to misuse their power for personal benefit at the expense of, for example, their organizations' effectiveness.

Nevertheless, organizational politics are often a positive force. FLMs striving to make needed changes often encounter resistance from individuals and groups who feel threatened and wish to preserve the status quo. Effective FLMs engage in politics to gain support for and implement needed changes. Similarly, FLMs often face resistance from other FLMs or managers who disagree with their goals for a group or team or for the organization and with what they are trying to accomplish. Engaging in organizational politics can help FLMs overcome this resistance and achieve their goals.

Indeed, FLMs cannot afford to ignore organizational politics. Everyone engages in politics to a degree—other FLMs, coworkers, and direct reports, as well as people outside an organization, such as vendors or supplies. Those who try to ignore politics might as well bury their heads in the sand because in all likelihood they will be unable to gain support for their initiatives and goals. Whether an FLM chooses to engage in or avoid it, organizational politics is a reality in the workplace.

How do people behave when they are engaging in political behaviors? Political behaviors include ingratiation, self-promotion, strong influence tactic, coalition building, the forging of connections with powerful allies, taking credit for positive events and the success of others, and the circumvention of legitimate channels to secure resources that would otherwise be unattainable.

Reasons for Political Behavior

We can identify at least five conditions conducive to political behavior in organizations. The conditions include the following:

- *Ambiguous goals.* When the goals of a group, team, department or organization are ambiguous, more room is available for politics. As a result, members may pursue personal gain under the guise of pursuing organizational goals.
- *Limited resources.* Politics surfaces when resources are scarce and allocation decisions must be made. If resources were ample, there would be no need to use politics to claim one's "share."
- *Changing technology and environment.* In general, political behavior is increased when the nature of the internal technology is nonroutine and when the external environment is dynamic and complex. Under these conditions, ambiguity and uncertainty are increased, thereby triggering political behavior by groups interested in pursuing certain courses of action.
- *Nonprogrammed decisions.* A distinction is made between programmed and nonprogrammed decisions. When decisions are not programmed, conditions surrounding the decision problem and the decision process are usually more ambiguous, which leaves room for political maneuvering. Programmed decisions, on the other hand, are typically specified in such detail that little room for maneuvering exists. Hence, we are likely to see more

political behavior on major questions, such as long-range strategic planning decisions.

▪ *Organizational change.* Periods of organizational change also present opportunities for political rather than rational behavior. Efforts to restructure a particular department, open a new division, introduce a new product line, and so forth, are invitations to all to join the political process as different factions and coalitions fight over territory.

Table 13.1 identifies the prevailing conditions for political behavior and the potential political behaviors

Because most organizations today have scarce resources, ambiguous goals, complex technologies, and sophisticated and unstable external environments, it seems reasonable to conclude that a large proportion of contemporary organizations are highly political in nature.

Political Strategies for Gaining and Maintaining Power

Imagine that you have watched your new manager, Malroy, climb up to the career ladder in your organization from an entry-level employee to an FLM and now to a more senior manager. You have witnessed him using various strategies to gain power, get others to support his ideas and follow him. These strategies, often known as office politics, have influenced Malroy's ability to lead the team toward company goals and enforce rules.

It is true that not all office politics are good and healthy for an organization, but you can see how the political methods, also known as political strategies, have influenced Malroy's ability to gain power. It is true that not all office politics are good and healthy for an organization, but you can see how the political methods, also known as political strategies, have influenced Malroy's ability to gain power.

TABLE 13.1 Conditions Conducive to Political Behavior	
Prevailing Conditions	**Resulting Political Behaviors**
Ambiguous goals	Attempts to define goals to one's advantage
Limited resources	Fight to maximize one's share of resources
Dynamic technology and environment	Attempts to exploit uncertainty for personal gain
Nonprogrammed decisions	Attempts to make suboptimal decisions that favor personal ends
Organizational change	Attempts to use reorganization as a chance to pursue own interests and goals

Gaining and Maintaining Power Through Political Strategies

There are many strategies that people such as Malroy can use to gain and maintain power. These strategies influence how individuals in the organization view the manager or leader. For Malroy, this can influence how much control he has over employees and how likely he is to get his direct reports and teams to work toward the organization's goals.

FLMs who use political strategies to increase and maintain their power are better able to influence others to work toward the achievement of group and organizational goals. By controlling uncertainty, making themselves irreplaceable, being in a central position, generating resources, and building alliances, FLMs can increase their power. Let's look at each of these strategies.

Control Uncertainty

Consider that your division has had two division heads in the past 5 years, and there are rumors that the division might be eliminated. There has also been secrecy surrounding the departure of the division heads, causing employees to feel confused about what is really going on inside the organization.

This uncertainty has damaged employee morale and productivity. However, as soon as Malroy took charge, he was open and honest with his direct reports. He explained why the previous division heads had left, and he held a meeting where he delivered a 2-year plan for the unit.

Malroy's decision to stop secrecy and deliver a 2-year plan likely alleviated stress within his unit and assisted employees in feeling more secure. By reducing uncertainty, Malroy has established himself as a good FLM in the organization and increased the trust of employees.

Uncertainty is a threat for individuals, groups, teams, departments, and whole organizations and can interfere with effective performance and goal attainment. For example, uncertainty about job security is threatening for many employees and may cause top performers (who have the best chance of finding another job) to quit and take a more secure position with another organization. When an R&D department faces uncertainty about customer preferences, its members may waste valuable resources to develop a product that customers do not want.

FLMs who can control and reduce uncertainty for other FLMs, teams, and departments as well as the organization as a whole are likely to see their power increase. FLMs in marketing and sales gain power when they can eliminate uncertainty for other departments, such as R&D, by accurately forecasting customers' changing preferences. FLMs who can control uncertainty are likely to be in demand and sought after by other organizations.

Making Oneself Irreplaceable

Over the past few years, Malroy has also worked hard to become an expert in the organization. He hasn't just spent time learning about his own area of expertise and projects he has worked on; he has also ensured that he understands how other groups, teams, departments, and the whole organization functions. Malroy is also on time to every meeting and has also taken the time to learn coworkers jobs and often filled in when others were not available. Because of this, Malroy has made himself a valuable asset to his department and the organization and made himself irreplaceable.

FLMs gain power when they have valuable knowledge and expertise that allow them to perform activities no one else can handle. This is the essence of being irreplaceable. The more central these activities are to organizational effectiveness, the more power FLMs gain from being irreplaceable. Employees who can position themselves as irreplaceable can quickly gain power in an organization. If a company sees the employee as someone they cannot replace, they have more incentive to promote them and give them more power in their department.

Being in a Central Position

FLMs in central positions are responsible for activities that are directly connected to an organization's goals and sources of competitive advantage and often are located in central positions in important communication networks in an organization. FLMs in key positions have control over crucial organizational activities and initiatives and have access to important information. Other organizational members depend on them for their knowledge, expertise, advice, and support, and the success of the organization as a whole is seen as riding on these FLMs. These consequences of being in a central position are likely to increase FLMs power.

FLMs like Malroy who have historically been outstanding performers, have a wide knowledge base, and have made important and visible contributions to their organizations are likely to be offered central positions that will increase their power. And, this was the reality given Malroy's promotions.

Generating or Bringing in Resources

As you can imagine, the first team and department Malroy worked for was struggling when Malroy first came on board. When Malroy was an entry-level employee, the work unit was just starting-up. Within the first few weeks, Malroy found various sources of help from across the organization, which helped the work unit meet their goals during some of its most difficult times. Malroy also played a vital role in bringing on new employees who had important technical and other skills that helped to increase the work unit's productivity and overall performance.

Organizations need three kinds of resources to be effective: (a) input resources such as raw materials, skilled employees, and financial capital; (b) technical resources such as equipment and computers; and (c) knowledge resources such as information technology, marketing, or engineering expertise.

Building Alliances

From the beginning, Malroy also made sure people would like and support him. He would bring coffee, donuts, and other treats to the work area, and would regularly help his co-workers and ask his FLM if there was anything he needed help with or other work that needed to be done.

When FLMs build alliances, they develop mutually beneficial relationships with people both inside and outside the group, team, department or organization. The parties to an alliance support one another because doing so is in their best interests, and all parties benefit from the alliance. Alliances give FLMs power because they provide the FLMs with support for their initiatives. Partners to alliances provide support because they know the FLMS will reciprocate when their partners need support. Alliances can help FLMs achieve their goals and implement needed changes in organizations because they increase FLMs' level of power.

FLMs should build alliances not only inside their organizations, but also with individuals, groups, teams, and organizations in the task and general environments on which their organizations depend for resources. These individuals, groups, teams, and organizations enter alliances with FLMs because doing so is in their best interests and they know they can count on the FLMs' support when they need it. When FLMs build alliances, they need to be on their guard to ensure that everything is aboveboard, ethical, and legal.

Political Strategies for Exercising Power

Politically skilled FLMs not only understand, and can use, the five strategies to increase their power, they also appreciate strategies for exercising their power. These strategies generally focus on how FLMs and other managers can use power unobtrusively. When FLMs exercise power unobtrusively, other members of an organization may not be aware that the FLMs are using their power to influence them. They may think they support these FLMs for a variety of reasons: because they believe it is the rational logical thing to do, because they believe doing so is in their own best interests, or because they believe the position or decision the FLMs are advocating is legitimate or appropriate.

The unobtrusive use of power may sound devious, but FLMs typically use this strategy to bring about change and achieve organizational goals. Political strategies for exercising power to gain the support and concurrence of others include relying on objective information, bringing in an outside expert, controlling the agenda, and making everyone a winner.

Relying on Objective Information

FLMs require the support of others to achieve their goals, implement changes, and overcome opposition. One way for an FLM to gain this support and overcome opposition is to rely on objective information that supports the FLM's initiatives. Reliance on objective information leads others to support the FLM because of the facts; objective information causes others to believe that what the FLM is proposing is the proper course of action. By relying on objective information, politically skilled FLMs unobtrusively exercise their power to influence others.

Bringing in an Outside Expert

Bringing in an outside expert to support a proposal or decision can, at times, provide FLMs with some of the same benefits that the use of objective information does. It lends credibility to an FLM's initiatives and causes others to believe that what the FLM is proposing is appropriate or rational thing to do. Although an FLM might think consultants and other outside experts are neutral or objective, they sometimes are hired by FLMs and other organizational members who want them to support a certain position or decision in an organization. For instance, when FLMs face strong opposition from others who fear that a decision will harm their interests, the FLMs may bring in an outside expert. They hope this expert will be perceived as a neutral observer to lend credibility and "objectivity" to their point of view. The support of the outside expert may cause others to believe that a decision is indeed the right one. Of course, sometimes consultants and other outside experts actually are brought into organizations to be objective and guide FLMs on the appropriate course of action.

Controlling the Agenda

FLMs also can exercise power unobtrusively by controlling the agenda, thereby influencing which alternatives are considered and whether a decision is made. When FLMs influence the alternatives that are considered, they can make sure that each considered alternative is acceptable to them and that undesirable alternatives are not in the feasible set. In a hiring context, for example, FLMs can exert their power unobtrusively by ensuring that job candidates whom they do not find acceptable do not make their way onto the list of finalists for an open position. They do this by making sure that these candidates' drawbacks or deficiencies are communicated to everyone involved in making the hiring decision. When several finalists for an open position are discussed and evaluated in a hiring meeting, an FLM may seem to exert little power or influence and just go along with what the rest of the groups want. However, the FLM may have exerted power in the hiring process unobtrusively by controlling which candidates have made it to the final stage. Sometimes FLMs can prevent a decision that they find unacceptable from being made by not including it on the agenda.

Making Everyone a Winner

Often, politically skilled FLMs are able to exercise their power unobtrusively because they make sure that everyone whose support they need benefits personally from providing that support. By making everyone a winner, an FLM can influence other organizational members to see supporting the manager as being in their best interest. Making everyone a winner not only is an effective way of exercising power but, when used consistently and forthrightly, also can increase FLMs' power and influence over time. That is, when an FLM actually does make everyone a winner, all stakeholders will see it as in their best interests to support the FLM and her or his initiatives.

Conclusion

Conflict is an integral part of organizational life and occurs because of disagreements or incompatibilities between individuals, or within groups and entire organizations. Conflict can be functional or dysfunctional and even destructive. Four types of conflict arising in organizations are interpersonal conflict, intragroup conflict, intergroup conflict, and interorganizational conflict. The conflict management strategies discussed in this chapter will help the FLM promote healthy conflict as well as resolve dysfunctional conflict.

Negotiation is a conflict resolution technique used when individuals or other parties to a conflict reach an impasse. There are the two types of negotiation (distributive negotiation and integrative bargaining) in our business and personal lives. Sometimes, these two usually distinct forms of negotiation can even overlap. By understanding these negotiating types, FLMs can be better prepared in different situations and in a better position to more effectively negotiate when the need arises.

Organizational politics, whether an FLM likes it or not, exists in almost every workplace. Effective FLMs realize that politics can be a positive force that enables them to make needed changes in organizations. FLMs can make use of various political strategies to effectively exercise power to minimize the destructive side of politics in their organizations.

14

Safety and Health

Truly Looking Out for Your Employees

O rganizations continue to be involved in safety and health management in response to many compelling influences, the most basic of which is a sense of social and humanitarian responsibility to ensure a safe and healthful workplace for employees. Other influences over the years include local, state, federal, and international government intervention, pressure from labor unions, and an increased awareness of safety and health issues among the general public. Finally, their experiences in issues of worker protection have led proactive organizations to appreciate the direct relationship between safety and health management and organizational effectiveness. When an organization protects the well-being of its employees, it is protecting the organization's most valuable resource and avoiding the staggering costs and negative public image associated with safety neglect.

Before taking a closer look at the key points of this chapter, consider the experience of one FLM, Kai Williams. The chapter then focuses on the importance of and the benefits of safety and health management. The next section takes an in-depth look at the Occupational Safety and Health

Succeeding as a Frontline Manager in Today's Organizations, pages 391–421
Copyright © 2021 by Information Age Publishing
All rights of reproduction in any form reserved.

Act (OSHA) and its implementation under the Occupational and Safety Administration. The chapter concludes with a discussion of behavior based safety as a critical way for FLMs and their organization to better institutionalize a safety culture.

Kai's Experience

Kai Williams has just filled out an OSHA accident report concerning the second major injury in his department this year. Both injuries occurred when an employee was trying to reach for something on a high shelf. First, Anzel Mason, standing on the top step of a stepladder in the storage room, lost her balance and fell. She was out for 3 weeks with a strained back. Next, Foster Gaines tried to reach a folder on a shelf and fell to the floor after the chair he was standing on slipped. He broke his arm in the fall and missed 12 days of work.

Kai sighs in frustration. If he had talked to his employees once about being careful, he had talked to them a dozen times! Kai simply cannot believe the stupid things his employees do. Why only yesterday he himself tripped over a pencil someone had left on the floor. Fortunately he caught himself in time. Whatever can he do to prevent more "useless" accidents? Kai Williams' impromptu talks with his employees have had little effect on reducing accidents. He now needs to implement a safety program in his department and encourage employee participation in the program.

A successful safety program starts at the very top of the organization. The owners, C-suite executives, and middle managers must all be committed to safety. FLMs like Kai Williams are the representatives of management who have daily contact with the employees and therefore critical to the program's success. A safety program is only one way FLMs contribute to safety and health in the workplace. Even in organizations that have a safety engineer or safety director, the FLM is responsible for seeing that any safety directives are carried out. It is the FLM who shapes the employees' attitudes toward safety: Employees take their cues from the FLM as to what is important.

As an FLM, Kai has a legal responsibility to ensure that the workplace is free from unnecessary hazards and that working conditions are not harmful to employees' physical or mental health. Although accidents can and do happen, Kai and other FLMs are on the front line to prevent them from occurring. Kai must be concerned about safety and health if for no other reason than unsafe and unhealthy work sites cost money. He therefore needs to focus his efforts on both preventive and corrective safety controls.

The Importance of Safety and Health Management

Today, safety and health management concerns go beyond the physical condition of the workplace to a regard for employees' mental and emotional well-being and a commitment to protecting the surrounding community, for example, from pollution and exposure to toxic substances. The concerns have led to an increased emphasis on safety and health management programs. One of the most effective ways to reduce workplace hazards and injuries is through a comprehensive, proactive safety and health management system. According to the OSHA (n.d.):

> A safety and health management system is a proactive, collaborative process to find and fix workplace hazards before employees are injured or become ill. The benefits of implementing safety and health management systems include protecting workers, saving money, and making all your hazard-specific programs more effective. (n.p.)

As a result of an increased focus on safety and health management, employees at all levels of the organization are now involved in promoting safety. Briefly, some of the health and safety activities of FLMs, human resource management (HRM) professionals, and other employees are listed below.

FLMs

- Make safety and health a major objective of the organization.
- Support the HRM professionals' efforts to train all employees in safety and health.

HRM Professionals

- Work with other professionals such as medical doctors and industrial engineers to develop new programs.
- Create HRM programs that train employees for safe and healthy behaviors and reward them for their success.

Employees

- Participate in the development and administration of safety and health programs.
- Perform in accordance with established safety and health guidelines.
- The importance of these activities is evident when one thinks of the benefits and costs of safety and health.

The Benefits of Safety and Health Programs

If organizations can reduce the rates and severity of work-related accidents, diseases, and stress levels, and improve the quality of work life for their employees, they can become more effective. The benefits of improved health and safety include:

- more productivity due to fewer lost workdays,
- increased efficiency from a more committed workforce,
- reduced medical and insurance costs,
- lower workers' compensation rates and direct payments because fewer filed claims,
- greater flexibility and adaptability of the workforce as a result of increased participation and an increased sense of ownership,
- better selection ratios when hiring new employees because of the enhanced image of the organization, and
- a substantial increase in profits.

Costs of Work-Related Accidents and Illnesses

The costs of work-related accidents and occupational diseases to American industry are known to be in the billions of dollars annually and are increasing in certain areas. These costs are both tangible and intangible. The tangible costs are measurable financial expenses. One major category of these costs is directly related to lost production. This category includes costs incurred as a result of work slowdown, damaged or idle equipment, damaged or ruined products, excessive waste, and any profit forgone due to lost sales. A closely related cost is the cost incurred for training new or temporary replacements. Another category covers insurance and medical costs. These costs are increasing due to large claims and other expenses incurred as a result of work-related accidents. This category includes the costs of worker's compensation insurance, accident insurance, and disability insurance.

The intangible costs of work-related accidents and illnesses include lowered employee morale, less favorable public relations, and a weakened ability to recruit and retain employees. It is only natural that employee morale will suffer in an unsafe environment. If a member of a work team is injured, the harmony of the team may be impaired by the absence of the injured employee. A bad safety record may also be a major reason for poor employee relations with management. If employees perceive that their FLMs are unconcerned about their physical welfare, employee–FLM relations can deteriorate. In fact, safety is often a primary reason for unionizing. A poor safety record is also harmful to an organization's public relations. It may deter customers from purchasing a business' products or services.

Frequently, organizations ignore or are not aware of these and other "hidden" costs of occupational illness or injury. The following list summarizes some of the costs that can be associated with a single accident in the workplace. In general, the more serious the accident, the greater the costs:

- the cost of wages paid to workers who are attracted to the accident site and therefore not working;
- the cost of slowdowns at later production stations caused by interruptions in the work of both the injured person and those who come to the scene;
- the cost of repairing damaged equipment;
- cleanup costs;
- payments to the injured employee in excess of workers' compensation;
- the cost of dispensary services provided by the plant nurse or infirmary;
- diminished productivity of injured employees after they return to the job, but before they regain the ability to produce their full work output;
- the cost of management time incurred to investigate accidents;
- extra overtime costs occasioned by the interruption of work;
- the cost associated with the recruitment, selection or transfer, and training of replacements for the injured workers;
- the costs due to the generally lower efficiency of replacement workers;
- legal costs for advice with respect to any potential claims;
- the costs of rental equipment placed temporarily in service while unsafe equipment is repaired or replaced;
- increased insurance payments that reflect the degree of safety and health risk containment;
- the costs associated with any loss of accreditation by national or international marketing or business associations, or any adverse impact on competitiveness within the global market; and
- the loss of market share from adverse publicity.

The Occupational Safety and Health Act

In 1969, in the aftermath of a tragic explosion that claimed the lives of 78 coal miners and amid reports of a high incidence of black-lung disease among miners, Congress passed the Coal Mine Health and Safety Act. The following year, continuing public and governmental concern about safety and health in the workplace was reflected in passage of the Occupational Safety and Health Act (OSHA). Its stated purpose is "to assure so far as possible every working man and woman in the nation safe and healthful working conditions and to preserve our human resources." Thus OSHA was designed to enforce safety and health standards to reduce the incidence of occupational injury, illness, and death. The Occupational Safety and Health Administration of the U.S. Department of Labor (DOL) enforces OSHA, which covers nearly all businesses with one or more employees. OSHA was created to

- encourage employers and employees to reduce workplace hazards and to implement new or improve existing safety and health programs;
- provide for research to develop innovative ways of dealing with occupational safety and health problems;
- establish "separate but dependent responsibilities and rights" for employers and employees to achieve better safety and health conditions;
- maintain a reporting and record-keeping system to monitor job-related injuries and illnesses;
- establish training programs to increase the number and competence of occupational safety and health personnel;
- develop mandatory job safety and health standards and enforce them effectively; and
- provide for the development, analysis, evaluation, and approval of state occupational safety and health programs.

The act covers most employers. The main employers it doesn't cover are self-employed persons, farms employing only the employer's immediate family members, and certain workplaces protected by other federal statutes. The act covers federal agencies. It usually doesn't apply to state and local governments in their role as employers.

Accident prevention is a major goal of safety and health management. OSHA requires employers to keep a log of on-the-job accidents, and accident investigation and measurement can supply useful data for developing effective safety programs and improving working conditions. These data can be useful to company safety specialists as well as to worker-management safety committees. State OSHA programs are found in those states that have assumed responsibility for administration of OSHA. Under special plans negotiated with the DOL, states agree to establish programs of inspection, citation, and training that meet or exceed the minimum standards enforced on the federal level.

Few laws have evoked as much negative reaction as OSHA. While most people would support its intent, many have criticized the manner in which it has been implemented. The sheer volume of regulations has been staggering, and many of them are vaguely worded. For example, the Occupational Safety and Health Administration developed the following 39-word single-sentence definition of the word exit:

> That portion of a means of egress which is separated from all other spaces of the building or structure by construction or equipment as required in this subject to provide a protected way of travel to the exit discharge.

In addition, many OSHA standards have been criticized as unacceptable, arbitrary, trivial, unattainable, excessively detailed, costly, or petty. For example, one regulation states:

> Where working clothes are provided by the employer and become wet or are washed between shifts, provision shall be made to ensure that such clothing is dry before reuse.

In response to definitions and regulations similar to the examples given above, many organizations have developed a negative attitude toward OSHA. As a result of these critics, legislation was enacted to soften some OSHA requirements. Many of the original standards were also subsequently revoked by the Occupational Safety and Health Administration itself. In spite of these changes to its policies and procedures, OSHA performs a job that today's FLMs must understand.

OSHA Standards and Record Keeping

OSHA operates under the "general duty clause" that each employer shall furnish to each of her (or his) employees employment and a place of employment which are free from recognized hazards that are causing or are likely to cause death or serious physical harm to her (or his) employees. To carry out this basic mission, OSHA is responsible for promulgating enforceable standards. The standards cover just about every conceivable hazard, in detail.

Under OSHA, employers with 11 or more employees must maintain a record of, and report, occupational injuries and occupational illnesses. An occupational illness is any abnormal condition or disorder caused by exposure to environmental factors associated with employment. This includes illnesses caused by inhalation, absorption, ingestion, or direct contact with toxic substances or harmful agents. Employers must report all occupational illnesses and occupational injuries (specifically those that result in medical treatment [other than first aid], loss of consciousness, restriction of work [one or more lost workdays], restriction of motion, or transfer to another job). If an on-the-job accident results in the death of an employee or in the hospitalization of five or more employees, all employers, regardless of size, must report the accident to OSHA. If even one employee is hospitalized due to a work-related incident, the employer must notify OSHA within 24 hours.

OSHA Inspections

OSHA enforces its standards through inspections and (if necessary) citations. The inspection is usually unannounced. OSHA may conduct warrantless inspections without an employer's consent. OSHA inspections are conducted by compliance officers. These inspectors are men and women from the safety and health field who have attended specialized training at one the training centers. They also take additional training courses once each year in specialized areas such as industrial hygiene, construction, or maritime safety and health.

The inspection process starts with the presentation of the compliance officer's credentials and a meeting with the appropriate employer representative. OSHA inspectors look for violations of all types, but some potential problem areas—such as scaffolding, fall protection, and inadequate hazard communications—grab more of their attention. If the inspection has resulted from an employee complaint with the complainant's name withheld, as well as copies of any applicable laws and safety and health standards. Before an inspection tour, the compliance officer will also want to meet with a representative of the employees if the company is unionized. If it is not, an employee representative will be selected by the members of the plant safety committee or by the employees as a whole. Both the employee and employer representatives typically accompany the compliance officer during the inspection. In addition to a planned inspection, the compliance officer is permitted to interview various employees at his or her discretion about safety and health conditions. OSHA gives the compliance officer the right to take photographs, make instrument readings, and examine safety and health records. Compliance officers must keep any trade secrets they observe confidential.

After the inspection, the officer should discuss any observations with the employer and review possible OSHA violations. The employer should estimate the time needed to correct any hazardous conditions noted by the officer. Citations and penalties are not issued at this time, nor can the officer order that any part of the business be closed down immediately. If an imminent danger exists, the compliance officer will ask the employer to abate the hazard and remove endangered employees. If the employer does not comply, OSHA administrators can go to the appropriate Federal District Court for an injunction prohibiting further work as long as unsafe conditions exist.

Violations and Citations

If after the inspection tour an OSHA standard is found to have been violated, the OSHA area director determines what citations and penalties, if any, will be issued as well as a proposed time period for abatement. An employer who believes the citation is unreasonable or the abatement period is insufficient may contest it. The act provides an appeal procedure and a review agency, the Occupational Safety and Health Review Commission, which operates independently from OSHA. Penalties generally range from $5,000 up to $70,000 for willful or repeat serious violations (although they can be in the millions). Criminal penalties are levied in the most serious cases. For example, a willful violation that results in the death of an employee can bring a court-imposed fine of up to $250,000 (or $500,000 if the employer is a corporation) or imprisonment for up to 6 months, or both. A second conviction can double these penalties. Falsifying records can result in a fine of up to $10,000 and 6 months in jail. Multiple violations or failure to correct prior violations can add up to enormous fines. The OSHA area director may enter into settlement agreements. Therefore, many cases are settled before litigation: OSHA then issues the citation and agreed-upon penalties simultaneously.

In practice, OSHA must have a final order from the independent Occupational Safety and Health Review Commission (OSHRC) to enforce a penalty. An employer can drag out an appeal for years.

OSHA inspectors don't look just for specific hazards but also for a comprehensive safety approach. Problems here would include lack of a systematic approach, sporadic or irregular safety meetings, lack of responsiveness to safety audit recommendations, and failure to inspect the workplace regularly.

OSHA had levied fines in the millions of dollars, although settlements have tended to be for lesser amounts, and do not always include an admission of wrongdoing. Companies usually can negotiate with OSHA on the final amount of fines levied. Companies also can reduce the amount of fines they pay by cooperating with OSHA and especially by being proactive in responding to OSHA investigations and recommendations. Other settlements—many of which do not include an admission of wrongdoing on the part of the company—include, for example, paying a fine and intensifying its training programs to settle a case.

OSHA's Hazard Communications Standards

Millions of U.S. employees are potentially exposed to one or more chemical hazards in the workplace. Because of the threats posed by these chemicals, OSHA has established a Hazard Communications Standard (HazCom). This standard is also known as the "right to know" rule. The basic purpose of the rule is to ensure that employers and employees know what chemical hazards exist in the workplace and how to protect themselves against those hazards. The goal of the rule is to reduce the incidence of illness and injuries caused by chemicals.

The Hazard Communications Standard establishes uniform requirements to ensure that the hazards of all chemicals imported into, produced by, or used in the workplace are evaluated and that the results of these evaluations are transmitted to affected managers and exposed employees. In 2016 HazCom was aligned with the Globally Harmonized System (GHS), a global hazard communication system developed by the United Nations that standardizes the way hazardous chemicals are classified and then communicated via safety data sheets and labels. With GHS alignment, the classification of chemicals includes categorizing hazards based on severity, a concept that didn't exist in HazCom 1994. It also meant significant changes to safety data sheets and labels.

The HazCom specifically required that employers maintain complete and updated Material Safety Data Sheets (MSDSs), for each hazardous material. MSDSs provide information on the nature of the hazards involved, and include appropriate handling procedures and remedies for unexpected exposure. Employers, manufacturers, or importers involved with the hazardous material were required to prepare MSDSs. With the HAzCom and GHS alignment labels now have six standardized elements: product identifier, manufacturer information, signal word, pictograms, hazard statements, and precautionary statements. Also under GHS, material safety data sheets (MSDSs) are referred to as safety data sheets (SDSs), the "M" has been dropped. More importantly, these SDSs must now contain 16 sections in a specific order.

OSHA developed a variety of materials to help employers and employees implement effective hazard communications programs. FLMs play a key role in these programs. FLMs should make certain that SDSs are available for chemicals that are brought into, used in, or produced at the workplace they supervise. If FLMs find that some information is missing, the suppliers of the chemicals and other hazardous substances should be able to provide it.

The FLM's Role Under OSHA

While OSHA has an impact on the entire organization, it also places certain responsibilities on the FLM. Although FLMs cannot be familiar with all of the thousands of pages of OSHA regulation interpretations, they do need to understand what kinds of practices are required to preserve health and safety in their departments. In addition, OSHA imposes some specific responsibilities on FLMs.

First, OSHA requires that FLMs keep specific records. One of these is OSHA Form 200-Log and Summary of Occupational Injuries and Illnesses. Each occupational injury and illness must be recorded on this form within six working days from the time that the employer learns of it. Furthermore, if fatalities occur or five or more employees require hospitalization, the organization must report them to OSHA within 48 hours. FLMs must also complete OSHA Form 101-Supplemental Record of Occupational Injuries and Illness within 6 working days from the time that the employer learns of the accident or illness. This form contains much more detail about each injury or illness required to be recorded. These are injuries and illnesses resulting in death, lost workdays, loss of consciousness, restriction of work or motion, transfer to another job, or medical treatment other than first aid. Injuries requiring temporary first aid do not have to be recorded.

Second, FLMs are often asked to accompany OSHA officials while they inspect the organization's facilities. Because many organizations and FLMs feel threatened by OSHA officials, they may tend to behave antagonistically toward them. This is not advisable. An uncooperative FLM could cause these officials to be more hard-nosed than usual, resulting in stiffer penalties than would have been imposed otherwise. It is in the best interests of the FLM and the host organization for the FLM to cooperate with visiting OSHA officials. During the inspection, it is important to be polite and cooperative. This is not always as easy as it sounds because the inspection may come at an inconvenient time and may be viewed as unwanted interference.

Third, FLMs should be familiar with the OSHA regulations affecting their departments. They should constantly be on the lookout for safety violations. It is the FLM's responsibility to see that the employees follow all safety rules. Naturally, these include all OSHA rules and regulations. As part of this role, FLMs must ensure that, as mentioned above, SDSs are available for all hazardous substances.

OSHA Responsibilities and Rights of Employers and Employees

Both employers and employees have responsibilities and rights under the OSHA Act. For example, employers are responsible for providing "a workplace free from recognized hazards" and for examining workplace conditions to ensure they conform to applicable standards.

Employees also have rights and responsibilities, but OSHA can't cite them for violations of their responsibilities. They are responsible, for example, for complying with all applicable OSHA standards, for following all employer safety and health rules and regulations, and for reporting hazardous conditions to the FLM. Employees have a right to demand safety and health on the job without fear of punishment. Employers are forbidden to punish workers who complain to OSHA about job safety and health hazards. However, they must still make a diligent effort to discourage, by discipline if necessary, violations of safety rules by employees.

Unsafe Personal Acts

Experts believe that unsafe personal acts cause the bulk of the workplace accidents. These unsafe acts include taking unnecessary chances, engaging in horseplay, operating or working at unsafe speeds, failing to wear or use protective equipment, using improper tools or equipment, taking unsafe shortcuts, making safety devices inoperative by removing them, lifting improperly, and throwing materials. It is difficult to determine why employees behave unsafely. There probably is no single reason. Some employees may be suffering from fatigue, haste, boredom, stress, poor eyesight, daydreaming, or physical limitations. However, these reasons do not explain why some employees intentionally neglect to wear prescribed safety equipment or to follow safety procedures. These employees may wish to impress others or project a certain image. They may think that accidents always happen to someone else. That attitude can easily lead employees to be careless or show off. Employees with low morale also tend to have more accidents than employees with high morale; low morale is likely to be related to employee carelessness. A company's poor safety record can adversely affect morale.

Finally, a reason often given for accidents is that certain people are accident-prone. It seems to be true that due to their physical and mental makeup, some employees are more susceptible to accidents than are others.

Accident-proneness may result from inborn traits, but it often develops as a result of the individual's environment. Given the right set of circumstances, anyone can be accident-prone. For example, a "normal" employee who was up all night with a sick child might very well be accident-prone the next day. A tendency to be accident-prone should not be used to justify an accident, however. Employees who appear to be accident-prone even temporarily, should be identified and receive special attention.

Unsafe Physical Environment

Accidents can and do happen in all types of environments: in offices, retail stores, factories, and lumber yards. Accidents are more likely to occur in certain locations than others are, however. Listed in order of decreasing accident frequency, these locations are:

1. wherever heavy awkward material is handled, using hand trucks, forklifts, cranes, and hoists;
2. improper handling and material lifting (about one-third of workplace accidents);
3. around any type of machinery that is used to produce something else, the most hazardous are metalworking and woodworking machines, power saws, and machines with exposed gears, belts, chains, and the like (even a paper cutter or an electric pencil sharpener has a high accident potential);
4. wherever people walk or climb, including ladders, scaffolds, and narrow walkways (falls are a major source of accidents);
5. wherever people use hand tools, including chisels, screwdrivers, pliers, hammers and axes;
6. wherever electricity is used other than for the usual lighting purposes, especially near extension cords, loose wiring, and portable hand tools; and
7. near outdoor power lines.

Just as there are certain locations in which accidents occur more frequently, certain conditions of the work environment also seem to result in more accidents. Some of these unsafe conditions are:

1. serious under-staffing;
2. unguarded or improperly guarded machines;
3. defective equipment and tools;
4. poor lighting;
5. poor or improper ventilation;

6. improper dress, such as clothing with loose and floppy sleeves worn when working on a lathe or any machine with moving parts;
7. loose tile, linoleum, or carpeting;
8. sharp burrs or edges of material;
9. reading while walking; and
10. poor housekeeping (e.g., cluttered aisles and stairs, dirty or wet floors that are slippery or have small, loose objects lying on them, improperly stacked materials, etc.).

How to Measure Safety and Health Rates

OSHA requires organizations to maintain records of the incidence of injuries and illnesses. Some organizations also record the frequency and severity of each.

Incidence Rate

The most explicit index of industrial safety is the incidence rate. It is calculated by the following formula:

$$\text{Incidence rate} = \frac{\text{Number of injuries and illnesses} \times 200,000}{\text{Number of employee hours worked}}$$

The figure 200,000 is the base for 100 full-time workers (40 hours per week, 50 weeks). Suppose an organization had 10 recorded injuries and illnesses and 500 employees. To calculate the number of yearly hours worked, multiply the number of employees by 40 hours and by 50 weeks: $500 \times 40 \times 50 = 1$ million. The incidence rate thus would be 2 per 100 workers per year.

Severity Rate

The severity rate reflects the hours actually lost due to injury or illness. It recognizes that not all injuries and illnesses are equal. Four categories of injuries have been established: deaths, permanent total disabilities, permanent partial disabilities, and temporary total disabilities. An organization with the same number of injuries and illnesses as another, but with more deaths would have a higher severity rate. The severity rate is calculated as follows:

$$\text{Severity rate} = \frac{\text{Total hours charged} \times 1 \text{ million (hours)}}{\text{Number of employee hours worked}}$$

Frequency Rate

The frequency rate reflects the number of injuries and illnesses per million hours worked rather than per year as in the incidence rate. It is estimated as follows:

$$\text{Frequency rate} = \frac{\text{Number of injuries and illnesses} \times 1 \text{ million (hours)}}{\text{Number of employee hours worked}}$$

None of these rates would mean much unless they are compared with similar figures. Useful comparisons can be made with similar figures from other departments or divisions within the same organization, from previous years, or from other organizations. These comparisons make it possible to evaluate an organization's safety record more objectively.

Other Safety and Health Concerns

Besides accidents, several common concerns about safety and health in the workplace are especially significant because they are widely occurring, or at least widely discussed. Some of these include substance abuse, occupational diseases including stress, and violence. Alcohol and drug abuse, prolonged job stress, and emotional illness are among the enormously costly problems that need to be addressed through programs within organizations as well as through broader community programs. These costs are of various kinds, and they include losses stemming from absenteeism, lowered productivity, and treatment expenses. What cost figures do not show, of course, is the mental and emotional anguish these problems cause fellow workers, friends, family members, and others. Obviously, drug, alcohol, and emotional problems off the job carry over into the job setting and vice versa.

Job Stress and Burnout

Problems like alcoholism and drug abuse stem from job stress. Concerns about stress and how to manage it have become major safety and health issues. Prolonged stress has been inked to subsequent physical injury, debilitation, and disease, including heart disease. There are also links between stress and gastrointestinal diseases, arthritis, and rheumatism, which are major sources of employee disability.

Many external factors can trigger stress. Some include work schedule, pace of work, job security, route to and from work, workplace noise, and the number and nature of customers. Many service workers (especially in fast food and retail stores) have unpredictable work schedules, often set at the last minute by their employer. This raises stress and reduces employee health.

Job stress has serious consequences for employer and employee. The human consequences include anxiety, depression, anger, and various physical consequences, such as cardiovascular disease, headaches, accidents, and possibly even early-onset Alzheimer's disease. Stress also has serious consequences for the employer as healthcare costs of high-stress workers are higher than those of their less-stressed coworkers. Yet not all stress is dysfunctional. Some people, for example, are more productive as a deadline approaches.

Burnout

Burnout is closely associated with job stress. Burnout is the total depletion of physical and mental resources caused by excessive striving to reach an unrealistic work-related goal. Burnout consists of three components, *exhaustion* (profound fatigue). *Cynicism* (a loss of engagement in what you do), and *inefficacy* (feelings of incompetence). Burnout doesn't just spontaneously appear. Instead, it builds gradually, leading to irritability, discouragement, entrapment, and resentment.

Depression

Employee depression is a serious problem at work. Depressed results in lost workdays, absenteeism, and lost productivity. Depressed people also tend to have worse safety records.

FLMs and their organizations should work hard to ensure that stressed, burned out, and depressed employees utilize support services. FLMs should be trained to recognize signs of stress, burnout, and depression and then work with others in the organization to make assistance more readily available through such things as employee assistance programs (EAPs).

Health Problems Associated with Computer Monitor and Ergonomics

Despite the advances in computer monitor technology there is still a risk of computer-related health problems. These problems include short-term eye burning, itching, and tearing, as well as eye strain and eye soreness. Backaches and neck aches are also widespread. Computer users may also suffer from carpal tunnel syndrome, caused by repetitive use of the hands and arms at uncomfortable angles.

Infectious Diseases

With many employees traveling to and from international destinations, monitoring and controlling infectious diseases has become an important safety issue as evident by the recent COVID-19 pandemic. FLMs and their organizations can take steps to prevent the entry or spread of infectious diseases. These steps include the following:

1. Closely monitor the Centers for Disease Control and Prevention (CDC) travel alerts.
2. Provide daily medical screenings for employees returning from infected areas.
3. Deny access for 10 days to employees or visitors who have had contact with suspected infected individuals.
4. Tell employees to stay home if they have a fever or respiratory system symptoms.
5. Clean work areas and surfaces regularly. Make sanitizers containing alcohol easily available.
6. Stagger breaks. Offer several lunch periods to reduce overcrowding.

Many of these steps are being used at the time of the writing of this book in response to the Coronavirus pandemic.

Violence in the Workplace

Historically, safety prevention has focused on the prevention of accidents in the workplace. Recently, however, violence in the workplace has become an increasing concern and a huge problem. Bullying, the "silent epidemic" of the workplace where abusive behavior, threats, and intimidation often go unreported in organizations. While there is no way to guarantee that an organization will be free from violence, a violence prevention program can greatly increase that probability. Violence prevention programs are described in the next section.

Programs to Promote Safety and Health

FLMs' and other managers' and leaders' first duty should be to formulate a safety policy, and then implement and sustain this policy through a safety or loss control program. The heart of any safety program is accident prevention. It is obviously much better to prevent accidents than to react to them. A major objective of any safety program is to get the employees to "think safety"—to keep safety and accident prevention on their minds.

These programs may include training, safety meetings, the posting of safety statistics, awards for safe performance, contests, and safety and health committees. Although these programs may be time-consuming, FLMs will ultimately benefit if their employees use good safety practices. Not only will there be budgetary and morale advantages, but increased safety will decrease the time an FLM spends filling out accident reports, attending meetings to investigate injuries, and making recommendations.

Many approaches are used to make employees more safety conscious. However, the following elements are present in most successful safety programs:

- *Clear terms and procedures.* Employees and FLMs should be trained in safety procedures and understand all relevant company rules.
- *A safety budget.* To reduce the frequency of accidents, management must be willing to spend money and to budget for safety. Accidents involve direct as well as indirect costs. Money spent to improve safety is returned many times over through the control of accidents.
- *The support of management.* Safety programs need the support of top and middle management. That support must be genuine, not casual. If upper management takes an unenthusiastic approach to safety, employees will be quick to realize it. Management's personal concern helps to show this support. This includes meeting with department heads over safety issues, on-site visits by top executives to discuss the need for safety, appointing high-level safety officers where appropriate, and offering rewards to FLMs based on their employees' safety records.
- *Good example set by management.* Management's good example is critical. If safety glasses are required at a particular operation, then all managers should wear safety glasses at the required work locations. If employees see FLMs or other managers disregarding safety rules or treating hazardous situations lightly by not conforming to regulations, some may feel that they, too, have the right to violate the rules.
- *Responsibility for safety.* One person should be in charge of the safety program and responsible for its operation. Typically this is the safety engineer or the safety director, but it may also be a high-level manager or the human resources manager. Safety should also be clearly established as a line organization responsibility. All LMs should consider safety an integral part of their jobs, and operating employees should be responsible for working safely.

- *Positive attitude.* A positive attitude toward safety should exist and be maintained throughout the organization. The employees must believe that the safety program is worthwhile and that it produces results.

In short, organizations show their concern for loss control by establishing a clear safety policy and by assuming the responsibility for its implementation. Organizations that fail to implement safety policies face being fined by OSHA for unsafe practices; or any failure to report job-related illnesses and injuries, as well as potential lawsuits or workers' compensation claims by employees.

Strategies for Promoting Safety

Uninteresting work often leads to boredom, fatigue, and stress, all of which can cause accidents. In many instances, job enrichment, discussed in Chapter 6, can be used to make the work more interesting and result in fewer accidents. Simple changes can often make work more meaningful to the employee. Job enrichment attempts are usually successful if they add responsibility, challenge, and similar qualities that contribute to the employee's positive inner feelings about the job.

The safety committee is a way to get employees directly involved in the operation of the safety program. A rotating membership of 5 to 12 members is usually desirable, including both management and operating employees. The normal duties of a safety committee include inspecting the work site, observing work practices, investigating accidents, and making recommendations. The safety committee also may:

- sponsor accident-prevention contests;
- help prepare safety rules;
- promote safety awareness;
- review safety suggestions from employees; and
- supervise the preparation and distribution of safety materials.

Reinforcing behaviors that reduce the likelihood of accidents can be highly successful. Reinforcers include non-monetary reinforcers such as feedback, activity reinforcers such as time off, material reinforcers such as company-purchased doughnuts during the coffee break, and financial rewards for attaining desired levels of safety. The behavioral approach relies on specifying and communicating the desired performance to employees, measuring that performance before and after interventions, monitoring performance at unannounced intervals several times a week, and reinforcing desired behavior several times a week with performance feedback. More will be said at the end of this chapter about the behavioral approach in the form of behavior-based safety program and culture.

Management by objectives was introduced in Chapter 4. This approach can be used in the safety area. Behavior modification programs are often linked successfully to management by objectives programs that deal with occupational health. The seven basic steps of these programs are

1. Identify hazards and obtain information about the frequency of accidents.
2. Based on this information, evaluate the severity and risk of the hazards.
3. Formulate and implement programs to control, prevent, or reduce the possibility of accidents.
4. Set specific goals that are challenging, but attainable regarding the reduction of accidents or safety problems.
5. Consistently monitor results of the program.
6. Provide positive feedback to promote correct safety procedures.
7. Monitor and evaluate the program against the goals.

The FLM's Role in Promoting Safety

FLMs are responsible for a great deal of what goes on day to day in the workplace; it's not just a position that solely assigns tasks. Because FLMs are the link between management and the operating employees, they are in the best position to promote safety and thus a safety culture. In addition to fostering a healthy attitude toward safety, an FLM who observes unsafe conditions should take one of the following actions, listed in order of priority:

1. Eliminate the hazard.
2. If the hazard cannot be eliminated, use protective devices such as guards on machinery.
3. If the hazard cannot be protected, provide warnings, such as labels on parts of equipment.
4. If the hazard cannot be removed, notify the proper authority.

Recommend a solution, and then follow up to make sure that the unsafe condition has been corrected.

FLMs should always take a proactive stance towards preventing accidents and promoting safety. It is up to FLMs to see that employees follow safety. It is up to FLMs who observe and are responsible for the day-to-day performance of employees. Unfortunately, some FLMs must witness a serious injury before they appreciate why they must enforce safety rules and procedures. FLMs who avoid enforcing these rules because they are afraid employees will react negatively do not understand why the rules exist. They fail to recognize the importance of their role in maintaining a safe and healthy workplace.

Violence Prevention Programs

A set of OSHA guidelines released in 1995, "Guidelines for Preventing Workplace Violence for Health Care and Social Service Workers," are still very relevant today and can serve as a guide for organizations to develop a written workplace violence prevention program as part of an overall safety and health program. Some of the guidelines' main recommendations are to

1. establish a policy of zero tolerance for workplace violence;
2. encourage employees to report incidents of workplace violence;
3. develop a plan for workplace security;
4. appoint a person with program responsibility and provide adequate resources to run the program;
5. ensure management commitment to employee safety; and
6. hold employee meetings on safety.

The FLM's Role in Preventing Violence

FLMs play an important role in the success of violence prevention programs. FLMs need to take responsibility for reducing or eliminating violence in the workplace. To this end, they must be sensitive to the causes of workplace violence. Many people feel pressured in their jobs and fear layoffs. When other stresses are added to these, such as negative performance appraisals, personality conflicts with coworkers or managers, or personal problems such as divorce, a potentially dangerous person may emerge. While FLMs cannot eliminate all of these pressures, which are realities of everyday life, they can make sure that employees are treated fairly. When employees are treated as though they are expendable, they will not feel a commitment to the company and could respond to such treatment with a violent reaction. FLMs should deal with performance problems by focusing on employee behavior and future improvement, rather than on past performance problems (see Chapter 12 on performance appraisals.) FLMs should never discipline employees in front of coworkers. This can be humiliating and incite a violent reaction.

FLMs should also take steps to reduce the possibility of hiring employees who might be prone to violence. For example, interviewers might ask job candidates to describe how they reacted to a past management decision with which they disagreed, and why. "What frustrates you?" And "Who was your worst supervisor, and why?" The responses to these questions and follow-up questions could be quite revealing. Interviewers should also check for evidence of substance abuse or emotional problems which might be indicated by careless driving or DWI (driving while intoxicated) entries on driving records. Unexplained gaps in a person's employment history should be carefully examined. In addition, other background circumstances, such as the following, may call for a more in-depth background checking:

- incomplete or false information on the resume or application;
- a negative, unfavorable, or false reference;
- prior insubordinate or violent behavior on the job;
- a criminal history involving harassing or violent behavior;
- a prior termination for cause with a suspicious (or no) explanation;
- history of drug or alcohol abuse;
- strong indications of instability in the individual's work or personal lies as indicated, for example, by frequent job changes or geographic moves; and
- lost licenses or accreditations.

Of course, FLMs in partnership with HRM staff can obtain an employment application, and check the applicant's employment history, education, and references.

Use Workplace Violence Training

FLMs and others in the organization can be trained to identify the clues that typify potentially violent current employees. Common clues include the following:

- an act of violence on or off the job;
- erratic behavior evidencing a loss of perception or awareness of actions;
- overly confrontational or antisocial behavior;
- sexually aggressive behavior;

- isolationist behavior with a threat of violence;
- insubordinate behavior with a threat of violence;
- tendency to overreact to criticism;
- exaggerated interest in war, guns, violence, mass murders, catastrophes, and so on;
- commission of a serious breach of security;
- possessions of weapons, guns, knives, or like items in the workplace;
- violation of privacy rights of others, such as searching desks or stalking;
- chronic complaining and the raising of frequent, unreasonable grievances; and
- a retributory or get-even attitude.

The guidelines below lists useful considerations FLMs can make use for firing high-risk employees:

- Plan all aspects of the meeting, including its time, location, the people to be present, and the agenda
- Involve security enforcement personnel.
- Advise the employee that he or she is no longer permitted onto the employer's property.
- Conduct the meeting in a room with a door leading to the outside of the building.
- Keep the termination brief and to the point.
- Make sure he or she returns all company-owned property at the meeting.
- Don't let the person return his or her workstation.
- Conduct the meeting early in the week and early in the morning so he or she has time to meet with employment counselors or support groups.
- Offer as generous a severance package as possible.
- Protect the employee's dignity by not advertising the event.

Finally, FLMs should learn the proper organizational procedures for reporting and dealing with different types of potentially violent situations. Comprehensive violence-prevention programs can be beneficial. For example, one organization created this type of program, which is run by a full-service loss prevention department, and includes extensive training, a 24-hour hotline, and an intervention policy. The program's primary purpose is to reduce violent crimes within the organization. It also addresses threats, harassment, and domestic violence targeted toward any member of the organization's workforce.

Employee Assistance Programs

Employee assistance programs (EAPs) are designed to help employees whose job performance is suffering because of physical, mental, or emotional problems. EAPs address a variety of employee problems ranging from drug abuse to marital problems to bereavement. Direct assistance or help through referrals for these employees is essential for humane reasons and for reasons of organizational effectiveness. Many organizations create EAPs because they recognize their ethical and legal obligations to protect not only their workers' physical health, but their mental health as well. Ethical obligations stem from the fact that the work climate, job change, work rules, work pace, and style frequently cause behavioral, psychological, and physiological problems for employees. Ethical obligations become legal obligations when employees sue the company or file workers' compensation claims for work-related illness. The success of EAPs depends on how well they are planned and implemented. There is also some evidence that EAPs are more successful with some types of problems than with others. For instance, EAPs appear to be more effective at dealing with alcoholism than with drug addiction.

The FLM's Role in EAPs

In the traditional alcoholism treatment program, the FLM had to look for symptoms of alcoholism and then diagnose the problem. Under an EAP, however, the FLM is responsible only for identifying declining work performance. If normal corrective measures do not work, the FLM confronts the employee with evidence of his or her performance and offers the EAP. Classic warning signs, such as chronic tardiness and absenteeism may be difficult to recognize, however, in companies where some employees telecommute, or where workers are geographically separated from their FLMs. Nevertheless, here are some recommendations on how to proceed.

- Once you suspect a problem, begin documenting instances in which job performance has fallen short. Absenteeism, including leaving early or arriving late for work, errors, a slackened commitment to completing tasks, and a rise in conflicts with other employees due to mood swings may be evident.
- Having assembled the facts, set up a meeting. Keep the discussion focused on performance, and do not try to make a diagnosis.

Outline the employee's short-comings, insist on improvement, and then say, "I need to bring you to the medical department...something isn't right here... I'm taking you to the experts."

- Often FLMs are scared of being wrong and of potential liability. They worry, "Can the person sue me?" As long as the discussion focuses on declining job performance, legal experts say that a defamation claim is highly unlikely. A focus on job performance is usually necessary for an effective confrontation in any event.

This approach leaves the diagnosis and treatment recommendations to trained counselors. FLMs can increase the odds of success by telling employees that if their performance doesn't improve they'll be disciplined. As difficult as it is, such intervention often works.

Wellness Programs

As health-care costs have skyrocketed over the last two decades, organizations have become more interested in preventive programs focused on maintaining worker health. Companies are encouraging employees to lead healthier lives and are attempting to reduce health-care costs through formal employee wellness programs. While EAPs focus on treating troubled employees, wellness programs focus on preventing health problems in the first place. A complete wellness program has three components:

1. It helps employees identify potential health risks through screening and testing.
2. It educates employees about particular health risks such as high blood pressure, smoking, poor diet, and stress.
3. It encourages employees to change their lifestyles through exercise, good nutrition, and health monitoring.

Wellness programs may be as simple and inexpensive as providing information about stop-smoking clinics and weight-loss programs or as comprehensive and expensive as providing professional health screening and multimillion-dollar fitness facilities.

Should FLMs attempt to change employees' bad health habits through a "carrot" or a "stick" approach? That is, should employees be rewarded for healthy behaviors (the carrot) or penalized for unhealthy behaviors (the stick) or both? Some companies prefer the stick approach. For example, one company refused to hire workers who smoke, and another company fired workers for drinking excessively after their shifts. Both companies claim their actions were justified by their interest in avoiding the higher health-care costs attributable to smokers and drinkers. Other organizations charge smokers more for health insurance. Still other organizations impose fines on employees with unhealthy lifestyles and make them pay more for insurance.

In contrast, one organization uses a carrot approach that includes lowering insurance premiums for employees with healthy lifestyles, including non-smokers who control their weight and blood pressure. Another organization pays employees to get a computerized health-risk appraisal and awards them up to almost $1,000 per year for participating in weight-loss and exercise plans.

A number of organizations have developed fitness programs which involve employees in some form of controlled exercise or recreation activities. Fitness programs range from subsidized membership at a local health club to company softball teams to very sophisticated company-owned facilities.

Evaluation of Safety and Health Programs

Safety and health programs have begun to receive more attention in recent years. The consequences of inadequate programs are measurable: increased employees' compensation payments, increased lawsuits, larger insurance costs, fines from OSHA, and pressures from unions. Evaluation of a safety management program requires indicator systems, such as accident statistics, effective reporting systems, clear safety rules and procedures; and management of the safety effort.

A safety and health program can be evaluated fairly directly in a cost-benefit sense. The most cost-effective safety programs need not be the most expensive. Programs that combine a number of approaches-identifying safety criteria like improvements in job performance and decreases in sick leave, safety training, safety meetings, providing medical facilities, and strong participation by top management-work when the emphasis is on the engineering aspects of safety. Conducting a cost-benefit analysis can be helpful in improving programs. An organization can calculate the costs of safety specialists, new safety devices, and other safety measures. Savings due to reductions in accidents, lowered insurance costs, and lowered fines can be weighed against these costs. Programs can be judged by other measurable criteria as well, such as improvements in job performance, decreases in sick leave, and reductions in disciplinary actions and grievances. At the same time, FLMs must realize that cause-and-effect relationships may be complex, and difficult to measure accurately. In addition, not all benefits of a health and safety program are measurable; many benefits are intangible.

FLMs must ensure a safe and healthy workplace for employees. Employees must be able to report unsafe or unhealthful workplace conditions or hazards to a supervisor without fear of reprisal. This means that FLMs have a major role to play in creating and sustaining a strong culture of safety in their organizations. Safety cultures are heavily influenced by metrics. How safety is measured by FLMs and their organizations can fundamentally change how safety is managed, and how safety is managed is a primary contributor to an organization's safety culture. In organization's with a strong safety culture, safety is embedded in daily management; it is part of the fabric of daily activity. It infuses every interaction, every decision and every behavior. One example of such an effort available to FLMs and their organizations is a behavior-based safety program and culture.

Behavior-Based Safety Program and Total Safety Culture

Behavior Based Safety (BBS) is a process that informs management and employees of the overall safety of the workplace through safety observations. As briefly discussed earlier, the behavior approach to safety focuses on reinforcing safety behaviors. The basic principles of BBS are:

- Define target behaviors.
- Develop critical behavior checklists to document instances of target behaviors.
- Design interventions to improve/prevent unsafe behavior.
- Chart progress consistently.
- Give effective behavioral feedback.

Like any effort or program BBS has both advantages and disadvantages. BBS has been referred to as the Swiss Army Knife of safety programs for its multi-functional uses. When approached correctly, BBS has a myriad of benefits available to FLMs that make work sites or places safe, productive, and improve morale. Here are just a few benefits FLMs can expect when implementing BBS correctly:

- focuses on the human side of safety,
- defines safe and unsafe behaviors,
- encourages safe behavior and discourages unsafe or destructive behaviors,
- involves employees in safety,

- requires management to put its money where its mouth is, and
- engenders commitment and passion especially in the early phases.

Many safety managers and experts have spoken out against BBS for not being worth the cost, not executing what it advertised, and not meeting even basic expectations, while others have criticized BBS for fostering a blame-the-employee attitude regarding accidents, injuries, and other safety failures. Because of this, BBS is often misinterpreted by operations that buy into the erroneous philosophy that people do dumb things and that's why accidents happen. One common flaw in BBS is that it focuses solely on employees' behavior, even when other things should be factored in.

As suggested earlier, BBS is intended to focus workers' attention on their own and their peers' daily safety behavior. The goal of the BBS program is to improve the employee safety of the organization. BBS utilizes evidence-based intervention strategies ranging from basic employee behavior audits to comprehensive safety management elements with the aim of optimizing an organization's safety culture and reducing incidents. BBS programs are generally comprised of the following elements:

- BBS program design (includes representation from management and frontline employees);
- identification of behaviors (from mishaps, near misses, safety audits and observation) to be changed;
- development of a safe and valid checklist or procedure for tasks in which unsafe behaviors have been expressed;
- behavior measurement system (usually the frequency of safe and risky behaviors during observations);
- behavioral observations (can include both single tasks and an entire workspace);
- observer-generated feedback that includes recognition of both appropriate behaviors and those that should be changed;
- application of behavior observation data to change management; and
- evaluation of program effectiveness.

The Basics of an Observation

When implementing a BBS program, it is important for FLMs to understand that observers (employees trained to conduct on-site safety reviews) conduct reviews of other employees with an eye on their behavior. These observers record safe and unsafe behaviors, in addition to noting safe and unsafe workplace conditions. The observer then shares the findings with the worker and provides feedback. Positive feedback is encouraged. Discussing the ways in which employees can perform their tasks in a safer manner helps workers and observers to become more aware of their behavior. BBS programs are based on a continuous feedback loop where employees and observers provide input on improving safety to each other and safety professionals utilize the data collected in conducting the observations to continually improve the BBS program.

The Behavior Based Safety Checklist

Organizations who implement a BBS program determine the appropriate list of behaviors to observe based on the unique behaviors and risks of their organization. Safety professionals in partnership with FLMs usually develop a checklist format that is easy and quick for observers to complete in the field and lists the target behaviors. Checklists often include the basics of the observation (time, date, location, behaviors observed, observer) and the number of safe and unsafe observations of the reviewer. The checklist also includes fields for any feedback and comments provided to the employee.

Based on your BBS goals and objectives, FLMs might also create a schedule that determines how many observations (and what type of observations) should be conducted throughout your organization on a weekly, monthly or quarterly basis. Schedules and observations can change based on the continuous feedback loop of a BBS program.

However as observation checklists and schedules become more in-depth, they also become harder to track and manage. FLMs can also make use of technology to improve management of their BBS program without sacrificing its effectiveness.

In the end, a successful BBS program requires the following pieces working in unison:

- dedicated involvement from every employee (even the CEO); including partners like vendors, contractors, and sub-contractors makes the program even stronger;
- a method for collecting and evaluating data;
- mechanisms for instituting change to policies, procedures, and systems; and
- FLMs and other leadership's willingness to admit that there's a better way and to start over.

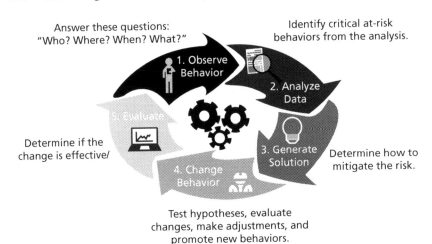

Figure 14.1 The 5 elements of a world class behavior based safety program. *Note:* Behavioral based safety is most effective when treated as a continuous loop, constantly adapting to your employee, safety, and business needs.

BBS is most effective when treated as a continuous loop, constantly adapting to your employee, safety, and business needs. These elements are part of the complete BBS process as shown in Figure 14.1.

When BBS goes as planned, employees are more engaged in their safety, and more willing to take responsibility for their safety-related behavior. They are also able to hold their peers accountable when unsafe practices occur. The result is a workforce that is acutely aware of safety protocols, are actively working to stay safe, and agree that the ultimate aim of a safety initiative is a "total safety culture" in which

- individuals hold safety as a "value" and not just a priority,
- individuals take responsibility for the safety of their co-workers in addition to themselves, and
- all levels of employees are willing and able to act on their sense of responsibility—they can go "beyond the call of duty."

Conclusion

FLMs' primary responsibility toward safety is to establish an environment where safety is emphasized. FLMs have a legal responsibility to ensure that the workplace is free from unnecessary hazards and that working conditions are not harmful to employees' physical or mental health. FLMs also have responsibilities to listen to employee complaints and suggestions, work closely with the safety committee (if there is one), and provide safety instruction.

The costs to an organization of accidents, injuries, and occupational diseases are both tangible and intangible. The tangible costs are the measurable financial expenses. The intangible costs include lowered employee morale, less favorable public relations, and weakened ability to recruit and retain employees.

The basic purpose of any safety program is to prevent accidents. Since getting employees to "think safety" is one of the more effective ways to prevent accidents, this is a major objective of most programs. Many strategies are available for promoting safety within an organization. These include making the work interesting, establishing a safety committee, periodically holding safety training and rewarding employee participation.

Prolonged stress is associated with enough health and accident problems for stress to be an important area of concern for organizations. Today's FLMs must learn to recognize the following warning signs of potentially violent employees: employees making threats or being threatened, employees with serious problems at home, employees with a chemical dependency, employees showing signs of paranoia, or employees fascinated with weapons.

EAPs provide avenues for FLMs and organizations to offer help to employees with problems in their personal and work lives. Wellness programs provide opportunities for employers to reduce healthcare costs.

FLMs can make use of BBS to develop a total safety culture in their organizations. This requires that FLMs and others assess (via surveys or focus groups) the safety culture and use the feedback to enhance the organization's safety.

Reference

Occupational Safety and Health Administration. (n.d.). *Worker safety in hospitals.* Retrieved from https://www.osha.gov/dsg/hospitals/mgmt_tools _resources.html

About the Author

Ronald R. Sims is the Floyd Dewey Gottwald senior professor in the Mason School of Business at William and Mary where he teaches leadership and change management, business ethics, and human resource management. He received his PhD in organizational behavior from Case Western Reserve University. His research focuses on a variety of topics including change management, leadership, business ethics, and human resources management. Dr. Sims is the author of more than 90 articles in scholarly and professional journals, and has authored and edited, alone or in collaboration 40 books and 80 chapters. Professor Sims has provided consultation, executive education, and employee training in the areas of change management, business ethics/reputation management, human resource management, and human resources development to organizations in the private, public, and not-for-profit sectors over the past 40 years.

Succeeding as a Frontline Manager in Today's Organizations, page 423
Copyright © 2021 by Information Age Publishing

Printed in the United States
By Bookmasters